Group Psychotherapy and Personality:
Intersecting Structures

The
DISTINGUISHED BOOK AWARD
Conferred by the Postgraduate Center for Mental Health
is presented to
Dr. Henry Kellerman
for this volume entitled
Group Psychotherapy and Personality:
Intersecting Structures
an original work that makes a fundamental contribution
to the psychological sciences and to the art
and science of psychotherapy.

Group Psychotherapy
and Personality:
Intersecting Structures

Henry Kellerman, Ph.D.

GRUNE & STRATTON
A Subsidiary of Harcourt Brace Jovanovich, Publishers
New York   San Francisco   London

Library of Congress Cataloging in Publication Data

Kellerman, Henry.
Group psychotherapy and personality.

Includes bibliographical references and index.
1. Group psychotherapy. 2. Personality.
I. Title. [DNLM: 1. Personality. 2. Psychotherapy,
Group. WM430 K29g]
RC488.K44   616.8'915   79-13049
ISBN 0-8089-1182-1

Grune & Stratton, Inc.
111 Fifth Avenue
New York, New York 10003

Distributed in the United Kingdom by
Academic Press, Inc. (London) Ltd.
24/28 Oval Road, London NW 1

Library of Congress Catalog Number 79-13049
International Standard Book Number 0-8089-1182-1
Printed in the United States of America

A GENERATIONAL CELEBRATION

All family groups contain an apparent size and an actual size. The apparent size refers to current membership of the group, while the actual size refers to present membership as well as to ancestral figures. This implies that all groups also contain generational continuity embedded in a genealogical framework.

This book then, is dedicated to generations—to those figures of my family that I love and have loved, including those I have never known. They comprise four generations of my family corresponding to the concept of a four-generation, full-group life span as described within this book.

The First Generation

To the memory of my maternal grandmother, my bubba Pessie Pellis, whom I knew for 20 years and whose profound sense of indestructibility greatly influenced me.

To the memory of my maternal grandfather, Chaim Pellis, a sensitive person whom I never knew; his respect for education and scholarship perhaps has influenced the creation of this book.

To the memory of my paternal grandmother, Mariam Koilerman, whom I never knew but whose unique good-natured humor and sense of irony surely contributed to the development of my perceptions.

To the memory of my paternal grandfather, Meyer Koilerman, whom I never knew but whose sense of great gentleness seemed to permeate my home.

The Second Generation

To my beautiful parents, Esther Kellerman, my mother, who is the personification of talent and, like sunshine, is the embodiment of color and warmth; and my father, Samuel Kellerman, a rare example of a person of pure authenticity and conviction. These central, caring, loving, and guiding figures of my life who share an irrepressible zest for life and are ultimately responsible for any capacity I have to work meaningfully, to acquire wisdom, and also to be loving; I hug you and kiss you and additionally dedicate this book to your 50th wedding anniversary in 1980.

The Third Generation

To my very beautiful wife, Linda Turkel Kellerman, painter, renaissance person, and mother of our four extraordinary children, who brings to my life the ability to struggle toward ever-increasing consciousness, whose great intelligence helps reveal that which matters in life, and who personifies the openness and the integrity so necessary in the survival of the human condition.

The New Generation

To my loving, joyous, and beautiful children—Max Kellerman, Sam Kellerman, Harry Kellerman, and Jack Kellerman. May you sing and dance, draw lots of pictures, study hard, and express all the qualities inherent in your generational heritage, in a peaceful and just world that is free from want.

L'Chaim

Contents

List of Tables

List of Figures

Preface

After 1945 it became clear to the contemporary world that group behavior as a phenomenon influenced by political causes was of singular importance in the persecution of large masses of people. What was it about a defined group of people that enabled it to perform mindless and heartless acts, engage in sadistic behavior, and then justify its purpose while its members renounced individual responsibility for such behavior? Social and political scientists knew that leadership was of central importance to the group's congealing identity and that groups could be galvanized to act on the basis of scapegoating and economic motivations. Yet the inner workings of the group, its infrastructure, personality, and process effects were not at all understood.

In 1958, 13 years after the war and during my first year in a professional clinical position, I conducted patient orientation groups at the Pilgrim State Hospital in West Brentwood, New York. It was there that I was able to see firsthand the power and complexity of group behavior. I became aware that, depending on its purpose, the group itself is neither inherently good nor bad. Rather, it is a potentially powerful agent in the implementation of goals and its character is determined on the basis of these goals. I became aware that the longer any group exists, the more defined its character becomes, and whether it is a good or bad group then becomes a highly relevant question.

One of the first phenomena I noticed about groups was that they became activated with a motive force quite quickly, were resistive to change, and were generally powerful influences with respect to membership loyalty. I became impressed with the observations that the group becomes different than the amalgam of its constituent membership and it develops pervasive attitudes and moods based upon its emerging traditions, culture, and diagnostic makeup.

Through my work during the past 20 years with groups at the Middletown (NY) State Hospital, at the Postgraduate Center for Mental Health, and in my private practice I have also noticed a few main group phenomena that exist with practically every group. First, the nature of leadership seems to set as well as to reflect the tone and ideology of the group, and second, group members share common defensive needs that seek to be reinforced. I was interested in examining the entire group process as it is embedded in a therapy framework; that is, I was convinced that the group process intersects the personalities of individual members at many points. In fact, it seemed to me that the group-as-a-whole contained personality features not unlike the personality structure of individuals. Yet there was no single unifying theory of group process either in the social psychological, group process, or psychoanalytic group therapy literature that elucidated this structure.

Simultaneous to my earlier work with groups, I became interested in the research of Dr. Robert Plutchik, who at the time was developing a psychoevolutionary theory of emotion. Since that time, many studies based upon various aspects of his theory have been published, including a personality test by Dr. Plutchik and myself entitled the *Emotions Profile Index*. I did not realize at first that I would ultimately be able to utilize the theory in part as a basis for analyzing the fundamental structure of individual personality and the structure of groups. My diagnostic training at Kings County Hospital, my psychoanalytic training at the Postgraduate Center for Mental Health, and my research on emotions led me to a unique position in which I could attempt to integrate these seemingly diverse areas of scientific discourse into a theory of the structure and function of groups. This book is the first formal statement of that integration.

Throughout these 20 years, I also have had the opportunity to teach in the doctoral programs at City University, New York University, the New School for Social Research, and in the postdoctoral fellowship program at the Postgraduate Center for Mental Health. Along with my supervision of students as Director of Psychology Internship Training at Postgraduate Center, these teaching posts have enabled me to present some of the ideas in this book to a new generation of students. These ideas previously were formally presented at professional meetings at the Psychiatric Institute, Yeshiva University, the Advanced Institute of Ethics and Psychoanalysis, and at the Postgraduate Center for Mental Health. Interactions with students and professional colleagues alike have helped me to refine many of the concepts so necessary to the final form of the manuscript.

There are two persons whom I wish to thank for their respective major roles in the development of my competence as a group psychoanalyst and in the development of my scientific thinking. They of course bear no scholarly responsibility for either the development and particular integrative nature of the ideas in this book, or for whatever the scientific and philosophical implications of those ideas may be.

I embrace Dr. Harold Leopold, former Director of the Group Process Department of the Bronx State Hospital, for allowing me to see that time is on the side of the therapy work. His deep respect for his patients and his wisdom provided a very special role model in the group therapy aspect of my psychoanalytic training.

To Dr. Robert Plutchik, Director of Program Development and Clinical Research of the Albert Einstein College of Medicine—scientist, teacher, friend, and brother—I offer my unending gratitude for his continued support over the years on my behalf. Our collaboration for these many years is largely responsible for my scientific education. Our work has given me the necessary conceptual boost to integrate and write this book. After years of gaining insights based upon the emotion theory, I am happy that I have finally been able to present it with something in return; the development of a system of personality and group structure that in part has been generated from its foundation.

There are other individuals who also indirectly contributed to this book. These persons influenced me during my psychoanalytic training in ways that helped me discern certain important problems of treatment, and they ultimately also influenced my professional stance as psychologist and psychoanalyst. I would like to extend my gratitude in this regard to Dr. Lucille Blum, Dr. Max Geller, Ms. Deborah Hample, and the late Dr. Emanual K. Schwartz, all of the Postgraduate Center for Mental Health. Mrs. Eleanor Wimble, Chief of Social Service at the Harlem Valley State Hospital in Wingdale, New York also influenced me early in my training with her profound concern for the needs of patients and her overall professional competence.

The research for various parts of this book led me at times to unexpected places, and it helped to convince me further that the laws of the physical and social sciences are similar and even share common properties with the arts. In this regard I would like to thank Professor Richard Pollack of the New York University Courant Institute of Mathematical Sciences for his help in analyzing certain thorny problems in the conceptualization of chapters 7 and 8 on the transformational shape of the group, and Professor Leo Silber of the Polytechnic Institute of New York, who also provided me with various materials for these chapters. In addition, I extend my sincere appreciation to Ms. Sandra Jamrog, dancer and choreographer, who introduced me to the work of Effort-Shape theory and directed me to the Dance Notation Bureau where I obtained materials that helped me to solve other problems of these specific chapters.

I would also like to acknowledge the help of Ms. Lee Mackler, Chief Librarian, and Ms. Amy Chalfy, Assistant Librarian of the Postgraduate Center for Mental Health, for their kindness and cooperation in providing me with research materials and citations of publications. I am grateful for the typing of materials by Ms. Michaele Bober and Ms. Diane Gross, and sincerely appreciate the efforts of Ms. Anita Nutrell for the typing of several chapters of the manuscript.

Writing this book was like an odyssey: it was accomplished over a three-year period in Bethel, Connecticut; Cape Cod, Easthampton, Long Island; Liberty, New York; and New York City. I would especially like to thank Mildred and Irving Turkel of Bethel, who always made it so comfortable for me to work there. During this period, several people critically reviewed portions of the manuscript. Dr. Robert Plutchik reviewed several chapters and made some especially astute suggestions with regard to content and format presentation. Mr. Robert Lampert contributed some timely and valuable suggestions with respect to various parts of the introductory statement of the book. I am especially grateful to Dr. Anthony Burry, who performed an arduous and thorough review of the entire manuscript. His thoughtful comments enhanced the work in a multitude of ways.

Finally, I would like to observe that in the formulation and integration of ideas that reflect the growing edge of any field of science, the difference between discovery and invention at times becomes unclear. Many scientists in diverse disciplines have made this observation. Piaget in developmental psychology, Bronowski in mathematics and in the history of anthropology, as well as scientists in other fields have observed that the difference between discovery and invention may not even be a relevant distinction to make. Since I also have experienced the vague demarcation between discovery and invention at various times in the writing of this book, I too must join ranks with those who would minimize the difference. Further, it seems to me that invention makes discovery more possible and consequently, without invention, a work may not be as fruitful, or generate as much additional interest and research, and perhaps would not be terribly exciting. For these reasons and because of the particular way in which the theoretical synthesis is cast, this book is entirely my responsibility.

Introduction

The central task confronting group psychotherapists consists of managing three main interacting components of the group. The components are:

1. the therapy itself,
2. the group process encompassing the group therapy, and
3. the personalities of individual group members that are affected by this process.

The aim of this book is to integrate these components into one theoretical construction; to show that group psychotherapy is embedded in a continuous group process and the group develops a personality force similar to the personality structure of its individual members.

Group psychotherapists occasionally feel that something affects the group other than conventional transference phenomena. This "something" sometimes resonates with the therapy work and sometimes interferes with it. It is perhaps the effect of the three interacting components on the group that therapists uneasily sense. In this book an attempt will be made to understand these interactions further.

What are some of the important issues of each component? Therapy issues consist of organizing and conducting the group, managing transferences, and supervising the entire process of working-through. In addition, the group develops an underlying infrastructure—its governing process. This process generates stages and phases of the group in which focal conflict themes are expressed. These are group process issues. Finally, the therapist needs to understand the character formations of individual group members, with respect to both structure and dynamics. These are issues of the psychology of personality.

Actually, the group therapy literature has not produced very much theoretical work on the connection between the personality forces of individual members and those of the group process. It is the purpose of this book to show that in the therapy group, personality and process are welded together to produce a therapeutic environment for each group member. A personality theory will be developed that organizes within a single network: emotions, traits, group roles, ego-defenses, dreams and nightmares, intrapsychic forces, psychosexual levels of development, and psychosomatic symptoms. The model will reveal that this personality structure is characteristic of both individuals and the group-as-a-whole.

It also is the thesis of this book to show that the group is located in a larger evolutionary context. In this context, the therapy group represents an evolutionary advance; a workshop for examining the interaction of all three components so that the self-defeating and irrational behavior of its individual members may be modified.

The group as an evolutionary product is more specifically considered here as a sociobiological and historical environment. Its ongoing history accumulates into group generations. Its sociobiological cast is reflected in an underlying role genealogy appearing throughout all generations of the group. This interaction of group process and individual personalities constitutes a merging of extremes: the group process, in the Skinnerian sense that emphasizes the powerful effect of environment, impinges upon the deeply rooted Freudian personality structure of individual group members. The question this book seeks to answer, therefore, concerns how the ritualized personality structure of individuals intersects with seemingly immutable group processes in a way that creates a therapeutic blending.

An integration of the pertinent literature on group psychotherapy, group process, social psychology, psychoanalysis, and personality structure has been brought to bear on the overall theoretical model so that the reader may see this emerging therapeutic blending from several points of advantage.

It is hoped that this book will stimulate further thinking and research into the interaction of all three components—group therapy, group process, and individual personality structure.

1

A System of Group Structure: Basic Elements of Group Composition

It is possible to form a therapy group based upon scientific principles of group process and group composition. The formation of such a group is not merely a matter of collecting people and "circling" them, even if the aim of the group is to ventilate feelings, discuss problems, and, in some free form, to interact. The apparently simple plan of forming a therapy group actually raises a complex set of questions.

The group therapy process ideally should be set into motion as an artistic creation, attaining its own genetic and organic maturity. The therapy group needs to be an enduring creation. Such a creation must achieve certain important aims, and its implementation should be guided by organizing principles. As an example of one such principle, the group must achieve a measure of balance.

The formation of the group raises some fundamental questions of the relationship between group composition and group function. A first obvious decision-making question refers to the issue of selecting an optimal number of patients for the therapy group. This issue of group size implies that at a certain point the group may contain too many members or fewer members than are needed. How many members then are too many and how many are too few, and on what premise is the size of the group based? In addition, is there a purpose to sitting in a circle? Does the circle contain a special structural value for group therapy or is it a symbolic physical shorthand for some other more complex shape? These questions represent issues that will ultimately influence the course of the evolving group.

The very nature of the group also will be influenced by the therapist's

1

motives in forming the group. Some therapists may view the group as an expedient treatment modality; others feel that to treat patients in a group is easier and less problematic, or requires only minimal training. Furthermore, there may be an economic advantage in treating groups, which may sometimes motivate therapists to form groups regardless of questionable membership composition. Reasons of expediency need no scientific rationale. A therapist who is prepared to form a group on the basis of approximating some ideal of group composition will utilize scientific guidelines. These theoretical formulations will provide the therapist with a framework in which to select patients based upon several specific criteria. Such formulations will help the therapist to decide on the correct number of patients for the group, and may also enable the therapist to see that there operates in the group a system of forces both implied by and guiding this selection process.

In this chapter a theory of group structure is presented that stresses the balance of forces within the group. These forces are generated by an underlying structure. The underlying structure constitutes an important existing condition which enables the group ultimately to become a therapeutic emulsifying agent for each of its members. Group members need to comprise a good therapeutic blend, and this blend may be generated by the contrasting personalities in the group. Thus, in addition to the issues of patient selection and a determination of the optimal number of patients for the group, this chapter also considers the diagnostic homogeneity–heterogeneity of group membership. Diagnostic variation as an important aspect to group balance constitutes a basis for the proposition initially posed: it is possible to form a therapy group based upon principles of group process and group composition.

GROUP SIZE

The group therapy literature concerned with size of therapy groups approaches this problem in two ways. First, some therapists decide on the ideal number of patients for a group on the basis of empirical and personal experience. These therapists gain a sense of ideal group size through a process of trial and error and they are not particularly guided by how group size may relate to group process. Second, researchers attempt to determine ideal group size based on certain theoretical considerations of group process and function.

The Empirical Position Regarding Group Size

From an empirical position, some group therapists who are psychodynamically oriented have suggested that three patients constitute the smallest possible group and ten patients may be considered an upper limit of group membership (Geller, 1963). Wolf and Schwartz (1971) have described groups of 6 to 15 patients, and Winick et al (1961) have cited research reporting up to 25 patients in an analytic group. On the basis of his experience, Foulkes (1964, 1973) considers the optimal number of patients for group therapy to be seven to nine persons. Yalom (1970) also considers seven patients to be a good number, and proposes a range of five to ten members. He feels that a group ceases to operate as a therapy group with only three or four patients. Winick, Kadis and Krasner (1961) report eight patients to be the preferred number, Hartley (1963) reports an ideal range to be eight to ten patients, and Schwartz (1965a) also suggests between eight to ten patients. In an earlier publication, Wolf and Schwartz (1962) originally proposed eight patients as the ideal number for a therapy group, with eight to ten patients representing a basic range for the group. Wolf (1963) adds that fewer than eight patients makes for a potentially dull group, and more than ten patients becomes unwieldy.

From a purely practical view, Kadis et al. (1968) suggests starting a group with five patients. These authors reason that with only five patients, a secure therapeutic environment may be established. It is further implied that the group can gradually be increased to a full complement of eight members.

The Theoretical Position Regarding Group Size

PERSONALITY VARIABLES

Several authors also provide a theoretical rationale indicating that eight patients constitute the ideal number for a group. Goldfarb (1953) considers the crucial variable of the group process to be intimacy, and implies that eight patients ideally satisfy this condition of intimacy. The joining of personality variables to considerations of group process provides a basis for investigating the entire problem of ideal group size. Authors who propose eight or fewer patients as the ideal number for a group consider this "rule of eight" to be based upon maintaining control over the group process. More specifically, these authors suggest that a chaotic group may develop with more than eight members, especially since the disruptive force of acting-out can potentially increase if the group is too large (Loeser, 1957). Hare (1952, 1962), in studies of differently sized groups, makes this general point in regard to a large group. The large group is seen as one in which cliques can easily develop, disruptive subgroups can form, and the group can become generally more dissatisfied and less consensus seeking.

The potential for acting-out in larger groups is more specifically understood as the acting-out of anger and aggression. Carter (1958) observes that the more aggressive types in the group will be able to express themselves at the expense of the less forceful types, who in turn will become quite inhibited and unable to express themselves at all. One aspect of Carter's observation implies that it may be necessary to understand and control the force of aggression in the group before any others. First, this may be done by keeping the group membership to about the generally accepted norm of eight members; and second, the group may be composed in a way that creates a balance of forces in which aggressive urges are not unduly represented in the overall repertoire of group responses. When the anger component in the group is correctly balanced, the group environment becomes one in which accumulated rage will be continually diluted.

This view of the group as an environment in which members can examine their feelings and work through emotional distortion is directly implied from object relations theory (Guntrip, 1969; Kernberg, 1970b; Winnicott, 1971). In an important theoretical paper, Kosseff (1975) relates group psychotherapy practice to object relations theory and he perceives the group to be endowed with qualities of transitional objects. Each of its members can work through dependency, helplessness, and inferiority feelings and therefore use the group to resolve problems of rage distortion. A balanced group helps, through introjection and identification, to rebalance each of its members.

To this theme of balance, Cartwright and Zander (1968) connect group size with group cohesion. Group cohesion may become noticeably affected when the number of members varies significantly above or below eight. Turquet (1974) suggests that overall task requirements should also determine the structure and composition of the group. The therapy group may be represented by a membership range of 6 to 16 patients, with a conventional size of 8 to 12 and an upper real limit of 12. It is felt that more than 12 patients make it difficult for any member to maintain a therapeutic attitude, and fewer than five or six patients create the circumstances for extra resistance phenomena to exist in the group.

Finally, Loeser (1957) offers a cogent argument for the size of the group to vary between four and eight members. Loeser feels that seven constitutes the ideal number of members in the group with the therapist presumably acting as the eighth member. Additional group members would create a different sort of group in which the therapeutic fiber might tend to disintegrate. Loeser considers seven members to constitute a better group because the group:

1. will contain diluted libidinal drives
2. will express intra-group transferences
3. cannot be destroyed by one or two people
4. will contain a heterogeneity of psychodynamic types
5. may handle acting out
6. can be a therapeutic environment where the therapist's activity may be held to a minimum
7. maintains only a few regulations, and
8. provides time and attention for each person.

Experienced group therapists would most likely agree with this formulation.

APPARENT SIZE VERSUS ACTUAL SIZE

In a more ambitious theoretical approach, Rey (1975) relates the size of groups to the early stages of spatial organization of the body-ego, and the number of internal and external objects as part of that body-ego. These cumulative inner objects of individuals add to the population of the existing group. The group has to contain this accumulated body politic and therefore will have to deal with a multitude of transferences. Thus, size of the group is vitally important.

> *Each member and the analyst are substructures of the group with their inner world of internal objects. It follows that the number of psychic objects as opposed to the number of members, i.e. apparent size, must be the decisive factor. Experience seems to indicate a smaller number than the traditional eight and one oscillating around five. (Rey, 1975).*

The question raised here is whether the group contains a true number of inner objects. One implication of this formulation is that too many inner object members may interfere with the group process. However, Rey's conservative estimate that five members constitute an ideal group may not take into account that a multiplicity of transferences in the group is frequently desirable. This transference matrix makes possible an extended inner-object group whose basic apparent membership is certainly more than five members.

The concept of inner-object endowment raises the theoretical possibility that determining the size of a therapy group can be based upon an examination of the family model, because each group member transports several additional inner-object figures into the group. These inner-object figures are historical family figures. Schindler (1973), indicating that seven or eight members constitute an ideal number of patients for a group, also suggests that seven or eight members similarly comprise a statistically average primary extended family. In terms of this family model as it relates to the development of inner objects, it may be hypothesized that the primary members include parents and children and the extended members include grandparents and a few other family members. Thus the inner objects of group membership also contain generational components. This issue of generational aspects of the therapy group will be explored in chapter 4.

The formulation of group inner objects also raises the question of the total number of such objects contained within the group. It is an issue of apparent size versus actual or implicit size. The apparent size of a group may be eight members, but the actual size in a transferential and inner-object sense may be far larger. An apparent group of eight members plus the therapist may contain an implicit supra-group of 72 or more members, with each member and the therapist hypothetically sharing an average of eight other inner-object figures in the group.

A distinction of apparent size versus implicit size suggests that any group maintains within itself the possibility of a multitude of transferences. This proliferated transference environment allows for a potentially rich therapeutic climate to exist in the group. The apparent group size and its expanded implicit group size also allow for a diversity of emotions to exist in the group, so that members of the group are able to express and share a wide range of feelings. This diversity of emotional responsivity is the basis of the group's interactional nature, and its existence in the group creates the possibility of great therapeutic ferment.

SESSION LENGTH AND GROUP SIZE

Foulkes and Anthony (1957) raise one final issue in the determination of group size. They also indicate that seven to eight members represent an ideal group size, and suggest that, ". . . numbers help to determine the size of the group circle and the amount of group time each member imagines is portioned to him. . . ." This is a novel way of seeing the problem of group size. It suggests some further ideas of group size in terms of the length of an actual group therapy session. For example, group members may imagine that an objective allocation of participatory time exists in the group, divided equally for each of them. This objective allocation of time may be based upon the actual length of the session divided by group membership. The authors further point out that 90 minutes, embraced by a range of 60 to 90 minutes, constitutes the duration of a typical group therapy session. Since a group may consist of eight members plus the therapist, nine in all, then each of the nine may be operating on the basis of an implicit and unconscious arithmetic. A 90-minute session divided by a membership of nine produces a time sense in which each member of the group assumes a ten-minute participation period. This becomes an objective individual allocation of time assumed by the therapist and each group member to be part of the group structure.

A second implication of this equation of length of session divided by group size relates to the difference between the objective ten-minute participation time assumed by each member, and the actual participation of each member. Although the members may share the calculation of participation time, in actual practice, because the group may be diagnostically heterogeneous, assumed participation time is quite differently calibrated than actual participation time. For example, aggressive, gregarious, and intellectualizing types may exploit the assumed talk-time of passive, depressed, and otherwise schizoid withdrawn types by monopolizing group interactions. This also suggests that actual participation time may not simply differ from that of assumed participation time but even by systematically different than assumed participation time, and this systematic difference is governed by considerations of diagnostic group composition.

This issue of the distribution of communicational interaction is discussed by Bales et al. (1951) and reviewed by Mills (1974). Mills asks whether a pattern exists in the distribution of interaction. He implies some design or structure to communicational networks. Bales discusses the distribution of member's interaction in terms of the extent to which every other member has already acted. These authors postulate a ratio of relative output of a member to total membership output. The assumed allocation of participation time calculated by members is probably a simple apportionment of talk-time. In actual practice, the arithmetic of interactional time may more correctly resemble the Bales ratio.

There is a third implication of an equation that relates length of session to group size, resulting in an assumed ten-minute allocation of participation time for each group member. This equation also implies that a small group size increases participation time for each member and a larger group size decreases this time. The equation applies if a session length of 90 minutes is held constant. If session length increases, group size also may increase, especially if the ten-minute cumulative participation period is considered to be an important constant. The communicational implications of group size and session length also may contribute to an understanding of time-extended groups, the scientific underpinning of which is currently in an embryonic stage.

It would seem that a group size of eight and a session length of 90 minutes probably constitutes an ideal group therapy condition and partially addresses the question of the rationale for a 90-minute session. This rationale is based upon the various criteria set forth by authors who are concerned with determining ideal group size based upon important group and personality variables. A review of these factors reveals a fourth implication of a ten-minute participation time period hypothetically allocated for each group member. In terms of face validity, it is perfectly reasonable to assume that an objective ten-minute apportionment of time which each member may use in some communicational form has at least two kinds of beneficial effects on the group and on individuals in the group. First, a 90-minute session divided among all members in terms of hypothetical, equal participation time does not allow any single member to be considered somehow especially privileged. This condition permits the control of undue aggressivity and the modification of acting-out behavior. Second, this sense of participation permits each member an adequate span of time, whether used intermittently or in larger clusters, to develop and express feelings of intimacy and trust, and eventually, to discover ways of attaining a significant measure of self-disclosure. The development of such qualities ultimately contributes to the overall therapeutic climate of the group. In addition, this ten-minute allocation time potentially ensures that all members may participate in the group. This maximum participation time, although recognized as a hypothetical condition, may help to generate the most therapeutic kind of group cohesion. Finally, when a condition exists that permits all members potentially to participate in the group, an opportunity for emotional diversity to exist is also maximized. It is precisely this goal of creating emotional diversity that characterizes the direction toward which a group strives.

Determining group size, then, has been related to issues of cohesiveness, intimacy, aggression, acting out, the apparent group versus the actual group, the apportionment of participation time for each group member, the length of group sessions, and the importance of ensuring a group climate that permits a diversity of emotion to exist, with the "rule of eight" representing an ideal group size.

Creating a group in which the entire emotional responsivity domain is sampled raises the question of the diagnostic composition of the group. If the diagnostic composition of the group is somewhat restricted, the emotional diversity of the group also may be restricted. The issue then becomes one of creating a basic diagnostic composition that in diversity of emotion and in the diagnostic balance of forces allows a structure to develop which will enhance the group process.

A question therefore needs to be raised in which the issue of emotional diversity is related to group function and group process. What constitutes emotional diversity and how may it be understood, especially with regard to the theoretical network of the therapy group?

EMOTIONAL DIVERSITY AS AN ELEMENT OF GROUP COMPOSITION

The Importance of a Full Emotion Range in the Group

Many authors agree that group therapy process becomes increasingly enhanced when, in the group, there are many emotions expressed. This proposition implies at least two basic themes. The first shows that therapy groups become potentially more therapeutic as a function of emotional diversity represented in role composition of the group and in member interaction. A corollary to this theme indicates that a group with emotional restriction is potentially less therapeutic and may contain inherently fewer growth features. Such a group may be one in which the membership composition is diagnostically restricted. A second theme proposes that the ideal condition of the therapy group is for a great variety of emotion to exist, provided the membership is composed in a specific way. A group composed of diagnostically heterogeneous members, that is, with a membership composition sampling the full range of emotions, may maximize the group's therapeutic potential.

Emotional Forces

The idea of the creation of a group in which a full range of emotion is sampled within the membership suggests that, in the ideal diagnostic composition of the group, a specific underpinning of emotional forces exists. The concept of diagnostic heterogeneity may be understood with reference to this system. Kadis et al. (1968) recognize this implication and state, "The group process is a tangled fabric of pushing and pulling, hate and love, aggression and passivity, coolness and warmth. All of these different emotional directions serve the purpose of strengthening the therapeutic cohesiveness of the group." This tangled fabric is similar to Darwin's (1859) tangled bank, in which seemingly endless variation is basically derived from only a few developmental strains.

The emotional dispositions that Kadis et al. cite may in fact not be tangled, but rather may be part of some specific emotion system. For example, in considering the forces of pushing and pulling, hate and love, aggression and passivity, and coolness and warmth, the authors are implying that at least some of the forces of the group are conflictual or opposites. The group may contain a system of forces theoretically understood to be one of polarities.

In formulating their sense of conflicting or opposite forces, Kadis et al. did not view the group as one that expresses emotion randomly. Rather, they implied that such forces, as they begin to operate in the group, create the possibility for a complex of interactions to exist. The emotional repertoire of the group experience may seem tangled, but only because the system allows for a maximum of emotional diversity to exist. Diversity and 'tangledness' are not necessarily synonymous.

Emotional Themes

At first glance, the group's interactional process seems quite unsystematic. However, results of a wide cross section of group therapy research indicate that the nature of such interaction may in fact be determined and understood with reference to a few basic underlying group themes. For example, Bion (1961) proposes a few "assumption cultures" that are common to all group therapy experiences. Categories of assumption cultures are really basic dispositional characteristics of the group structure. They determine the predominant emotional and interactional nature of the group at any given time. They are designed to help members avoid the experience of anxiety. These cultures assume that all behavior and emotionality of the group may be understood with reference to two basic conditions. One condition is called the assumption group, in which members function with regard to an overall resistance theme. The second overall group condition is called the work group, in which members are motivated by a desire to know, to gain insight, and to understand.

There are three distinct assumption groups containing corresponding and prevailing emotions. The dependent group is one in which the emotions of guilt and depression are expressed. These emotion themes are reflected in the wishes and behavior of group members who look to the leader for security. The pairing group is one in which the emotions of hope and sexuality characterize the basic underlying theme of the group interaction. Group members express such emotion themes by identifications with any two members who constitute a romantic heterosexual couple. The third pattern of the assumption group is called the fight–flight group: hate and anger determine interactions of the group and thematic material of extreme hostility or phobic withdrawal characterizes the overall group interaction. The fight part of this group is expressed when the group as a whole continually attacks the therapist, disregarding any concern with realistic justification. The flight part is evident whenever avoidance behavior characterizes the group's interactional nature. The group may only be influenced by one of these cultures at a given time; that is, when the group operates on the basis of any one assumption then the other so-called assumtion groups are temporarily dormant. For all practical purposes the terms assumption cultures and assumption groups may be used interchangeably.

Bion correlates basic cultures to six emotions: guilt, depression, hope, sexuality, hate, and anger. The six emotions, as they express basic phases of group culture, also may be considered to comprise Bion's basic emotion structure of therapy groups. This sort of underlying emotion structure for groups also is recognized by Thelen et al. (1954). The authors derive four classes of emotionality and four corresponding qualities of work behavior to represent the basic underlying group organization. The four classes of events were derived originally from Bion's three basic assumption cultures. The basic assumption cultres may actually reflect a greater aggregate of emotion than originally suggested by Bion. It may be hypothesized that the fight group is characterized by the emotion of anger, while the flight group is motivated by the emotion of fear as well as perhaps by some variation of loss or hopelessness. Thus Bion's notion of basic emotion forces which are contained within the assumption cultures increases from a total of six—guilt, depression, hope, sexuality, hate, and anger—to perhaps seven or eight forces, adding fear and hopelessness. This structural approach to understanding group interaction and process implies that the alleged tangle of forces in the group really may be only a manifestation of a few basic categories comprising an underlying system of emotion.

BASIC EMOTION SYSTEMS

The idea that basic emotions may be different from mixed or complex emotions has its historical roots in the description of basic mood reactions implied by Aristotle (Nowlis, 1970) and in the basic emotions noted by Descartes, Spinoza, Hobbes, McDougall, and more recently by Plutchik (1962) and Milenson (1967). An adaptational evolutionary approach to the understanding of basic emotions has been made by Murray (1954), Turner (1957), Scott (1958), and Plutchik (1962). Although these approaches are based upon the conception of individual behavior, nevertheless they resemble quite closely the categories derived by Bion in his analysis of group phenomena. In Table 1-1, a

Table 1-1. A comparison of the Bionian system of group behavior with other emotion systems conceived for individual behavior

BION	DESCARTES	SPINOZA	HOBBES	McDOUGALL	PLUTCHIK
Hope	Love	Joy	Love	Tender	Acceptance
Depression	Sadness	Sorrow	Grief	Subjection	Sadness
Sexuality	Desire	Desire	Desire	Elation	Joy
Hate	Hatred		Hate	Disgust	Disgust
Anger			Aversion	Anger	Anger
Guilt					
	Admiration				
	Joy		Joy		
				Fear	Fear
				Wonder	Surprise
					Expectation

comparison is made of Bion's basic emotion system for groups with other basic emotion systems developed with respect to individual functioning. Inspection of Table 1-1 shows that only the emotion of guilt in Bion's system is not specifically duplicated anywhere else as a basic tendency. Although hope also is not precisely indicated by other authors, it is nevertheless closely allied to emotions such as love and joy, which are generally seen to be basic states. Both love and joy contain elements of optimism and anticipation of pleasure, and therefore in an indirect way they resemble Bion's hope. Except for these few differences, an examination of Table 1-1 indicates that the formulation of basic emotion systems for individual behavior corresponds quite closely to an emotion system developed to account for group behavior. Implicit in this comparison is the idea that additional parallels may be drawn between individual and group behavior. Implications generated from these comparisons may provide a basis for the further understanding of the phenomena of group infrastructure.

The comparison between individual emotion systems and group emotion systems also was viewed as a potentially fruitful avenue of research by Bach (1954). Bach utilized Bion's basic assumption cultures as a basis for proposing that a therapy group contains a membership composition that may express an amalgam of basic emotions. This conception is also cited by Johnson (1963), who points out that specific behaviors of the group correlate to the emotions of fear, rage, and guilt. The correlation of these emotions to behavioral patterns is determined by how well fear, rage, and guilt are managed. Apparently Johnson considers that a proliferation of behavioral patterns in the group results from the difficulty in managing these few basic emotions.

A further attempt to develop a reductionistic approach toward understanding group therapy interaction has been made by Schutz (1958), who suggested that the group evolves in terms of a developmental sequence. This development is guided by three major needs: the need for inclusion, the need to control, and the need for affection. These are related to basic Freudian psychosexual themes of oral, anal, and oedipal development. Schutz's need system may also be interpreted as an attempt to define basic emotional inclinations of the group.

Emotion and Group Diagnostic Composition

The relation between emotions expressed in the group and individual personality is noted by Durkin (1964) who indicates, ". . . each member's valency for the group emotion and his mode of reacting to it are products of his character, and therefore of his genetic history." Furthermore, there is a connection made between the roles occupied by group members and basic emotions. The essence of roles are the basic emotions that become expressed by the propensities contained within the roles. This view is proposed by Foulkes (1964) who, in addition to indicating that individuals express specific emotions in their roles, also notes that these roles and emotions are polarized within the group. Such views provide a bridge between the domain of emotion expressed by group members and the system of diagnostic composition of the group.

The relation between basic emotions and the diagnostic composition of the group implies the primary issue that diagnostic group composition should not be a fortuitous creation. The group may develop and evolve a healthy complexity based upon the existence of basic underlying forces of emotion. As various authors have pointed out, there may be certain basic emotional propensities that should be represented in the group composition in order for the group to develop its natural complexity and ultimately to realize its therapeutic goals.

Diagnostic Group Composition: An Introduction

There exists a general theoretical agreement with regard to the problem of diagnostic group composition. Most authors consider diagnostic pluralism to contain the greatest potential for the achievement of therapeutic goals. This issue of group composition has been elaborated by Locke (1961), Mullan and Rosenbaum (1962), and Whitaker and Lieberman (1964). Although Wolf and Schwartz (1962) point out that the nature of the homogeneity of the group is an important aspect of group functioning, it seems clear that their conception of group homogeneity refers to the process of patient selection, in which the disparity between degrees of pathology is kept to a minimum. These authors go on to indicate that heterogeneous groups are essentially more therapeutic than groups that are homogeneous. Foulkes and Anthony (1965) also address this issue in noting, ". . . according to some authorities, too wide a range of diagnostic reaction types may build up into a self-disruptive force. . . . Bringing compatible people together certainly makes for a more comfortable group life, but whether it makes for better group therapy is only to some extent true." The authors imply that there may be a hypothetical full diagnostic range that can be approximated in the composition of the group which is neither disruptive nor inbred.

PROBLEMS OF A DIAGNOSTIC SYSTEM

The issue of a diagnostic system has been disparaged by many authors. Yalom (1970), for example, indicates that ". . . the psychiatric diagnosis based on the American Psychiatric Association official manual is . . . spectacularly useless as an indicator of interpersonal behavior." Yalom calls it "diagnostic folly." The reliability and validity problems of this diagnostic system are revealed by Beck et al. (1962), who studied judges' agreement of psychiatric diagnoses. Results showed that agreement was low for diagnoses of neurotic depression, anxiety reaction, schizophrenia, and personality trait disturbance. The main difficulty of such diagnostic descriptions is that their original formulations were based upon atheoretical and strictly empirical observation. The psychiatric nosology as it is currently formulated (Gruenberg, et al., 1968) is largely based upon an operational approach to the problem of diagnosis. Its "diagnostic folly" is generated from the formulation of a system based upon an arbitrary nosological classification along one or two lines of diagnostic commonality.

To classify a series of diagnoses as to whether patients do or do not experience anxiety, or do or do not express affect appropriately, lacks a firm theoretical foundation, and such an approach is not embedded in any significant nomological network. To be useful, classification of diagnoses should be based upon a multitude of factors that in turn are systematized by organizing principles. The folly of an empirical nosology becomes especially obvious in comparison to a classification system generated from personality theory, in which diagnoses are implied by underlying organizing categories.

In Support of a Diagnostic Model

The importance of the diagnostically heterogeneous group has been noted by Rosow and Kaplan (1954) and by Slavson (1953, 1957). Glatzer (1956) indicates that this heterogeneity includes basic diagnostic polarities which create a productive counterpoint for each other. As an illustration, Glatzer offers the example of how the hysteric and compulsive types are interesting and good for each other. This idea of diagnostic polarity is also recognized by Foulkes and Anthony (1965) who, in discussing principles of patient selection, elaborate the importance of the heterogeneous group and introduce the concept of blending diagnoses. They indicate that "the greater the span between polar types, the higher the therapeutic potential" existing in the group.

Diagnostic polarity has also been called complementary transactions. Anthony (1960), who rejects general diagnostic classification, nevertheless has come to recognize six complementary transactions. These general characterological dispositional states or inclinations which are expressed in many groups are: exhibitionistic–voyeuristic, heterosexual–homosexual, sadistic–masochistic, penis pride–penis envy, manic–depressive, and progression-regression. Johnson (1963) also suggests that in the selection process, a sampling of neurotic classification will produce enough diversity of diagnosis to provide for a suitable group composition. This selection of suitable patients diagnosed as neurotic include: depressive reaction, obsessive-compulsive, anxiety reaction, conversion hysteria, and phobic reaction. It is also emphasized that none of these diagnostic states occur in pure form because frequently personality structure is mixed. The implication for group structure is that a distinction must be made between basic diagnostic dispositions and the more mixed diagnoses. Mixed diagnoses may be composed of only a few basic dispositional states. Any theory of group composition needs to account for the relationship between primary or basic dispositions and more secondary or mixed states. This point historically has been made in emotion theory by Descartes, who postulated that there is a difference between a few primary emotions and the other more mixed emotions which are generated from these few primaries, as well as by Spinoza, who made this point sharply, even postulating that all emotions are derived from only three basic states (Plutchik, 1962).

Creation of a basic group structure is reflected by the expression of all the basic emotions in the group's role repertoire. This completed role repertoire implies that a full complement of diagnostic possibilities exists in the group. Thus, expressions of all basic dispositions reveal the full complexity of emotional interaction in the group. Stock and Thelen (1958) underscore this point by indicating that a group having a wide range of valency types deals with a wider range of emotional issues.

In postulating a basic organization of dispositional states of the group, many authors outline certain central criterion issues. One of the these central issues leads inexorably to the conclusion that a system of basic dispositional states seems to consist of opposite or polar forces. A second major issue suggests that a theory of group composition should be able to distinguish pure states from mixed or more complex states. In terms of a similarity structure of diagnosis, a theory of group composition should also be able to enumerate a diagnostically heterogeneous range that is related to basic emotions—one that clarifies the concept of diagnostic blending.

These issues raise some immediate questions. What are these basic emotion states that become expressed through basic diagnostic dispositional types? How many basic emotion states are there? Is there any way of measuring them? How do they relate to each other in terms of their polarity? What is meant by a good diagnostic blend? The following chapter will explore some of these questions.

2

A System of Group Structure: Measurement and Emotion Structure

In order to elaborate the basic group diagnostic composition, it is first necessary to investigate the basic underlying emotion structure of the group. Just as a system of group composition needs to distinguish certain dispositional phenomena, so too must an emotion theory address itself to several additional important questions. The emotion theory should be analyzed with respect to its similarity structure; that is, with respect to the relation of one emotion to another. Second, the theory should elaborate its implicit system of polarities. Finally, this emotion model should be based upon evolutionary adaptational considerations so that its relevance to human groups is increased. The emotion model should be governed by a method or system of organizing principles that can reveal the connections between emotions, roles and diagnostic structure of human groups.

The following section will describe a method that permits the ordering of concepts with regard to the question of how one concept relates to another. In particular, the relationship of one emotion to another will be considered along with the relationship of each emotion to its polar opposite. The method employed demonstrates the utilization of organizing principles. A description of a theory of emotion then will be presented that allows for basic emotion categories to be related to basic dispositional or diagnostic types.

A CIRCUMPLEX STRUCTURE OF FORCES

According to Cartwright and Zander (1968), "when a group acquires some stability in the arrangement of relationships among members, it may be said to be structured." This arrangement of relationships implies some method of por-

15

traying the degree of similarity and disparity of relational components. When a set of concepts are systematically related, then they are also said to possess an organizing principle. This sort of idea was proposed by Schaefer and Plutchik (1966), who hypothesized that a circular configuration—a circumplex—could be found for personality traits, emotion signs, and diagnostic constructs. The authors postulated that together these universes form "a conceptually differentiated but highly integrated system of inter-connected signs." Plutchik (1974) describes the circumplex as "an ordered series of correlations in a matrix. When the elements of the correlation matrix show a range of correlations from high positive to high negative, then a factor analysis of the data will usually reveal a circular ordering of the variables." Therefore, the circumplex is a mapping of configurational relationships. It is considered to be an important method for viewing concepts because it creates a relational matrix. Whatever the variation of components in this matrix may be, the basic relational network remains the same.

The circumplex has no beginning and no end. Concepts may be ordered in terms of a similarity–disparity gradient. Thus the system generates general laws of relationship. One law may be described as a law of neighboring: it states that the forces located close to one another in the circle share common properties and are most similar. Another law indicates that any two forces that are most disparate in their location in the circle may approximate a position of polarity. Thus, the second law in this similarity structure is the law of polarity. This general system was first studied by Guttman (1954). It also has been used in the ordering of personality concepts (Block, 1957; Lodge, 1953); in the study of the social behavior of children (Becker and Krug, 1964); by Freedman et al. (1951), who studied the interpersonal dimension of personality; by Lodge and Gibson (1953) to develop a map of personality; by Lorr and McNair (1963), who devised an interpersonal behavior circle; and in a series of studies by Schaefer (1957, 1958, 1959, 1961), who related maternal behavior with child behavior and investigated a model of personality development.

Figure 2-1 is an example of a circular ordering of emotions as portrayed with the primary dimensions of facial expression (Schlosberg 1952; Woodworth and Schlosberg, 1954). The circular plot was used to locate 72 Frois-Wittmann pictures, and it shows that each of the pictures may be related to every other picture in terms of an implicit similarity structure.

Another portrayal of the circumplex is shown in Figure 2-2. Schaefer (1961) demonstrates that interpersonal behavior and personality traits may be organized in a circumplex. Figure 2-3 is a more complex example of the circumplex, showing the similarity structure and implicit system of polarities of a measure of emotion terms as compared with a universe of personality terms (Schaefer and Plutchik, 1966).

In Figure 2-4, Kellerman (1965) demonstrates that the circumplex allows for an evaluation of basic changes in the implicit structure of a personality trait domain as a function of degree of maladjustment. In this study, a matched sample of normal subjects with an absence of symptoms was compared to a sample of moderately and severely disturbed subjects who showed a wide variety of symptoms. Results revealed a systematic shift in the implicit arrangement of trait behavior on the circumplex as maladjustment increased. Thus a group of anger-related traits cluster in the severely disturbed group. The relation of traits such as resentful, sullen, gloomy, and impulsive reflect a syndrome of anger in this disturbed group.

Within the circumplex, two independent dimensions emerge from the data. These dimensions are used to help organize a given domain of concepts in a more systematic fashion. They may be considered to be a single heuristic device in the organization of the data. For example, Shostrom (1971) and Shostrom and Kavanaugh (1971) used the Leary (1957) two-dimensional system of anger–love and strength–weakness as a fundamental way of understanding mate selection and all mate pairings. Figure 2-5 shows this circular similarity structure of mate selection and pairings. Despite certain theoretical difficulties in the formulation of this system (Kellerman, 1977b), Shostrom nevertheless has attempted to organize a great body of data into a more parsimonious scheme through the use of a circumplex-like approach.

Carson (1969) reviewed the literature that uses this approach to derive a few factors in the study of interpersonal behavior. Underlying factors of interpersonal behavior were also studied by Dunphy (1974), who used a principal components factor analysis to derive common trends of content in groups. Dunphy formulated the idea that role differentiation, fantasy activity, and group development fall into one inclusive framework. Bales (1970) also used a factor analysis to study interpersonal behavior. He produced a three-dimensional interpersonal space in which status and power, likeability, and task commitment constituted the major factors. Most of the research on interpersonal behavior that uses factor analytic techniques or circumplex plotting of data have derived either two or three major factors within which all interpersonal behavior may be located.

There are several other studies that further illustrate two-dimensional circular systems. Diamond (1957) designated extraversion–intraversion and love–hostility as two independent dimensions. Freedman et al. (1951) derived dimensions of love–hostility and dominance–submission; Schaefer (1958) derived the dimensions of love–hostility and autonomy–control; Stagner (1948) derived dimensions of excitement–depression and pleasantness–unpleasantness; and Leary (1957) used dimensions of love–anger and strength–weakness as the basis of a test designed to measure aspects of personality.

In terms of the use of two-factor studies with groups, Bennis and Shepard (1974) describe group phenomena or barometric events of the group in the following way. They indicate that group development is influenced by a group's internal uncertainty. This subgroup pattern consists of two factors. The first is a dependence factor in which authority relations influence the

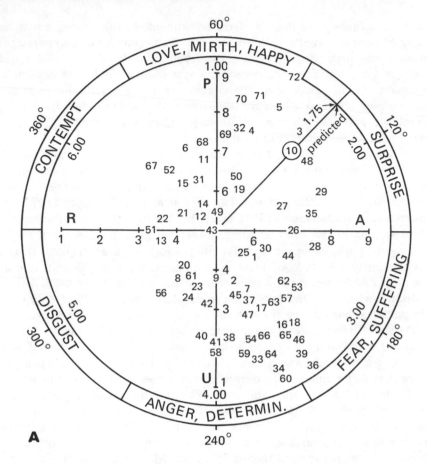

Figure 2-1.   A circular ordering of emotions portrayed as primary dimensions of facial expression. (A) The location of each of the 72 Frois-Wittmann pictures on an oval surface. Picture No. 10 (encircled) serves as an example of the method used. It is plotted at axis values of P-U = 7, A-R = 7, as determined by the rating scales. A thread is then stretched from the intersection of the axes (5.5) across the plotted point, and its position read off in degrees. Dividing by 60 yields the predicted circular scale value (1.75), which is compared with that obtained earlier by direct sorting on the scale (1.65). This picture might be called "pleased surprise," and both predicted and obtained values place it in the appropriate step of the Woodworth scale (Woodworth and Schlosberg, 1954). (B) The location of typical pictures of the Frois-Wittmann series. This display includes

group. The second is an interdependence factor which involves personal relations that are qualitatively different than member-to-member authority relations. These two factors are essentially the power and love dimensions noted by Leary, and together they generate the group's "internal uncertainty."

    In the study of diagnostic nosology (Plutchik and Platman, 1977) and in studies of emotions and personality traits (Kellerman and Plutchik, 1968) the

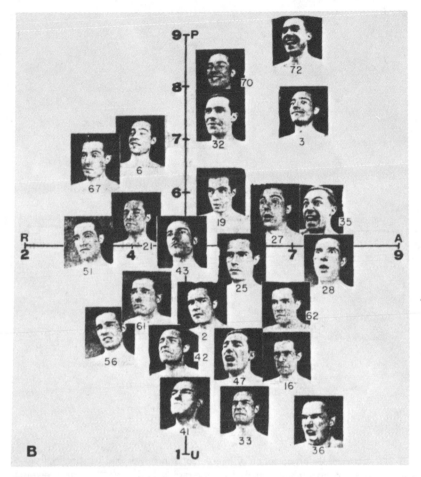

facial expressions reflecting emotions which are shown around the margin of the surface in Fig. 2-1B, and as many of the more centrally located ones as could be mounted. The average error of prediction for these 24 pictures is a half-scale step, just as it is for the whole series of 72. The picture with the worst prediction of the whole series is No. 43 at the intersection of the axes. The plots show that each of the pictures may be related to every other picture in terms of an implicit similarity structure. (From Schlosberg, The description of facial expressions in terms of two dimensions, *J. Exp. Psychol.* 1952, 44:229–237. Copyright 1952 by the American Psychological Association. Reprinted by permission.)

circumplex has produced a consistent and similar network of personality components. Figure 2-6 represents the study by Plutchik et al. (1977). It shows the implicit circumplex structure of diagnostic categories as judged by a sample of psychiatrists.

The circumplex system of analyzing a set of concepts therefore has been used to locate interpersonal behavior, emotions, personality traits, and diag-

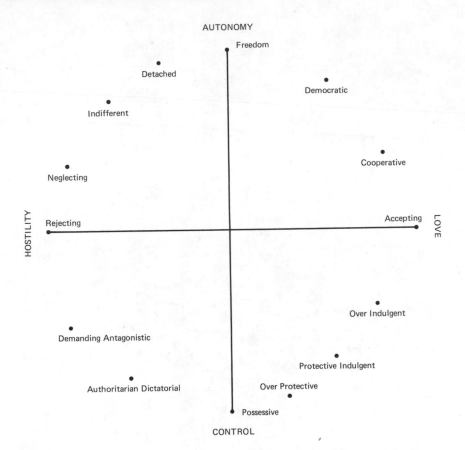

Figure 2-2.   A circumplex organization of interpersonal behavior and personality traits. (From Schaefer, Converging conceptual models for maternal behavior and for child behavior. In: Glidewell, J. C. (ed.), *Parental attitudes and child behavior*. Springfield, Ill., Thomas, 1961, with permission.)

nostic constructs. It even has been used to locate therapy group members in terms of the group's similarity structure of membership (Kellerman and Plutchik, 1978). In this study, all members of a therapy group were tested with the Emotions Profile Index (Plutchik and Kellerman, 1974). The EPI is a test of emotion and personality. The group members were drug addicts. Each member took the test as the items applied to self, and then rescored the test by applying the items to each other member of the group including the therapist. This technique produced a personality circumplex matrix based upon underlying personality trait forces. Each of the group members were located on the circumplex in terms of an implicit similarity structure. The locations were then correlated with diagnostic dispositions; the final circumplex shows member location related to diagnostic location. This approach allowed the subjects to

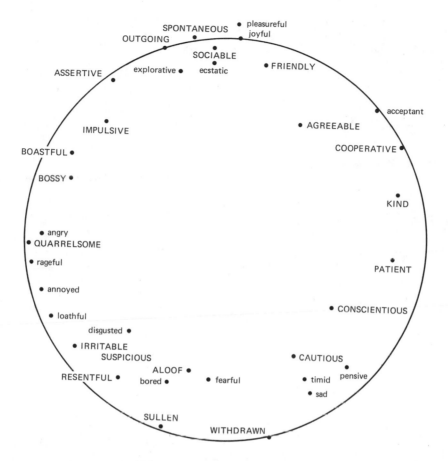

Figure 2-3.   A circumplex organization of emotion terms and personality traits. (Reprinted with permission of authors and publisher from: Schaefer, E. S. and Plutchik, R. Interrelationships of emotions, traits, and diagnostic constructs. *Psychological Reports,* 1966, *18,* 399–410.)

be arranged on the circumplex grid based upon the interaction of total group dispositional forces. Figure 2-7 shows the circle of members and their diagnostic points of reference. From these plots, certain predictions regarding prognosis and treatment outcome may be made.

The results of these many studies suggest that despite a variety of approaches, most authors derive overlapping or similar dimensions in both the study of individual personality and the study of personality features of group behavior.

The circumplex is a methodological advance. Its use and the application of two-dimensional models demonstrate the correlations among and similarity structure of emotions, diagnostic constructs, traits, and tendencies. This is an important methodological feature that may be used to examine the construc-

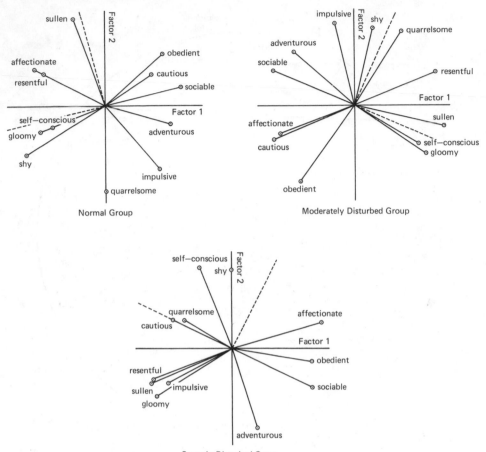

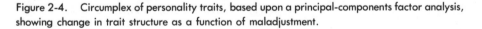

Figure 2-4.   Circumplex of personality traits, based upon a principal-components factor analysis, showing change in trait structure as a function of maladjustment.

tion of a theoretical group composition, since authors of group therapy texts (Johnson, 1963; Kadis et al., 1968) do not usually distinguish between diagnostic, emotion, trait, and "tendency" language in the conception and formulation of basic forces of the group. Any system that could show implicit relationships between these languages would go far to facilitate a conceptual refinement.

Thus the circumplex system portrays in a circular form a structural organization of forces. Such an organization as it relates to emotion can portray the arrangement of basic emotions, create a logic for understanding the balance of forces, and show the arrangement of polar forces. A theory of emotion that uses a circular system, considers the idea of basic states as an underpinning for more mixed states, and, considers the idea of polarity, may also ultimately be related to a group structure in which emotion becomes expressed through roles that in turn contain implicit diagnostic correlations.

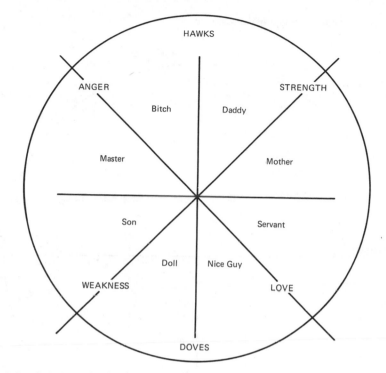

Figure 2-5. Pair Attraction Inventory categories arranged in a circular model, showing a two-dimensional structure of anger—love and strength—weakness. (From Shostrom, 1970, with permission.)

Figure 2-6. A circumplex organization of diagnostic terms based upon a factor analysis of psychiatrists' definitions. (From Plutchik, R., and Platman, S. R. Personality connotations of psychiatric diagnosis. *Journal of Nervous and Mental Disease*, 1977, 165:418—422. Copyright 1977, the Williams & Wilkins Co., Baltimore.)

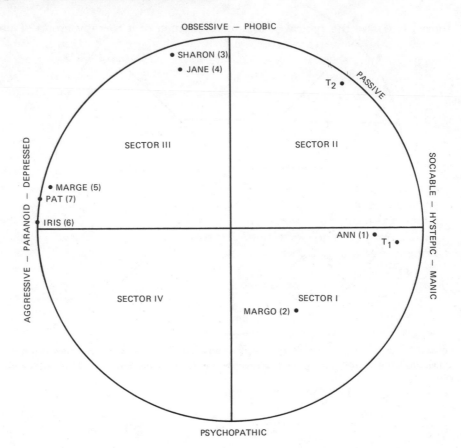

Figure 2-7.   Location of group members determined by rotated factor loadings and based upon personality profiles. A hypothetical underlying diagnostic structure is also presented. (From Kellerman and Plutchik, 1978, with permission.)

Foulkes and Anthony (1965) indicate that a circular system is of special theoretical significance. They say that there is psychological meaning to the circle. To some extent, circle has some special meaning in language as seen in the expressions "magic circle, best circles, circle of friends, wheels within wheels." In addition, the authors indicate that there appears "in the language of the emotions an ambivalence of positive and negative—attracting and repelling, loving and hating—forces." In discussing group behavior, Mills (1974) proposes a similar metaphor. He writes, "much of the iceberg of group process is below the surface: feelings of pleasure or displeasure; wishes to affirm or to disaffirm; evaluations of others as good or bad, and of their actions as appropriate or inappropriate," characterizes the group setting.

The circular system is ideally suited to represent the operation of such forces. It is also the typical seating configuration of a therapy group. This circular seating pattern has been traditionally used because it offers all members the greatest communicational and interactional possibilities, and in addition it tacitly assumes a 'democracy of visibility'. To these traditionally accepted tenets of the circular seating arrangement, a new criterion must be added. The circular seating configuration of a therapy group seems to be a primary arrangement, one that is ideally suited to the nature of the therapy task. This circular pattern may have its own intrinsically compelling nature. When a therapy group convenes, the nature of the task inclines the group to arrange itself in a circle. Underlying personality forces may 'need' to express and synchronize their so-called positiveness and negativeness, their attractingness and repellingness, their lovingness and hatingness, and their overall "pushingness" and "pullingness." A circle may be the correct organizing structure that facilitates this synchronizing process. Forces expressed through membership composition locate each other and their polarities crystallize; and even though opposite forces may not be literally sitting opposite each other, their expression as opposites is nevertheless represented in the circle.

It should be noted that a circle is a two-dimensional representation. It is possible that any truly complex conceptualizations such as those of group psychotherapy or personality require relationships to be visualized in three dimensions. Bales (1970) and Borgatta and Crowther (1966) discuss this point and indicate that a three-dimensional plot of complex interpersonal data increases its inferential possibilities. In the following section, the basic formulation of group forces will be presented in terms of a two-dimensional model. Chapters 7 and 8 will explore how the two-dimensional circular group shape is actually a simplified representation of a more complex shape. This more complex transformational shape may permit further implications to be drawn about the structure of the group.

INTRODUCTION TO AN EMOTION THEORY

Emotional Tendencies

An overall response style may be reflected in the group process. The therapy group can be a mini-lab experience—a microcosm—of the stimulus conditions found in life generally. A characteristic personality style may become consistently expressed both in and out of the group. When certain conditions of the group environment resemble conditions outside the group, this consistency of behavior may be most clearly seen. In forming a group, it becomes necessary to help create conditions that parallel those existing outside the group. One such condition is inherent in the nature of the group composition. The group must contain a certain diagnostic structure so that any group member may have the opportunity to respond with a full range of emotion.

Response patterns are organized so that opportunities exist for each person to express a multitude of emotions. Whether each group member chooses to express these emotions or is unable to express them is a potential therapy issue. However, the fact remains that the group experience can be constructed for similar conditions to exist for each member inside the group that also exist for these members outside the group. Thus, the group setting provides potential experiences that enable each person to express a multitude of emotions; that is, exposure to a heterogeneous group of people increases the likelihood that emotional responsivity will not be restricted. The main element of the group composition, therefore, is to construct conditions that permit the full range of emotion to exist. Many authors consider this group condition to be an important feature of the therapy process and they relate it to the concept of a group diagnostic heterogeneity. Bennis and Shepard (1974) indicate that, "The more heterogeneous the membership, the more accurately does the group become for each member a microcosm of the rest of his interpersonal experience." Stock and Thelen (1958) propose that the group should contain the greatest range of valency types. Some of these types were described earlier. Foulkes and Anthony (1965) imply that the group consists of members who produce an emotional underpinning of positive and negative, attracting and repelling, and loving and hating forces. Kadis et al. (1968) also point out that group tendencies include forces of hate and love, aggression and passivity, and coolness and warmth. Other authors such as Glatzer (1956) imply that specific diagnostic types may be good for each other. In this same vein, Johnson (1963) even suggests that the group may contain an ideal potential diagnostic structure of depressed, obsessive, anxious, hysteric, and phobic dispositions.

An analysis of these sorts of theoretical data suggests that the heterogeneous underpinning of group forces may be categorized with reference to only a few basic tendencies or propensities. If the membership of a group contains a certain mix of personalities, then the group may be germinating within itself an ideal underlying organization of emotional tendencies. A supporting theoretical feature to this ideal emotional organization, and hence this ideal group membership, is the importance in the group for members to experience and express a full range of feeling and emotion. By composing a correct mix of members, it is possible to produce the conditions that define the group as a microcosm of the outside world. The group then becomes a viable therapeutic environment for all its members.

Of the various emotional tendencies or propensities cited, many may be seen in the context of a basic two-dimensional scheme. For example, the tendencies of positive and negative, pushing and pulling, attracting and repelling, and coolness and warmth may be located on a two-dimensional surface with one axis labelled active–passive and the other labelled good–bad. The specific diagnostic and emotional propensities of hate and love, aggression and passivity, depression, phobia, hysteria, and anxiety may be similarly located on a two-dimensional surface with one axis labelled active–passive and the other labelled pleasure–pain.

A PSYCHOEVOLUTIONARY THEORY OF EMOTIONS

The Primary Emotions

The literature cited previously on two-dimensional models suggests that certain diagnostic theoretical formulations may be analyzed in terms of personality models and trait structure theory, which in turn may provide new ways of investigating and understanding elements of group composition. In this section a theory of emotion will be presented that may be used as a basis for organizing the entire personality-diagnostic system. This theory utilizes some of the important personality trait structure principles cited earlier in the organization of basic tendencies. It is a system that conceives of primary emotions that contain basic properties or tendencies. It is an emotion system that may also be applied to the construction of a basic group composition.

This emotion theory, formulated by Plutchik (1962; and in press) and presented in a series of earlier papers (1955, 1958, 1960), is called a psycho-evolutionary one. It specifically enumerates the underlying dispositional tendencies of basic emotions. For example, the emotion of fear contains an inhibitory property, and its tendency would be one of withdrawal. The emotion of anger or aggression contains an energizing property, and its tendency would be one of activation or assertion. This approach is relevant to the problem of investigating the system of pushing and pulling and attracting and repelling forces found in all well-constructed therapy groups. The behavioral tendencies found in small therapy groups also suggest that there may be a few polar forces which are really basic and common to all organismic systems. Essentially, these forces or tendencies consist of pushing–pulling forces and attracting–repelling forces, and perhaps only a small number of other opposing states.

The emotion system to be described here postulates basic states determined by adaptational and evolutionary concepts. In this system, an emotion that is considered primary must somehow be related to a corresponding primary behavioral state seen at all phylogenetic levels (Plutchik, 1962, 1970). Thus, the idea of an adaptational evolutionary basis for the appearance of emotions is used as a framework to determine which emotions are considered primary. Since these behavioral emotion states may be identified at all phylogenetic levels, they may be expressions of basic prototypical patterns of behavior. These prototype patterns contain characteristic behavioral tendencies and can be expressed in several languages:

1. A functional language identifies each pattern. For example, protection is considered to be a universal prototype pattern.
2. A behavioral language essentially describes the basic tendency of the prototype pattern. For example, the behavior of withdrawal describes the tendency of the protection pattern.
3. The subjective language describes the specific emotion associated with a given prototype pattern. For example, fear is the subjective emotion associated with the protection pattern.

Table 2-1 lists the basic categories described in the three languages. This system generates a structure of eight basic patterns. These patterns are seen in all organismic forms but on higher levels may be expressed as emotion. For example, destruction in the functional language is a prototype pattern and its tendency is attack or fight behavior. In the subjective experience, the emotion associated with this pattern is anger. Each basic prototype pattern is represented by an emotion which is also considered to be primary.

The structural organization of these categories are arranged in a circular fashion in which the eight basic patterns are located in terms of four polar pairs. In this way a similarity structure of the system may be portrayed. Figure 2-8 shows the circular arrangement of the primary emotions. The emotions close to one another on the circle are similar only insofar as their positions are determined by the sharing of some common properties. For example, the emotions of acceptance and fear are clearly different; yet they appear adjacent on the circle because they share elements of passive tendencies. The emotions of disgust and anger are also clearly different, yet they are adjacent on the circle because they share elements of agitation. Emotions on the circle that are further apart share fewer properties and are therefore more conflictual. The emotions that are polar opposites or furthest apart on the circle are most dissimilar and most conflictual. The system therefore generates implications for a conception of emotional conflict.

In terms of this conflict implication, the theory assumes that basic emotions are capable of joining to form mixed states. Any state produced by the mixture of two primary emotions which are adjacent on the circle constitutes a low-conflict mixture. A state produced by two primary emotions once or twice removed on the circle constitutes an increasing state of conflict. Mixtures of opposite emotions produce states that generate maximum conflict. This suggests that the theory may be seen as a dynamic system as well as a structural one.

Table 2-1.   Three languages used to describe emotional states.

FUNCTIONAL LANGUAGE	BEHAVIORAL LANGUAGE	SUBJECTIVE LANGUAGE
Incorporation	Injesting, eating	Acceptance
Rejection	Riddance reaction, i.e., vomiting	Disgust
Exploration	Sensing, contacting	Expectation
Orientation	Alerting, 'dyscontacting'	Surprise
Protection	Withdrawing, flight, escaping	Fear
Destruction	Attacking, fighting	Anger
Reproduction	Possessing, mating	Joy
Reintegration	Losing and attempting to regain	Sadness

Based upon Plutchik and Kellerman, 1974. (Copyright 1974 by Western Psychological Services. Reprinted by permission.)

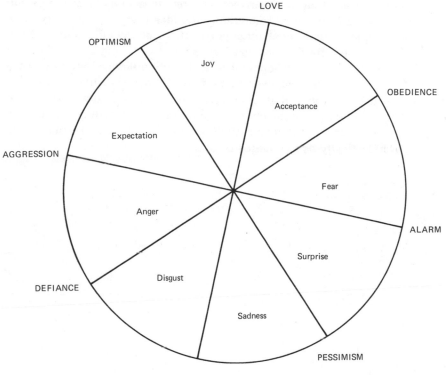

Figure 2-8. The emotion circle showing the primary emotion categories, their arrangement as bipolar dimensions, and the states produced by combining adjacent primary categories. (From *The emotions: facts, theories and a new model*, by Robert Plutchik. Copyright 1962 by Random House, Inc. Reprinted by permission of Random House, Inc.) The ordering here of anger and expectation is reversed and the ordering of fear and surprise is reversed. This represents an internal refinement of the original sequence of primary emotions around the circle.

The mixed states produced by the fusion of two or more of the primary emotions comprise the personality traits or character traits of everyday life. They are enduring states as compared to the emotions which are transient reactions.

Figure 2-8 shows the appearance of low-conflict traits, each generated by the mixture of two different primary emotions adjacent on the circle. It should be noted that the theory shows an internal consistency. Polarities exist both with respect to emotions and traits. Acceptance and fear produce obedience and their respective opposites, disgust and anger, produce the opposite of obedience—or defiance. The proposition that personality or character traits are generated by the habitual fusion of specific primary emotions also has been implied by Reich (1949) in his formulation of character trait development. Reich suggests that traits develop as a response to early demands and represent a coping adaptation. In addition, the idea that a few primary emotions are the basic elements of all other personality trait development has been historically suggested by Spinoza and Descartes.

The essence of trait development as an adaptive device based upon the fusion of primary emotions suggests that a basically normal emotion structure may be affected by various degrees of maladjustment. In a study cited earlier of the effect of maladjustment on changes in emotion structure, Kellerman (1965) and Kellerman and Plutchik (1968) found that the structure of emotion changes systematically as the degree of maladjustment increases. Figure 2-9

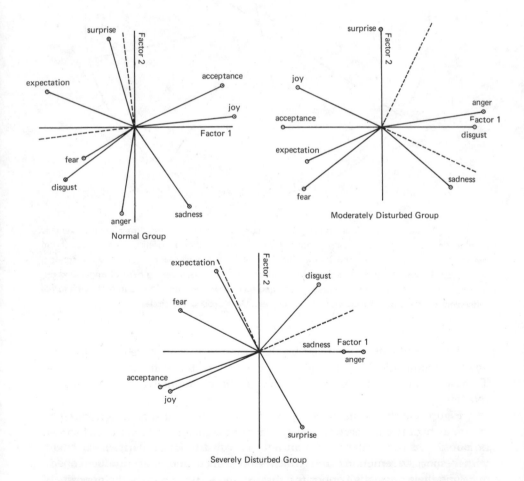

Figure 2-9. A circumplex of primary emotions, based upon a principal components factor analysis, and showing change in emotion structure as a function of maladjustment. (Referred to in Kellerman, 1965).

shows these changes in the primary emotion structure of three groups who were divided on the basis of degree of maladjustment. It may be seen from these data that as maladjustment increases, the emotions of anger, disgust, and sadness seem increasingly to form a cluster. This formation suggests that as pathology increases, a confusion develops in the discrimination of certain negative emotional states. Maladjustment may tend to decrease the development and utilization of coping devices. Distortion of historical events becomes an effect of such maladjustment.

The Prototype Categories of Analysis

The relation of the eight basic categories is shown in Table 2-1. Incorporation is a taking-in pattern, and rejection is a riddance pattern. In lower organisms, incorporation is an injesting of food, and rejection is an ejecting of something already taken in and interpreted to be noxious. Thus incorporation and rejection constitute a polarity. On the emotional level in higher organisms, the incorporation pattern is expressed by the emotion of acceptance. The qualities of ingathering, tolerance, and absorption characterize the underlying syndromal tendency of acceptance. The rejection pattern is expressed by the emotion of disgust. A riddance or repelling force underlies the disgust emotion. Thus the emotions of acceptance and disgust constitute a polarity, as do their underlying respective tendencies or forces of absorption and repulsion.

A second pair of polar categories are the exploration and orientation patterns. Exploration refers to moving in the environment and is somewhat synonymous with wonder, play, and curiosity. The emotion associated with this pattern is expectation. Expectation or anticipation contains a quality of goal orientation. The tendency that underlies the emotion of expectation is reflected by the force of moving or mapping. It is ultimately a need to order information by traversing the terrain. The orientation pattern represents a response to an unexpected and unevaluated stimulus, and it tends to stop or divert the organism during initial contact. It is an attempt at orientation during a disorienting moment. Associated with this prototype pattern is the emotion of surprise. Its underlying tendency is to cease or avoid contact. Thus the emotions of expectation and surprise constitute a polarity, as do their respective underlying tendencies of contacting and 'dyscontacting'.

A third set of polar behavioral prototypes includes the patterns of protection and destruction. Protection is characterized by flight reactions and represented in higher organisms by the emotion of fear. The tendency underlying fear is reflected by a pulling-away force from any stimulus object interpreted as threatening. Destruction may be defined as acting to overcome barriers that frustrate an organism's need. It is a behavior characterized by fight rather than by flight. At higher levels it is expressed by the emotion of anger. The tendency underlying the emotion of anger is reflected by the organism pushing toward an object interpreted to be frustrating. Thus the emotions of fear and anger constitute a polarity, as do their respective underlying tendencies of pulling and pushing.

The fourth set of polar behavioral dimensions are the prototype categories of reproduction and reintegration. The reproduction category includes behavior associated with sexual activity or the activity of possessing. On the emotional level, pleasure or joy characterize the quality of this dimension. Underlying the emotion of joy is an attraction force. The reintegration pattern is opposite to the reproduction pattern, since it is equivalent to deprivation and represents a loss of something previously possessed. During the period of deprivation, an attempt is made to reestablish a sort of homeostasis or balance. The attempt to reestablish a balance constitutes the nature of the reintegration pattern. On the emotional level, the deprivation quality of this reintegration pattern is expressed by the emotion of sadness. The tendency underlying this emotion is reflected by a yearning or neediness. Thus the emotions of joy and sadness constitute a polarity, as do their respective underlying tendencies of attraction and neediness.

The circular arrangement in Figure 2-8 shows the eight primary emotions ordered in relation to each other. This arrangement also shows a similarity structure displaying four pairs of polar opposites. The scientific rationale and support for the ordering of the primary patterns and the formulation of specific polarities are offered by Plutchik (1962; and in press).

TENDENCIES AND ROLES

This formulation has attempted to show aspects of the theory of emotion suggesting one way of understanding some basic propensities or tendencies that may influence interactional systems. These basic forces arranged in terms of four pairs of polar opposites are: absorbing and repelling forces, pulling and pushing forces, moving and stopping forces, and attracting and needing forces. This formulation agrees with and closely parallels the aggregate of forces suggested by several group therapy authors cited earlier. Tendencies such as loving and hating, considered to be basic group forces by other authors, actually may be semantic equivalents of those included here, or they may be secondary states essentially formed out of a mixture of more basic tendencies.

The emotion theory used here generates eight basic emotions that also correspond to basic character roles of the group. Hypothetically, eight basic character roles of group membership will in turn represent a full complement of basic group character roles from which all other personality trait behavior in the group may be derived. With this full complement of character roles, the group may be composed of members who convey the maximum expression and the fullest range of trait behavior and emotion in their interactional behavior. Under such circumstances, the group experience allows members to

express transient emotional reactions and to establish more habitual or characteristic behavior patterns. Foulkes (1973) refers to this point and states, "The
total interactions of the individuals are in fact the result of . . . emotions [and]
character dispositions."

This proposition implies a new and perhaps basic rationale for group construction based upon a group composition of eight members: therapists may
sense the importance of including a sufficient number of members in a group
so that the entire primary emotion spectrum is sampled within the group
membership. This attempt to ensure that a full emotional range will emerge in
the group may be satisfied by the use of selection criteria which help to organize the group with reference to certain basic character styles. Thus the aim
of composing a group of eight members may be first and foremost related to
the importance of creating a complete primary emotion system in the
group—a function that may be analogous to the completion of a protein chain.
Furthermore, just as primary emotions may mix to produce more complex
states, primary character roles also may mix to enable more complex interaction to occur in the group.

The theory of emotion by Plutchik presented here illustrates how a wide
range of behavior may be derived from only a few emotions. It also proposes a
range of intensity levels for each primary dimension. For example, fear represents only a middle intensity level for the protection pattern. A high level of
intensity representing this pattern would be experienced as terror, and a low
intensity level would be represented by apprehension. Another example of
this intensity dimension is easily seen by examining the destruction dimension. This pattern is represented by the emotion of anger, which reflects a
middle intensity. Annoyance might be a lower level of intensity and rage
might represent a high intensity level. Table 2-2 indicates a sampling of three
intensity levels for each prototype category. Each of the primary emotion dimensions therefore contains an implicit intensity component, and the circular
model also may be seen to exist in the shape of half an orange. Figure 2-10

Table 2-2.   Emotion intensity levels for each behavioral prototype pattern.

Prototype Patterns	INTENSITY DIMENSION FOR EMOTION		
	Low	Medium	High
Incorporation	Agreeableness	Acceptance	Voraciousness
Rejection	Dislike	Disgust	Revulsion
Exploration	Set	Expectation	Vigilance
Orientation	Startle	Surprise	Amazement
Protection	Apprehension	Fear	Terror
Destruction	Annoyance	Anger	Rage
Reproduction	Cheerfulness	Joy	Ecstasy
Reintegration	Gloominess	Sadness	Grief

Figure 2-10.   A multidimensional model of the emotions showing the intensity dimension. (From *The emotions: facts, theories and a new model* by Robert Plutchik. Copyright 1962 by Random House, Inc. Reprinted by permission of Random House, Inc.)

shows this arrangement, "with the emotion terms that designate each emotion at maximum intensity at the top. The vertical dimension represents intensity, or level of arousal" and the range is from a maximum state of excitement at the top to a state of low arousal at the bottom. "The shape of the model implies that the emotions become less distinguishable at lower intensities." If successive cross sections are taken, then the emotion circle becomes duplicated "with progressively milder versions of each of the primaries" (Plutchik, 1962).

The intensity-level feature of the emotion theory may be applied ultimately to the identification of character roles and diagnoses insofar as any individual may be expressing varying degrees of intensity of a particular character disposition. Furthermore, the mixing of primary emotions may be drawn from a multiplicity of intensity levels. The introduction of this variable permits a more cogent understanding of the great variation of emotional reactions and trait behavior that can occur among members of the group.

Some Factors Influencing the Blending of Group Forces

CONFLICT STRUCTURE

Another implication of the circular structure of the emotion model suggests how dispositional forces of the group blend. As the group is composed, the variety of character roles form an implicit similarity structure that also generates polarities. Yalom (1970) in quoting Foulkes and Anthony (1965), points out that "Blending together is a mixed bag of diagnoses and disturbances" designed "to form a therapeutically effective group. The greater the span between polar types, the higher the therapeutic potential." These polarities contain a high level of conflict. If the group is composed on the basis of sampling the entire emotion circle, then certain member-to-member interactions will reflect very little conflict, while other member-to-member interactions will reflect maximum conflict. This issue has prompted Taylor (1961) to point to a kind of implicit conflict structure, suggesting that in the process of group composition a condition needs to be accounted for in which each member has some paired equal or similar personality present in the group. The special issue of how to understand and measure this conflict will be discussed in chapters 7 and 8. At this point, the blending of forces in the group as a means of understanding and regulating conflict needs to be explored.

GROUP EFFECTS ON INDIVIDUALS

The blending of character styles in the group produces a certain personality of the group (Kellerman and Maliver, 1977). This group diagnosis suggests that the group is different than the sum of its parts. This difference is discussed by Durkin (1964), who cites the work of Emil Durkheim and reports on Georg Simmel's theory of the relation of opposing forces as a reflection of this difference. It has prompted McDougall (1921) to use the concept of "group mind," Freud (1921) to apply psychoanalytic precepts to group psychology, and Lewin (1951) to elaborate a theory of field composed of forces or vectors that reflect various influences of the field.

The process of blending group forces that ultimately defines the difference between the total group in contrast to its individual membership is discussed by Cartwright and Zander (1968) who indicate that, "The coordination of group activities requires that the behavior of each member be adjusted to that of others." This adjustment of one member to the others tends to promote a group cohesion. It begins to be shaped by the therapist but also may be generated by the structural underpinning of the group itself. If the group is well constituted, its performance will be superior; and according to Cartwright and Zander, groups with superior performance show greater cohesiveness. To this point Bach (1954) indicates that "the group has demonstrable effects on the individuals without our being able to specify the cause of this effect as 'residing' in any one independent member of the group." A co-variant point is made by Foulkes (in Kadis et al., 1968), who says "in therapeutic analytic groups it is of course, eventually the individual alone who counts—a point which is sometimes misunderstood. The analytic group as such has only an ad hoc existence as a therapeutic instrument." Whether Bach senses a new organismic organization in the group formation, or whether the group is merely seen as existing in an ad hoc state, its effect on individuals nevertheless is noted by many authors.

The idea of group effects on individuals also has been explored by Kellerman, Buirski, and Plutchik (1974) in a study comparing baboon groups and human groups. These authors describe a homeostatic balance of the group. They indicate that the emotions comprising the homeostatic force of the group center around the traits of assertion, caution, and agreeableness: "what probably happens in successful group therapy is that there is a rebalancing of the forces of assertion, caution and agreeableness in the individuals who comprise the group without altering its overall stability." The group has a kind of implicit personality based on the overall balance of personality forces. In a successfully functioning group, this group personality is more stable than the personalities of individual members of the group. This position is similar to the one expressed by Bach, in which the group effect on individuals is considered to be somehow different and separate from the effect of one individual member upon another.

The homeostasis of the group as an infrastructural mechanism also is discussed by Kadis et al. (1968), who consider the group to be a suprasystem containing its own infrastructural mechanisms. These mechanisms allow it to become a separate and distinct influence on its members. Bach (1954) states that:

> According to modern physical theories, particles may exist in "virtual" states in which they may have observable effects although they do not actually exist as independent observable particles. In an analogous sense, eight human beings together may form a virtual state, a social field, in which it, the social field, may have observable effects on each member, although the state or social field, or "group" is not actually existent as observable, independent of each member.

It is the intention here to describe the composition of this presumed virtual-state called a group.

GROUP COMPOSITION: PROLOGUE

Yalom (1970) writes, "Only when clinical practice begins to take advantage of some of the more sophisticated diagnostic techniques can we really scientifically compose a group." This concern with group blending and balance is discussed by Yalom and Rand (1966) in terms of the blending of interpersonal styles. Despite certain objections to composing groups based upon clinical diagnosis (Powdermaker and Frank, 1953), many authors are interested in learning more about diagnostic clinical role categories as a method for increasing the understanding of a good group blend. These role categories will be outlined in the following chapter. Yalom wonders further, "Are there guidelines available to assist the therapist to form . . . the ideal group?. . . If we are to talk intelligently about group composition, we must speak of composing the group in such a way that the members will interact in some desired manner." In another reference to group composition, Yalom states in a welcome simplification, "whether or not the group 'jells' is only in part related to the competence or efforts of the therapist or to the number of good patients in the group; in large part the critical variable is some, as yet unclear, blending of the members."

It may be possible to address both of Yalom's concerns about group composition on the basis of the emotion model presented here and its role and diagnostic implications to be presented in the following chapter. The answer to the first concern is affirmative: there are indeed guidelines available, based upon underlying emotion structure, to assist the therapist in forming the ideal group. Furthermore, the second issue of the "jelling" of the group, or the question of its membership blend, may be better understood both in terms of these role and emotion relationships and in terms of a theory of role conflict which will also be presented in the next chapter.

In this chapter it was pointed out that an underlying emotion structure of the group may be discerned. This structure is related to an ideal number of group members. A major proposition is drawn connecting the idea of basic assumed roles of the group to this underlying structure. It indicates that the relation between roles and basic underlying emotion structure ultimately permits the greatest diversity of emotional reactions to exist in the group and constitutes the most important criterion of group structure and group composition. The exposition of role structure and diagnostic correlates of this structure will be explored in the following chapters.

3

Basic Character Roles of the Group

This Chapter will present a theory of group composition that relates a member's role in a group to a particular diagnosis. A system of basic emotions provides the connective underpinning of the correlation between role and diagnosis. This emotion system suggests that individual underlying emotions constitute emulsifying agents between specific roles and specific diagnoses. The central thesis proposes that all three states—roles, diagnostic disposition, and underlying basic emotion—express cross-sectional levels of specific patterns or strains in the overall group composition. The group is considered to be composed of a few such basic strains or role lineages.

Within this construction, an ideally composed group is one in which membership role repertoire and membership diagnosis ensure the potential expression of all the basic emotions in the group. Because of this ideal condition, i.e., the potential expression of all basic emotions, the group must contain the possibility for great emotional diversity. The overall diagnostic composition of the group will therefore reflect its emotional composition in a highly specific way.

Any group member's diagnosis may contain as an underlying expressive force one or more of the basic emotions. The total group diagnostic composition thus will yield a hierarchy of group emotion. This hierarchy of emotion may be expressed as a frequency ranking of basic emotions as they are implied across group roles. For example, the emotion of anger may be implied in the diagnoses of aggressive personality, psychopathic personality, and paranoid personality. Particular emotions may also be implied in other group roles. Certain emotions will be expressed more frequently while others become expressed less frequently, and this emotion frequency index is a function of the role composition of the group. The ranking may be conceived as a cumulative emotion-frequency measure derived from the responses of all group members. If the group composition is constructed with reference to specific organizing principles, then this emotion-frequency ranking will be better balanced. Difficulty in group construction arises when the group is formed more or less randomly with regard to diagnosis. Such a random group composition is likely to produce an imbalance in the emotional repertoire of the group. This sort of emotional imbalance invariably generates a restriction in the emotional range of the group.

Once a basic group composition is formed, its role repertoire will guide the therapist in selecting patients whenever a role needs to be filled. The idea of maintaining a basic role composition has been suggested by Bach(1954). Freedman et al. (1951) agree that knowing the role repertoire of a group, and in time the changes that occur in this repertoire, is vital group information. When the role repertoire of the group is understood, the therapist is able to keep the underlying emotional organization of the group intact.

The issue of an ideal role composition has appeared in the literature in discussions of whether or not roles naturally emerge in the group and whether or not they affect the group process (Bogdanoff and Elbaum, 1978). Grinberg (1973) considers that the appearance of roles in the therapy group is assumed by members automatically: ". . . we should bear in mind that the emergence of roles is a natural phenomenon that takes place in every group automatically from the moment in which the group is formed." Kellerman, Buirski, and Plutchik (1974) also suggest that ". . . therapy groups are more stable if the members perceive themselves, overtly or covertly, as having clear roles within the group." This position essentially supports a group-process psychotherapy and implies that within the group composition, a fundamental balance of roles may be created.

Yalom (1970) is not satisfied with either the arbitrary naming of roles or the notion that roles automatically may emerge in a group. He asks whether fixed and underlying roles do indeed exist from group to group, and implies that an elaboration of such a system would be useful as a guide to group therapy composition.

In the following sections, a review of prevailing role theory will be described and a universal role framework will be proposed.

ROLES OF THE GROUP: A LITERATURE SAMPLING

Stereotypic Roles

An examination of the literature on role stereotypes suggests that a more parsimonious role system than now exists needs to be formulated. Many authors have noticed what might be called the stereotypic roles of the group. As a matter of fact, so many role stereotypes have been proposed that a cumulative listing would almost constitute a separate domain of psychological discourse. Most group therapists consider these roles to be universal and stereotypic, and common to all therapy groups.

Here is a partial sample of role stereotypes. Bach (1954) lists five roles: the guardian of democracy, the time-keeper, the aggressive male, the leader, and the humorous member. Luchins (1967) considers the roles of disruptive patient, patient with active symptoms, silent patient, overtalkative patient, exploitative patient, seductive patient, and do-gooder patient. Yalom (1970) adds the monopolist, a person who is either an angry or a manic type. This person creates disruption, off-target fighting in the group, absenteeism, dropping out, and subgrouping; and must eventually develop an observing ego as a main goal of therapy. Pines (1974) also describes the monopolist as a borderline type needing constant attention. Yalom further lists the help-rejecting complainer who is a monopolist type asking for help in order to reject it. Yalom's other role types include the star, the group hysteric, the executive leader, the great man, the paranoid type, and the self-righteous moralist who needs always to be right. Yalom makes certain fine personality distinctions of role character. For example, his self-righteous moralist is a person who wants recognition for noble character, not for achievement, and who is dealing with underlying shame and anger. Others who have described the self-righteous moralist include Berger and Rosenbaum (1967), Frank et al. (1952), and Rosenthal et al. (1954). Berne (1964) describes this type as a "yes but" person. Finally, Yalom's list considers the doctor's assistant who gives advice freely, the schizoid patient, and the silent patient. The silent patient is also described by Johnson (1963). Kadis et al. (1968) further cite the role of the silent member, the exhibitionist, the assistant therapist, and the provocateur. Abrahams and Varon (1953) describe the passive-dependent lackey type who is helpless, indecisive, clings to others, and can't say no; and Foulkes and Anthony (1965) describe roles of the favorite, the attention seeker, and the deputy leader. Wolberg (1978) adds the "the habitual latecomer" to a list that includes most of the other roles described above.

Other authors tend to predict role behavior in the group on the basis of diagnostic considerations. Wolman (1960) suggests that the group is especially good for obsessive, psychopathic, and manic-depressive types. Kadis et al. (1968), on the other hand, warn against including the psychopathic type. These authors suggest that the inclusion of bona fide psychopathic types in the group should be limited, and they also point out that more than one member with psychosomatic problems may create an acute subgrouping phenomenon in the group. Bach (1954) further suggests that the psychopathic type as well as the monopolist type are simply not good for the group, and Yalom (1970) indicates that schizoid types and somatizers cannot achieve satisfaction from the group. Finally, Aronson (1964) indicates that a good group composition should neutralize acting-out tendencies. This view supports a general agreement among the group therapists who would limit the presence of psychopathic types.

Group Roles and Group Process

The previous citations were concerned with group roles as a cast of characters. Another body of research influenced first by Redl (1942) and advanced by Bales (1950) and others at Harvard University is chiefly concerned with group roles as they relate to group process. The Harvard research was designed to study developmental processes that determine the formation of roles. For example, Bales and Slater (1953) suggest that roles are likely to be similar across groups and become differentiated early in the life of a group. Gibbard et al. (1974) add that although roles may be differentiated during formative group stages, some of these roles dissipate as the group works through focal conflicts. According to Stock and Lieberman (1962), these focal conflicts are really underlying group tensions which may be experienced throughout the life of the group, although they are most palpable during formative periods. The Harvard researchers are particularly concerned with this idea of the life of the group. They relate role formation and role differentiation to developmental issues and to group focal conflicts, and this correlation represents a broadening of group role theory. Durkheim (1933) offers a further theoretical underpinning by implying that role composition is the medium through which groups achieve their work distribution functions.

The idea that focal conflict of the group may be affected by the gradual emergence of roles has also been noted by Stock, Whitman, and Lieberman (1958) and by Whitaker and Lieberman (1964). The relation between focal conflict and role development is well illustrated by Bogdunoff and Elbaum (1978). The authors propose that role stereotypes are generated from the group's reactive focal conflicts. They present a theory of the development of eight roles. The authors propose that common group concerns produce reactive focal conflict issues that can be temporarily resolved by the emergence of one of these eight basic roles. For example, one theme may revolve around concerns of disclosure. These concerns generate reactive focal conflict issues of *revealing* versus *concealing*. One way in which the group resolves this focal conflict theme is by the derivation of a role of basic mistruster.

Another problem theme concerning one's expertise produces focal conflict issues of *competency* versus *incompetency*. These issues are resolved by the role function of professional patient. The general problem of control generates focal conflict themes of *dominance* versus *submission* and becomes managed by the appearance of the role of monopolizer. Authenticity as an existentially disturbing problem causes a focal conflict theme of *sincerity* versus *deceptiveness*. This conflict is managed by the development of the role of performer. Caring, as an initial concern, produces conflict themes of *help* versus *hurt*, which is ultimately resolved through the appearance of the role of helpful Hannah. The disturbing issue of violence or war produces focal conflict themes of *war* versus *peace*. This theme is in part resolved by the development of the war-lover role. Another presumably disturbing issue is fate. This concern generates the focal conflict theme of *good luck* versus *bad luck*, and it is ultimately addressed through the appearance of the role of misfortune hunter. Finally, the problem of feeling alienated generates focal conflict themes of *involvement* versus *separation*. The role that emerges in the group from such conflict is the isolate. The personal psychodynamics of the group members who are endowed with these roles roughly match the dynamics defined by the focal conflict themes.

The relationship between group roles and focal conflict also raises the question as to whether group roles shift as a function of group process, or rather, as suggested by Bales and Slater (1955), they remain fundamentally invariant across groups. This is one of the essential conceptual issues raised by the Harvard group. A review of this research reveals that the issue of role as seen from a developmental viewpoint becomes transformed into one of a more complex and general nature. The transformational question asks whether the basic model underlying group process is epigenetic or evolutionary (Gibbard, 1974).

Epigenetic versus Evolutionary Group Role Process

Several authors discuss the bridging roles of the group; that is, roles appearing as a function of group need during various phases of the group (Herbert and Trist, 1953; Stock, 1964; Stock and Thelen, 1958). This idea suggests that certain roles exist as virtual-states and are called forth by the group's need at the appropriate time. The ever-present yet dormant nature of such roles represents a tacit epigenetic phenomenon. Actually, Bennis and Shepard (1956) suggest this epigenetic phenomenon quite specifically. They postulate that certain kinds of roles continually exist but are inactive until invoked by the group process.

The contrasting evolutionary position is presented by Bales and Slater (1953). These authors propose that diffuse roles become differentiated over time; they do not simply exist, fully developed, awaiting their manifest destiny. According to Gibbard (1974), role differentiation as an evolutionary phenomenon serves as a motivating force of the group, as well as being generated by the group process itself. Only in this reciprocal sense is role differentiation an adaptive force of the group. However, whether roles exist fully developed or whether they become differentiated in a developmental sense can only represent one issue in the overall role function of the group composition. The epigenetic and evolutionary positions may be reconciled within a sociobiological framework. From this point of view, the group process may consist of certain underlying propensities which are determined by its evolutionary history; that is, the original adaptational emergency of group life contained mechanisms of survival upon which the group was based, and through which groups in part, continue to function. Some of these mechanisms help to generate roles. In a sociobiological framework, the role balance of the group corresponds to inherent adaptational group forces. Thus the group may be viewed epigenetically. However, its evolutionary nature may produce role variation, which as a function of adaptation and time becomes the basis for role differentiation. Therefore, it seems that when considered separately, epigenetic and evolutionary formulations fail to consider fully the basic underlying matrix of emotional polarities that ultimately generate all the roles of the group.

There are several authors, however, who do recognize that the developmental aspect to group role theory may relate to the group's underlying polar forces. For example, Dunphy (1968) and Mann et al. (1967) indicate that impulse expression and impulse suppression constitute a group polarity which is central to the entire role differentiation process. Gibbard (1974) adds that the development of specialized roles is an attempt to resolve the basic polarities of group life: positive versus negative feelings, especially toward authority; rational versus irrational responses to conflict; and solidarity versus fragmentation. Although they propose rather generalized polar conflicts, these authors do recognize the existence of an underlying polar matrix. It is this particular matrix, which is not sufficiently considered by the proponents of either the epigenetic or evolutionary positions, that needs to be explored further.

Central Figures

Conceiving central figures who emerge with specific role behavior is an idea that applies both to an epigenetic and evolutionary framework. The central-figure role was originally formulated by Redl (1942) and it constituted a distinctly different and more complex perception of role types.

Redl indicated that the group emotion is equivalent to the instinctual and emotional events taking place within members of the group under the pressure of group formative processes. Members will develop group emotions about each other reflected in their focus on a central figure. Redl describes ten central figures: patriarchal sovereign, toward whom members look for approval; leader, who members want to emulate; tyrant, with whom members identify in terms of identification with the aggressor; love object, who is a common external figure for all members; object of aggressive desires, where all members agree upon a scapegoat; organizer, toward whom members can depend for decision making; seducer, who acts out vicariously for all other members; hero, whose courageous behavior reduces the anxiety of all other members; bad influence, who takes responsibility for all acting out; and the good example, toward whom all members look as a guide to correct behavior. Members of the group will relate to each other in terms of the emotional responsivity that is based upon the common agreement regarding these central figures.

Five central stereotypic roles are enumerated by Dunphy (1968): idol, instructor, seducer or manipulator, scapegoat, and aggressor. Mann et al. (1967) and Ringwald (1974) further identify the role of hero, and define clusters of central figures or roles that fall into six categories: anxious participators, respected enactors, sexual idols, leaders and fall guys, outsiders, and prophets. Gibbard (1974) makes the point that, "the group's first and most pressing need is for a central figure who can be utilized as a point of orientation," thereby indicating the importance of the central figures to the group.

The general issue of central figures has produced a theoretical controversy. Gibbard (1974) indicates that conflict in the group creates a disequilibrium which leads to a differentiation of roles. This differentiation in turn ultimately leads to a regaining of group equilibrium. Role differentiation therefore becomes partly defensive and partly restitutive. The Gibbard correlation of role differentiation and group equilibrium is primarily an issue of group boundary. It constitutes an infrastructural mechanism of the group process.

Other authors (Bennis and Shepard, 1956; Dunphy, 1968; Mann, 1967; Ringwald, 1974) have suggested that central figures have interlocking functions both in the acting-out and in the resolution of focal conflict. The theoretical debate revolves around the question of whether the group model is viewed as a pendular process, constantly increasing in tension and then resolving tension; or whether it is viewed as a linear process, involving some inexorable development goal.

The function of central figures in the pendular model has been related to Bionian concepts of basic assumption groups. Here the central figures express the basic emotion of the assumption group, defined as an attempt to resist the Bionian work group. In this sense, central figures serve the resistance of the group as in the expression of purely Freudian resistance phenomena.

The function of central figures in the linear group model represents a Freudian resolution of resistance as the group moves to establish higher-order therapeutic goals. Thus the central figure may serve acting-out purposes or appear as a focal conflict resolution feature of the group. In either case these models do not elaborate a system of underlying conflict even though they do expand and deepen the understanding of role function in the group process. What they lack is the necessary theoretical bridge to specific emotional conflict. In addition, the interest in central figures is a focus on temporary role assignments of the group, but it tends to minimize the importance of all other group members. Overlooking other members minimizes the understanding of most polar role conflicts as they affect the ongoing group process. As Gibbard (1974) points out, "while the central figures may serve as symbols of the principal polarities in the group, they do not provide a precise reflection, a mirror image, of those polarities." Conceiving central figures offers a theoretical advantage to the study of group composition but it cannot qualify as a bona fide theory of group composition.

One other major work by Bales (1970), based upon two separate factor analyses of a domain of personality, produced 26 basic personality types. These data were collected from subjects involved in self-analytic groups at

Harvard University. Data derived in this study were plotted in a three-dimensional space so that the structure of the group could be viewed in terms of its topological features. A partial sociometry of the group was plotted with subjects located within this three-dimensional space.

> *The types are defined in terms of the way the acting person is perceived and evaluated by others in the group. These perceptions and evaluations depend upon his personality, his behavior, and his position in the group, as well as those of all the other members of the group. . . . The ratings an individual receives from others are usually related to his personality as well as his group role.*

The derived roles contain attitudinal, emotional, and diagnostic elements. Obviously 26 roles cannot really be considered basic types. Rather, some of the types are basic and others are mixed and more complex. A role entitled "Toward Failure and Withdrawal" may be paranoid or depressed in nature, or both. Another role entitled "Toward Withholding of Cooperation" may reflect passive, or aggressive, or both passive-aggressive elements. The research by Bales does not claim to provide the formulation of a new role typology. Rather, it is an attempt to broaden the conception of viewing interpersonal relations in a given space matrix, and it may suggest a new way to view the structure of psychoanalytic groups.

Typologies and Roles

In addition to viewing roles in three-dimensional space, and in addition to central figure conceptions, there are the Frommian (1941, 1947) and Horneyian (1950) typologies. These typologies offer general social, psychological, and characterological meanings to role. Frommian marketing, receptive, hoarding, and exploitative types correspond to Horney's conception of character types. These character types include: the moving-toward type with a self-effacing solution, who uses love as currency; the moving-against type, who uses an expansive solution in the search for mastery; and the moving-away type who is resigned and withdrawn, but in whom the search for freedom is central. The moving-against type is further subdivided into the narcissistic, perfectionistic-arrogant, and vindictive types. The moving-with type is a cooperative, mature collaborator.

These lists of roles comprise more than 50 examples of role types cited by various authors. The cumbersome theoretical structure of so many lists implies the need for ordering these data. Several of the role types are exactly duplicated by different authors, and others such as the leader type produce interesting variations; for example, executive leader, deputy leader, and rebellious leader; or with respect to the idol type, sexual idol and love object are produced as variations.

Yalom (1970) implies that many of these types are correlated to each other and even correlate to group phases. For example, the Bionian fight group corresponds to the Hornyian moving-against type, and the flight group corresponds to the moving-away type. The Bionian dependency group correlates to the moving-toward type and Bion's work group corresponds to the moving-with type. An elaboration of such general and dispositional roles has been offered by Abraham (1927), Fenichel (1945b), Freud (1908, 1931), Kernberg (1970a), and Reich (1949). This elaboration essentially represents a concern with role types spanning at least 50 years, with the last 25 years devoted to a concern with group roles.

Hardly any theoretical formulation has been applied to the group therapy literature on roles. A notable exception is Grinberg (1973) who states,

> Apart from the personal traits predisposing a participant to a given role, as a rebellious leader, a submissive member, a scapegoat, or a "radar" screen, his behavior or attitude on playing the role will depend predominately on the remaining members who will largely determine the emergence and functioning of the role which is deeply or unconsciously viewed as necessary for the group's current situation. . . . the role ultimately springs from the projective identifications of part of the group or of the whole group.

Most other commentary on group role assignment has been an exercise in pragmatic empirical labeling. A method is needed that enables this body of data to be organized in a more parsimonious framework and in a way that demonstrates some correlational matrix for all of these proposed roles.

BASIC EMOTIONS AND BASIC ROLES

To show that this randomly selected list of role stereotypes may be organized with reference to a few basic underlying categories, it is necessary to describe a system of roles that have been generated from the theory of emotion described in chapter 2. In relating basic emotions to basic roles, a system emerges in which eight basic roles are graphically arranged in a circular fashion as four polar pairs. As previously noted, each of the eight prototype patterns may be expressed in several clinical languages. These patterns may be expressed at various levels of organismic development, including the level of group process. Table 2-1 (p. 28) lists a functional, a behavioral, and a subjective language to describe respectively, the prototype categories, dimensional qualities, and emotions for each pattern.

Plutchik and Kellerman (1974) have suggested a trait language that correlates to each of the basic emotions. This trait language also may be a bridge to understanding the corresponding diagnostic dispositions and roles. For example, the emotions of acceptance and disgust may be expressed on a trait level as trust versus distrust. The emotions of fear and anger may be understood on a trait level as timidity and aggression. The traits of gregariousness and depression correspond to the basic emotions of joy and sadness respectively. The emotions of expectation and surprise relate to the traits of controlled and dyscontrolled behavior respectively. A lexicon of each prototype pattern is thus created that ultimately reaches into the group system in the form of a basic character role structure. This trait language as it enjoins the levels of each basic dimension, i.e., emotion and emotional tendency to diagnostic disposition and corresponding role, is presented in the next section.

The Enjoining of Basic Dimensions: Diagnostic Disposition and Role

Dimension I: The Emotion of Acceptance

The emotion of acceptance contains an absorption tendency as an underlying property. On the trait level, acceptance is expressed as trustful behavior in which idealization experiences, high suggestibility, and—in the extreme form—perhaps naive behavior are characteristic attributes. The diagnostic disposition defined by these qualities is that of the hysteric. Any member in the group, who typically expresses such personality features may frequently assume the role of the romantic, the one in whom critical faculties seem to be suspended. Thus the emotion of acceptance contains an underlying absorption tendency which generates the trait of trust. On a role level, this trusting quality produces the behavior of the romantic. The romantic in turn expresses the basic dispositional diagnosis of the hysteric. The role of the romantic in the group constitutes a basic infrastructural type. The romantic role, with acceptance as its basic emotion, has its corresponding opposite role which also is generated from a basic emotion category; i.e., the emotion of disgust.

Dimension II: The Emotion of Disgust

The emotion of disgust contains the tendency of repulsion as its underlying property. On the trait level, disgust is expressed as a distrust quality characterized by experiences of irritability and criticality. The diagnostic disposition defined by these qualities is that of the paranoid. A group member who assumes this sort of critical stance may be described as the scrutinizer. The romantic and the scrutinizer roles constitute polar opposites and reflect their respective opposite diagnostic dispositions of hysteric and paranoid.

A second pair of basic roles of the group are generated from a second pair of basic emotions. Fear and anger ultimately generate their respective equivalent role styles of the innocent and the scapegoater.

Dimension III: The Emotion of Fear

The emotion of fear contains a pulling-away tendency. On the trait level, fear is expressed as timidity which in turn is characterized by inhibitory behavior, obedience, and even lethargy and withdrawal. The diagnostic disposition embodying this fear dimension is passivity. A group member behaving in this manner may be described as the innocent. This sort of person will not initiate contact or take any responsibility for group functioning. This behavior reflects a sterility of intent.

Dimension IV: The Emotion of Anger

The emotion of anger contains a pushing tendency. On the trait level, anger is expressed as aggression. Aggressivity is characterized by attack or predatory behavior which is correlated to a general energized need. The diagnostic disposition expressing the anger dimension is aggressivity. A member assuming this stance in the group may be described as the scapegoater. Such a person will express an overabundance of anger and will confront those who are more likely to absorb the anger. The innocent and the scapegoater roles correspond to the passive and aggressive diagnostic dispositional types, and they constitute a second set of opposite role states of the group.

A third set of basic group roles are generated from a third set of emotion dimensions. Expectation and surprise generate role styles of the intellectualizer and the child.

Dimension V: The Emotion of Expectation

The emotion of expectation contains a mapping tendency. This tendency reveals a need for boundary-control which is established through exploration of the environment. On the trait level, expectation is expressed as control behavior. The trait of control is expressed through needs for decorum and reason as a way of monitoring the environment. The diagnostic disposition corresponding to the expectation dimension is that of the obsessive. A group member who expresses this disposition may be described as the intellectualizer; the person who rationalizes and who gains power by use of controlling measures.

Dimension VI: The Emotion of Surprise

The emotion of surprise contains a stopping tendency. The tendency of "stoppingness" needs to be avoided. Thus contact with an unexpected and unevaluated stimulus is a disorienting experience which is frequently likely to release impulsive behavior as a typical coping response. This impulsive or dyscontrolled behavior is an attempt to defend against the "stopping" tendency and integration of new experiences. It is a reorienting homeostatic attempt. On an intrapersonal level, the dyscontrol behavior stops one from knowing or thinking and promotes "doing" behavior. The dyscontrol favors action as a characteristic response. Acting-out behavior may be expected of a person who expresses this dispositional style. A corollary problem with this type is the appearance of a poorly developed attention span. A psychopathic diagnostic syndrome is associated with such behavior. Any member assuming this posture in the group will express behavior that is immature and impulsive. The role type in which this disposition is reflected is that of the child.

Thus the intellectualizer and the child constitute a third set of role opposites in the group and reflect the polar diagnoses of obsessive and psychopathic types. The fourth set of basic roles of the group are puritan and reintegrator, derived from the basic emotions of joy and sadness respectively.

Dimension VII: The Emotion of Joy

The emotion of joy contains an underlying tendency of attraction. On the trait level, joy is expressed as gregariousness. This gregarious behavior is characterized by altruism, excessive energy, a sense of possession, and a zest for interaction which is galvanized by a pure work ethic. The diagnostic disposition expressing the joy dimension is the manic personality. In the group, this member behaves with excessive tension and needs to ventilate an inexhaustible amount of work energy. A display of salvation fever provides the bridge between the manic quality and the derived work-ethic role called the puritan.

Dimension VIII: The Emotion of Sadness

The emotion of sadness contains underlying reintegration and restitutional components designed to repair loss experiences. The reintegration response simply attempts to reestablish a previous condition. The restitutional attempt represents a compensatory striving aimed at this reestablishment of a previous condition. Since loss experiences may reignite inferiority feelings, the compensatory element also reflects a self-aggrandizing attempt to conceal feelings of self-doubt. On the trait level, sadness is seen as depressive behavior. It is expressed either through crying in its extreme form, or, in its compensatory form through excessive self-aggrandizement. The diagnostic disposition associated with this behavior is the depressed personality. In the group, a member behaving either with morose or excessive crying behavior or with compensatory behavior may be described as a reintegrator.

The manic and depressed diagnostic personalities are thus transformational opposite role styles of puritan and reintegrator. The use of emotion theory as the basis for the development of a role system also yields an implicit diagnostic model. This diagnostic model in turn contains an inherent construct validity from which basic role behavior of the group may be better understood.

The work by Bales (1970) provides partial support for the system of emotion and diagnostic polarities as they become located in a three-dimensional space. The Bales study showed manic–depressed types to be located in opposite spheres. This was true also for the controlled–impulsive (obsessive–psychopathic respectively) and for the passive–aggressive (or inert–aggressive) types. The hysteric–paranoid polarity also was located in distinctly different areas of the space. In a separate study by Kellerman and Plutchik (1978), this same diagnostic matrix was found to apply to a group of drug addicts who participated in a study designed to relate emotion and diagnostic disposition.

The diagnostic model presented here may provide a basis for the development of a new theory-based diagnostic nosology. This model resembles the basic diagnostic types proposed by Schmertz (1976). Four propositions emerge from this analysis:

1. *All trait behavior may be analyzed with reference to eight basic emotions.*
2. *All differential diagnostic states may be generated from eight basic diagnostic dispositions.*
3. *All roles expressed in the group contain elements of only eight basic role styles.*
4. *The group infrastructural personality consists of emotional tendencies which are the properties of a system of basic emotions.*

The basic emotions produce all trait behavior expressed through the roles of the group. In their intense form, these role types of the group become clinical diagnostic dispositions. These are dimensional continuities that may be considered to be families or lineages of basic roles of the group. Just as Schmertz (1976) proposes that "it is . . . not farfetched to think of human temperament as an evolutionary product, a product functioning specifically as a mechanism for maintaining interpersonal equilibrium," it may also be proposed that dimensional continuities constitute an evolutionary adaptational phenomenon. The dimensional continuities of group role styles are seen in Table 3-1, in which all dimensions are separated into four polar types.

Table 3-1.   Families of basic polar role dimensions.

EMOTION	EMOTIONAL TENDENCY	TRAIT	DIAGNOSTIC DISPOSITION	GROUP ROLE TYPE
Acceptance	Absorption	Trustful	Hysteric	Romantic
Disgust	Repulsion	Distrustful	Paranoid	Scrutinizer
Fear	Pulling away from	Timid	Passive	Innocent
Anger	Pushing	Aggressive	Aggressive	Scapegoater
Expectation	Moving in the service of control.	Controlled	Obsessive	Intellectualizer
Surprise	Moving in the service of preventing control.	Dyscontrolled	Psychopathic	Child
Joy	Attracting	Gregarious	Manic	Puritan
Sadness	Reintegrating	Depressed	Depressed	Reintegrator

Group Composition: A Theoretical versus an Intuitive Approach

It is assumed that an ideal group composition will be based upon the theoretical criteria previously set forth. The question arises as to how group therapists actually form groups. It is quite apparent that most group therapists may not be fully conversant with the theoretical position presented here. Yet most group therapists in the process of forming a group seem to know intuitively whether or not the emerging group contains theoretically correct congealing elements. Group therapists who know their patients well can select those patients who will essentially enable the group to become a therapeutically crystallized environment. These therapists try to include some members who are active and others who are passive; some who are expressive, and others who are shy. It is obvious that Darwin's idea of a tangled bank discussed in chapter 1 hardly affects therapists' intuition in creating the personality structure of the group. Therapists are usually not confused by an endless variety of diagnostic choices. They simply select those patients that can be interesting for each other in the potential group interaction. Such a group composition contains an underlying matrix of a few polar emotion forces reflected in the diagnostic meaning to each role. In the composition of the group, the therapist functions with an implicit criterion which closely parallels the theoretical formulation presented here. Therapists, to whatever extent they are conscious of their goals in the composition of the group, desire a distribution of emotional forces. These forces or emotional inclinations include happy versus sad, trusting versus suspicious, passive versus aggressive, and rigid versus spontaneous—dimensions described earlier. They constitute underlying basic emotion polarities and permit the full range of emotional expression to exist in the group in the form of a basic role composition. The theoretical formulation presented here simply explicates and systematizes what therapists knew all along. Thus, the end result of an ideal group therapy composition is to create a basic infrastructural emotion system.

A SIMILARITY ANALYSIS OF ROLES

More than 50 roles listed in the group therapy literature are referred to by authors as role types. Each type has been used to describe roles as they apply to group behavior. These role types include: aggressive type, guardian of democracy, time keeper, aggressive male, leader, executive leader, rebellious leader, deputy leader, humorous one, monopolist, help-rejecting complainer, group hysteric, great man, star, paranoid type, self-righteous moralist, doctor's assistant, assistant therapist, schizoid type, silent member, favorite one, attention seeker, exhibitionist, provocateur, passive-dependent type, idol, sexual idol, love object, instructor, seducer, manipulator, scapegoat, object of aggressive desires, aggressor, hero, anxious participator, respected enactor, fall guy, outsider, prophet, patriarchal sovereign, tyrant, organizer, bad influence, good example, submissive member, radar screen, psychopathic type, somatizer, and manic type. At least 25 percent of these roles are duplicated on several lists. An examination of 50 role types reveals that at least three languages are used to describe them. Some authors use a diagnostic language to determine roles; others use a trait language; and still a third group describes roles in terms of an abstracted role-type language. There are also authors who list role types of the group using all three languages.

In the language of diagnosis, a syndromal formulation of roles is used that includes manic, paranoid, aggressive, hysteric, schizoid, passive-dependent, psychopathic, and somatizer roles. The language of traits used to describe roles is composed of attributes of personality that are enduring and become each member's individual behavioral signature. They include the aggressor, anxious participator, submissive member, silent member, humorous one, aggressive type, help-rejecting complainer, self-righteous moralist, attention seeker, exhibitionist, provocateur, and manipulator. The third language used to describe roles is an abstracted group-role language which seems based upon the concept of central figures rather than on representing personality characteristics of any individual member. These roles include: favorite, idol, sexual idol, love object, instructor, leader, guardian of democracy, time keeper, monopolist, great man, star, doctor's assistant, assistant therapist, aggressor, executive leader, deputy leader, rebellious leader, seducer, scapegoat, object of aggressive drives, hero, respected enactor, fall guy, outsider, prophet, patriarchal sovereign, tyrant, organizer, bad influence, good example, and radar screen.

Without some theoretical delimitation in the formulation of role types, these 50 types could be expanded to include any amount at all. The value to a system of group composition that generates a few basic role types is that all other possible roles may be located with reference to one systematic theoretical formulation. Figure 3-1 represents a similarity structure of all 50 role types. These types are located on a circumplex that has reference to the eight basic role types generated from the theory of emotion.

Figure 3-1 demonstrates that a role type may be located at several points of the circumplex. For example, the monopolist may be expressing the role of the child by acting out and generally seeking attention; or may be expressing the role of puritan, exhorting members to participate; or may be expressing the role of intellectualizer, simply by leading all interactions. The monopolist may be paranoid, manic, psychopathic, or obsessive. As a role type, it needs further definition; it cannot be understood well from a simple role designation. There are several other such overgeneralized types on the circumplex. In contrast, the basic role categories derived from emotion theory constitute more discrete formulations and are embedded in a more meaningful theoretical network. From this theoretical network, the eight basic role types are rather specifically related to other aspects of personality.

There is a structural consistency to this theoretical formulation. The eight basic role types are distributed into four pairs of polar opposites. The romantic accepts all, the scrutinizer rejects all. The innocent renounces intentionality as a way of hiding, the scapegoater asserts intentionality as a way of confronting. The intellectualizer needs to control impulse, the child needs to express impulse. Finally, the puritan needs to possess, and the reintegrator needs to regain something lost or perceived as lost.

Any group that accumulates these basic role forces in its composition will

Figure 3-1. A similarity structure of 50 role types sampled from the group therapy literature and listed outside the circle. These are related to the basic role types expressing emotions and diagnostic dispositions which are listed inside the circle. Role types listed with an asterisk are duplicated at another point on the circle.

also generate a basic emotional wellspring. This kind of emotional organization will provide for the conditions that produce the greatest diversity of emotionality. A group that is composed of persons expressing either these basic role styles or more complex role assignments containing elements of the basic types may be considered to possess an approximate ideal group composition. Bach (1954) underscores the importance of such a polarity of roles in the group. He states, "selection procedures [should] take cognizance of the need of the group to increase its role repertoire in order to obtain better complementation between roles."

This role organization creates the special condition of the group that defines it as a therapeutic setting. The group becomes a transformational environment. Therapeutic possibilities become maximized because of the complete constellation of basic emotions that conflict and coexist. The importance of this diagnostic heterogeneity characterized as the presence of opposite dispositions has been called the "signaling response" in interpersonal relations by Bach (1957) and the "interpersonal reflex" by Leary and Coffey (1955). It is hypothesized that when any group is less than ideally composed, the group will arrange itself so that most or all the basic roles can be expressed; that is, members will actually attempt to role play in order to establish what is sensed as a more normal composition.

THE GROUP AS CHANGE AGENT

The Issue of Role Shift

Bales and Slater (1953) imply that the basic diagnostic role model of the group is fundamentally an evolutionary one. They propose that the most basic, relatively diffuse roles become more differentiated over time. This view suggests that basic diagnoses are related to basic role types, and these categories become established as a function of adaptational considerations. This evolutionary understanding of role and diagnostic development illuminates the special function of the group modality in producing such profound role and diagnostic changes. In terms of role shift, the role and diagnostic functioning of individuals becomes qualitatively and differently expressed in the group. This idea that one's behavior in a group seems dispositionally different than the same person's behavior in an individual encounter has been noticed by Borgatta and Esclenbach (1955), Bell and French (1955), Bishop (1951), Goldstein et al. (1966), and Moos and Clemes (1967); and discussed at length by Yalom (1970). These authors investigate a wide variety of research issues using data from Rorschach variables, mother–child interactions, and patient–therapist and leadership interactions in groups. They suggest that group behavior cannot be predicted accurately from behavior during an individual interview. This finding again implies that the group becomes a transformational environment. The group not only has an effect on individuals, but it also perhaps expresses its own personality. This group personality is determined by the unique complexion of cumulative role behavior of members. Members may shift and exchange role behavior and yet the group can maintain its basic personality because each of the basic role dimensions retains its presence in the group. The basic roles remain constant; it is just that their location and embodiment may change from person to person. In this way persons may change, but the group's "personality of emotions" remains the same.

The mechanics of role shift provide clarification of the dilemma proposed by Bogdanoff and Elbaum (1978) with respect to overcoming role-lock effects and facilitating role fluidity. Thus, the group environment may generate profound, evolutionarylike change conditions.

Role Transformation

A further suggestion that group behavior may be related to basic group role types is offered by Knobloch (1968). Knobloch introduces a theme suggesting that persons may possess "relatively permanent dispositions" that become expressed in their reactions. This thesis postulates that "it is most feasible to study [these reactions] as products of social learning, although it cannot be a priori excluded that some inborn social releasers are also present."

This position also raises a theoretical role paradox. On the one hand, Knobloch implies that roles may be modified and evolve as a function of some learning intervention such as therapy; on the other hand, roles may constitute "relatively permanent dispositions," presumably resistant to change and practically genetic in nature. Yet despite any person's resistance to change, object relations theorists postulate that the group as a transitional object affords each patient a chance to experiment with different roles. Experiences such as these tend to expand one's identifications and to repair whatever split-object problems may exist. Thus, the group as transitional object (Kosseff, 1975) permits a multiple transference environment to exist (Greenacre, 1971). Role shifts and role relocations become possible in this environment.

The system of roles presented here supports both parts of Knobloch's implication. Roles may change, become more complex or less problematic, intensify, become more or less severe, or transcend typical clinical states. However, this system also suggests that roles are not unrelated to deeper structures; they may reflect deeply ingrained genetic codings which tend to retain residual qualities even under the most profound change conditions. In this sense, the system contains sociobiological implications. Any role that metamorphoses into another implies that some basic personality tendency was transformed, which in turn modified a basic emotion. This change of emotion further implies that a trait representing some enduring personality characteristic is relinquished, and a given diagnostic disposition has been similarly significantly altered. Such a process may constitute a genuine geneticlike advance. It is a transformational phenomenon which despite some research to the contrary reveals the group therapeutic endeavor to be one of truly profound evolutionary power.

Yalom's (1970) antipathy toward traditional diagnostic nosology seems to be reasonable. His suggestion is that group therapy *art* needs a basis in group therapy *science* in the form of an interpersonal nosological system. The system presented here is one attempt to provide a scientific nosological underpinning to group therapy art. The family of dimensions of this system may satisfy Yalom's requirement that new diagnostic procedures should directly sample group-relevant behavior. What remains to be elaborated is the specific selection criteria used by therapists to select members for group therapy. The use of selection criteria should produce an adequate group composition that reflects a comprehensive role structure.

SELECTION CRITERIA USED TO FORM A GROUP

Individual versus Group Effects

In order to form a group that will blend in terms of member role and diagnostic structure, certain criteria of selection must be met. There exists in the group therapy literature a plethora of issues raised by authors regarding suitable selection norms for patients of therapy groups. Authors such as Wolf and Schwartz (1962) consider issues of personality structure to be of major importance in the selection of patients for group therapy. However, the varieties of diagnostic dispositional states constitute only one aspect of selection criteria. The functional aspects of selection criteria cut across diagnostic states. Topologically speaking, the surface of the group must be smooth and not characterized by discontinuous changes in surface texture. In this sense, patient selection must account for a measure of ego development or ego-strength that is more or less equal for all group members regardless of diagnostic disposition or role type. Whether or not roles are interpersonally accessible or show great interpersonal impedance, an equal measure of ego-strength or personal resilience must be present in members expressing any role. Durkin (1957) provides a partial reference for understanding this ego-equating phenomenon by stating, "group interaction must proceed through that part of the member's ego development that we call character or personality. It is, if you will, ego interaction."

Despite the fact that members enter therapy groups with different motivations, they must somehow be able to recognize that they all share a reasonable range of stability or ego. All group members should be, diagnostically speaking, either neurotic or character disorder types. None should be floridly psychotic. Slavson (1955) indicates that patients should have experienced minimal satisfaction in early relationships; they should not be unduly sexually disturbed; they should possess basic ego-strength; and they should possess adequate superego development. Although Slavson focuses on individual effects in the development of selection criteria, patients selected for group therapy based upon these criteria will be able to participate in the group therapy enterprise in a manner that facilitates group effects.

According to most authors, the single most important selection criterion is ego-strength or ego equality among group members. This ego equality may exist even though members demonstrate quite distinct and varying motivations in the group. An example of the variety of motives among patients with roughly equivalent ego-strength is offered by Benne (1958). Three separate motivating styles are described. First, some patients seek form and structured work production. Second, some resist structure and seek a more extemporaneous interaction. This second type needs to ventilate feelings and to discuss relationships. A third type generally tries to strike a compromise between the first two types. Benne's motivating styles are essentially similar in that the three styles are all inclined toward interaction. However, the basic role composition which has been proposed here suggests that a fourth type is necessary. The scrutinizer and innocent types are both very guarded against interaction. They represent critical and highly inhibited types respectively. A fourth motivating type to add to Benne's conception would be characterized as the patient who is resistant to interaction despite a stated desire to be included as a member of the group. This fourth type may reveal an inherent element of motivation within the resistance itself.

A Focus on Group Process

The motivating styles described by Benne also suggest that affiliation needs are of utmost importance to the members of the group. Members who are eager to work with or without structure or to strike a compromise in order to work have some emotional investment in the group as a whole. This issue of affiliation with the group is considered by Kadis et al. (1968) to be the most important feature of patient selection criteria. These authors describe four criteria of selection based upon a measure of affiliation or identification with the group. The criteria are generated out of a concern with the overall group process, and with seeking to preserve a viable therapeutic group atmosphere.

1. The group must be able to cope with the tension of a newcomer to its ranks; and, secondarily, the newcomer's anxiety level should be appropriate to the ongoing process.
2. It becomes important to predict whether a new member will fit with the other members of the group. This fit is an index of identification and empathy with others.
3. Any newcomer to the group must be reasonably able to tolerate the nature of group activity. This tolerance is an overall index of ego-strength.
4. A new member's defense system needs in some way to be equivalent to the defense system of those members already part of the group. This criterion is an index of the interlocking of patients' defense systems.

The focus on group process in determining selection criteria is elaborated by Leopold (1957). Although interested in diagnostic attributes of individual members, Leopold is fundamentally concerned with the ongoing group climate. He suggests four major selection criteria:

1. Patients should have full reality contact. Those who repeatedly inject their distortions and irrationalities in the group are generally unreachable by other members.
2. A member should have the capacity for being reached emotionally in the group in terms of group interpersonal relationships. Monopolizers of group time inhibit and render useless most group interaction.
3. Members should have the flexibility for acting to increase or decrease group tensions.
4. Any member should periodically be able to catalyze the group.

Leopold's focus on group effects includes the issue of ego equality among members. Primarily, members should not be psychotic. Second, in insisting on the emotional reachability of each group member, Leopold remembers that the group can be a transformational work environment. Third, his concern with group tension regulation reflects an implicit sense of boundary concerns as a group process feature. Finally, the criterion that each member should be able to catalyze the group indicates that Leopold implies a quasi central-figure presence as part of either an epigenetic or evolutionary group process model.

The focus on group effects is also discussed by Durkin (1964). She cites the importance of pure group effects as reflected in the work of Sherif on group norms and in the work of Lewin on field tension. Implications of such social psychological studies consistently imply that group effects on individuals are quite strong. Couch (1961), who studied the personality needs correlating most with patients' behavior, discovered that of all personality variables it was the behavioral press—the overt behavioral acts directed toward the individual—that related most. This finding implied that the role composition of the group exerted great influence on member behavior.

Many authors apparently feel that group effects can be most effective across role types, provided that all members share a range of adequate ego-strength. An adequate group role composition in which a roughly equivalent ego-strength characterizes the personality development of each member further sets the stage for a therapeutic transformational environment to exist in the group. This transformational group environment also may imply that group roles shift from member to member although the personality of emotion remains the same for the group as a whole. The role shift signals some ongoing personality alterations among members. These individual role and personality alterations have been related to psychoanalytic transference interpretation and to the working-through process of individual members with the group therapist.

In terms of group effects, role shift is also a function of the social-psychological and sociological aspects of group organization. How roles shift becomes an important question in this social-adaptational framework. These powerful individual and social forces that produce personality alteration may be understood as part of the group's social structure.

SOME ISSUES OF ROLE SHIFT IN THE GROUP SOCIAL SYSTEM

The Group as a Social Structure

Schaffer and Galinsky (1974) postulate that a concern with the group as a social system may produce different results than concern with the group as an interpersonal relationship model, in which emphasis is on the relationship between the therapist and each individual member. It would seem that from both a group dynamics and psychoanalytic point of view, the change in role constitutes an extremely important part of the therapeutic process. This shift of role as an expression of the working-through process cannot occur just from emotional ventilation or catharsis. The shift of role must be characterized by a corresponding change in the status implied by a group member's particular role; that is, it must signal a change in the social-desirability value of a membership role position. Therefore, roles also may be understood in terms of social and psychological desirability. Each role may contain some unconsciously agreed-upon value in the overall social structure of the group. The value in the role implies a role meaning, or a status element of role. For example, in chapter 1, objective theoretical participation time in the group was compared to actual participation time. It was suggested that actual participation time by members is based upon specific diagnostic role meanings. It is such role meaning that is the equivalent of a role-status element. As an illustration, the actual vocal participation time of the scapegoater will be far greater than that of the innocent. The scapegoater who expresses aggressive urges obviously claims a different and unconsciously agreed-upon status among group members than does the innocent. In order for role shift to occur, status needs first must be suspended. In group psychotherapy this becomes accomplished along with the ever-increasing level of each member's self-disclosure. Therefore, role fluidity as a measure of successful psychotherapy (Bogdanoff and Elbaum, 1978) may mean role-status change.

Mullan (1963) indicates that role behavior becomes more undifferentiated as the resolution of status need increases. This undifferentiation process may be a necessary precursor to role shift. Thus role and status are different. Role becomes the dynamic part of status (Cartwright and Zander, 1968) and both constitute elements of social structure. As the dynamic part to status, roles are also cultural mechanisms similar to conventions, customs, and taboos. They may be used to regulate the group social structure (Jaques, 1955). It is this regulation feature of the group social structure that constitutes the important issue in the life of a group.

The Sociobiology of Groups: An Introduction

The role shift in the group is based upon the reworking of defenses so that status needs may be altered. The alteration of status needs creates the condition for a temporary undifferentiating role process to take place. This alteration process raises the issue of examining the group as-a-whole as a social structure. It is within this social structure that roles and status needs as transformational ingredients may be better understood. The transition constitutes a movement from role status issues to one of investigating the group sociology. This sociology contains historical as well as generational and genealogical elements and therefore may be more accurately represented as a sociobiology. Such elements of the group process define the group as a psychosociological environment embraced by a biological framework; and in terms of structure, perhaps even embraced within a biophysical framework (Kellerman, 1976b). Thus the group may be an environment in which inner forces affect its boundary.

In the context of a germinating group infrastructure, chapter 4 will present one possible theoretical approach in the formulation of a sociobiological underpinning to a psychoanalytic group therapy process.

4

Psychotherapy Group Process: Genealogical and Socio-Adaptational Forces

An overall theoretical consensus proposes that the family system represents the basic underlying model of group therapy; that is, knowing more about the vicissitudes of family life provides therapists with a greater understanding of patients' behavior in a group. This position is cited by psychodynamically oriented clinicians (Bach, 1954; Grotjahn, 1973; Kadis et al., 1968; Wolf and Schwartz, 1962), by social psychologists concerned with group dynamics (Bonner, 1964; Cartwright and Zander, 1968), and by group development experimentalists investigating teaching and self-analytic groups (Gibbard, Hartman, and Mann, 1974). It is assumed that this sort of model provides one basis for transference interpretations. There is, of course, much indirect evidence to support this family model hypothesis. For example, clinicians generally find that children from families with no other siblings experience greater difficulty and increased tension upon entering a group. These patients find it difficult to be spontaneous, frequently show derivative oedipal problems involving issues of privacy and loyalty, and see the group as a cold and unfriendly place. They may seek the protection of the therapist and may usually be seated in close proximity to the therapist during their initial entry to the group.

Apparently not having sibling experience during formative periods contributes to this difficulty at a later time. A second illustration of the group as transference family involves actual and frequent reminders by patients themselves. For example, patients respond to each other with somewhat prosaic yet intense comments such as, "you remind me of my mother," or "you remind me of my father." Experience also teaches that the most dramatic interactions frequently invoke old family memories and the reactions to these memories become replayed. There are many other examples that could be cited to suggest that the apparent and very useful model existing in the group is the family system. There are also some authors who best understand a member's behavior in a group when they view the group as a family system (Bion, 1955; Ezriel, 1950, 1952; Foulkes, 1960; Haley, 1968; and Rabkin, 1970).

Most psychodynamically oriented group therapists use this family model to understand forces operating in the group. However, there may be more to this model than simply the existence of a system frozen in time. The family is not a static system. It expands, experiences loss, grows older, incorporates new members, and generally develops a history all its own. It develops as a function of time, so to speak, generationally. The monitoring of the family as a basis for understanding the group process therefore implies a temporal variable reflecting growth, history, membership acquisition, and a generational quality. Given this longitudinal condition of family life, the group also may be traced generationally. This implies that the group contains an underlying genealogical aspect which may be characterized as having a sociology composed of legends, myths, specific traditions, folklore, mores, and aspirations.

In this chapter, the geneaological property of therapy groups will be examined and outlined. The purpose of this construction is to develop a hypothetical model from which certain practical implications regarding therapy groups may emerge. The theoretical context suggesting this formulation develops from an evolutionary adaptational view; that is, questions of adaptational issues arise from the investigation of the fundamental purpose of the family. The model has psychosocial and sociobiological implications.

An attempt will be made to trace conditions leading to the maximizing of the group process. Adaptational concepts will be related to the infrastructure of groups, especially with regard to the life of the group and with reference to the appearance of normative thematic material as part of group generationality. The central question of this particular formulation that will be raised is, what is the purpose of the group? It is a question to be answered at the conclusion of this and of the following chapters on group defense structure.

The hypothetical system presented here in which the variable of age is controlled, may be said to have a potential existence which in a practical sense could become more or less approximated. Its expositional value, however, lies not in whether group therapy is in fact perfectly congruent with this model, but rather that the model may generate many implications and hypotheses, and in so doing may serve to increase general knowledge in the field and to stimulate further thinking.

THE CONCEPT OF GROUP GENERATIONS

Traditional therapy groups, if successful, may continue for many years even though the patients who comprised the original group are no longer in attendance. The length of time most patients spend in traditional psychodynamically oriented therapy groups is approximately two to three years. There are, of course, many patients who either spend less time or much more time in a group. However, empirically it seems that more than 50 percent of patients in groups will terminate before three years. Yalom (1970) reports that 18 to 24 months constitutes the period of time for most patients to undergo significant therapeutic change. If a group continues for four to five years, most of the membership will probably have changed twice. If the group continues for six or eight years, most of the membership will probably have changed three or more times. Should the group continue for eight to ten years, most of the membership will probably have changed at least four times.

Thus, a generation may be defined as a period of time in a group lasting about two years and characterized by an approximate new membership; that is, all or most of the original members have left, and new members have been added to the group. In this way, eight years would be the approximate period of time represented by four generations. If the group is well composed, generations may last longer—perhaps three or four years or more. The equivalent time periods of generations related to individual development is generally considered to be 20 to 25 years for each generation. In terms of individual development then, four group generations would total approximately 80 to 100 years. For whatever implications are derived from this formulation, the ratio of individual generations to group generations equals about ten years to one year respectively. Simplifying this ratio, it might be said that a group lasting eight to ten years is equivalent in age to an individual of 80 to 100. This comparison also has been suggested by Bennis and Shepard (1974) who, in outlining problems for a theory of group development, state, "maturity for the group means something analogous to maturity for the person."

Such a comparison is not frivolous, and may contain important implications. For example, an individual at 25 struggles with different problems than the same person does at 35. At 35 this person is concerned with issues that are frequently far different than the issues dealt with at 45 or even at 55. Similarly, a group that lasts for eight or ten years or more, will probably have a different experience-shape during each of its four generations. This is especially true if the average age of the members increased in each succeeding generation. The importance of elapsing time as a critical variable in the process of change also has been cited by Lorr (1962) and by Yalom (1970). The idea that the group needs an extraordinary time span in which to develop its full potential as a change agent is also suggested by Mills (1964) who considers the group's aims of achieving intimacy and modifying authority relationships to reflect a process that is a protracted and enduring one.

To pose a hypothetical condition, if a group were begun with all members in the early adult years, with a mean age of 23, the next generation of members about two years later might consist of some people in their 30's with an average age in the group of about 28 or 30. The following generation, about two years later, might consist of members in their 30's and perhaps some in their late 30's or early 40's, with a mean age in the middle to late 30's. The fourth generation, about two years later, could consist of most members in their late 30's and 40's and perhaps some who are about 50, with a mean age of about 40.

The increase in mean age of an ongoing group as a function of generational development has its practical rationale and is seen as an adaptational feature of groups. In this hypothetical condition when a therapist starts a group in which the average age of the membership is about 22 or 23, the maturity and experience quotient of this group is more or less low. True enough, it is a young adult population, but nevertheless persons at 22 or 23 are experiencing their first adult metamorphosis with all its attendant tensions and normative conflicts. As these people work in the group they become less neurotic, more assertive, more mature, and more sophisticated in the use of therapy tools to facilitate their own progress. Such qualities are not easy to acquire. After two or three years, some of these members will leave the group and others will be invited to join the group. On a purely practical level, in order for the group to sustain the interest of the remaining members, all new individuals can no longer be uninitiated 22 or 23-year-olds. Furthermore, those members that remain in the group who are now 24 to 26 have also experienced a highly specialized and maturing experience so that newer members not having had the opportunity to develop in the same way need to be somewhat older. If they are older, perhaps in their mid to late 20's, their lack of group experience is in part compensated by their increased life's experience and maturity. Theoretically, this state of affairs suggests that there may be an inexorable force operating in the group that inclines the group chronologically upward in age.

It is suggested here that a full group generational cycle consists of four generations, and in time will last approximately eight to ten years. This cycle constitutes one group life span. In groups that are superbly constructed, hardly any members leave the group in two or three years. In such cases, each generation can last four to five years. Such groups are quite exceptional however.

GROUP GENEALOGY

There are at least two further implications of this generationality of groups. The first is the idea that groups may be thought of as containing a genealogical component; that is, that the group has an ancestry, and that there may be so-called hereditary lines in the group. Hereditary lines might be described as lines or lineages of particular member roles. For example, a group that lasts eight years may always have at least one member that carries the motive force of the group. This person will be well motivated, and may work in therapy with obvious authenticity. After some time when this person leaves the group, the therapist may eventually add a new member who either in motivation and or actual appearance is reminiscent of the "replaced" member.

This same kind of unconscious organization of membership which may be part of group infrastructure applies to various member-roles in the ongoing group. As was shown in the earlier chapters on character roles and group composition, there may always be present an assertive member, a passive member, an introspective type, etc. and these roles remain filled by different people who ultimately make up role lineages across four generations. As is frequently the case, members who have been in the group for two or even three generations are sometimes heard to say that some new member is reminiscent of either one or two previous members from different generations, and may attribute conscious motives to the therapist for "keeping up that type." The fact that there may be stereotypical roles in the group has been cited by Berger and Rosenbaum (1967) and by Yalom (1970), and outlined in the earlier chapter on character roles.

The idea of role lineage also has relevance to the concept of central figures (Redl, 1942). The question raised is whether central figures of the group exist in some dormant state waiting to be expressed, or whether role lineage is actually expressed generationally in the group as a function of the therapist's efforts to maintain a basic and ideal group composition. In certain respects, leadership qualities are also provided by group members who act as catalysts to the group process. These catalysts are also central figures. Bennis and Shepard (1974) indicate that "Leadership from the standpoint of group development can be defined in terms of catalysts responsible for group movement from one phase to the next." This structural aspect to the group process involving a central figure provides one basis for determining the membership roles that are needed for group development.

A person who is in the fourth generation of the group may have had two or three role descendants from previous generations, i.e., persons who occupied the same role position in the group. This role inheritance may be analogous to the genetic transmission of a trait but it must be remembered that it is the therapist who maintains this basic group organization. The concept of system genealogy is also implied by the work of von Bertalanffy (1969) and Miller (1969), and a transgenerational effect on a system is discussed by Ehrenwald (1974).

NORMATIVE THEMATIC MATERIAL OF EACH GROUP GENERATION

The second implication of a four-generation group life span containing a genealogical component is that there may be normative thematic material that is more germane to a given generation than to any other generation. The concerns of 20-year-olds are quite different from the concerns of 50-year-olds. Although persons from both of these age levels share some similar problems, they are nevertheless concerned with different aspects of even similar problems. For example, at 20 one may be struggling to compete, to create a career, to search for a spouse, and to strive for advantage and excellence. At 50, one still struggles, but the existential condition and experiences may have a different complexion. Striving is still an issue, but the question becomes to what end? Is it worth it? In one's 20's the striving may be more oedipal with issues of victory, loyalty, and competition quite prominent. In one's 50's the striving theme may contain elements that are more oral, including feeling deprived, defeated, or if victorious, perhaps unfulfilled. Empirically, therapists see conflict material being expressed in any group generation that includes elements from all psychosexual stages. However, just as different age levels may contain material more from one psychosexual stage than from another in individuals, so too, it is proposed here, will each group generation be characterized as containing as its general group theme, derivative issues from given psychosexual stages.

The Group's Phases and Stages

To understand the developmental sequence of group process and to generate derivative psychosexual material from this process, it must be first established that the group therapy condition itself represents an attempt to create an enduring social structure, one that assumes an institutional life. In the therapy sense, this establishment of a social structure is partially a reworking or restructuring of historical reference points. Kaplan (1967) refers to this in postulating that "any small group of individuals who have their formal relationship to social structures temporarily suspended have as one of their primary needs the reestablishment of a social structure in order to communicate and to achieve agreed upon tasks." Kaplan and Roman (1961) and Kaplan (1967) further propose that this sort of group formation develops three main phases: a dependency phase in which leaders are idealized, a power phase in which there is an exaggerated view of the leader's power and concomitant concern that it may be used punitively, and an intimacy phase in which pairs of group members develop an affinity for one another.

These stages of group development illustrate the overall idea that group formation occurs in a sequence of developmental phases. This sort of conception has also been suggested by Applebaum (1963), Bion (1959a), Ezriel (1950), Foulkes and Anthony (1965), Redl (1942), and by Stock and Thelen (1958). Applebaum (1963) particularly states the case for the recapitulation in small groups of early instinctual experiences. Phases of development are "a progression through infantile psychosexual stages." This idea of group stages that are sequentially progressive has also been cited by Erikson (1959) who correlates group formation to psychosocial phases of child development. Gibbard (1974) further suggests that any sort of structural differentiation of the group, whether psychological or sociological, can be understood only in a developmental context.

Models of Group Development and Psychosexual Themes

The models of group development presented in the literature especially with reference to self analytic groups may be roughly divided into three categories. Gibbard, Hartman, and Mann (1974) call these models: (1) linear-progressive, (2) life-cycle, and (3) pendular. An analysis of the thematic content of each of these models indicates that they are not easily reconcilable. This is true especially with regard to the sequential way in which each considers oedipal and pre-oedipal issues in the development of group process. The authors state that "the group situation, unlike the dyadic situation in individual therapy, dictates that oedipal and pre-oedipal themes may influence group process at the same time and in ways that make it difficult to relate the two processes."

The following review and analysis of each model will be made in order to account for the interweaving of oedipal and pre-oedipal themes in the development of group life, and to provide a framework by which the models may become more related to one another.

LINEAR-PROGRESSIVE MODELS

In this model of group development, the group moves from its initial starting point to a conflict stage and, resolving this conflict stage, to cohesive behavior and the goal of "task accomplishment." Tuckman (1965) provides one example of a linear-progressive model. The group development shows five subphases. Testing is a formative stage in which dependency problems emerge. Intragroup conflict and emotional expression is a second group phase. It is code named "storming." A third phase of group cohesion is code named "norming." A fourth stage is characterized by role relatedness, and the fifth stage comprises the performance of the group task.

Bennis and Shepard (1956) offer a second example of the linear-progressive conception of group development. They suggest a two phase process with various subphases. The first major phase is an authority phase. This phase deals with issues of dependency. The second phase is an interpersonal one in which the group deals with interdependence. Phase one includes subphases in which there may be a submissive solution to authority problems, or the solution may reside in the working-through of rebellion or a compromise solution may emerge in which the dependency-authority problem goes through a perfunctory adjustment. Rebellion needs to be worked-through adequately however, so that the mood swing between enchantment in the group—and disenchantment—a function of the concern with individual identity—may also be in turn resolved. Only with this resolution, the resolution of authority problems, may the group proceed to the second major interpersonal phase.

These conceptions of group development are linear because the group process works toward ultimate goals. They are also considered progressive because dependency characteristics imply developmentally earlier implications than later interdependence. The linear-progressive model of group development stresses this sort of sequence and both implies and is supported by the conception that individual development is replicated in the development of the group-as-a-whole. The transition or developmental sequence begins from childhood, the dependency stage, and leads to adulthood where possibilities of intimacy exist.

This conception of a linear-progressive process in group development does not consider the issue of the decline or termination of the group, and therefore lacks a substantial theoretical analysis of the group's end phase. In addition, the concern with authority as well as dependency issues as characterizing early group life suggests that oedipal elements are also being expressed in the initial group phase, a point not adequately considered. For both of these reasons, the issue of decline of the group and the issue of oedipal conflicts existing in the initial group phase, a simple linear-progressive approach does not seem to offer the best explanatory model of group process development.

LIFE-CYCLE MODELS

This second type of theoretical model of group development emphasizes the importance of the terminal or termination phase of group process. Mills (1964) identified five periods of group development. They are termed: (1) encounter, (2) testing boundaries and creating roles, (3) creating normative system, (4) production, and (5) separation. Mann (1966) and Mann et al. (1967) also discuss the terminal phase of life-cycle models. This terminal phase stresses both separation and what is termed "terminal review." Others who discuss the terminal phase of the group or the death of the group include Dunphy (1968) and Slater (1966). Both authors focus on the return to the "outside world" as a function of the increased permeability and ultimate dissolution of group boundaries.

Life-cycle models only add the terminal phase to the linear model. The life-cycle model is still progressive, reflecting the movement of the group from the dependence of childhood to the decline of old age. There is a serious question whether such a sequence reflects the true structural makeup of a group and this shall be discussed later.

PENDULAR MODELS

This sort of model stresses the evolution of boundaries of the group. The ambivalence of members generated both by the fear of and the wish for boundaries in the group, and the ever present problem of group equilibrium constitute the focus of this sort of model (Slater, 1966). An example of a pendular process in group development is the shift of Bion's dependency group to pairing group to fight-flight group. Gibbard, Hartman, and Mann (1974) imply that the pendular process keeps the group tension calibrated to the equilibrium-disequilibrium balance as generated by such boundary concerns. Anxiety, guilt, and depression consitute disequilibrium phenomena, and these emotions need to be managed in order to reestablish the group equilibrium. The pendular process occurs throughout the life of the group and is an adaptational response to both introjective and projective elements in the development of the group boundaries.

An Integration of Models

Each of these models leaves the analysis of certain issues incomplete. The linear-progressive model considers the group to be a replication of individual development and views group development as an ever increasing process of differentiation, but it does not integrate the end phase of the group with any theoretical construction. The life-cycle model ultimately considers the demise of the group to be essential to group development, yet it too is progressive. It implies the termination of the group once the group has accomplished its task. The pendular model is concerned with recurring patterns in the life of the group and considers an entirely different set of problems than either of the other models. How then may all three models be integrated so that what appear to be theoretically disparate positions between models may be reconciled without positing the group's demise?

Authors who have developed conceptions of group development represented within each of the three models begin with the assumption that the group recapitulates individual development in the sense that groups begin at the beginning; that is, at the vital stage or at a point containing oral elements, seen in the derived form as dependency features. Once this assumption is accepted these models cannot be integrated so as to account for a time extended psychotherapy group.

However, it is not necessary to accept this assumption. A new assumption is offered which considers that groups actually do follow a developmental sequence. It is one defined, however, as a psychosexual regression. The group therefore, begins in the oedipal period and not in the oral period. It expresses oedipal problems during its formative periods. During first sessions of newly formed groups it is quite usual for individuals to reveal their anxieties and their hopes that members of the group will offer them understanding. Compassion, sympathy, and the fear of rejection constitute much of the stated concerns of members during initial sessions and these concerns do seem to reflect oral derivative needs. However, if one carefully observes the sequence of interaction during such sessions, quite a different sense of interactional meaning emerges. For example, as soon as two members begin to develop some contact, they will frequently be interrupted or their interaction will be interfered with by another member.

In the first session of a newly formed group, when David and Gina began to develop their interaction beyond a formal and perfunctory question and answer

encounter, Bob, during a pregnant pause, suddenly and quite abruptly began
speaking to yet a fourth member while referring to Gina. The verbal content
of the group session to that point seemed, psychosexually speaking, to be oral; that
is, members were expressing needs for understanding. However, its style was oed-
ipal; that is, members of the group were covertly feeling competitive

The prevailing style of groups during formative periods will frequently
show such underlying oedipal-competitive urges here illustrated by Bob's behavior. The group then, perhaps evolves regressively from the oedipal toward
the phallic stage expressing problems derived from each psychosexual phase.
The anal and then the oral stages are experienced as the group ages further.

One major hypothesis arising from this conception is that in group development, the group process of maturation is equivalent to psychosexual regression; that is, in terms of the group recapitulating individual development,
a maturing group is inversely correlated to psychosexual maturation, and positively correlated to psychosexual regression. It is a developmental process
characterized by a "dematuring."

Bennis and Shepard (1974) tacitly refer to this idea when they posit their
linear-progressive conception of group development. The movement from a
preoccupation with authority relations to a preoccupation with personal relations certainly seems at face value to suggest oedipal problems before oral
ones. The distribution of power occupying the group in its original phase
moves to a distribution of affection which occupies the group during its later
stages. In the development of group life, this kind of sequence seems to reflect
a psychosexual regression better than it does a linear progression. Even authors such as Bennis and Shepard (1956), Gibbard and Hartman (1973b), and
Slater (1966) who are identified with these three major models of group development feel compelled to consider oedipal issues in the group's formative
stage. Gibbard, Hartman, and Mann (1974) indicate that the "group situation
recreates basic nuclear family conditions that spawn the oedipus complex . . .
The oedipal paradigm is also a progressive one in the sense that, in individual
development the resolution of the oedipal crisis leads to guilt and the internalization of the paternal superego, which is accompanied by a more stable
identification and a period of work and task orientation." In addition, Freud
(1913, 1921), Holmes (1967), Lundgren (1971), and Whitman (1964) all notice
the oedipal paradigm in the construction of ongoing group process especially in
the initial work on the revolt against the leader.

Kaplan (1967) and Kaplan and Roman (1961) derive a linear-progressive
model previously cited as containing developmental stages of dependency,
power, and intimacy. This model however, may actually be one that is more
linear-regressive than it is progressive. For example, the dependency stage
seems to be an oral phase, yet the idealization of the leader contains oedipal
and hysteric features. In addition, the power phase which at first glance seems
to reflect anal concerns over the leader's ability to punish, and which may be
correlated to effects such as displacement of anger, repression of fear, and

general ambivalence toward the leader, seems even more suitably characterized by phallic concerns, castration anxiety, and issues of assertion. The intimacy phase in which "pairing" reflects the predominant affectionate mood may actually contain oral elements. It may be a truer dependency phase than the one the authors formulated characterizing the dependency of the first group stage. The developmental sequence according to Kaplan, as it is expressed in group formation, may therefore also imply that the group process may evolve in a psychosexually regressive sequence; that is, the oedipal phase leading ultimately to the oral phase.

It should be remembered that adult groups are composed of mature people, and this is also true during group formative periods. As a matter of interest, Scheidlinger (1968) distinguishes between group formative regression which is considered to be normal, and neurotic regression characteristic of individual defensive operations. Assuming this condition of maturity of members during the formative group stage, it would seem that the probability of oedipal problems existing and reflecting the initial concern of the group is at least as likely as that of oral problems. Furthermore, a general psychoanalytic treatment position assumes that pre-oedipal issues arise only when repressive barriers recede, and this process implies a time-extended treatment condition, not one concerned with termination features.

Gibbard, Hartman, and Mann (1974) propose a less extreme view than is represented either by the linear-progressive model of group development, or by the psychosexual regressive model presented here. These authors recognize that oedipal elements in the early formative period of group development cannot be overlooked. They indicate that the group is both mature and primitive: "the group is composed of enough disparate and irreconcilable components to make it an imperfectly integrated entity. Thus group members have available a continuum of alternative behaviors, ranging from the more regressed to the more mature, while the group-as-a-whole as it matures becomes more like a symbiotic mother with whom the members are ambivalently fused." There are two issues that emerge from this position. The first implies that the group recreates family nuclear conflicts insofar as the vicissitudes of psychosexual problems affect to varying degrees any productive work in the group. The second issue implies that boundary problems of the group, that is, problems of disequilibrium, result from part object transferences and defensive operations, and this suggests pre-oedipal problems. The authors finally state "We are not, however, in favor of an integration which simplifies the issue. We are more than ever impressed with the complexity of group life. In our view, issues on different levels do occur simultaneously and must be seen that way."

This view of the complexity of group life is quite valid, yet the need for a conceptual framework offering the possibility of reconciling and integrating the variety of observations on group development is necessary. Scheidlinger (1964) refers to this problem and recognizes that the newly formed group creates the possibility for psychic disruption and that intrapsychic and inter-personal tensions are generated by the threat of this potential disruption. The result of these particular tensions is to implement reparative efforts in order to master initial tensions. That is precisely what is meant by the early phase of group development producing a group formative regression.

The unusual sense of time generated by and in a group also has been mentioned by Kaplan (1967) who indicates that a group time sense may pro-duce a tendency toward regression. "The time-limited span of a training group, which is considerably shorter than the usual life span of a therapy group, has a significant effect upon the emergence of regressive group emo-tions." Here Kaplan refers to the time-sense imbalance of groups while simul-taneously noticing that groups contain strong regressive forces in their de-velopment.

The developmental-regressive model presented here offers the possibility for an overall integration of models. First, it considers that derivative mate-rials from all psychosexual stages are expressed in all phases of the group process. Second, it identifies the group process as regressive insofar as the group begins with a predominance of oedipal issues, and as the process of group development evolves, psychosexual themes move toward the oral phase. Thus the group process is, psychosexually speaking, regressive or retrogressive.

Therefore, to the proposition that the group life-span consists of four gen-erations must now be added that each of these generations is characterized by a major psychosexual theme and by all other psychosexual subthemes. This conception of the retrogressive evolution of groups takes into account the issue of the death of the group which will be further examined in the following sec-tions, and which is conspicuously absent in the progressive linear model. Furthermore, the regressive model establishes a new conception of the de-mise of the group, a feature of the life-cycle models, and expands this concep-tion in an important way. Third, the regressive model also accounts for the recurring pattern of moods and themes cited by authors who propose a pendu-lar model. Thus the regressive psychosexual model of group development im-plies that the group may be truly linear, life-cyclic, and pendular.

In this present work, the hypothetical condition illustrating this retrogres-sive process of group development is the formation of a group of young adults. However, the retrogressive process of group development occurs even if groups were to be composed of members of various ages, or of members in their 50's or even 60's; that is, derivative material of the oedipal period would absorb the group's attention in the formative period and move toward oral problems as the group evolves. The difference would be that in a group with members in their 50's or 60's, the initial oedipal period would contain a more intensely coexisting oral subtheme.

The general principle governing the appearance of major themes and subthemes during a given stage of the group reflects in part this mixture in ages of group members. For present purposes, to illustrate the retrogressive process of group development, the age of group members will remain constant. This is what is meant by the young adult group constituting a hypothetical condition.

It should also be pointed out that despite the two to three year period a member spends in a group, there are some groups in which two or three members maintain their membership for up to eight years or more—a full four generational cycle. Although this sort of commitment to the therapy is sometimes thought to reflect unnecessary dependence, it is perhaps the unusual position presented here that an ideal group is one, in fact, in which at least one or two members may maintain their group membership for at least eight years. Such patients have the opportunity to experience the entire regressive sequence of psychosexual themes. This offers them the unusual opportunity to experience and utilize a full character analysis. Such an exposure tends also to keep the entire group climate especially fertile and compelling.

Group Generation and Psychosexual Themes

The first group generation of young adults in their early 20's is frequently dealing in a central way with oedipal themes. Issues of competition and loyalty abound. The second generation of the group with members in their late 20's or early 30's is frequently preoccupied with career issues, issues of assertiveness and passivity, and what might be called phallic envy. This second generation of the group cycle may then be centrally related to the phallic period. The third generation of the group with members in their late 30's or early 40's is concerned with issues of control, acting-out, or dyscontrol. Marriages are disintegrating, the whole issue of how one feels about money, and an overreaction to demands are examples of concerns in this time period. Thus it may be that the third generation of group life correlates to issues of the anal period. Finally, the fourth generation of the group with members in their 40's and 50's and some perhaps still in their 30's, but with a mean age of mid 40, may be somewhat depressed during critical periods. Career disenchantment, feeling deprived of love, and feeling generally quite needy seem to preoccupy members during this time and may characterize this generation of group life as one corresponding to issues of the oral period.

Thus, on a theoretical level, it may be seen that an inverse relationship develops between the aging process of group generations and the emergence of derivative conflict material of psychosexual stages. First generation is oedipal, second is phallic, third is anal, and fourth is oral. As the group ages then, a psychosexual regression takes place. Extrapolating from this implies that termination of the group will result from the natural progression of the group's generational cycle. This is perfectly logical and will occur provided something adaptational does not take place. The proposition here is that something adaptational does take place, and that the group does not expire, rather becoming restored with a new and opposite force. This force shall be discussed in a later section of this chapter.

Diagnosis, Group Generation, and Psychosexual Content

Another implication of the connection between the appearance of psychosexual stage thematic material with that of group generations relates to the kind of therapeutic work each patient does for the period of time spent in the group. For example, if each group member functions in the group for two to three years, perhaps a substantial part of the therapeutic work done by that patient is largely determined by the prevailing themes during that particular stage of group development. Despite the fact that patients struggle with all derivative psychosexual material, the only significant work that may be possible for any one individual refers to underlying thematic material absorbing the group's attention at a given group phase; a psychoanalytic and Bionian intersection.

This idea has been suggested in various forms by Bennis and Shepard (1956), Bion (1961), Foulkes and Anthony (1965), Leder and Schwartz (1969), and by McDougall (1921). Bennis and Shepard (1956) refer to an isomorphic relation between group development and ego correlates of psychosexual stages. Bion (1961) discusses three universal underlying "cultures" existing as independent of the conscious work of the group. Foulkes and Anthony (1965) describe three phases of the group. They indicate that "the group tends to speak and react to a common theme as if it were a living entity. . . . All contributions are variations on this single theme, even though the group are not consicously aware of that theme and do not know what they are talking about." Leder and Schwartz (1969) also refer to group stages as they relate to the psychosexual stages postulated by Freud (1905). Finally, McDougall (1921) outlines five conditions of the group environment that must be met during the group process in order to provide a complete experience for its members.

As the age composition of the group becomes more heterogeneous, underlying themes may create a more complex set of forces in the group. This implies that despite therapists' search for group heterogeneity, it may be therapeutically facilitating to form groups, or include members in existing groups, who fall within the total generational age range already existing in the group. It may be that the therapeutic process is maximized for each member when the group age composition is more congruent with generational themes.

The generational movement of the group may also reveal a corresponding diagnostic polar structure that was suggested in Chapter 3 on group roles. For example, oedipal themes of loyalty and disloyalty characteristic of first generation issues are also characteristic of the hysteric-paranoid polarity. In fact, the paranoid nature of the first group generation has been indicated by Gibbard, Hartman, and Mann (1974). Scheidlinger (1968) also recognizes that the initial plase of the group takes on a paranoid flavor, and Fried (1976) states that the paranoid mood "is the prevailing condition during the initial narcissistic group base." The second generation of the group in which phallic themes of assertion and passivity are seen may be diagnostically characteristic of the polar dispositions of passive-aggressive. The third generation of the group expressing anal themes of control and dyscontrol reflects polar diagnostic dispositions of the control of the obsessional type and the dyscontrol of the psychopathic type. In the fourth generation, oral themes of possessing and losing are generated, and correspond to the polar dispositions of manic and depressive types. Thus, the issue of the diagnostic nature of the group may be expanded to include a systematic organization of diagnostic dispositions unfolding as a function of group generationality.

ADAPTIVE FORCES OF THE GROUP PROCESS

Creating the Group Motive force

In forming a group, certain conditions should prevail so that the life of the group is viable. The therapist interested in maintaining such a motive force in the group begins with ground rules that are made explicit to all members (Spotnitz, 1973; Yalom, 1970). These are not arbitrary. They are designed to facilitate the group's coalescing as a functioning system.

The group must maintain its integrity by maintaining its boundary. This suggests that the group becomes a suprasystem; more than just the sum of its parts. The idea of a group being more than the sum of its parts has been suggested by Emil Durkheim in the 19th century and by other researchers implying similar hypotheses (Bonner, 1964; Cartwright and Zander, 1968) and has been reviewed by Durkin (1964). Systems concepts such as "suprasystem" and "group boundary" have also been discussed by von Bertalanffy (1969) and by Miller (1969). The group develops a membrane much like a living organism. To take the analogy one step further, this organism contains a nucleus and even a cytoplasm represented by the therapist and by the therapeutic ambiance in which the members interact respectively. The issue then becomes how to best maintain the integrity of the group boundary so that the motive force or tension level inside the group is sustained. The ground rules of the group are generated on the basis of one major criterion—helping to maintain the inner working condition of the group. First, members in the group are encouraged to be on a first name basis only. This tends to promote anonymity and creates a special serious and working environment in the group. Further, this guideline is designed so that reality conditions are kept in a secondary role. The general idea is to discourage personal interaction between members outside of the therapy session. It leads to the second guideline, that extracurricular meetings of members, cliques, socializing, and travelling home together should be discouraged (Foulkes and Anthony, 1965). This may seem to be a severe principle and it is acknowledged that members talk to each other before and after sessions, and do perchance travel together when going home in the same direction, but because of each member's understanding of the importance of this particular guideline, the group will not be unduly affected by violations. If members report and discuss this extragroup contact, the breach is assuredly only minor. Therapists have found that group members having extra-group contact are generally more resistive and will function for shorter periods of time in the group.

The extra-group contact is one way of prematurely leaving the group. It is a form of alliance seeking-subgrouping behavior. Most analytically oriented group therapists agree that subgrouping tends to produce detrimental effects in the group. An exception to this principle is considered by Yalom (1970) who feels that subgrouping may be harmless provided that the goals of the subgroupers are consonant with the goals of the overall group. Other researchers such as Bion (1961) consider subgroup socializing as satisfying one of the underlying assumption cultures of the group and as interfering with the overall work culture of the group. The acting-out nature of subgrouping, such as its significance as an expression of undischarged hostility to the leader in addition to its other deleterious effects, is cited by Frank (1957), Lindt and Sherman (1952), and Yalom (1966). The subgrouping phenomenon within the group is also discussed by Bach (1954) and Redl (1944).

The prohibitions cited—omitting surnames unless voluntarily reported and the prevention of extra-group contact—generally serve to keep the tension between members vital and palpable in the group. They help prevent a drain of energy which would in turn create a decrease in the heartbeat and blood flow of the group. Members who search for ways of negating the guidelines will generally be expressing tension that they find difficult to express in the group. They simply look for ways of getting out. These same members are usually the ones who engage in alliance seeking behavior and subgrouping, are chronically late or miss sessions, and may ask for physical and touching experiences in the group. When therapists enforce group guidelines, these members may finally be able to experience and verbalize their tensions, or if tensions are too great, they may terminate. If so, it may be that such members were prematurely invited into the group or that their acting-out urges are in any case too great. They may not be able to function in this kind of therapeutic framework. Yalom et al. (1967) review termination issues inherent in acting-out. Frequently those group members who are unable to establish enduring relationships in their lives also engage in acting-out behavior in the group. In this way they are able to recreate a neurotic condition in the group resembling the one that brought them to the group in the first place.

Grace was a 30-year-old woman who came to therapy because of a disquieting romance in which her boyfriend suddenly left her. A 15-year history of feeling consciously inhibited and competitive with other women characterized an important aspect of her experience which also included many brief sexual encounters with men. Dressing seductively so that her large breasts were displayed to the best advantage, she set out to conquer. She entered the group with this "conquering" aim and immediately began to cultivate those same conditions that usually produced her typical neurotic pattern.

After some time in the group, it was noticed that Grace and another woman Barbara, would never speak to each other. Barbara, an attractive and stylish person, was popular in the group primarily because she was pregnant. She was a shy and frightened woman overly concerned with what she considered to be her imperfections. It was one of the male members of the group who casually observed that Grace and Barbara never spoke to one another. In a characteristic expression of self-defense Barbara blurted out, "but we talk, we talk outside . . . Grace always waits for me after group . . . we walk to the bus together . . . Grace has been giving me some of her bras . . . I'm getting large and Grace had some bras she wanted me to have . . . we talk a lot." This seemingly innocuous extra-group contact is an example of acting-out in which Grace managed to nullify the competitive threat posed by Barbara's presence and was indirectly asserting her "breast-power" over Barbara. One may see from this illustration how extra-group contact may, quite automatically and unconsciously, affect the nature of verbal interaction in the group.

During this discussion other group members began indicating that Grace was having quite specific and separate innocent little contact with them either before or after the session. It gradually became clear that Grace was introducing an antitherapeutic element into the group and involving herself with people in a self-defeating way. Her behavior was controlling and manipulative. For the first time, Grace was presented and provided with an ongoing conscious laboratory in which she could have some real possibility of working on her conflicts instead of characteristically short-circuiting many of her relationships.

A third guideline reflects the idea that each member of the group is responsible for each session; that is, when a member misses a session no other person may be temporarily substituted. This rule of responsibility to the group is consonant with the group's respect of any person's inviolable membership and serves the principle of maintaining firm group boundaries. When a new member is introduced, the group is notified well in advance and this allows for discussion among current members regarding a new addition. It does not, however, generally imply permission by the group. The idea here is that the group must become pregnant with the idea. New progeny is never sprung on a family. The family lives with the idea for a while and then prepares for the appearance of the new member.

A fourth guideline established for the group may be called the rule of no physicality. Talking instead of physical contact is the keynote of the group. To verbalize feelings is the aim of the work. This, of course, is not designed to encourage puritanical and schizoid features. Rather, it implies that therapy supports any attempt to crystalize intuition into thought, to articulate feelings, and to continue working towards making the unconsicous more conscious.

These four guidelines will help the therapist establish a healthy functioning group which implies that avenues of acting-out have been structurally undermined. When the quantity of group acting-out remains low, the group termination force which always exists correspondingly remains weak. These guidelines needn't reflect countertransferential aspects of therapist functioning as suggested by Schwartz (1965b) and Schwartz and Wolf (1964). The notion of the therapist's countertransference shall be elaborated on in a later chapter. The guidelines outlined here relate strictly to the maintenance of a viable group motive force, a necessary boundary condition.

With the formation of the group, the first generation begins to evolve. This process as previously described can lead to a complete life cycle of the group which becomes approximated toward the end of the fourth generation, about eight years later. At this point two issues become immediately important. The first relates to the ongoing process of selection of members throughout the life of the group. With what principle are members selected to ensure the future generations of the group? This question is different from the one in chapter 3 that asked what are the basic character roles of the group. The second issue refers to the actual termination of the group at the end of the fourth generation. The fundamental question constitutes a dialectic; that is, since the group is veering inexorably toward its eventual demise, can another force be introduced which, at least on a theoretical level, enables the generational direction of the group to become reversed? These issues are the unanswered ones raised by the difficulty with life-cycle models. They relate to the entire genealogical infrastructure of the group and are the basic elements of adaptation in evolution. They are elements of selection and mutation.

Adaptational Elements of Selection and Mutation

Two main features in the theory of evolution are selection and mutation. Species develop in an adaptational framework and such evolution is guided by principles of selection and phenomena of mutation. It is proposed here that the genealogical infrastructure of the group exists largely because issues of selection and what might be termed mutational equivalents take place in an adaptational context.

SELECTION

In terms of group generations, members are selected during any generation in a way that facilitates the basic motive force of a group. Sound selection principles have been pointed out by Kadis et al. (1968), Leopold (1957), and

Slavson (1955) and were discussed at length in chapter 3. Should a therapist select a new member based upon whether the group will be good for the particular individual, it is hypothesized that the group life is weakened, and this selection criterion is not adaptive. For example, therapists are sometimes heard to say that they will place passive people in a group based upon the idea that group treatment is best for the resolution of passivity problems. This introduces an unnecessary and potentially deleterious complexity into the group life. After a while these same therapists are lamenting that their group is "falling apart" because of its resistive and passive nature. Evolutionary selection as applied to group life is determined more by group requirements and less by considerations of individual needs, even though the group's vitality is frequently sustained by its altruistic focus on individual members. In most animal flocks, troops, or groups, membership is based upon the criterion of whether the member is good for the group. Similarly, in therapy groups, therapists will usually include new members who will enhance the complexion of the group wherever it is felt that the group needs a role filled. Bach (1954) suggests that new members be selected by asking "what role is open in the group?" Foulkes and Anthony (1965) also consider this idea. They feel the individual will be cared for only if group considerations are primary. Grotjahn (1973) also has arrived at the theoretical position that to invite a new member into a group needs to be based upon whether or not this new person can "fit into the specific cohesive and well working family." This implication of patient selection for therapy groups is also suggested by Kellerman, Buirski, and Plutchik (1974) in an ethological study of a baboon troop. It is a selection criterion that assumes equivalent ego-strength in the diagnostic variation of the membership.

Sometimes a new member will be a passive person, sometimes an assertive person, sometimes a person who is frightened or guarded or isolated, and sometimes a person who is angry, enthusiastic or gregarious. The selection principle then implicitly helps the therapist maintain a viable group composition which will ensure generational movement. This group composition reflects the model of character roles outlined in the previous chapter. Furthermore, as long as the group climate is as viable as possible, then every member will benefit from the therapeutic nature of the group. Many writers agree apparently that current and future individual needs may be best served when the group need is primary. This principle ensures generational movement so that even when members leave, newer persons can avail themselves of similar benefits. The soil of the group, so to speak, should always be kept fertile.

MUTATION

The issue of selection as an adaptational element in the evolutionary process was relatively clear as it related to group development. However, the issue of mutation as it occurs adaptively is not as simple. The clue to locating a mutational point had to be related, it seemed, to termination. The selection principle alone would only allow the group to function through about four generations. It was apparent, therefore, that another force would have to be brought to bear on the generational direction of the group in order for there to be created a dialectic of forces. This new dialectic of forces would symbolize some mutational-equivalent if only because it could modify the inexorable aging of the group.

Again in this particular instance, the mutational quality exists within the element of selection. The way to have the group further adapt naturally during the fourth generation is to introduce two or more newer members of young adult age. This process may serve to create a new tension. One such member is not sufficient. Two or more individuals serve to convey to the membership that another serious force exists in the group with which the group needs to deal. The newer members need to be of first generation age in order to strike a stark contrast with the existing mood. Hypothetically speaking, the thematic or psychosexual conflict material is then constituted as first generation oedipal issues intersecting fourth generation oral issues. This intersection reflects a greater dialectic than would a condition with new members of third generation age bringing with them thematic material of an anal nature—not terribly disparate from oral themes. The mutational effect needs to be startling. Gradually newer members are introduced who are of first and second generation age, and the mean age of the group will be reversed. Thus the dilemma introduced by life-cycle model theorists who imply the ultimate demise of the group is resolved within a genealogical linear-regressive model that integrates the linear-progressive, pendular, and life cycle positions. From a theoretical point of view, most animal groups that endure contain these elements in their group life, and even in families, as children grow up they begin to have children of their own who in turn also make families. Generational direction as far as age is concerned is constantly moving back and forth from older to younger to older to younger. A somewhat related idea is presented by Ehrenwald (1974) who posits a transgenerational treatment effect. This analogy to families is not intended to be a perfect fit but it does seem to make the observation that naturally functioning groups from an adaptational point of view can be guided by elements of selection and equivalent mutation conditions.

Leadership

A third and essential force of the group is, of course, located in the position of the therapist. Much has been written regarding the qualities of leaders (Schwartz and Wolf, 1964; Strupp, 1960). Issues of leadership will be confined only to implications for the therapist based upon the particular theoretical formulation described. It is assumed that the generational direction of a group will at least in part be advanced by the therapist's concern with some of the issues discussed here.

LEADERSHIP AND THE LIFE OF THE GROUP

In the present model the leader must make provision for leadership succession, for if the leader were to become incapacitated or to die, the group would terminate and this usually occurs in traditional therapy groups when leaders die. Aronson et al. (1962) discuss the impact of the death of a leader on group process. A therapist who uses the genealogical model as a way of understanding group infrastructure will most likely arrange for some alternate therapist to take over the group in the event of some permanent incapacity or death. This is actually not such a farfetched idea. Individual heads of families frequently create mechanisms such as wills and generally arrange some provision for the family in the event of unforeseen tragedy. For therapists to be truly involved in the life and direction of the group, some arrangement needs to be made to ensure the group's continued existence if it is to be valued as an adaptive institution. This is one way the group becomes a suprasystem.

LEADERSHIP AND GENERATIONAL TRANSFERENCE THEMES

The therapist's role in the group generally remains the same throughout any group life cycle. However, depending on the particular group generation, a member's relation to the therapist may be different, and this change may reflect generational mood differences. Despite the fact that members from each group generation may experience a full complement of emotions and moods, members from each generation may also express issues relating to a specific psychosexual conflict stage, and mood may be a reflection of this correlation. The implication here as far as the leader is concerned is that transferential reactions can be fundamentally influenced by these mood states. For example, although the therapist is the same person and behaves quite authentically in each generation, members may nevertheless respond to the therapist in a stereotypic manner based somewhat on generational considerations. First generation members may compete for and against the therapist, and may be highly suggestible or quite guarded. These behaviors are simply effects of the oedipal period which relate to first generation themes. Second generation members may relate more to the therapist on the basis of passive-aggressive issues which correspond to material of a phallic nature. Third generation members may relate to the therapist with great control or impulsive dyscontrol. Such behavior is in part stereotypic derivative anal material. In the fourth generation members may seek support and understanding and appreciate all identifiable links to the therapist. Such behavior may be derived from oral needs. Therapists who use this model may have a better understanding of transference in the group, they will at least have a broader entree to communicational channels other than more traditional knowledge such as dominance hierarchies, overt transference interactions, or the maintenance of diagnostic heterogeneity.

LEADERSHIP AND GROUP INTELLIGENCE

Another and more exotic function of the therapist as it emerges from this model refers to how a leader may maximize group intelligence. According to the formulation reached here, groups mature and actualize their life cycle much faster than a maturing and aging individual. The analogy between maturity for groups and for individuals has also been made by Bennis and Shepard (1974). The hypothetical age ratio between individuals and groups was theoretically derived as approximately ten years to one year respectively. This ratio may suggest some interesting hypotheses with respect to the intelligence of a group. It is known, for example, that animals maturing to adulthood within one or two years or even sooner do not develop any great intelligence. This is in contrast to humans, who take much longer to mature but who develop great intelligence. Similarly, a group that reaches its full life cycle in eight to ten years may not really generate any great group intelligence although it can have powerful effects on individuals. Therefore, like many enduring animal groups, a therapy group needs to depend on ritual and on the operation of systematic mechanisms of its infrastructure to keep it aging naturally. This aging process is equivalent to high order "intellectual" development; that is, the extent to which a group facilitates its natural processes becomes a partial index of its intelligence. The therapist can help the group achieve this aim. Furthermore, Bennis and Shepard (1974) indicate that "the group can resolve its internal conflicts, mobilize its resources, and take intelligent action only if it has means for consensually validating its experience." This consensual validation of the group experience in part becomes expressed in the transgenerational nature of group life. The notion of group intelligence has been discussed by Cartwright and Zander (1968) and a further explanation of the therapist's role in the group is given in the following chapters. Other forces also contribute to the group's intelligence and these shall be presented.

One of these forces is the transformational effect experienced by group therapists in their role as leader. There is some surprising agreement among many group therapists regarding the difference in their own abilities as leaders in the group context versus their overall abilities outside of the group context. Group therapists are heard to say that there are times in the group when they can sense a profound understanding of whatever is occurring and can often make a sweeping integration of a wide array of behavior. Therapists frequently feel as though they are physically located in the eye of the storm, enabled therefore to offer wisdom in the midst of a tangled and sometimes chaotic fabric of feelings, problems, and human frailty. Such reports by therapists resemble peak experiences that persons report from time to time. The group therapist, however, usually generates these feelings as a standard mode of experience.

What is it in the basic nature of group life that transforms the personality of even the therapist, so that the therapist's perceptual and empathic responses contain such lucidity? The answer may lie in the analogy between individual age development and group age development. In a sense, the group ages approximately ten times faster than does an individual. This ratio was discussed in the previous section on the aging of the group as a function of generational development. The unique position of leader of the group may allow the therapist to exist, as it were, in two different time zones: a seemingly metaphysical phenomenon with some theoretical and empirical anchoring. The therapist both is and is not a member of the group and thus may have access in an amorphous sense to the relativity of what might be termed psychological evolution. Because of this special access, the therapist may be provided with the advantage of acquiring and expressing psychological sense that is usually described as wisdom: something acquired by individuals only as a function of experience and perhaps even acquired only by advanced age. It is this wisdom that the therapist expresses with lucidity, which is not duplicated by the therapist anywhere else except in the group context.

Such an unusual formulation is somewhat supported by Rey (1975): "The therapist is a special inner object of the group. . . . He is the genius of the group in the true primitive sense of the word. He generates. He is a meta-system with regard to the system of members." The leader represents continuity. The position of leader may be in itself equivalent to the evolutionary force which can be abstracted in physical terms as *time*.

LEGENDS AND GROUP CULTURE

One of the phenomena accumulating in the group-memory contributing to its aspiration level and intelligence is the emergence of myths and legends, especially during the third and fourth generations. The group as a genealogical suprasystem, containing a generational direction, also expresses itself as a culture that has a sociology of legends and even folklore. Adaptation takes place through this medium of culture.

Culture and Myth

CULTURE

Arlow (1961) and Winnicott (1953) agree that the development of myth serves an especially adaptive function in the group. The generational movement in groups is part of this culture and the group process may even be considered acculturation or adaptation of new elements; that is, moving from one generation to the next represents an expansion of culture. The concept of group culture has been found to be a useful one even by such diverse authors as Bion (1955) and Yalom (1970). McDougall (1921) also refers to a shared system of traditions, habits and customs in the group. The importance of group culture in the entire group developmental process has been elaborated by researchers studying self-analytic and teaching groups as well as by group psychoanalysts. Jaques (1955) sees the importance of group culture to be its mixture of conventions, customs, taboos, and rules that are utilized in the organization of relations among members of a particular social structure. Group culture may be defined as an amalgam of individual and group values. This implication of the definition of group culture as an interaction of individual and group values is crystallized by Bion (1959b): "The 'culture' or manifest structure of the group reflects a collective compromise formation. The conscious aims of individual members and the unconscious and disavowed aims which group members have 'pooled' by means of the group mentality are brought together, however tenuously, into an equilibrium. . . . The group culture represents the intersection of individual and group psychology." Therefore, the culture of the group is equivalent to the sharing among group members of values and unconscious fantasies about the experience of the group, especially with regard to generational direction. Culture is the sense of work in the group and the struggle for new meaning as a function of the working-through process. It is a finding of truths through the interpretation of experience.

MYTH

Gibbard, Hartman, and Mann (1974) state that "Groups are replete with mythological assumptions about themselves. Members and leaders make use of conscious fantasy productions, involve their fellows in issues of political faith and ideology, have rituals and ritualistic activity, and invent religious-like beliefs as well." This idea of the group's pooling of abstracted images of itself is also suggested by Dunphy (1974), who proposes that the group myth serves the purpose of an "overarching symbol system"; that is, a system that unifies all small group interaction in the very pooling of group member fantasies. Hartman and Gibbard (1974a) further suggest that myth and ideology are congruent insofar as myth binds group members to a common purpose sewn by "a similarity of belief." Their basic idea is that the development of myths contributes to the maintenance of social structure and culture.

GROUP MYTH AND GROUP ROLE

According to Arlow (1961) the myth is an instrument of socialization insofar as it contributes toward ultimate group cohesion. Dunphy (1966) elaborates upon this concept and ties it to the idea of central figures: "development of the group proceeds by the emergence and working-through of these 'myths' shared by the group at large and portrayed by a few key members." In another reference to this point Dunphy (1974) indicates that role specialists in the group function as symbols of focal conflict, but that group development is based more upon the "salience" of a given member at any point of the group process rather than by some variation in a role itself. Role specialists become reference points for other members as the direction of group culture evolves.

The major focus of myth construction in the group revolves around the figure of the leader. Kaplan (1967) refers to this point. "The role of the leader as part of the mythological construction of the group-as-a-whole and the rituals that the group weaves about him is one facet of a process through which a social structure is achieved." This system of mythopoeisis constructed around the leader is an important point to grasp because it is part of the entire transference-theme shift from one group generation to the next.

GROUP MYTH AND GENERATIONAL THEMES

In conceptualizing the development of self-analytic groups, Dunphy (1974) states, "It appears . . . that the chief elements in each of these myths are prototypical images of the group and of the instructor and that these images derive primarily from the inner emotional experiences of the group members at successive stages in the cultural evolution of the group. . . . It seems therefore that each of the major periods in the evolution of the group is accompanied by a myth which represents an ideal-typical image of group relationships and of the instructor and that the role specialists function as important symbols in these myths."

Here Dunphy interweaves several major ideas of group development. Myths or themes may be characteristic of specific group generations, and roles are a reflection of a group mythology which has as its basic motive force the formal authority figure of the group—the therapist. The key issue, however, is that "myth is a shared, rather than individual fantasy, built up over time out of events in the history of groups" For example, the Bionian pairing group's motive is to produce something. Myths and even legends will arise during this group culture regarding the creation of something in the group ensuring the future existence of the group. The myth contains a hope for group survival and for the maintenance of the group social structure. Turquet (1974) indicates that what endures in the group for the viability of future generations are the myths created by the group itself.

Evolving from one generation to the next thus implies a change in the characteristic thematic material emerging in the group. The assimilation and incubation of such changes represents a broadening aspect of the culture and constitutes an adaptation of the group. This sort of process operates in families, in societies, and apparently also in therapy groups.

An example of the creation and existence of myths, legends, and folklore frequently becomes expressed in the group when in the second, third, or fourth generation, a member's name from the first generation is still referred to as an example of just how effectively the group helps people. Although no current member has ever known or seen this "legendary" member, this member's name and successes are transmitted—handed down as it were, as the oral history of African tribes was handed down. Interestingly enough, groups will tend to develop only positive folklore. Failures or rejections are mostly aborted from the group memory. They do not become transmitted although occasionally they may be referred to parenthetically.

Apparently the group uses such legendary or even mythical figures as a way of developing a folklore serving the interest of generational directionality or aging. Members seem to relish such legends. It becomes a great source of motivation and work in the group. The college dropout eventually accepted into law school, the dependent 35-year-old son who finally married, and the timid woman who became an architect, her secret ambition, are examples of legends echoing through later generations of the group in a way that exhilarates members and creates a heightened sense of positive identification and affiliation with the group. Such legends are profound sources of motivation and constitute an affirmative manifestation of group life. They act as a countertermination force and they have been noticed by other researchers (Yalom, 1970). In this same context, Astigueta (1977) refers to the concept of group history.

TERMINATION ISSUES

Issues and elements of termination begin with the formation of the group and are constantly in question. Whether it is the increase in termination urges as a function of the group's aging process, whether acting-out is taking place, or whether resistance in the group becomes solidified, termination forces are always dormant and impending. Yet given the guidelines outlined in the formation of the group and the considerations involved in ensuring the infrastructural mechanisms leading to the process of generationality, these factors of group structure militate against termination and in fact make the termination issue less than immediate.

Termination problems will increase when guidelines are not adhered to, when the energy emanating from the therapist becomes diffused or deflected, as may sometimes be the case in cotherapist models where transference is being split, or even in the creation of the alternate group; that is, an extra-group session in the absence of the therapist. In cotherapy groups Yalom (1970) indicates that the positive effect on group members as part of this model lies in its potential as a modelling experience. It may be important for patients to see "parents" occasionally disagreeing but still maintaining their love for each other. A discussion of the pros and cons of the cotherapy model is elaborated upon in Spitz and Kopp (1957). Issues that contraindicate a cotherapy model include: First, patients split therapists; that is, they undermine their relationship and relate in a confused way to two authority figures. Second, it may be suggested, since many people marry for the wrong reasons, that therapists may also get together for the wrong reasons. The group then has to deal with this marriage, a problem which may become central and tend to absorb too much group energy. Third, cotherapists frequently tend only to agree with each other. Fourth, a cotherapy model may split the group into two distinct camps. Fifth, instead of one patient taking on the task leadership and another patient taking on the emotional leadership, which is usually the case, each therapist may assume those roles. Yalom (1970) asks, what then is left for the patients? The position here contraindicates the use of cotherapy models for group psychotherapy.

Extra-group sessions may have value insofar as members deal with issues of independence, assertion, and superego transference to the therapist (Dworwin, 1969; Kadis, 1956b; and Mullan and Rosenbaum, 1962). They also may help the members cumulate group ego-strength as a way of meeting the strength of the superego energy imputed to the therapist. Despite such apparent positive aspects to the alternate group session, it is proposed here that the alternate group drains further energy from the motive force of the group, contributing to the accumulation of termination energy. An elaboration of the issue of alternate sessions is made by Seligman and Desmond (1975). Lindt (1958) and Zicferstein and Grotjahn (1956) also agree that the alternate session is contraindicated by the group therapy model. They share the opinions of Bieber (1957) and Slavson (1964) who stress the key issues opposing the use of alternate sessions. They indicate that the difference between socializing and therapy becomes obscured, and although sessions may seem therapeutic, they actually may be simply cathartic. The alternate session is considered to generate acting-out and premature termination urges. Furthermore, members cannot convey in the actual session all that happens in the alternate session. In addition, what members do or do not consider important in the alternate session is up to question (Yalom, 1970). The conclusion drawn here is that the alternate session should not be employed, a position contrary to the one enunciated and developed by Wolf and Schwartz (1962 and Schwartz (1965b), who suggest that opponents of the alternate session encourage dependency and unduly prolong the course of therapy.

Termination of the group is actually a moot issue in this genealogical model. With a genealogical view of group psychotherapy that includes phenomena of generational directionality, acculturation, and the emergence of evolutionary adaptive elements of selection and mutation, the termination of the group becomes less than a relevant concept. Termination of individual members of the group is an entirely different issue than the possibility of a total group termination. Factors leading to termination of individual members have been discussed by Bross (1959), Grotjahn (1950), Kadis and Winick (1960), and Kauff (1977). Individual member termination is viewed here as consisting of the intersection of group dynamic factors with considerations of individual dynamics.

The group infrastructure as created by the therapist provides for the eventual introduction of a dialectical struggle designed to maintain the group as a suprasystem. Termination may not be a viable concept of a suprasystem. Thus, the fundamental question originally posed, "What is the purpose of the group?" has a simple answer. *The purpose of the group is to stay alive.* This answer has also been implied by Kadis et al. (1968) and by Yalom (1970), who state that open groups may, in theory, perpetuate themselves indefinitely. Foulkes and Anthony (1965) also refer to this stated purpose of the group when they say "it is important for the group to have no occupation and no reason for existing beyond itself." This somewhat cryptic reference needs further elaboration or at least some further definition. In the following chapters on the anatomy of group defense structure a resolution of this question of the purpose of the group staying alive is offered. The question is then posed: to what end is the purpose of the group to stay alive?

POSTULATES OF PSYCHOTHERAPY GROUP PROCESS

A series of postulates can be formulated to explicate the genealogical and socioadaptational view of psychotherapy group process.

The postulates related to generationality are:

1. *A group tends to age both in terms of longevity and mean age of its membership.*
2. *The age of a group may be defined in generational terms with about a two- or three-year span representing one generation.*
3. *Four generations, about eight years, beginning in the young adult period, constitute a generational cycle or one full group life span.*

The postulate related to group genealogy is:

4. *Groups contain a genealogical component expressed by hereditary lines or role lineages reflecting an unconscious organization of membership throughout the life span of the group.*

The postulates relating to derivative psychosexual thematic material and generationality are:

5. *Derivative thematic material from all psychosexual stages is expressed in each generation of the group process.*
6. *Each group generation contains a major psychosexual theme and subthemes from all other psychosexual stages.*
7. *Major thematic material of psychosexual stages is produced in each succeeding generation of the group in an inverse relationship, constituting a psychosexual regression.*
8. *An organization of group character roles containing diagnostic implications evolves as a function of group generationality.*

The postulates relating to the group motive force are:

9. *Principles of group formation ensure the integrity of group boundaries and help maintain tension within the group.*

10. *Maintaining the tension in the group reduces acting-out behavior and weakens the group termination force.*

The postulate related to the adaptive element of selection is:

11. *In order to ensure a viable group climate and maximize generational movement, therapists should select members based upon the principle: the patient should be good for the group, not only that the group should be good for the patient.*

The postulates related to the adaptive element of mutation are:

12. *A dialectic is generated during the fourth generation represented by the introduction of first generation members. Now the group is composed of two disparate generations.*
13. *This dialectic reverses the generational direction of the group and is considered to be the mutational point in the group life.*

The postulates related to the adaptive element of leadership are:

14. *Therapists need to make provision for their succession as a way of ensuring the group life span.*
15. *Transference to therapist changes thematically as a function of generationality.*
16. *The group's intelligence is maximized if a full life cycle is realized.*
17. *Intelligence of the group is not equivalent to individual intelligence necessitating a complex infrastructure to keep the group acting as an adaptive entity.*
18. *The therapist has access to the relativity of psychological evolution. This access contributes to the therapist's skills and wisdom, enabling the group to further exercise its intelligence.*

The postulates relating to group culture are:

19. *The group contains a cultural element through which myths, legends, traditions, and group folklore become transmitted as a function of generationality.*
20. *Moving from one generation to the next represents an expansion of culture.*
21. *Myths, legends, and overall group culture act as a countertermination force.*

The postulates relating to termination are:

22. *The termination germ exists in the group from its inception.*
23. *The genealogical infrastructure of the group acts to minimize the effects of the termination urge.*
24. *The use of cotherapists and the use of alternate sessions drain undue energy from the motive force of the group, leading to the group's accumulation of termination energy.*

25.   *Termination of the entire group is only a peripheral concept in this genealogical formulation of group therapy life.*

The postulate relating to the purpose of the group is:

26.   *The purpose of the group is to stay alive.*

5

Ego-Defense Structure of Groups: The Nature of Group Tension

Earlier sections of this work described an infrastructural underpinning that governs the group process and a specific theory of group composition indicated that a system of personality forces exists in the group. These forces were shown to be arranged in terms of their inherent polarity and to have the property of generating conflict. The systematic interaction of these personality forces form part of the group infrastructure. The personality forces are arranged into four polar pairs. They constitute eight basic character or dispositional types. Suitable balancing of these forces produces a correct structural organization in the group of character roles, and this implies a diagnostic composition that affects group movement. An analysis of the emotion theory underlying the proposed roles of the group has attempted to show that through diagnostic selection criteria therapists may more or less approximate a homeostatic balancing of these personality forces in the group. This theory of group composition guides initial patient selection influencing the ultimate character role composition of the group.

The group evolves a genealogy and emerges as a suprasystem. This system was described as functioning according to generational development. It contained the idea of dialectic conflict which was also shown to influence the nature of generational direction and the appearance of subsequent psychosexual themes in the group.

The issue explored in this and the following chapter concerns the group's transformation into a functioning system in contrast to its description as an inert body. The environment of the group becomes a compelling one for each of its members and it is this compelling quality that will be examined. This element infuses the group process with energy, constitutes the core of cohesion, and fuels the motive force of the group. This compelling quality can be defined as the cumulative effect of the anxiety or tension experienced by each member of the group. Tension provides the group with movement force, thereby allowing for the appearance and operation of the group's underlying mechanisms.

This group tension is examined in this and the next chapter. First, an analysis of the nature of tension is presented. A specific view of tension correlates emotion and ego-defense, and core tension themes are revealed through an analysis of this relationship. These tension themes are also related to the basic role composition of the group. The next chapter is devoted to an analysis of tension resolution. Issues of transference-resistance and working-through are related to the core tension themes and to the regulation of overall group tension. In the final part of the chapter, group and family systems are compared and the importance of this relationship for both models is shown.

Implications of this new synthesis are related to the final postulate presented in chapter 4 on the genealogical view of groups which posited that the purpose of the group was to stay alive. The question now asked is, to what end does this staying alive relate? What, if anything, is served by the group staying alive? A final analysis reveals whether this "staying alive" postulate is ultimately an aimless axiom or whether it provides the context for an analysis of a further dynamic process.

THE GROUP REQUIREMENT

Entering a group frequently produces acute tension even among patients of considerable experience in individual treatment. "They'll see me for what I really am" is a likely approximation of the private and silent fears experienced by many persons who consider group treatment. In individual treatment, immaturities and neuroses may either be analyzed, tolerated, or overlooked; in a sense they may even be forgiven. Parents sometimes forgive. But can one expect forgiveness in peer relationships? Can you be immature or appear perverse or ugly, or reveal embarrassing feelings to group members: "I am the best, the worst, the brightest, the most naive, the most beautiful, the most repulsive?" Will you be understood and accepted in the group or be ultimately scalded by its effect? A beginner's apprehension may be that success will be elusive and understanding not forthcoming. Such apprehension suggests that patients entering therapy groups carry with them an instruction, whether implicit or explicit, regarding their functioning in the group. The central theme of the instruction is that to be in a group means both to reveal oneself and to be revealed. It is this particular expectation that creates a special condition of tension in the therapy room duplicated nowhere else. To have one's behavior so closely monitored, both by the therapist as authority figure and by one's peers, in the context of a reveal-yourself work ethic is especially difficult. Bogdanoff and Elbaum (1978) consider this fear of self-disclosure to reflect a central focal conflict of the group.

This special tension condition and its apparent effects raise a question as to whether the group therapy enviroment is more reminiscent of conditions and effects existing in marriage rather than those existing in one's original family. This tension may, in fact, reflect the precise kind of tension found in marital relationships at least to the same extent as that experienced in original families. Functioning in the group therefore may be as relevant to the treatment of reciprocal peer contact as it is to the repair of original family relationships.

First sessions produce a variety of physiological and emotional changes (Kellerman and Plutchik, 1977). Patients report feeling nervous, sweaty, aroused, upset, and stressed. Some report dry mouth and increased heart beat and acknowledge feeling anxious and tense before the group session. Patients also begin to notice distinct differences in member interaction between waiting room contact before a session, and therapy room contact in the presence of the therapist. In the waiting area, patients engage in general social conversation. Sometimes an expectant, hyperkinetic quality seems characteristic of the pre-group time period. As patients enter the therapy room, in the presence of the therapist, they may become less talkative, and may at times even become silent. This phenomenon of silence also has been noticed by Yalom (1970). The transition from waiting room to therapy room frequently produces a serious attitude change. Previous waiting room activity seems implicitly recognized as play and prelude and not as work. Work begins when activity is infused with direction.

The difference between waiting room and therapy room behavior can be conceived as the fundamental ambivalence of all patients in therapy. As Kadis et al. (1968) indicate, the patient wants change and doesn't want change, and this ambivalence is exquisitly projected onto the therapeutic work condition. The waiting room represents a no-change condition and so waiting room tension lacks a therapeutic charge. The therapy room represents the "change" side to the ambivalence reflecting the "something serious" that occurs. Spotnitz (1973) describes this serious work condition: "In the group the patient is asked to engage in the special action of talking in the presence of other patients . . . is called on to help them talk, and to get them to help him understand what he is saying." Spotnitz implies that this partially agreed upon complicity generates a highly charged condition. He attributes this supercharge to the nature and amount of feedback patients receive, and to the presence of additional transference figures in the group setting.

This idea of the group providing each member with many transference figures suggests that the group becomes a system resembling a family or potential family. It generates a boundary, develops a work ethic, and creates a set of operating rules. The group assumes the character of an institution to

which each member is affiliated. The nature of this family affiliation, however, produces a therapeutic impasse, the roots of which exist in the patient's
family history and are reflected in the reciprocal peer nature of group therapy.

One's relationships in a family are governed by fixed rules and regulations. These rules allow only certain patterns of relations to exist and exclude
others. Transcending the therapeutic impasse requires the breach of such historical rules; that is, the overall transference behavior of any member of the
group must become transformed so that alternatives are developed toward
previously fixed patterns of relating. Accomplishing this goal requires that
group members not be unduly governed by historically determined family
rules, or at least that they work strenuously at re-examining these rules. The
group itself also becomes transformed as a function of its evolving distinction
from transference family to new family. It is this familial metamorphosis that
contributes to the development of an especially interesting and therapeutic
climate in the group.

THE NATURE OF EGO-DEFENSE

Tension and Ego-Defense

Generally, the effect of tension on the group is to generate greater membership interest and this occurs despite each member's discomfort with the
experience of tension. The presence of tension, however, creates resistance to
therapy. The implicit demand of self-disclosure with which members enter the
group and the basic ambivalence of wanting to change and simultaneously not
wanting to change operationally defines this resistance phenomenon. Resistance causes group members to behave in well defined ways. For example,
frightened members, generally wary of confrontation will engage in alliance-
seeking behavior or in appeasement behavior. Those members of the group
who are more angry may become provocative or even hypercatalytic. In
either case these behaviors may be considered defensive operations designed
to deflect feelings of inner discomfort or tension. It is an indirect and secondary way of reacting, and provides a clue to the cause of overall group tensions
(Kellerman and Plutchik, 1977).

Patients learn quickly that it is permissible to proceed at whatever pace
seems comfortable. Members also see that the aim of the work is to uncover,
confront, and reevaluate typical defensive patterns. It is this goal of the work,
to look at defensive behavior, that constitutes the essence of the tension and
creates a work dilemma: to react directly or to react in a secondary way,
thereby reducing tension.

In a discussion of the effect of defensive operations on tension, Durkin
(1964) recognizes this dilemma. She cites Anna Freud's position indicating
that since the defensive system is composed of primary defense mechanisms

and ingrained character traits it may protect therapy patients "from the eruption of unbearable anxiety." It is this self-protection that forms the basis of therapy resistance. The resistance is the unique interaction of a variety of defensive operations. Durkin further indicates that transferences of all types constitute the major form of resistance and that transference resistance includes the transference of character defenses.

Kadis et al. (1968) also indicate that the use of defense mechanisms represents the basic resistance to character change, and that the primary purpose of the defenses is to fend off anxiety. This need to remain hidden both from the therapist and the group by utilizing defenses has also been aptly noted by Ezriel (1952, 1956). Reich's character defense (1949), Freud's repetition compulsion (1914b), and even Ezriel's avoided relationship phenomenon (1973) all share the idea that defense represents an attempt to suppress potential threat. Ezriel (1973) especially points out that "the analyst can demonstrate to each member his particular defense mechanisms in dealing with his individual unconscious tension dominant in that session."

The goal of relinquishing defense as a means of raising consciousness, however, is not a simple task. Suspending ego-defense patterns is equivalent to the relinquishment of one's only coping patterns. As Reich (1949) so correctly elucidated, one's defensive structure was developed to eliminate either real or imagined threats to the personality. To be asked to give up such safety then, is to court a high degree of tension.

The relationship of tension to defensive operations may be represented by a formula. This equation roughly implies that low tension indicates low defense confrontation, and as defense confrontation increases, tension increases. Thus the implicit instruction with which patients enter a group may be translated into a demand to relinquish typical defenses. Although such an aim will tend to increase understanding, it will also raise one's anxiety or tension level.

Suspending Ego-Defense Patterns

There is general agreement that the primary task of the group is to resolve defenses (Rice, 1963; Turquet, 1974). However, the overall tension of the group is based upon the challenge to the cumulative system of defense. This correlation of defense and tension raises the question of the fundamental purpose served by a defense system in the functioning of each individual. In addition, tension itself needs to be defined.

It has been suggested that defense patterns of behavior generally, and defense mechanisms specifically, have developed in order to deal adaptively with the presence of particular emotions (Kellerman and Plutchik, 1977; Plutchik, Kellerman, and Conte, 1979). For example, the defense mechanism of displacement and related displacement behavior has developed to manage the emotion of anger. This has been stated in the ethological literature (Kaufman, 1960; Lorenz, 1966), in the personality-psychological literature (Kellerman, 1977), in social psychological studies of scapegoating and hate (Bychowski, 1968; Lasswell, 1952), and in a comparative study of animals and humans (Kellerman, Buirski, and Plutchik, 1974). Without mechanisms of defense, a continual and direct expression of emotion would occur producing a protracted state of tension. Defenses deflect, modify, inhibit, and redirect emotions. A direct and unmodulated quality of emotion will be expressed when members agree to relinquish defense. Bach (1954) and Powdermaker and Frank (1953) further indicate that defenses cover underlying feelings and that the purpose of the group is to permit feelings to emerge to undo defenses. The direct expression of emotion is not regulated by rules of propriety and convention. A sense of propriety encourages the use of typical defense patterns and in the therapeutic context serves the resistance. Direct emotional expression facilitated by the suspension of ego-defense patterns is part of a therapeutic process in the service of change. Bennis and Shepard (1974) state that "the moments of stress and catharsis, when emotions are labile and intense, are the times in the group life when there is readiness for change." Under conditions where ego-defense patterns are suspended, tension within the group will increase.

The Relation of Ego-Defense to Emotion

The proposition that the expression of emotion unencumbered by defenses is threatening raises an evolutionary issue. It has been suggested that emotions developed during evolution to deal with particular types of survival crises (Plutchik and Kellerman, 1976). To relinquish defenses may reveal emotional states associated with historically threatening events. This position is entirely consistent with the Reichian view of character formation (Reich, 1949). Reich viewed the development of character traits as an attempt to nullify and cope with threat. This suggests that certain historical events could not be directly managed. As a result an attempt is made to modify emotional expression. This process creates a matrix for the development of character traits; that is, patterned compromise behavior is designed to gratify needs without any accompanying threat or anxiety.

The view of emotion-defense interaction as an evolutionary advance does not imply that people can function well without any defenses at all. In the absence of defense, transient crises accompanied by intolerable levels of tension would be experienced from moment to moment. The nature of emotion is that it is a transient adaptive reaction seeking to reestablish a kind of behavioral homeostasis (Plutchik and Kellerman, 1976). The interaction of emotional states generates these enduring patterns called personality traits and ego-defenses.

The major implication of this formulation is that all defenses have historical antecedents, and that relinquishing a defense may generate the emotional state associated with an original condition. This is precisely what Goldman (1963) implies in discussing how people strive to avoid anxiety within the historical context. For example, if displacement behavior is given up, then the real source of threat must be faced, i.e., the person who could not be attacked originally without the serious possibility of reprisal.

Another implication of the idea that ego-defense is related to emotion lies in its application to Ezriel's concept of the avoided relationship (Ezriel, 1973). In Ezriel's formulation, the defense is correlated to the avoided relationship that if not avoided could produce a calamity. Ezriel's "calamity" is reminscent of the Reichian conception relating historically threatening memories to the development of ego defense. Similarly, Bion conceives of the group as containing basic assumption cultures. These cultures offer a framework for the expression of a few basic categories of emotion, and they imply the idea of defense (Bion 1959b; Sherwood, 1964).

It may be seen that the correlation of defense to emotion has been pointed out in a wide variety of sources. Bach (1954) added the interesting notion that just as the past influences the present, so too may the present influence the past, especially insofar as memory is frequently unreliable. Current needs, emotions, and defenses may shape the nature of past memories. This idea has also been posited by Goffman (1959) and by Rycroft (1966).

The Group as a Treatment Setting for Resolution of Defense

In a discussion of transference therapy work as a function of particular treatment modality, Durkin (1964) reports that an analysis of defensive transference is especially applicable to group therapy and says that defenses "guard what Kubie called the patients' central emotional position." In a more recent paper, Durkin (1974) reports that Ezriel considered the relation between emotion and defense to be so important that he taught "that every individual's reaction (defenses) to the group emotion should be clarified." What this meant to Ezriel was that the therapist clarifies to the entire group each role and each respective defensive posture taken by a given member. Also, Fenichel (1941) considered that working on ego-defense offered the best chance of resolving resistance, especially since resistance is integrally tied to the patient's defenses. To this Durkin and Glatzer (1973) add, "Intensive feelings are reawakened whenever transference resistance is brought into the open." Glatzer (1962) also suggests that "the group is helpful in penetrating tenacious primitive defenses." It is apparent that the group is considered by many writers who are conversant with the psychoanalytic theory of transference-resistance to be uniquely suited as a defense-resolution treatment setting.

THE THEMES OF TENSION

The importance of managing emotion relates to the nature of tension. If poorly regulated, direct emotionality produces consistently high levels of tension in the personality. If well managed, emotionality can be transformed in various ways, ultimately producing low levels of tension. It is this regulation feature in the management of emotion that constitutes the adaptational nature of personality defense. Regulating tension also raises the issue of maintaining optimal levels of tension. Not only is tension a desirable characteristic of the therapy, but its existence also provides evidence that members of the group are, at least to some extent, maintaining their basic obligation of membership (Kellerman and Plutchik, 1977). Tension implies that members are indeed confronting bothersome issues, and to do that they must begin to hold in abeyance their defensive operations. Furthermore, the extent of the tension indicates whether typical defenses are being dealt with by members. An inverse relationship is thus revealed between tension level and defense confrontation.

A Model of Emotion and Defense

Ego-defenses and ego-defense operations may be understood by outlining basic themes of group tension. It may be assumed that all tension content of the group is composed of a few basic themes. These themes refer to specific categories of defense designed to manage specific emotion dimensions. Since it is the anticipated giving up of defenses that produces tension, it may be useful to consider those emotional dimensions managed by specific defense mechanisms. The relationship of emotion to character roles has been referred to in chapter 3, and the laws governing the structural relationship between one emotion and another have also been referred to elsewhere (Plutchik, 1962; 1970 and in press). The relationship between specific emotions and ego defense mechanisms has been proposed by Kellerman (1977), Kellerman and Plutchik (1977) and Plutchik, Kellerman and Conte (1979).

The emotion theory by Plutchik (1962), described in chapter 2, postulated that there exist eight basic emotions structurally arranged as a model of four bipolar pairs. To the conception of four basic bipolar emotion dimensions correlated to bipolar character roles in the chapter on character roles may now be added basic defensive conditions conceived as forming four bipolar defense categories or eight basic defense categories. It is proposed that these eight basic defenses are designed to manage the eight basic emotions, reflecting an adaptational element of personality development. All defensive functioning in group interactions, no matter how complex, may be understood with regard to these eight basic defensive postures.

An interesting implication derived from this system is that varieties of experience may be understood in terms of a few basic dimensions. The idea that roles contain a central defensive core (Durkin, 1964) is translated by Teicher (1972) to mean that roles tie character defenses to events of life. "They become the individual's answer to the demands made by external reality." In terms of Adlerian psychology these demands relate to issues of inferiority (Dreikurs, 1963). To Jung the defensive operations concern maintaining individuality (Illing, 1963), and to Horney they include the conflict between a need to belong and the feeling that others are hostile (Rose, 1963).

Table 5-1 shows the emotion-defense relationship at a glance, and Figure 5-1 shows the organization of emotion-defense structure. This figure also corresponds to Figure 3-1 (p. 53). Some of these conceptions have been discussed in terms of general group development theory (Bennis and Shepard, 1956; Ehrenwald, 1974).

Table 5-1. Basic bi-polar emotion and defense dimensions.

EMOTION	DEFENSE
Trust (acceptance)	Denial
Distrust (disgust)	Projection
Control (expectation)	Intellectualization
Dyscontrol (surprise)	Regression
Passivity (fear)	Repression
Aggression (anger)	Displacement
Gregariousness (joy)	Reaction Formation
Deprivation (sorrow)	Compensation

Figure 5-1 portrays a circumplex organization of emotion and defense. The central idea here, also referred to in chapter 2 on group composition, consists of two elements. First, those emotion and defense categories that are adjacent on the circle share more variance; that is, they are more similar. Any two emotion-defense categories further apart on the circle are more dissimilar. The second element of this circumplex organization concerns the notion of polarity. Any two emotion-defense categories opposite on the circle are most dissimilar. The usefulness of this circumplex system in conceptualizing relationships has been described by Burt (1950), Guilford and Zimmerman (1956), Guttman (1954), and Schaefer (1958), and more fully elaborated in chapter 2.

An examination of Figure 5-1 will indicate that the circumplex organization is actually an emotion-defense similarity structure (Kellerman and Plutchik, 1977; Plutchik, Kellerman, and Conte, 1978). The following section will provide a rationale for these specific emotion-defense correlations, and the development of a schema or mnemonic device will be described that provides a useful way of viewing the similarity structure of defenses.

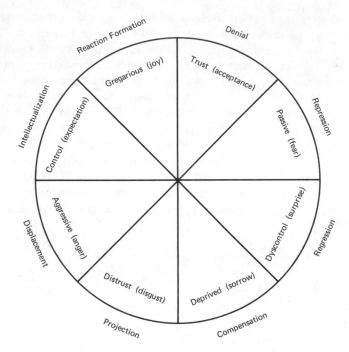

Figure 5-1.   A circumplex ordering of emotion categories on the inside of the circle with corresponding defense mechanisms on the outside of the circle. This structure reveals an organization governed by the law of neighboring and the law of polarity.

The "It" Device

In Figure 5-2 a schema or mnemonic "it" device is portrayed, in which each defense is defined in terms of function; in this instance, in terms of the "it." This "it" invention is an attempt to generate a sense or statement of defenses as they relate to each other and as they correspond to emotions. The "it" may be an impulse, a person, or an event. Tracing the "it" around the circle in Figure 5-2 creates a tentative logic or similarity structure for the entire system of defenses. The "it" device may be examined at any point of the circle with respect to its function. For example, the statement describing the defense of denial is "don't see it." The way to use this device then, starting from the point of denial on the circle, is to follow each image in a clockwise direction. In this way, not only is each defense defined by its statement or image, but each succeeding defense then becomes a logical aternative to its predecessor. What this means is that as one defense follows another around the circle, a new "defense logic" is continuously created. This "defense logic" may be illustrated by starting with "denial" and following a hypothetical thought process in a clockwise direction around the circle. In the following

Figure 5-2.   The "it," a mnemonic device to create an image of each defense mechanism. A similarity structure of defenses is revealed by the continuous images around the circle. Corresponding emotions also are indicated.

illustration each defense is defined by this mnemonic "it" device or image which may be visually traced in Figure 5-2.

Denial is *don't see it*. If that doesn't work then insulate yourself and *don't feel it*. If that doesn't work then repress it and therefore *don't remember it*. If that doesn't work then *do something else about it* like act-out; or you could regress and *cry for it*, or you could compensate and *try to get it back*. If none of these methods work then you might fantasize or *daydream about it*. If even this doesn't work then you might as well criticize or project and *blame it;* or, even better, you might displace it and *attack something that represents it.* When these attempts are also inadequate you might as well *join it.* How?; well, you might identify with it or *be like it.* A good way to be like it is to introject or *take it in.* Once you've finally taken it in, you'd better not show it—rather you could *recategorize it* by intellectualizing it. How is that possible?; well, you might rationalize or *make an excuse for it,* or whenever you commit yourself you could undo it by *retracting what you said about it.* Another good way to hide it, is to sublimate or *transform it.* Perhaps the best way of transforming it is simply to use reaction-formation in order to *reverse it* altogether. Once it's reversed you surely won't see it and therefore you can deny it.

This clockwise progression of images and corresponding defense mechanisms is one way to examine the similarity structure of the defense system; that is, it is one way of determining the placement of defenses in a structure based upon some organizing criteria. In Figure 5-2, locations of the basic emotions on the outer rim of the circle correspond to defense locations and offer additional theoretical support for the relation between emotions and defense mechanisms. The "it" invention is intended here to present one possible method of understanding the interrelation of defenses and of defenses and emotions. In the following presentation, an attempt will be made to offer clinical illustrations of emotion-defense-role correlations in the context of group therapy events.

The Basic Polar Emotion-Defense Dimensions

TRUST VERSUS DISTRUST

Trust

The emotion of acceptance or, on the behavioral level, taking in, is a trust dimension. The particular character role that expresses this dispositional quality is that of the romantic. The romantic is perpetually trusting and accepting and is essentially naive. On the defense level the romantic uses the mechanism of denial. The denial of threatening feelings relates to an overly trusting attitude. Such individuals are characteristically uncritical. For the romantic to relinquish defense operations means to deny less and to "face the facts." In the context of group participation this work may produce much tension. On a clinical diagnostic level, if the denial is intense then the romantic may be seen as an hysteric character. In this trusting and suggestible type, the emotion of acceptance or trust is managed by the defense of denial. Lachman and Stolorow (1977) relate the defense of denial to idealization needs and to the trait of suggestibility. In this sense, patients of this type tend to idealize all relationships.

Although she was often reminded of her short-lived enthusiasms, Josephine, a 35-year-old single woman would insist that each of her new relationships was the ideal one. She was quite unable realistically to evaluate any of her romantic involvements. This idealization of relationships was also occurring in the group. She professed only the most positive feelings for all group members, who in turn generally found it difficult to relate to her. As one member pointed out, she was always smiling. Her obvious suggestibility angered other members who insisted that she cease nodding her head in approval at any opportunity. She was, in spite of this behavior, a highly competent person. Part of her work in the group consisted of efforts to express even remotely felt dissatisfactions. The general therapeutic goal was to help her gain access to the introspective process and to reduce passive-aggressive behavior.

In this clinical illustration, the major defense of denial was extensively utilized to manage intense needs of acceptance and love. The emotion of trust or acceptance is thereby maintained by a quality of high suggestibility and managed by the defense of denial.

Distrust

The emotion of disgust or on the behavioral level, rejection, characterizes the distrust dimension. The particular character role that expresses this dispositional quality is that of the scrutinizer. The scrutinizer is always critical and never trusting. On the defense level the scrutinizer uses projection. The task for the scrutinizer of giving up defensive operations in group interaction is to begin confronting underlying feelings of self-criticality and low self-esteem. In a group context this demand may also be quite tension producing. On a clinical diagnostic level, if the projection is intense, the scrutinizer may be seen to be a paranoid character. As far as emotion and defense are concerned in this distrust type, the emotion of disgust or feelings of inferiority are managed by the defense of projection. In the psychoanalytic literature (Freud, 1911, 1912) the emotions of disgust, loathing, and criticality are related to the paranoid disposition and to the defense of projection. The emotion of disgust is managed by the defense of projection so that the object of the disgust remains alien to the personality. Here patients will manage to find fault with everything and everyone as a way of not seeing personal imperfections which presumably are unconscious and profound.

Herman was a 27-year-old single man who, by virtue of his exquisitely sensitive eye could detect even the most hidden imperfections in people. Never seriously involved in any lasting relationships, he usually discovered something to criticize in each group member. He would actually rate the behavior of group members and evaluate this behavior with reference to his own private sense of standards. He also demonstrated an intense "buyers regret" in any relational contact; that is, sharing an opinion with another group member seemed to make him angry and would force him to verbally withdraw any explicit support or responsibility for the shared opinion. Because of his unmalicious and natural display of superiority, he could not acknowledge any corrective observations made by other group members concerning his functioning in the group. Only after Herman was fully convinced that a respected older woman of the group truly admired him was he able to yield. He finally admitted feeling shy and harboring a personal sense of incapacity. Herman's work in the group consisted of relinquishing projective defenses and further confronting feelings of self-criticality, low self-esteem, and inferiority.

In this clinical illustration the emotion of distrust or disgust was managed by the defense of projection through the expression of a chronically critical attitude.

The opposition of trustful vs. distrustful emotions also reveals the opposition of the defenses denial and projection respectively. The polarity of defense represents one part of an implicit model of defense that may be seen in Figure 5-1. The model also enables a comparison of the hysteric and paranoid dispositions with regard to features of suggestibility and criticality respectively.

CONTROL VERSUS DYSCONTROL

Control

The emotion of expectation or, on the behavioral level, exploring, constitutes a control dimension. The particular character role associated with this type is that of the intellectualizer. The intellectualizer shows strong needs for control and for maintaining decorum. It is this type that frequently calls for reason. Persons of this type may be highly sublimated and are powerful rationalizers. The object of giving up defensive functioning by the controlled type and thereby decreasing intellectualization may ultimately lead to greater spontaneity and to an examination of control needs. The examination of such needs, however, may produce an inordinate amount of tension. On a clinical diagnostic level, if the intellectual defense is overdeveloped, the intellectualizer may be seen as an obsessional character who needs to prevent the expression of any sudden impulse. In this particular type, the need for control as expressed in the emotion of expectation or anticipation is managed by the defense of intellectualization.

Lawrence, a 50-year-old divorced father of three was frequently accused by group members of "coaching from the side lines." He would interpret and mediate conflict, yet was the object of scapegoating. Group members would implore him to recognize their perceptions. Instead, he would lecture to them that although he knew that they had the best intentions, nevertheless he felt they were misguided. The unrelenting pressure on Lawrence to acknowledge his obvious needs for control and to recognize more spontaneous or even irrational feelings was also a plea for him to become less intellectualized. The intellectualizer is quite miserly and this was certainly characteristic of Lawrence. Working on relinquishing some intellectualization caused Lawrence to experience a silent period in the group, especially since he was now less rehearsed. He later became more generous and relaxed.

This clinical illustration attempts to show that the emotion of control or expectation is managed by the defense of intellectualization as well as by other secondary obsessional defenses, e.g., rationalization, undoing, and sublimation. The relation between these obsessional defenses may be seen in Figure 5-2.

Dyscontrol

The emotion of surprise or, on the behavioral level, responses reflecting behavior of disorientation constitutes a dyscontrol dimension. The character role showing this dispositional quality is that of the child. The child shows regressive behavior and is impulsive and undercontrolled. Behavior of the child is not governed by the usual pauses and punctuations of social intercourse. When impulsive types are confronted with their regressive defense they may feel compelled to examine their inability to "sit still." Although sitting still for this type may reflect more mature behavior it may also be experienced as feeling trapped and therefore may be terribly anxiety-provoking.

On a clinical diagnostic level the child may be seen as a psychopathic character, one disposed to acting-out. In this dyscontrolled type, the disorientation or surprise is managed by the defense of regression. Patients of this type are frequently opting for action rather than for talking. Attention span is generally impaired here.

Cissey, a 23-year-old woman, joined a group composed of young adults. Her attempt in any interaction was to be seen as the little girl. She was a very impulsive person whose attempts to endear herself seemed rather silly and immature. She participated in the group, in a rambling fashion, never quite sticking to the point. Her immature style of relating tended to alienate those around her. Only after some difficult sessions in which she was called "superficial" did she become visibly frightened. Realizing that the group would not support her regressive defense, she desperately tried to recreate within the group a situation that resembled her outside life. Group members were quick to notice her inability to hear them and her incessant need for action. Despite her resilience and apparent ego-strength, qualities not usually found in such persons, she would not be cornered and, unannounced, she suddenly terminated. The group requested that she return. Upon her return it was pointed out to her that she usually assumed an inferior role in any family scene and that she really couldn't imagine having equal footing in adult relationships. Hence, she would engage in antics designed to deflect attention from her real anxiety; that is, if she behaved as an adult, she would have to be denied immediate gratifications and her motoric action-orientation could no longer be expressed. After some time, and continued reassurance, Cissey's excessive acting-out decreased and her phobic inability to sit still subsided. The acting-out, however, was not eliminated. This dyscontrolled type is more fragile than other types and therefore the prognosis here is usually somewhat guarded.

In this clinical illustration the expression of impulsive behavior was facilitated by the defense of regression. Regression was used to manage the emotion of dyscontrol by preventing any controlling or stopping behavior from occurring.

The opposition of control vs. dyscontrol emotions again contributes to the idea that in the implicit system of defense structure, the defenses of intellectualization and regression constitute opposite states.

PASSIVE VERSUS AGGRESSIVE

Passive

The emotion of fear, or on the behavior level, seeking protection, may be conceived as a dimension mostly characterized by an inhibitory component. This inhibitory element is the diagnostic bridge between the emotion of fear and the passive dimension. The particular character role associated with this type is that of the innocent. The innocent shows fearfulness, timidity, passivity, lethargy, and obedience. Persons of this type are frequently highly repressed. The emotion of fear generates escape as well as withdrawal feelings and the defense of repression acts to eliminate threatening material from consciousness. The special nature of repression suggests a postulate with respect to the relation of defense to emotion. *It is proposed here that although repression is the vital quality of all defensive structure, it is most prominent in the management of fear.* The object of resolving the repressive posture may enable persons of this type to examine their inability to be assertive. On a clinical diagnostic level, if the repression is quite overdeveloped, the passive quality becomes central to the development of the passive character.

An extremely passive, almost mute 35-year-old man attended group sessions regularly for two months. When addressed by group members he would respond. However, he would not initiate any exchanges and denied having emotional responses to any of the ongoing interactions. It was only when one or two group members began noticing his unconscious motoric behavior that Simon did admit to feeling flushed. He would bother his cuticles, shift in his chair, and finger drum absentmindedly. He daydreamed and appeared bored and in need of personal attention. No amount of confrontation could modify Simon's passive-isolative stance, even though under an intense inquisition he finally admitted to feeling apprehensive and awkward. He felt that what he had to say would be meaningless and it became quite clear that Simon's repression was terribly entrenched. The repression and passivity problem led him into the role of the innocent quite by default. After a group member described his wife's very bloody childbirth did Simon suddenly and for the first time interrupt the proceedings with the announcement that he was about to faint. The group mobilized instantly and individual members suggested to Simon that he lower his head to the floor. Some members tried to convince Simon that his reaction was a psychosomatic one, proving he was repressing emotion. After several minutes Simon recovered, and seeming quite composed, stated he was certain that the story of the bloody childbirth caused his "spell." The group seemed collectively astonished by his outright acknowledgement of the apparent cause-and-effect relationship which induced his spell. The story of the bloody birth may have both frightened and angered Simon, causing him to hyperventilate. This hypothesis suggests that in the passive syndrome, repression may be managing fear but also covering a deeply ingrained secondary response to the feeling of helplessness. During the following two years Simon was responding more readily in the group. While remembering grammar school experiences he recounted an interesting memory in which he felt angry toward a classmate, and in a suspended moment, pushed this classmate down. It was his only childhood memory of expressing feelings. Simon would also periodically refer to his fainting spell two years earlier, remembering that it was prompted by the story of the bloody childbirth.

In this clinical illustration, the passive condition in which fear is the primary emotion is managed by the defense of repression. The passive repressive condition may also appear in diagnostic withdrawal syndromes that include schizoid and borderline states.

Aggressive

The emotion of anger, or on the behavioral level, attack or destruction, describes the aggressive dimension. The character role expressing this dispositional quality is that of the scapegoater. The scapegoater shows displacement behavior, is quite angry, and is drawn to people who will absorb hostility. This displacement defense does not allow the scapegoater any opportunity to confront frustrations directly or simply. On a clinical diagnostic level the scapegoater may be seen as an aggressive character.

An erudite man of 37 would frequently and angrily attack any woman of the group older than he, whenever he thought this member was showing only perfunctory interest. He accused passive members of the group of having opportunistic motives, but he also avoided the more dominant group members. He would consider corrective criticism but would resume his usual provocative behavior unaffected by group pressure. Attack or be attacked was his talismanic view of the world. He was cynical. His inability to engage any of the more dominant members of the group revealed a defense against handling his insecurities more directly. A significant change occurred when it was pointed out by a dominant female member that he conspicuously avoided all other vocal members of the group. He was somehow able to accept this criticism and then expressed hatred toward an older sister who was a mother surrogate in his childhood. This sister was quite punitive and demanding, and was the one who nicknamed him Peanuts. The displacement defense deflects anger, and in addition, permits extra anger to be released toward other transference figures. This man of 37 nicknamed Peanuts embodies these dynamics—he was always directing anger toward those members of the group who would not or could not retaliate.

In this clinical illustration, the defense of displacement manages the emotion of anger. The opposition of passive vs. aggressive roles further suggests that in the system of defense structure, the defenses of repression and displacement are polar opposites.

GREGARIOUS VERSUS DEPRIVED

Gregarious

The emotion of joy, represented for example as sexual behavior, also reflects the gregarious dimension. In this category response to stimulation and an energized potential of personality is quite strong. The particular defense associated with this type is that of reaction-formation. The defense of reaction formation regulates sexual urges and determines the degree to which sexual motives remain suppressed. The character role associated with this type is that of the puritan. The puritan demonstrates unsullied altruism and the purest of motives. Great energy, a sense of bearing, and a sense of self-possession characterize this type. The energy level of the puritan is far too high. It is as if reaction-formation permits the sublimation of sexual energy into social non-sexual activity. Ostow (1959) has indicated that reaction-formation may deflect instinctual energy from the forbidden activity to its opposite. It should be added that the reaction-formation is utilized because the forbidden activity contains pleasure-attraction ingredients. On a clinical diagnostic level the excessive energy and persistently good intentions of the puritan suggest the manic character. Thus in this type, reaction-formation manages the emotion of joy in the sense that an energized quality constitutes the major ingredient of the joy.

Florence was a 45-year-old woman raised in a moralizing and religious home. She became earth mother to all group members. A strong sense of responsibility and a sobering conscientiousness allowed her to become the embodiment of the group work ethic. Group members would criticize her for being such a moralistic type. Yet there was something compelling about her and other women recognized and admired her. Her insistence that devotion, love, and fidelity was the goal of marriage caused a frequent stir in the group. Members either rallied to her or challenged her. She denied sexual fantasies, insisting only on the primary relationship she enjoyed with her husband. Her attitudes were generally received by the group with curious skepticism. She would be reminded that her many activities made it impossible for her to be at home, and contact with her husband was quite meager. Florence was constantly involved in a spate of projects. Some members noticed a seductive quality to her style and the group became reluctant to tolerate her acquired role as assistant therapist. She described her husband as a well intentioned, although remote, person and, in recounting her family concerns, she began experiencing anxiety. First, her abundance of energy was not achieving its release in the group, and second, she was feeling deprived and in need of more affection. Florence was favored by many members of the group, and the change in her defense structure was aided by this measure of group support. The experience of depressive feelings signalled a change in the defensive reaction-formation.

In this clinical illustration the defense of reaction-formation regulates the degree to which sexual energy may be experienced.

Deprived

The emotion of sorrow, or on the behavioral level, reaction to loss, characterizes the deprivation dimension. The particular character role of reintegrator shows this dispositional quality. The reintegrator is involved in a good deal of adolescent fantasy serving to suppress feelings of inadequacy or depression. It is proposed here that the typical defense mechanism used to manage such feelings is compensation. Such persons are frequently reporting heroic deeds, boasting, and yearning for recognition and applause. In depressed persons, even the most minimal compensatory acts signal the beginning of a restitutive process. For the deprived type to relinquish this compensatory defense means to abandon adolescent fantasy and meet issues of loss in a more realistic fashion. When this suspension of compensation occurs in the context of analyzing loss experiences, a resulting depression may be part of a reconstructive process in the service of the ego. However, when compensation becomes suspended independently of the reconstructive process, a resulting depression may then create suicidal risk. Relinquishing the compensatory defense should be part of a transformational transference-resolution process and not a just doing well process. A cathartic doing well process can include compartmentalization mechanisms and these may increase suicidal potential (Kellerman, 1976a). The compensatory behavior is designed to regain something such as a realistic lost object, help create a defense against feelings of incapacity, and aid in the development of a sense of well being. During object-loss experiences, identification with the object as an internalized symbol produces a sense that something "inside" was lost. This identity loss experience needs to be replaced, or in some way regained. The compensatory mechanism manages, through fantasy or through behavior, to accomplish this aim. It is an attempt to overcome the effects of a real or perceived loss. On a clinical diagnostic level, if compensation is the characteristic defense style, an underlying depressive character is sure to exist.

Jesse, a 22-year-old college student was referred for treatment because of a suspected suicide attempt. The onset of an insomnia condition related to difficulty he was experiencing studying for final examinations. Already on probation, any additional failures would end his college career. Deprived of sleep, feeling lonely and desperate, he injested a half dozen stay-up pills. Whether he intended to end it all or simply to stay awake was ultimately unclear to him. Jesse used the group setting as a forum in which he could spin tales of his intellectual and sexual power. Describing with great relish that many girls were attracted to him, he also admitted that it was really the abstract recognition that interested him and not the actual social contact. His consistent boasting produced a compensatory transparency that group members were quick to point out. Fortunately, Jesse was resilient enough so that some of his defensive bravado became moderated and his interaction with other members assumed less of a declamatory stance. He also became somewhat depressed. At first, Jesse was astonished by this very obvious change, but was relieved to see other members examining their own relationships and fears so easily. As anxiety of exposure and expected ridicule subsided, the use of the compensatory mechanism was less necessary.

In this clinical illustration the defense mechanism of compensation was utilized in the management of deprivation and inadequacy feelings. The opposition of the gregarious vs. deprived emotions also reveals the opposition of reaction-formation and compensation defenses respectively.

The above discussion on the relation between emotion and defense is intended to be one framework within which defensive operations may be understood. For example, the defense of compensation is actually a condensation of a whole host of childhood experiences in which loss, sorrowful feelings, feelings of inadequacy, and attempts at reintegration were occurring, but which culminated in a character defense that became etched in the personality. The compensatory defense, then, creates the possibility that original tensions of deprivation may be avoided and not consciously experienced.

This model of emotion-defense and its relation to character roles again implies that other role types may be composed of the basic role types described above. This point is underscored by Kadis et al. (1968) who state that "The form of each patient's defense mechanism is expressed in the role he wishes to assume in the group." Some of these types have been noticed by Powdermaker and Frank (1953) who illustrate role and defensive correlates to the withdrawn or passive patient, the antagonistic or aggressive patient, and the intellectualized patient. Bach (1954) also discusses the patient's "preferred mode of defense;" one member is sensitive to sexual themes, another to injustices, another to the controlling behavior of others, another to critical members, and another to special communications to the therapist. Bach states, "In realistic social life, people react to the overt defense patterns of others, that is, to the patterns of social role behavior." Finally, Yalom (1970) as well as Argyris (1968) refer to the idea that defense mechanisms are part of a system that produces "typical behavior."

Introductions to these tension themes are given in Kellerman and Plutchik (1977) and in Plutchik, Kellerman, and Conte (1979). These authors suggest that the eight basic defense mechanisms discussed here are essentially the major defenses described as adaptive structures in evolution to manage the basic emotions. All other defense mechanisms are seen to be secondary or to be qualitatively different than the basic eight. Other defenses such as identification or internalization function more as process mechanisms, while defenses such as undoing and rationalization, are variants of the defense of intellectualization and are all part of the obsessional defense syndrome. Other secondary defenses also may be part of diagnostic syndromes. It is proposed that the "process" defenses or the identification-introjection mechanisms function to cement and reinforce character or personality trait development. In contrast, the defenses examined in this chapter are designed to regulate emotions that become expressed as transitory reactions.

Emotion Defenses versus Trait Defenses

Emotions as transitory reactions seem to be regulated by the mechanisms of defense usually referred to as ego-defense mechanisms. These include for the most part reaction-formation, denial, repression, regression, compensation, projection, displacement, intellectualization, rationalization, and undoing. Other defensive operations such as indentification, internalization, and introjection seem to be utilized more in the development of enduring personality traits. A review of the "defense" literature produces lists of defenses that are proposed by various writers. Freud (1926) listed regression, repression, projection, isolation, introjection, undoing, and reaction formation. Anna Freud (1937) adds sublimation and displacement to this list. Healy, Bonner, and Bowers (1930) propose a variety of defenses or "dynamisms:" displacement, transformation, symbolization, idealization, unconscious fantasy, repression, reaction-formation, projection, isolation, undoing, conversion, introjection, identification, sublimation, rationalization, and dream work. Brenner (1975) lists the defenses of undoing, denial, reaction-formation, displacement, repression, identification with the aggressor, isolation, projection, compensation, identification, and introjection. Other authors, such as Coleman (1956), list 17 ego-defense mechanisms; Frazier (1975) lists 23 ego-defenses and Vaillant (1976) lists 18 ego-defenses.

Many writers apparently agree on a basic complement of defenses but each includes some defenses not included on the lists of others. An analysis of these conceptions suggests that defenses that may function in the development of character or personality trait formation include introjection, idealization, identification, and identification with the aggressor. These may be part of the defensive operations that generate personality styles and illustrate what is meant by the appearance of more enduring traits. Other defenses that are listed such as transformation, symbolization, unconscious fantasy, conversion, and dream work seem rather to be definitions of defensive processes or, in the case of transformation, to be a synonym for the term defense itself. The remaining defenses of displacement, repression, reaction-formation, projection, isolation, undoing, sublimation, rationalization, denial, and compensation may be utilized most often in the personality to manage the so-called transitory emotional reactions. In the following section and in chapter 10 an attempt will be made to distinguish between blocking and releasing functions of those defenses considered here to be basic and related to the primary emotions.

Accessible versus Impedance Defenses

This system of defense and emotion generates at least three major principles. First, it is proposed that as an evolutionary adaptational product, specific defenses have evolved to manage particular emotions. Second, it is proposed that this development was highly selected. Although a given defense evolved to manage a specific emotion, the defense system was flexible enough so that any given defense or group of defenses could be employed in virtually any clinical syndrome. Third, it is proposed that the eight primary defenses are divided into two major categories. One category may be termed "accessible." The defenses in this category are designed to manage those primary emotions that permit healthier and more accessible interpersonal contact to occur. Another category may be termed "impedance." The defenses in this category are designed to manage those primary emotions that produce more conflict in the personality.

The terms "accessible" and "impedance" were suggested by the findings of a study of maladjustment (Kellerman, 1965; Kellerman and Plutchik, 1968). In this study a group of normal subjects was compared to moderately and severely disturbed groups on the basis of which of the eight primary emotions was selected by subjects as reflecting best self-descriptions. The emotions were selected from paired adjective choices on the Emotions Profile Index (Plutchik and Kellerman, 1974). Results for subjects in the "normal" group indicated that the emotions of trustful, gregarious, timid, and controlled (reflecting acceptance, joy, fear, and expectation respectively) were activated to higher levels than the levels to which their opposite emotions were activated. In contrast, those emotions hardly activated in the normal group became more highly activated in the disturbed groups; these included emotions of distrust, deprivation, dyscontrol, and aggression (reflecting disgust, sorrow, surprise, and anger respectively). As maladjustment increased, therefore, a significant shift in the emotions profile occurred. This finding implied that the emotions of distrust, deprivation, dyscontrol, and aggression, if highly activated, may reflect more pathological states in the personality or greater maladjustment. The term "impedance" was therefore applied to suggest that the diagnostic states reflecting emotions of distrust, deprivation, dyscontrol and aggression as their main dispositional quality reflected greater resistance. These diagnostic states are paranoid, depressed, psychopathic and aggressive, respectively. They were viewed as potentially causing greater disturbance in day-to-day living. The term "accessible," on the other hand, was applied to suggest that the diagnostic states reflecting emotions of trustful, gregarious, timid, and controlled as their main dispositional quality, reflected less interpersonal difficulty for people in day-to-day living. These diagnostic states are hysteric, manic, passive and obsessive, respectively. One implication of the difference between the accessible and the impedance diagnoses with respect to prognosis is that it is probably better to be hysteric, manic, passive or obsessive than paranoid, depressed, psychopathic or aggressive. A further analysis of this difference is presented in chapters 7 and 8.

In the division of accessible and impedance states, the timid (fear) emotion reflects a more positive prognostic sign than the aggressive (anger) emotion. This finding is based upon the ratings of social desirability of trait terms on the Emotions Profile Index. Those fear-mixed traits such as obedience and caution were rated by judges to be highly socially desirable while anger-related trait terms such as quarrelsome and resentful were judged to be of lower social desirability value. In the division of accessible versus impedance emotions, it is proposed here that defenses designed to manage the accessible emotions have a different function than those designed to manage the impedance emotions. Defenses in the accessible group for the most part act to block impulses as a way of handling threatening feelings. Defenses in the impedance group for the most part act to release impulses as a way of handling threatening feelings. Table 5-2 lists the accessible and the impedance states.

Table 5-2.   The nature of accessible and impedance defense mechanisms.

 EGO-DEFENSES: ACCESSIBLE CATEGORY

1. Intellectualization. Logic and reason are used to *block* feelings that contradict prevailing attitudes. To maintain control is the defensive aim of the intellectualization mechanism.
2. Reaction-Formation. A feeling of attraction is *blocked* by a transformation to its opposite feeling. Management of sexuality is the defensive aim of the reaction-formation mechanism.
3. Denial. Psychological blind spots are used in order to "not see" or to *block* unpleasant realities. To maintain a condition of trust is the defensive aim of the denial mechanism.
4. Repression. Unacceptable memories are rendered unconscious and impulses to escape or withdraw are *released*. Passivity is the effect of the defensive aim of the repression mechanism.

EGO-DEFENSE: IMPEDANCE CATEGORY

1. Regression. A retreat to an earlier level of development results from *release* of impulse and more immature behavior. To maintain a condition of dyscontrol is the defensive aim of the regression mechanism.
2. Compensation. A feeling of loss or inadequacy is covered by the expression of self-assurance and by the *release* of impulses seeking extra-gratification. Depressive restitution is the defensive aim of the compensation mechanism.
3. Projection. Feelings of blame and criticality are *released* toward others as a way of not acknowledging one's fallabilities and insecurities. To maintain a condition of distrust is the defensive aim of the projection mechanism.
4. Displacement. Hostile feelings are *blocked* toward figures who are directly threatening. To maintain open channels of aggression toward less threatening figures is the defensive aim of the displacement mechanism.

Ego-defenses therefore are acting either to block or to release. In this sense they are like timing devices designed to manage emotionality. An analogy that may apply is that defense is to emotion as RNA is to DNA. The intrapsychic implications of accessible versus impedance types and the blocking-releasing function of defenses are offered in chapter 10 on the intrapsychic group.

Several postulates may be proposed with respect to the function and structure of defense mechanisms and their relation to emotions, roles, and diagnostic states.

Postulate 1: *Specific defenses are designed to manage specific emotions.*

Postulate 2: *There are eight basic defense mechanisms that have evolved to deal with the eight basic emotions.*

Postulate 3: *The eight basic defense mechanisms show properties both of polarity and similarity.*

Postulate 4: *There are other secondary defense mechanisms chiefly utilized in the ongoing formation and reinforcement of character trait development. These are the identification-introjection-internalization defenses.*

Postulate 5: *Defenses act to block or to release impulse.*

Postulate 6: *Major diagnostic personality types are related to particular defensive styles, roles, and emotions.*

Postulate 7: *Although all defenses contain a repressive element, it is the passive dispositional diagnosis with the emotion of fear as its chief underlying component for which the defense of repression was originally developed.*

Postulate 8: *An individual may utilize any combination of the defense mechanisms.*

THE APPEARANCE OF DEFENSE AS A FUNCTION OF GROUP GENERATION

The outline of a defense model relates also to the group generational system described in chapter 4 on the genealogy of groups. A four generation group was postulated, in which the first generation consisted of members of early adult age. This was considered to be a hypothetical system designed to examine phenomena of group process in a "pure" condition. It was accomplished by controlling age as the key variable in producing pure hypothetical generations. This theory of group generations proposed that the first group generation produces oedipal themes of loyalty-disloyalty and competition. The second generation of the group with members in their 30's generate themes of a phallic nature characterized by passive and aggressive issues. The third generation of the group with members in their 40's produces themes of an anal nature composed of control and acting-out or dyscontrol issues. The fourth generation of the group with members in their 40's and 50's was seen to generate themes of an oral nature including those of deprivation.

Some immediate implications develop from this analysis of group generations and the appearance of derivative psychosexual thematic material. Based upon such thematic material the operation of specific defense postures may now also be related to group generations. For example, during the first group generation, oedipal themes of loyalty versus disloyalty are quite prominent and correlate to the emotion-trait dimensions of trust versus distrust. On a diagnostic level this polarity is expressed as the hysteric character and the paranoid character. On a defense level, then, the first group generation may promote oedipal themes and these themes are maintained through the use of defensive functions represented by denial operations governing the focal theme of trust and by projection operations governing the focal theme of distrust. Although Klein (1948) correlates denial and idealization to the defense against depressive anxiety, she also accounts for the appearance of paranoid fears and suspicions as a cover to the depression. Thus a Kleinian would understand the first group generation as one that generates derivative paranoid themes.

During the second group generation, passive-aggressive phallic themes may be correlated to the passive-aggressive emotion-trait dimensions. On a diagnostic level this polarity is expressed as the passive character and the aggressive character. On a defense level, then, the second group generation may promote phallic themes which are maintained through the use of defensive operations represented by repression reflecting passive themes and displacement reflecting aggressive themes.

During the third group generation, anal themes of control vs. impulse and the general issue of demands constitute this generational concern and correlate to the emotion-trait dimensions of control vs. dyscontrol. On a diagnostic level this polarity is expressed by the obsessive character and the psychopathic character. On a defense level, then, the third group generation may promote anal themes which are maintained through the use of defensive operations represented by intellectualization reflecting control themes and by regression reflecting dyscontrol themes.

During the fourth group generation oral themes of possession, sexuality, and loss experiences are prominent, and correspond to the emotion-trait dimensions of gregarious vs. deprived. On a diagnostic level this polarity is expressed by the manic character and the depressed character. On a defense level the fourth group generation may be mostly concerned with oral themes utilizing defensive operations represented by reaction-formation sexual themes and by compensation reflected in themes of deprivation.

There is a second implication that emerges from the relation of defensive operations and psychosexual thematic material as a function of group generations. As the movement from the first to the fourth group generation constituted a psychosexual thematic regression, so too it may be hypothesized that defensive operations are part of a hierarchical system. The first generation oedipal stage corresponds to denial and projection defenses. The second generation phallic stage corresponds to repression and displacement defenses. The third generation anal stage corresponds to intellectualization and regression defenses, and the fourth generation oral stage corresponds to reaction-formation and compensation defenses. A new way of considering the development of defense is thereby suggested.

This system further implies that denial and projection represent the most advanced defense development because they correlate to the oedipal stage. Repression and displacement reflect a lesser advanced defense development because they correlate to the phallic stage. Intellectualization and regression reflect next to the earliest level of defense development as they correlate to the anal stage, and reaction-formation and compensation represent the earliest or most primitive stage of defense development correlating as they do in this formulation to the oral stage. The listing of the hierarchy of defenses in this present system is different from the hierarchical conception of defenses proposed by Fenichel (1945b) and Anna Freud (1937) among others. This is especially indicated in the case of the defense of denial. In traditional psychoanalytic thought denial is considered as a primitive defense mechanism. Yet there are very few good examples in the psychoanalytic literature to support the idea of denial as a primitive mechanism. Many examples of denial seem to be better illustrations of rationalization. Furthermore, even when examples of the

Table 5-3. Correlation of personality and group structural elements.

GROUP GENERATION	EMOTION DIMENSION	TRAIT DIMENSION	DIAGNOSTIC TYPES	ROLE TYPES	DEFENSE MECHANISMS	PSYCHOSEXUAL STAGE THEMATIC MATERIAL
1	Acceptance	Trust	Hysteric	Romantic	Denial	Oedipal
	Disgust	Distrust	Paranoid	Scrutinizer	Projection	Oedipal
2	Fear	Passivity	Passive	Innocent	Repression	Phallic
	Anger	Aggression	Aggressive	Scapegoater	Displacement	Phallic
3	Expectancy	Control	Obsessive	Intellectualizer	Intellectualization	Anal
	Surprise	Dyscontrol	Psychopathic	Child	Regression	Anal
4	Joy	Gregariousness	Manic	Puritan	Reaction-Formation	Oral
	Sorrow	Deprivation	Depressed	Reintegrator	Compensation	Oral

use of denial as a primitive defense in children are given, upon closer scrutiny these children are usually beyond infancy. It should also be noted that no single system has been agreed upon by psychoanalytic writers with respect to a hierarchy of defenses.

The entire issure of a hierarchy of defense, as well as even whether defense mechanisms may only be considered defenses of the ego, is a complex one and will be further discussed in later chapters. These issues relate directly to the concept of an epignetic personality program. It is proposed that in such a program the defense system may be encoded or engraved in the substrate of emotion and may become more differentiated during salient developmental periods. This is a sociobiological concept that becomes explored in psychoanalytic terms in chapters 9 and 10.

Table 5-3 illustrates the relationship of group generation to derivative psychosexual stages, emotion dimensions, trait dimensions, defense mechanisms, role type, and diagnostic type.

This table implies that structural elements of the group are integrally related to personality forces. It may also be more clearly seen at this point that a preponderance of one role type in a group produces an accumulation of one defensive pattern. If there are too many passive people in a group, especially during the second group generation, an accumulation of repression may lead to the group's premature termination. The issue of role balance and patient selection in any generation, therefore, becomes highly important. Selecting any patient for a group is a powerful element of group functioning. In terms of this conception, then, any patient contributes to the role complexion of the group and to its accumulated defense structure in a highly specific way. Durkin (1964) points out that "defenses common to each period and the character traits based upon them. . . . [are] registered indelibly in the personalities of the members."

The relative conflict and the relative intrapsychic impact of each of these defenses is examined in chapters 7 and 8 on the transformational shape of the group, and in chapter 10 on the intrapsychic group.

How to resolve the indelibly registered attributes or defensive conflicts of group members is explored in the following chapter on tension resolution and regulation. It is a problem of the management of defenses.

6

Ego-Defense Structure of Groups: Tension Resolution and Regulation

In this chapter the working-through process will be analyzed in terms of its effect on repetitive defensive behavior. The resolution and regulation of tension based upon working-through of defense will then be used to view the structure of group and family systems. The purpose to the group's indefinite existence is then proposed.

The success of defensive operations determines the extent to which original tensions may be suppressed. Under conditions of high suppression neurotic interaction in the group is reinforced and repetitive defensive behavior is maximized. If the role complexion of the group is reasonably balanced, accumulation of any given defense pattern is minimized. Repetitive neurotic interaction is generally referred to as the repetition compulsion and is evoked in the context of transferential relationships.

EMOTION AND TRANSFERENCE—THE REPETITION COMPULSION

Freud (1914b) indicated that patients in treatment automatically exhibit the compulsion to repeat certain behavior. In a recent paper Spotnitz (1973) adds that "the group setting is an even more efficient incubator" of acting-out forces. The meaning here as it relates to defense structure implies that defenses do not permit direct confrontation of feelings but lead rather to the repetition of neurotic behavior. Patients will tend to resist "knowing" a feeling and one method of resistance is to act-out. According to Schwartz (1965a) defense and resistance operate so automatically that the repetition compulsion does not become unduly influenced by the presence of other people in the group. The idea is that transference represents a standard condition of the group regardless of group role composition. Schwartz, then, sees both the group interpersonal dimension and the individual intrapsychic one as intersecting axes. It is quite consistent with his position that group therapy may be viewed as the analysis of individuals in groups. A second implication of the seemingly immutable nature of the repetition compulsion is that since basic character structure reflects intrapsychic organization, then character roles in the group may not be easily changed; that is, trait behavior remains entrenched in the personality. Durkin (1964) further equates character with that of the structure of the ego, implying the permanent disposition of character traits. Thus the repetition of behavior is a symptom indicating that defenses are operating well and that the tension products of defense remain unconscious.

The literature on emotion, defense, and transference suggests that therapy must provide what Alexander and French (1946), Frank and Ascher (1951), and Freud (1937) refer to as the corrective experience. The central idea is that the relation of the transference to defense mechanisms "brings the past into the present" (Durkin, 1964) and this synchrony of past and present may modify the repetition behavior (Fried, 1973). The past-present connection creates an opportunity for the corrective experience to occur.

Transference: Relating the Present to the Past

In Ezriel's (1973) formulation, defense generates behavior that produces an "avoided relationship that if not avoided could produce a calamity." This avoided relationship condition implies a defended underlying experience. It suggests that current behavior is highly correlated to historical events, memories, and expectations. This past-present correlation is also discussed by Durkin (1964) who indicates that the need to maintain repression creates a parallel need for defense to operate revealing that the past exists in the present. Rycroft (1966) and Yalom (1970) have correctly pointed out that the object of relating old and new is to focus the meaning of history onto present problems. An understanding of ties to the past allows for new behavioral alternatives in the present. One implication of this past-present correlation is that the repetition of current behavior in the light of historical material is the soil in which defensive operations are nourished.

The Historical Imperative

REMEMBERING

Relating the new to the old means that patients begin to remember more clearly. In order to remember better, defense patterns must be surrendered. These "old things" generally relate to "old feelings" and portions of one's history that are suspected to contain revelatory material. History, therefore, is seen as integral to the therapist's and the patient's sense of the overall therapy work (Wolf and Schwartz, 1962). The ongoing struggle between "the defense which is on the side of forgetting one's history, and the relinquishment of defense which is on the side of remembering one's history" comprises one part of the historical tension (Kellerman and Plutchik, 1977). It was those historical events that produced original intense feelings that were then hidden from view by the appearance of defensive behavior. Relinquishing defenses will reveal emotional states associated with these historical events. When repression is lifted an historical synapse is evoked which creates greater differentiation between the emotions and attitudes of the past and repetitive patterns of the present. When repression was maintained, past and present were not distinguishable.

The importance of remembering does not necessarily refer to any one specific memory. Recapturing lost memory has both literal and figurative meaning. The long-range task of member interaction in the group is the recreation of history, the therapeutic separation from it, and ultimately the development of a new relationship with it. The giving up of defensive behavior is a reflection of the giving up of one's history or at least the distorted, unfinished, and incomplete work of that history. The task of recreating history, separating from it, and then establishing a new link with it defines this differentiation process. It allows members to understand their history from new and fresh vantage points and permits a modification of historical distortion. This sharpening of the distinction between past and present ensures that repetitive automatic reactions may no longer be compelling. Under such conditions new alternatives of relating will replace the compulsion to repeat behavior (Fried, 1965).

The degree to which past and present are differentiated determines the extent to which defensive operations may be modified. This differentiation is fostered, as Fried (1973) says, "by the group's insistence that self knowledge be used to move ahead towards new modifications of emotions, new reactions, and fresh ways of coping with life." This is one conception generated from group therapy process. What is learned from the nature of the group is that defenses, or vested interests that people are reluctant to give up because of fears of survival, can in fact be changed. Self-defeating ritualized defenses can be modified to help produce more insightful and healthier functioning.

Ultimately, each person must reevaluate the vested interests that their ancestors created for them. When it is no longer necessary to deal with the conflicts and biases of the past and with the distortions and consequent tensions that those conflicts generate, then a rebalancing of forces becomes possible for the present and the future (Kellerman and Plutchik, 1977). Old values, needs, and historical imperatives may then be modified or refreshingly reaffirmed.

ACTING-OUT

Distinguishing the historical from the present has been discussed by Fenichel (1945a,b) who proposes an equation relating historical differentiation to acting-out. According to Fenichel, acting-out probability is high when the differentiation between past and present is minimal. Acting-out probability may decrease as differentiation between past and present increases. Fenichel defines acting-out as a relief from inner tension and considers it to be a derivative effect of repressed memory. Acting-out, then, is an attempt to maintain repression or not to know something, and this "something" consists of historically suppressed emotion. Not to know is not to remember some historical material. Acting-out behavior implies that memories are threatening to surface, causing the activation of typical defense patterns (Glatzer, 1958).

Ackerman (1963) suggests that the group environment, because of multiple transference possibilities, increases the urge and possibility of acting-out. To this it may be added that while the group environment does indeed increase acting-out urges, this occurs because in the context of multiple transference possibilities there exists the cumulative pressure on each member to relinquish typical defenses. Intense pressure exists in the group for emotion to be expressed, for memory to be freed, and for tension to be tolerated—a difficult task, yet one in which expression of the historical imperative is a necessary and vital condition for personality restructure and reintegration.

This formulation positively indentifies the group therapy milieu as an historical environment. It contains historical essence for each group member, as well as containing a developing group history based upon generational movement. The controversy between the "here and now" position of group therapy (Bach, 1954) and the historical position (Wolf and Schwartz, 1962) may be seen to be quite pointless. The current group reflects the here and now as well as having historical relevance. It therefore becomes quite artificial to eliminate historical underpinnings of any psychodynamically-oriented treatment enterprise. The use of historical referrants provides the key to the working-through process.

Working-Through in the Group

Relating the new to the old and maintaining a condition of remembering implies that typical defenses have been suspended, overall repression is lifted, acting-out is either absent or only minimally relevant, and tension is intense and fluid. Under such conditions one's coping patterns are confronted and this confrontation may seem to be life threatening. Since emotion is experienced in the full measure of its historical impact, it is no wonder that the simple act of entering a therapy group produces such significant amounts of tension. The implicit instruction each member assumes that defenses are to be given up may now be seen to contain existential ingredients and to possess great depth of meaning. Defenses are composed of historical anticedents. To give them up in the group transferential context provides an opportunity to rearrange feelings and to deal with fixed ideas and irrational responses. This process may be intuitively perceived as potentially painful.

The working-through process, then, may only be understood by tying the present into the past (Durkin and Glatzer, 1973). It is governed by the principle that current repetitive behavior, which in the context of transference-resistance may be inappropriate or irrational, at one time may have been quite appropriate and even highly rational. It may have been quite rational for a child to develop passive-aggressive procrastination as an enduring character trait when the act of defiance or even assertion carried with it dire consequences. However, to repeat this passive-aggressive procrastination in the "here and now" reveals that the current perception of reality has been determined elsewhere. The importance of remembering is that it produces the link between the here and now and the historical roots of any character pattern.

The working-through process allows original emotions such as defiance or anger to be expressed directly to the on-target transference figure. The therapist is usually this on-target figure, but in the group setting multiple transference opportunities exist. In the group, therefore, tension generated by direct emotionality may be evoked by more than one source. These multiple sources of tension create a group dilemma characterized by patients' decisions either to work-through or to act-out (Ackerman, 1963; Durkin, 1964; and Fenichel, 1964). This decision, to work-through or to act-out, constitutes the fundamental choice that all members experience. Anxiety and tension increase in the group when the decision is to work-through, and decrease when the decision is to act-out. The acting-out supports character defense by keeping tension bound. Working-through releases anxiety for reconstructive work. The corollary idea that character patterns bind anxiety was considered by Reich (1949) to be instrumental in creating character defense. Releasing this anxiety creates the working-through condition.

Anxiety and tension will shift when an aspect of working-through takes place or when acting-out takes place. The difference, however, is that neurotic repetitive behavior will continue to recur when tension is reduced by the acting-out. The resolution of tension based upon a working-through process extinguishes the compulsion to repeat, so that original tensions no longer need to be desperately mastered.

The working-through experience also allows patients to view termination of treatment as part of an understandable process. The end of treatment may be traced in terms of the entire therapeutic endeavor and the resolution of the working-through process ushers in the sense that one may now act as one's own therapist. This is quite different from a termination resulting from an acting-out urge (Leopold, 1959). The importance of working-through therefore considers, in part, that history is process and not necessarily, event.

Working-through is considered here to represent the most profound achievement in therapy because it holds out the hope for reconstructive modeling to occur. Members of the group become historical figures for each other, and in this special sense they also endure for each other. In addition, because of the working-through process, the fixed form of the family scene—its neurosis—may be transcended.

Working-Through and Defense

The themes of tension previously described comprise the basic defense dimensions that are affected by the working-through process. As transference distortions become worked-through, one's history becomes less threatening. The proposed relationship between these tension themes and their historical correlates may be described in the following ways in connection with the personality dispositions previously developed. These historical connections are hypothetical but they may offer, however tentatively, some interesting insights between basic dispositions and historical antecedents.

TRUST VERSUS DISTRUST

Trust

Denial represents the defense mechanism of this disposition. Individuals who are high deniers, nonintrospective, and defensively trusting may have been at one time quite guarded. Painful family encounters and early relationship failures may have created the need not to see. The working-through process can enable such persons to be less naive and less compulsively social. Working through helps such individuals to be more discriminating and decisive. Derivative psychodynamic issues of loyalty and disloyalty here may become transformed into the basic realization that one may have likes and dislikes, and the dislikes need not be threatening.

Distrust

Projection represents the defense mechanism of this disposition. Individuals who are high projectors and distrustful may experience a greater sense of self-worth after working-through persistent feelings of inferiority, self-criticality, and self-attack. Their identification as the accused is the main historical issue that needs to be dealt with. The distrustful person at one time may have been quite accepting. Original receptivity allowed for the unsuspecting and vulnerable absorption of perceived abuse and criticism, constituting the historical root of the projection. The working-through process may reduce the need to project and to criticize. Self esteem can increase in such instances and historically unhealed injury to the ego can become pried loose from current relationships.

PASSIVE VERSUS AGGRESSIVE

Passive

Repression represents the defense mechanism of this disposition. Repressed individuals of the passive type are timid, shy, self-protective, and remote. They are generally not introspective and they are unaware of the subtleties in interpersonal relationships. They find it difficult to understand latent communication and are exclusively informed by manifest content. Although repression is the universal element of all defenses and found in all character types, it is nevertheless also the central defense of the passive person. Fear of rejection and physical harm and even underlying feelings of rage may characterize the historical condition of the passive person and these feelings may emerge during the working-through process. As repression lifts, expression of need and affection surface and may further develop. Fear of being angry can decrease, positive identity features can then develop, and assertive behavior may begin to appear.

Aggressive

Displacement represents the defense mechanism of this disposition. Fear of losing control characterizes the historical lever of this condition in which direct expression of anger may have threatened to evoke intense reprisal. There is a possibility that great provocation on the part of historical figures produces both the desire to aggress and the simultaneous fear of aggressing associated with a feeling of impotence. On-target figures are perceived as possessing the power to punish, and a rationale is automatically developed that justifies anger toward off-target figures. As the working-through process takes place, off-target reactions and volatility may decrease and excessive anger feelings may in turn subside. Personal doubt may be expressed more easily and potential fear of humiliation may no longer determine behavior. In this type, aggression can be transformed into healthier assertion.

CONTROL VERSUS DYSCONTROL

Control

Intellectualization represents the defense mechanism of this disposition. Individuals who are rationalizers, objectifiers, and classic undoers at one time may have been embroiled in chaotic and emotionally dyscontrolled situations. These historical situations could have created the need to control all the inconsistencies of relationships. Working-through allows more spontaneous behavior to exist as well as permitting a freer experience of feelings. The giving up of control defenses also reflects a regression in the service of the ego insofar as ambiguous emotional events may then be better tolerated.

Dyscontrol

Regression represents the defense mechanism of this disposition. Individuals who are acter-outers and who are generally immature may have at one time been immobile and phobic. The historical condition may have required a regressive defense so that continual motoric behavior could nullify any fear of immobility. This use of regression to avoid the experience of immobility also may contain life-saving properties. The possibility of becoming immobile carries with it the dread of a more pathological condition primarily because immobility can retard object development. The derivative fear of the dyscontrolled person is that relationships imprison. Working-through can produce dramatic change in this type. As fear of "stopping" or becoming immobile decreases, acting-out may also decrease and attention span, in part a relational quality, can improve.

GREGARIOUS VERSUS DEPRIVED

Gregarious

Reaction-formation represents the defense mechanism of this disposition. An excessively stressed moral code may characterize the early history of this type. The historical hypothesis suggests that parental figures were both over-stimulated and over-stimulating, and that this condition characterized the early environment. The use of reaction-formation enabled an ever present sexuality to be transformed into a nonsexual sublimated social attitude. The working-through process here can only be effective after a good deal of historical reminiscing takes place and when previously undesirable sexual ruminations that occasionally spring into consciousness are acknowledged. As the effect of reaction-formation decreases, individuals of this type may begin to feel less pressured to be perfect. Humor, previously dormant, may become available, and thus emotions of sexuality, tenderness, and affection can emerge more easily. In addition, energized and frantic behavior may become moderated. The working-through process also permits underlying depressive feelings to surface and to be explored.

Deprived

Compensation represents the defense mechanism of this disposition. The historical condition may have been one in which either there existed a lack of adequate object identifications or a parental over-focus on proficiency and performance. Unnecessary parental anxiety, the protest against any show of inefficiency and incapacity, may have been perceived by this compensatory type as reflecting an existing yet denied condition of inadequacy. The compensatory behavior, then, may have developed both as a defense against revealing personal inadequacy and depressive feelings and as a means of preserving parental approval. To be unhappy could imply failure and underachievement. Above all the compensator must in some way be an achiever. A depletion of energy occurs in the acting-out of the compensatory defense especially since facade posturing is so overused. In the working-through process, energy utilized previously in the service of defense may now be applied to realistic goals and may facilitate some solid achievement. Working-through implies that feelings of self-worth previously tied to parental approval now may be examined in more realistic fashion. Furthermore, a more realistic view of personal imperfections, access to sorrowful feelings, and an existential acceptance of vulnerability may for the first time allow for a mature and complete identity. When the historical condition is reflected by inadequate object identifications, then the compensatory mechanism is frequently insufficient to guard against the appearance of a gloomy disposition and an overall depression will be seen.

The working-through of all defensive operations is continuous and gradual. It produces fluctuating levels of group tension. In order for the group to maintain its homeostasis, mechanisms for the regulation of this fluctuating group tension level need to be established and identified.

THE EFFECT OF WORKING-THROUGH ON GROUP TENSION LEVEL

The working-through process effectively broadens the range of emotion that is both experienced and expressed. It does not eliminate the use of defense or even completely transform any particular defensive disposition. With the working-through of conflict, emotion previously attenuated by defensive operations may now be more accessible. Furthermore, character patterns that were self-defeating become less frequently seen and cannot persist. Tensions are more conscious and may be handled more maturely.

This issue of the group's fluctuating tension level implies that the group contains a cumulative consciousness. This idea is referred to by Slater (1966) who, in a reapplication of Bionian theory, states, "Group development thus rests on the gradual substitution of conscious for unconscious bonds." The group process reflects this increased awareness resulting from the raised consciousness of group members. It is a group consciousness that emerges as a separate entity based upon a differentiation of parts and function.

In this respect, each therapeutic resolution affects the overall interplay of forces in the group, moving, however unsteadily, toward ever increasing consciousness. As patients work-through particular conflict and as resistance both intensifies and recedes, the tension level of the group will change accordingly.

The rise and fall of tension level as a phenomenon of therapy groups has also been cited by Powdermaker and Frank (1953), and Foulkes and Anthony (1965) indicate that the rise and fall of tension is the central therapeutic element of the group. Since most groups are concerned with maintaining an optimal level of tension then some kind of feedback mechanism must exist in the group system to act as a regulator force. This means that the group tension must not lead to permanent and fixed patterns of friction or conflict (Plutchik and Kellerman, 1976).

Regulating Tension in the Group

As defense confrontation crystallizes for group members, the group develops its boundary. It becomes a system. The boundary serves to keep the tension within the group and at an optimal level. This idea of group tension level has also been cited by Kadis et al. (1968) who indicate that the group develops a homeostasis, the purpose of which is to keep the anxiety of members on a tolerable level. The sense of effective tension level is seen by Bach (1954) as referring to the need to maintain the group's equilibrium to the extent that it is threatened.

The idea of tension level has also prompted Ezriel (1952) and Sutherland (1952) in tandem studies to hypothesize that group tensions equal the algebraic sum of individuals having the same personal motive. The correlation of boundary development and group tension level is also discussed by Slater (1966) who postulates that overall group development is a function of both individual and group boundaries. The tension level of the group in this conception depends upon a desire on the part of members to establish boundaries and a simultaneous fear of losing individuality in the gradual coalescing of the group as a whole. In a wide-ranging conceptual integration, Slater attempts to unify Bion's nondevelopmental scheme, Piagetian cognitive stages, and other group models with that of his own group development theory. Slater's group tension level may be observed to change under the various cultural conditions existing in the group. Slater argues that the developing group increases its consciousness of both individual and group identity, and this increase in consciousness presumably affects tension level. Hartman and Gibbard (1974b), in a paper on anxiety, boundary evolution, and social change, actually equate boundary evolution with the struggle of group members to manage identity shifts. These authors indicate that social change is derived from a shift in the social equilibrium of the group and that these shifts create tensions that cause the appearance of defensive operations. It is the working-through of these defensive operations that leads to social change. This is essentially a theoretical position identical to the one suggested by Jaques (1955) who relates social change to anxiety and the resolution of defensive operations. The basic assumption activity of the group consists of mechanisms that are infrastructural elements of the group, or elements that generate the group's underlying conflict themes. These are elements that act to maintain both individual and group boundaries. They are part of the overall group tension regulation mechanism; that is, the appearance of conflict themes sets into motion the process of defense confrontation that ultimately leads to attempts at tension regulation.

This Bionian conception of basic assumptions as they relate to tension regulation distinguishes between the variation of tension and tension level. The assumption groups are directed toward instant reduction of tension and are devoted to the immediate avoidance of all effective distress. The work group on the other hand may tolerate an increase of tension and may have more tolerance for frustration and delay. It is a view that considers the group process to be a generator of defense against tension while containing within it an equivalent potential work ethos. The group, therefore, in its natural makeup has the need both to reduce tension and to increase it. This position is also cited by Bales (1955) and by Mills (1964) who indicates that "group equilibrium is chronically unsteady, and efforts are constantly made both to undermine and to maintain that equilibrium."

Group members who need to maintain a low degree of tension will act-out or try to generate extra-group activity with each other. They may be expressing elements of the basic assumption group of fight-flight, pairing or dependency. Under these conditions the group boundary may become fragmented. If this low tension condition continues, the group will expire. No system can exist without tension. The basic problem in the life of a group, therefore, is for it to sustain an optimal tension level needed to support its basic functions (Kellerman and Plutchik, 1977).

There are several factors which act to stabilize tensions at optimal levels or to maintain the tension homeostasis of the group. Among those are some important group social and cultural forces that are discussed by Kellerman and Plutchik (1977) and that have relevance to the Bionian work group culture. They are presented in the following section.

Tension Regulators

LEADERSHIP

The main force in regulating group tension is the nature of leadership. For purposes of maintaining tension homeostasis, unambiguous leadership becomes a necessary force in the group. The leader as regulator controls the internal permeability of the group as well as its external boundary (von Bertalanffy, 1969). This internal permeability refers to the climate of maximum information and interaction exchange within the group, as well as the group's ability to absorb new developments. The idea of the group system needing to maintain its boundary condition has also been implied by Kernberg (1975) and Miller (1969). If the group leader is unclear about the leadership role, confusion and acting-out behavior may develop. The central job of the leader in the small group context is to act as a regulator of group tension levels (Astrachan,

1970; Bach, 1954). The reaction of members to inconsistent or biased leadership is often to exhibit various forms of acting-out behavior such as the basic assumption behavior of pairing, seductiveness, or even termination of therapy. A leader's support of one member over another invariably produces a tilt in the tension. Occasionally therapists may unintentionally promote this tilt either by the nature of an interpretation or in some other way. However, equanimity is again established when tension level changes have occurred.

The therapist in the leadership role is also a mediator and clarifier. When difficult conflict arises the leader may need to identify implicit and explicit themes in the group in order to sort out sources of conflict. According to Kellerman and Plutchik (1977), any strong emotional confrontation such as insult, humiliation, sarcasm, and sexual references tends to provoke defensive behavior. During confrontational encounters group tension will sharply rise. This condition is evoked generally when members are involved in acute transference struggles. It may appear that such struggles are decided by who is right and who is wrong. The therapist must offer another way of looking at the conflict—an analytic way (Schwartz and Wolf, 1964, 1968). Wolf (1975) indicates that the "therapist analyzes bilateral intrapsychic pathology without taking sides." The frequency of such confrontations is one index the leader uses to guage the tension level of the group. Since a persistent undercurrent exists in the group for members to express their feelings (Spotnitz, 1973), therapists have to be alert to the sudden mobilization of feeling which can alter the group tension level; that is, more frequent confrontations may increase group tension level. This issue of the mobilization of group emotion has also been elaborated by Redl (1942).

RULES

A second force of group tension homeostasis concerns the explication of clear rules of group functioning. This includes the notion of limiting extragroup contact and maintaining the boundary condition of the group as discussed by Fried (1973). Clear rules of group functioning, especially with regard to the shared group work ethic, form the basis for the development of group cohesion and stimulate the work culture of the group. The integrity of the group system depends on the uniformity of these rules. At times, much of the therapy work relates to the monitoring of these rules and their attempted modification by group members.

COMMUNICATION

A third force in the stabilization of group tension is the availability and use of communication channels. Maintaining maximum communication is equivalent to maintaining the conditions for good reality testing. With conditions existing that allow for maximum communication the leader may take practical steps to regulate tension. When members believe that certain themes are not appropriate for discussion, then the operation of certain defensive behavior will remain untouched and unanalyzed. The variety of available communicational channels in the group is elaborated on in the later chapters on communicational interaction.

DOMINANCE HIERARCHY

A fourth force of the group that influences tension level is the nature of the dominance hierarchy within the group. Dominance issues in their relation to group tension have been especially prominent in the ethological literature (Buirski, et al. 1973; Delgado, 1969; Kellerman et al. 1974; Lorenz, 1966; and Sparks, 1969). It has been well documented in this literature that dominance hierarchies tend to increase the stability of a group in terms of establishing fixed patterns of behavior. With the establishment of these behavior patterns, tension level decreases. It has also been documented that when conflicts erupt over the issue of dominance it is usually between members of the group who are relatively close to one another in dominance rank (Kellerman and Plutchik, 1977). The dominance rank is expressed even in the spatial relations among members as reflected in seating arrangements (Buirski, 1975). Ritualistic seating in the group is also further examined here in a later chapter on group communication.

A fixed seating pattern in the group usually develops quickly. If the leader permits these ritualistic behaviors to remain fixed, the tension level of the group decreases and the group may become infected with the germ of termination. If the leader challenges this group defense and facilitates a fluid group interaction, tension increases and members will work on relinquishing defense. Aronson (1967, 1975) recognizes this sort of entrenched resistance. He has developed a special technique to understand it called the Core Behavioral Sequence. It is a technique designed to make more visible the repetitive fixed patterns in the group. Aronson sets specific tasks in order to vary procedures in the group. His aim is to undermine the group resistance. The affirmation of a patient's fixed position in the dominance hierarchy often acts to prevent conflicts from breaking out into the open (Kellerman et al. 1974). The leader, therefore, needs to be aware of the dangers inherent in maintaining a fixed dominance hierarchy.

NARCISISM AND HUMILIATION

Finally, an absence of narcissism is extremely important to the functioning of the group and to regulation of group tension (Fried, 1973). This absence of narcissism is the equivalent of not needing to save face. It usually begins as a characteristic of the leader's behavior and then gradually becomes part of the group ethos. The lack of narcissism makes conflict resolution more possible and allows members to relinquish typical defense patterns more readily. To be concerned about losing face indicates that defensive posturing is still of central importance to any group member. Losing face is seen as losing dignity. It is equivalent to identity loss. When defensive posturing subsides, patients may see that concerns about losing face are ultimately self-defeating.

Tension regulation may therefore be understood as constituting an extremely delicate feature of group therapy life. In one sense, it may be the central life force of the group infrastructure. It is proposed that the extent to which this regulation of group tension is successfully implemented and the extent to which a viable group boundary condition exists is reinforced by the existence of a group that is approximately ideal in its diagnostic composition.

IMPLICATIONS FOR THE FAMILY

Group System and Family System

Tension regulation refers to the optimal level of tension that is needed to support basic functions of the group. If these basic functions operate well, the group fulfills its proposed purpose to stay alive. These basic functions include the principle of minimal restriction on the nature of relationships inside the group. The object of group work is to confront role expectations, to transcend role type, and to modify fixed patterns of relating. An atmosphere of change possibility exists in the group and possibility for change ensures the group's survival. The group then, despite its embeddedness in a family model, may be everything the family is not, a point elaborated more fully by Bell (1975). In the family, restriction of relationships is quite important, role type is fixed, and patterns of relating become rigid. Survival of the family depends inextricably on the fixed nature of relationships designed to prevent undue upheavals. The family depends on what von Bertalanffy (1969) calls a steady state homeostasis.

Foulkes (1951) also sees a distinction between the group and the family. He states, "It is true that the family is a group but not that the group is a family." Similarly, Bion (1949) suggests that the group is like a family but not the same thing as a family. These authors concur that the group may be designed to do what the family cannot do—resolve fixed ways of relating. Survival implications, therefore, indicate somewhat different goals for therapy groups and for family groups. An understanding of this difference in goals may help generate new insignts into the relationship between family system and group system. Each contains adaptive elements, although a paradox develops regarding the disparate goals of each system. One is designed for change and one is designed not to change.

Family Therapy: A System Approach

The family is designed in such a way that conditions influencing change are minimized. The steady state condition of the family ensures that it remains a minimum change environment. Bowen (1965) refers to this concept by coining the phrase "undifferentiated family ego mass." This means that the family is unable to repair its own problems. In a later work, Bowen (1971) discusses what is termed the "functional helplessness" of the family. The rigidity of the family's symptoms and pathology created the need for and the development of family therapy as a new treatment modality. This treatment method focuses on the family system, rather than on the pathological symptoms of any single family member (Aponte and Hoffman, 1973; Haley, 1968; Jackson, 1957; Rabkin, 1970; Speck and Attneave, 1973; and Zuk, 1971). Treating the system is considered to be such a compelling formulation that a separate school of group treatment has developed to address this issue. The formulations of Bion (1948, 1949), Ezriel (1952, 1956), and Foulkes (1948) provide a philosophical underpinning of a systems approach to family therapy.

The integration of a systems theory model stressing group infrastructure with a psychoanalytic approach that stresses transference interpretation has been made by Ackerman (1967), Boszormenyi-Nagy (1965), and Grotjahn (1960), and an exposition of the value of this integration is cogently described by Fieldsteel (1974). The integration of these conceptualizations allows for the group and family to be understood both in terms of intrapsychic forces as well as in terms of a systems language.

The treatment modality of family therapy is designed to assume certain conditions of the therapy group. For example, Jackson (1959) points out that the notion of homeostasis is one integrally tied to the regulatory function of the family system in much the same way that the previous discussion of homeostatic regulation of tension in the group was seen. A similarity between families and groups, or as Mendell (1973) says, between the family and the "ad hoc family," is expressed by the concept of the multigenerational continuous nature of each system. This idea of the generational nature of groups was discussed in chapter 4 on the genealogical structure of groups, and is also referred to by Bloch (1974) and by Ehrenwald (1974), who specifically discusses generational influences in the family.

THE SPECIAL NATURE OF THE GROUP THERAPY MODEL

The fact that in group therapy the family model is generally considered the basic prototype of therapy interactions is most relevant to understanding how defenses were originally developed. Typical defense-resistance in groups is also witnessed in families. Many authors have pointed out that even when members of either therapy groups or families are explicitly instructed to change interactional patterns, the instructions are disregarded (Handlon and

Parloff, 1962; Jackson and Weakland, 1961). The defense structure in therapy groups and in families operates quite automatically.

Family interaction provides the setting and context for the development of character traits. The family model enables the group to become a laboratory recapitulating the family setting and context. However, the family model is not able to provide a technology for the resolution of defense and conflict. In this sense, the family provides the group with an underlying model, and the group in turn becomes an underlying model for the resolution of conflict in the family. The use of the group as a model for the family aids in the undoing of self-defeating defense postures, provides a context for the reevaluation and rediscovery of repressed emotion and repetitive behavior, and generally alows for, as Rosenbaum (1974) states, a "constantly changing dynamic movement" to take place in the family. Kadis (1956) and Yalom (1970) indicate that the group can recapitulate the primary family in a corrective way, eliminating the maladaptive relationships that may have existed. Growth-inhibiting relationships are not allowed to become ritualized as they become manifested in the group in the way that rigid relationships ultimately develop and become characteristic in a family.

The Group as Evolutionary Advance

The therapy group is the only family-like system designed to achieve a defense-free condition as a means of restructuring personality. The motive force of the group and the group's work ethic is based upon the need to relinquish defensive operations. Yielding of defense creates the conditions of a flexible environment where the cultivation of ritualistic and repetitive behavior cannot thrive. The family system, on the other hand, with its power struggles, its opportunistic relationships, its neurotic interplay, and its structural inability to tolerate the shifting of forces, constitutes a rigid environment where ritualistic and repetitive behavior, especially in the absence of a therapist, can thrive. In this sense, the group acts as alter-ego to the family. It provides the possibility of creating change within the family and is a modality in which this change may be accomplished.

An example of the difference in change possibility as a function of either group or family system can be illustrated by examining the phenomenon of subgrouping. In therapy groups subgrouping may be quickly identified and prevented. It becomes exposed as an undermining feature of the group. Members begin to feel that subgroupers contribute to the termination energy and interfere with the growth process of the group. Subgrouping is a restricting involvement occurring when members want tension to be low and when underlying historical emotions threaten to emerge. Subgrouping as an acting-out phenomenon reveals that a therapeutic moment has been successfully avoided and defended against. As group consciousness increases, the attention of the group becomes quickly mobilized and the group will effectively intervene to prevent the acting-out.

The subgrouping phenomenon also appears in the family as a firmly entrenched interactional phenomenon. In the family, however, an established subgrouping becomes an important element of the family balance. To maintain it is to maintain the necessary homeostasis level of the family. The phenomenon of one parent acting as translator or "switchboard operator" (Rosenbaum, 1974), controlling and mediating all family interaction is essentially a variation of this subgrouping phenomenon. It may also be the basis for Bion's pairing assumption group, and cannot be easily recognized or changed since the family relies on a fixed status-quo arrangement of forces to maintain its equilibrium. In this way family members know what to expect from family relationships.

The status-quo equilibrium provides family members with an immutable continuity of past and present, implied in the concept of system equilibrium cited by Homans (1950) and by Lewin (1951). The therapy group continuity of past and present, however, must not remain immutable for it is the stuff of which transference resolution and character trait modification are made. In the therapy group, continuity becomes restructured and this is precisely what is meant by an evolutionary advance. The particular family-like cohesion and affiliation that membership in the group implies also provides members with an opportunity to undergo the corrective experience (Alexander and French, 1946; Frank and Ascher, 1951; Yalom, 1970). In the group, therefore, the continuity of past and present must be constantly evaluated.

Both the family and the therapy group create relationships that endure. These relationships do not dissolve as a function of one's geographical location. In contrast, general friendships are sometimes important only in the environment and time frame that spawned them. When the environment changes and as time passes, friendships frequently dissolve. Group members and family members, however, retain their importance either on a reality or a fantasy level. They may be subject to the vicissitudes of time and place but they always retain a measure of importance. They constitute one's relation to the significant family past. The possibility that unrealistic repetitive behavior may be corrected in the group depends very much on this continuity. It is a transference continuity.

The group may transcend patterns of interaction that are fixed and self-defeating. It is the work of the group to continually increase tension, then to provide working-through experiences, and then to again increase tension for further working-through. It is this fluctuation of tension that characterizes group therapy homeostasis. It reveals the discovery that the group is a system in tension as seen by Lewin (1935, 1936, 1951).

The group can be a self-healing system. This idea of self regulation of the group was expanded upon by Lewin (1944) in the proposition that leadership functions are distributed throughout the group, thereby contributing to the capacity of the group to sustain itself. The self-healing nature of the group is uniquely determined by the operation of its infrastructural mechanisms. These include the fluctuating nature of group tension which is based upon the work of ego-defense resolution. In addition, maintaining the integrity of the group boundary and its internal permeability allows communicational shaping to develop. This means that loyalty in the group refers to interaction and communication and not to any particular member-to-member subgroup. The group's infrastructural mechanisms prevent a random fragmenting from occurring. This negentropy (Miller, 1969) indicates that as an ongoing process the group contains evolutionary implications which, as von Bertalanffy (1969) suggests, do not allow a prediction of the future course of the system.

Since the group may be able to avoid self-defeating influences, and since it may be considered to be a self-healing system, then it also may be understood as a self-perpetuating system. Perhaps the family system as it now exists is not adaptive enough to ensure evolutionary survival (Plutchik and Kellerman, 1976). From a social-psychological viewpoint, therefore, the advent of group treatment and then of family treatment was a necessary adjustment in the adaptational nature of the family system to ensure its survival.

THE PURPOSE OF THE GROUP'S SURVIVAL

The question originally posed in this chapter was based upon a principle formulated in chapter 4. This principle proposed that the purpose of the group is to stay alive. The question based upon this principle asked: To what end is the purpose of the group to stay alive? An answer to this question may now be proposed. The group as a natural human habitat (Gibbard, Hartman, and Mann, 1974) and as a self-perpetuating and self-healing system provides a model and treatment modality in which family pathologies may be repaired and restructured. The purpose of the group's staying alive is therefore *to ensure the evolutionary path of the family*. To look within the group is possibly to catch a glimpse of the future.

7

The Transformational Shape of the Group: Transformational Imperatives of Role Variation

In his explorations of field theory, Lewin (1951) proposed that all elements in a field are influenced by all other elements. The nature of such an interaction ultimately produces a variation in the tension level of the entire field. Lewin refers to this phenomenon as the spread of tension of a field and indicates that the tension tends to be evenly distributed. The therapy group is an example of one such interactional field. The issue of the spread of tension within such a field has been referred to by von Bertalanffy (1969), Kellerman and Plutchik (1977), and Miller (1969). These authors relate the variation of tension level in the group to structural factors as well as to factors involving the overall therapeutic process.

The hypothesis that tension is somehow evenly distributed in therapy groups has been tacitly and widely accepted. It has provided a rationale for the circular seating arrangement format considered by most therapists to display the tension of the group to the best therapeutic advantage.

The assumed evenly distributed spread of tension within the group implies a smooth circular structure and constitutes the group's apparent shape. Yet therapists are also aware that any group is composed of members of differing conflicts, emotions, defenses, and diagnoses. Each member of a group exerts a distinctly different force toward the group's work. This suggests that although the group may be an evenly distributed tension field, it cannot be a smoothly and evenly distributed conflict environment. As a matter of fact, the group is an interactional environment in which conflict distribution is probably never even, is always varied, and is subject to acute and sudden changes.

Based upon the diagnostic composition of the group, the nature of polar role conflict is determined by factors implicit in each member's diagnosis, as well as by the interaction of complementary and antagonistic relationships that exist and become expressed in the group. This implicit variation of the nature of conflict among group members implies that there are at least two basic ideas involved in the issue of group tension. One is overall group tension level and the other is polar role conflict which is based upon the group's diagnostic composition.

An evenly distributed permeating tension is one that best corresponds to the properties of a smooth circular group shape, but an adequate group composition is one in which conflict is quite unevenly distributed in the group. Therefore the actual structural shape of the group based upon conflict forces that are uneven still remains to be defined. Member to member visibility, the openness of the circular seating arrangement, and the maximum potential of communicational access between members are the conventional therapeutic criteria that cause groups to become arranged in such a circular shape. However, in view of the difference between conflict and tension and in view of a group's meta-communicational system, a more complex underlying shape to the group may better reflect the group's conflict variation. This other group shape is a transformational shape largely determined by the profoundly uneven distribution of conflict between members.

The circular shape of the group, then, may be considered to be an apparent shape based solely on the presumed uniform spread of tension, while the transformational group shape, representing a complex compositional texture, may be considered an actual or implied abstract shape. In this chapter, an attempt will be made to outline the elements that distinguish the apparent from the implied shape of the group. Elements of a transformational group shape shall be proposed and it shall be hypothesized that this transformational shape constitutes an actual underlying structure of the group. It is hoped that implications derived from the analysis will further contribute to the understanding of group structure.

THE UNEVEN DISTRIBUTION OF GROUP CONFLICT

Although group therapists and researchers have not yet begun to search for the group's transformational shape, some nevertheless have noticed several important compositional features of the group that imply the wide variation of conflict levels "around the room." In chapters 1 and 2 on group structure and group composition the basic diagnostic and emotion structure of the group was shown to reflect this variation.

Spotnitz (1976) indicates that a balance of polar forces, such as the blend of placid and volatile persons and those who arouse excitement with those who check it, tends to equalize the divergence in personality structure in the group.

This occurs despite differences in each member's tension level or defensive posture. Such a view raises the question of the relative difference in weight or magnitude of conflict members bring to bear on the overall group tension level. For example, does a placid person actually balance a volatile one? Can a regulator type really balance an instigator type? What then is the meaning of balance?

It seems quite obvious that a volatile group member conveys far more conflict-weight than a matching placid member. A psychopathic dyscontrolled type expresses far more conflict than a complementary obsessionally controlled one. These reflect complementary or polar diagnostic types, but the amount of tension implicit in their polarity is certainly not equal. Ackerman (1959) even refers to "right and wrong emotions" and Spotnitz (1976) refers to "toxic emotions" in terms of balance. Even here, however, complementarity and balance may have special meaning. Can hopefulness ever really balance despair? Does timidity balance ferocity? Are "happy" and "sad" emotions that contain an implicitly equal amount of conflict? Apparently, polarity does not imply equal weight even though the emotions involved are opposite and reflect a measure of balance. Antagonistic or polar matching of group members' personalities suggests a meaning more complex than the heuristic meaning of balance connotes.

Approaches to Group Balance

The focus on balance, complementarity, and antagonistic matching of group member's personalities is one that recognizes the importance of variation and range of personality style (Gerscovich, 1976). The issue of balance is based upon the diagnostic criteria examined in previous chapters, and relates to the idea that a maximum expression of the entire range of emotions facilitates the group process.

The formulation of an ideal group balance is addressed by Spotnitz (1976). He states, "In comparing heterogeneous groups . . . some therapists regard diagnosis as an inadequate source of information on how patients will function together. These practitioners therefore try to assertain the types of defenses that each candidate for a group activates in interpersonal situations. An assessment of current impulses and defenses is one aspect of achieving a balancing of personality types; this facilitates the functioning of the group as a unit." Here, Spotnitz is searching for different ways of creating balance through the construction of an ideal group composition. It may be determined by focusing on diagnosis. If this is not feasible, information on the nature of impulses in group members may provide sufficient guidelines; if not, then the formulation of an ideal group composition may depend on information about ego-defenses of the members.

The attempt by Spotnitz to find alternate routes to an ideal group composition is interesting in view of the discussion of emotion and defense in chapters 5 and 6. The discussion in these chapters showed that diagnostic, emotion, and ego-defense structures are linked in a systematic way so that virtually an identical ideal group composition may be derived whether the focus is on one personality domain or the other.

PERSONALITY TYPE AND CONFLICT-MAGNITUDE

In order to understand the complexity of the meaning of balance it is necessary to consider that a sense of the weight or magnitude of conflict inherent in any personality type must be included in formulations of member matching in the group composition. Authors and group therapists have generally perceived the overall nature of conflict within the group and considered its expression as a necessary one for maintaining a group therapeutic condition (Frank, 1955). However, the effects of the magnitude of conflict inherent in any personality type on the infrastructure of the group has not been examined. The importance of such conflict-effects are implied by Yalom (1970) who states that "patients should be exposed to a variety of conflict areas, coping methods, and conflicting interpersonal styles and that conflict in general is essential to the therapeutic process."

Yalom refers to the importance of the heterogeneous nature of the group composition. He considers that the heterogeneous group will produce a group dissonance and generate conflict. The conflict in turn will need to be resolved. Yet a detailed examination of the effects of such conflict on group structure has not been pursued in the group psychotherapy literature.

There is general agreement in the group therapy literature that in order to generate conflict, group composition should be based upon a diagnostic heterogeneity that includes polar role styles or complementary interpersonal styles. It is this diagnostic heterogeneity that constitutes the accepted definition of balance in the group. Foulkes and Anthony (1965) consider that the "degree of conflict determines the amount of involvement and hence degree of tension in the group." They indicate that the degree of conflict is based upon a "resonance" of group dispositional types: complementary relationships such as those between members expressing dominance versus submission, elation versus depression, and voyeurism versus exhibitionism. The question raised by such formulations concerns the effect different "weights" of dominance, submission, elation, depression, voyeurism, and exhibitionism have on the underlying structure and actual balance of the group. For example, if one were to plot these differing weights in order to represent them as a geometric shape, would the shape that is produced resemble a circle? The answer can be in the affirmative only if each dispositional type contains the same conflict-weight. Otherwise differing conflict-weights or magnitudes among dispositional types must imply a particular underlying conflict matrix that assumes some representational shape other than a circle.

GROUP STRUCTURE: A FUNCTION OF DIFFERENCES IN PERSONALITY
CONFLICT-MAGNITUDE

When Yalom (1970) considers cohesiveness to be a cardinal principle
guiding the group composition one may wonder whether such cohesiveness is
not really a group texture based upon the correct balance of personalities and
the correct configuration of conflict. Foulkes and Anthony (1965) obliquely
refer to this idea. They state, "The living portrait of the group is most
uniformly painted in terms of conflict which is evident in manifest or latent
forms in every group situation." Group cohesion may refer to the balance of
conflicts in the group.

A useful macrocosmic analogy relating group conflict to structure refers to
the principle that inner forces of a space determine its actual shape. This principle was also implied by the general theory of relativity formulated by Einstein. Einstein postulated that mass determines gravitational forces in space. As
applied to groups, the Einsteinian position would attempt to predict the actual
shape of the group from the interaction if its inner forces. The circular shape
therefore may not accurately reflect the variation of inner group forces. The
spirit of this latter view is shared by Ezriel (1957) who indicates that "the
common group tension which may be regarded as consisting of the various
unconsciously determined pushes and pulls exerted by the members of the
group on one another and on the therapist . . . make the patients react to one
another, make them select, reject, and distort one another's remarks, model
and remodel one another's interventions, until gradually a certain common
group structure emerges. The common group structure is thus a vector, the
resultant of the individual contributions of all members of the group." Ezriel is
careful here not to define this vector as a mean or average vector of all individual contributions, tensions, or conflicts. Thus Ezriel implicitly recognizes
that group balance is a complex phenomenon. His position suggests that
cumulative conflict may be represented by some mathematical function. Such
a mathematical statement would reflect the uneven distribution of conflict-
weight inherent in the various role types of the group. The vector or vectors
comprise a "common group structure." They may be visualized as points of
reference of the group shape. This group structure may be made more understandable if represented as a geometric model or shape reflecting its inner
forces.

Both Lewin and Ezriel imply this correspondence between group structure and group shape, and scholars of group therapy research indicate that one
way of deriving a sense of group vectors or group structure is to examine polar
role conflict of group members.

ROLE DIFFERENTIATION AS AN ASPECT OF OVERALL GROUP FORCE

The function of polar role conflict in the formation of the group structure
also has relevance to the understanding of group role differentiation process.
Dunphy (1968) and Mann, Gibbard, and Hartman (1967) consider impulse-

expression and impulse-suppression to be one such core polar dimension. Gibbard, Hartman, and Mann (1974) indicate that, "All of these psychodynamic models of role differentiation assume that specialized roles, especially the more visible leadership roles are reflections of and attempts to resolve the basic polarities of group life: positive versus negative feelings, especially toward authority; rational versus irrational responses to conflict and complexity and solidarity versus fragmentation."

What is overlooked in this view of the polarities of group functioning is the extent to which comparable role structures can be identified across groups. Each of the polar forces is weighted differently and may produce effects not immediately apparent from its opposition. For example, although an aggressive member of the group can create more apparent shifts in the group mood, the presence of an opposite passive member frequently creates the possibility for other group members to project fantasies onto this person more easily. Thus the presence of the passive member sometimes creates effects in the group that, although less conspicuous than those generated by the aggressive member, may sometimes be more profound. The point is that whatever the role ingredients may be, they can be seen to be part of the group structure, and researchers can learn more about the entire process of differentiation through them. In constructing an implied group shape, the process of role differentiation may be understood to be embedded in a similarity structure. This similarity structure is revealed within the true group space; that is, all group roles can be related on the basis of their particular conflict magnitude.

It is this goal of determining the implied group shape and thus of identifying the true group structure that shall be attempted here. An understanding of conflict variation of specific group polar role types will provide a method for determining the transformational group shape; that is, determining the specific conflict-weight for each polar role type will provide mathematical imperatives that lead inexorably to the actual abstract geometric shape: a transformation of the group circle.

CONFLICT-WEIGHTS OF GROUP DISPOSITIONAL TYPES

Eight basic dispositional types were described in earlier chapters and each type was analyzed with respect to its emotion, trait, ego-defense, and diagnostic component. These elements of the personality structure found in each dispositional type constituted an internally consistent theoretical network. For example, in the controlled type, the ego-defense of intellectualization ensures the condition of control, while in the dyscontrolled type the ego-defense of regression ensures a generalized impulse condition. Control is opposite to dyscontrol just as intellectualization is opposite to regression. The internal consistency of the theoretical network may be demonstrated with regard to each of the polar dispositional pairs at all levels of personality.

TRUST VERSUS DISTRUST

By inspection, and through a content analysis of the polar dispositional pairs, a distinct pattern of variation in conflict-weight emerges in each type of a pair. For example, the trusting type expresses a personality tendency of absorbing stimuli from the environment. Acceptance is the emotion that contains the absorbtion inclination. On a diagnostic level, the hysterical disposition best reflects this syndrome, and the ego-defense of denial manages the tendency to want to absorb and accept. A person who responds in this manner may find difficulties in interpersonal relationships. Yet such difficulties are certainly not those that generate great conflict. The trusting type is a low conflict-weight type. The amount of conflict-force this member exerts in a group is relatively mild.

In contrast, the distrustful type expresses the need to reject. Disgust is the emotion that contains this repulsion tendency. On a diagnostic level, the paranoid disposition best reflects this syndrome, and the ego-defense of projection manages the tendency to want to repel and reject. A person who responds in this dispositional or habitual way usually experiences significant difficulties in interpersonal relationships. They are the sort of difficulties that generate great conflict and may be considered to be heavily conflict-weighted. The distrustful type, therefore, is a relatively high conflict-weight type and the amount of conflict-force exerted by such a member on a group is relatively great.

From the standpoint of theoretical consistency then, role polarity cannot also mean equality of conflict-weight or magnitude in terms of group balance. The trustful-romantic and distrustful-scrutinizer types are polar opposites, represent antagonistic matching, and meet the criteria of complementarity set forth above. Yet, they demonstrate that complementarity of role matching, or ego-defense matching, will invariably produce an imbalance in the conflict forces exerted onto the group by the presence of any two such members.

It is hypothesized here that of the eight basic dispositional types, four represent types that express lesser conflict-force onto the group, while their opposites reflect types that exert significantly greater conflict-force onto the group. Any group composed on the basis of complementary or antagonistic matching will not produce a balance of conflict-force in the group. Instead, it is proposed that such matching produces a group which exists in quite a state of conflict imbalance.

The remaining polar dispositional types exert differing degrees of conflict-force on the group as described in the following.

TIMID VERSUS AGGRESSIVE

The timid dispositional type expresses a kind of "pullingness." What this means is that the timid type may express withdrawal and inhibition behavior. Fear is the emotion that contains this "pulling" tendency. On a diagnostic level, the passive disposition best reflects this syndrome, and the ego-defense of repression manages the tendency to want to "pull away." Such a person may be quite troubled, yet the amount of conflict-force exerted on the group by this member's presence is low. This timid type is an unobtrusive group member.

In contrast, the aggressive type expresses the need to "push." Anger is the emotion that contains the pushing tendency. On a diagnostic level, the aggressive disposition best reflects this syndrome, and the ego-defense of displacement manages the pushing tendency. A person who habitually responds in this manner usually has great difficulty in conducting interpersonal relationships. This person exerts a great amount of conflict-force onto the group environment.

Thus, in terms of conflict-weight, the opposite dispositional role types of timid-innocent versus aggressive-scapegoater are quite unevenly balanced. Timid types exert low conflict-force onto the group while aggressive types exert a high amount of conflict-force onto the group.

GREGARIOUS VERSUS DEPRESSED

The gregarious type expresses the personality tendency of attraction. The emotion of joy contains this attraction tendency. On a diagnostic level, a manic disposition reflects this syndrome, and the ego-defense of reaction-formation manages the tendency of attraction insofar as attraction is equated with sexuality. A person who responds in this dispositional manner generally enjoys highly stimulating interpersonal environments. The amount of conflict-force exerted onto the group by this gregarious type is low. Such types are generally work oriented.

The opposite dispositional type is the depressed personality which is one that expresses the tendency of "needingness." Sorrow is the emotion that contains the loss and need elements. On a diagnostic level, the depressive disposition reflects this feeling. The ego-defense of compensation manages the tendency to want to regain loss and to relieve "needingness." A person who responds in this dispositional manner finds difficulties in most interpersonal interactions. This person exerts a great deal of conflict-force onto the group.

The polar dispositional role types of gregarious-puritan versus depressed-reintegrator are thus quite unevenly balanced in terms of conflict weight. Gregarious types exert a relatively low conflict-force onto the group while depressed types exert a high amount of conflict-force onto the group.

CONTROLLED VERSUS DYSCONTROLLED

The controlled type expresses a tendency to move in the environment in order to know it and to control it. The emotion of expectation expresses this tendency. On a diagnostic level, the obsessive disposition reflects this syndrome, and the ego-defense of intellectualization manages the tendency to-want to know and to control. A person responding in this dispositional manner can adapt to interpersonal interactions in a relatively uncomplicated way and such a type exerts a low level of conflict-force onto the group.

The opposite dyscontrolled type expresses the tendency of stopping when disoriented. In order not to become disoriented therefore, continual movement is aimed for. Surprise is the emotion expressing this tendency. On a diagnostic level, the psychopathic disposition with its impulsive, and dyscontrolled behavior characterizes this type. The ego-defense of regression manages the tension of disorientation and helps maintain the overall impulse condition. A person who typically uses regression responds in an immature manner and expresses a great deal of conflict-force. This type generally experiences a whole host of difficulties in interpersonal affairs.

The polar dispositional role types of controlled-intellectualizer and dyscontrolled-child are thus also unevenly balanced in terms of conflict-weight. Controlled types exert a low level of conflict-force onto the group while dyscontrolled types exert a great amount of conflict-force onto the group. The effect of these high and low conflict types on group tension level will be discussed in the following section.

TENSION LEVEL VERSUS CONFLICT FORCE

Tension level of the group may be affected equally by high or low conflict-force personality types. The difference between tension level and conflict-force may be understood through the nature of the relationship between emotion and defense mechanisms. Defensive behavior as described in chapters 5 and 6 on ego-defense structure of groups, helps sustain tension at a rather low level irrespective of the presence of either high or low conflict-weight types in the group. When defenses are maintained, emotion becomes attenuated and tension level decreases. When group tension level is too low, the resistance of members increases so that therapeutic motivation also remains relatively low. It is only when defensive maneuvers are confronted that group tension level will tend to rise. The expression of defense mechanisms in both high and low conflict-weight types therefore tends to produce a minimum of group tension. Despite the even distribution of group tension, either at lower or at higher levels, the varied conflict inherent in polar role types remains in a state of imbalance due to the presence of high conflict-weighted types and low conflict-weighted types. The group may regulate tension level (Hebb, 1966), but the imbalance of conflict structure exists whether the tension level of the group is high or low.

Another way to understand the difference between group tension level and conflict-force is by means of considering the implicit difference in diagnoses between members (Kellerman and Plutchik, 1978). Some diagnoses are inherently more problematic than others. For example, a psychopathic dispositional type will encounter more difficulty in interpersonal contact than will the opposite obsessional dispositional type. As indicated previously, the basic group diagnostic structure is divided into high and low conflict types. Since the tension level of the group is determined by the nature of ego-defenses as they manage emotions, then the tension level of the group is an ego-defense level of the group. This suggests that when group therapists discuss the balance of forces in any group they are probably referring to the ego-defense structure of the group, or to the character level of the group. Group therapists even characterize psychotherapy of individuals as an analysis of intrapsychic forces and group psychotherapy as an analysis of character or ego-defense structure.

The expression of ego-defenses tends to produce the even spread of tension irrespective of diagnostic type. Conflict, however, is not evenly spread. The weight or magnitude of conflict refers, essentially, to the relative degree of social adaptation reflected by the various diagnoses, of which ego-defense is only one aspect. Tension, therefore, is regulated by ego-defense, and the conflict-weight inherent in any diagnostic type is determined by the intrapsychic nature of any particular diagnostic disposition.

Implications for the Group Shape

It may be that the circular apparent shape of the group is a reflection of the ego-defense level of personality; that is, the cumulative operation of defenses among members of the group tends to spread tension evenly through the group. This is true even if some members are highly defended while others are not so defended. Changes in any member's defensive posture will simply affect the overall group tension level so that tension tends to rise and fall accordingly. A therapy group also tends to find its own tension level. This means that as the overall defense organization of the group becomes established, tension level becomes regulated and stable. In this sense, the spread of tension is even, and Lewin's contention that the spread of tension of a field tends to show a regular distribution is perhaps supported by this formulation.

In summary, it is important to remember that the organization of conflict-magnitude distributed throughout the basic dispositional role types of the group reveals four high conflict-weight types that exert a high degree of conflict force onto the group, and four low conflict-weight types that direct a low conflict-force onto the group. The gregarious, timid, trusting, and controlled types exert less conflict-force onto the group while the depressed, aggressive, distrustful, and dyscontrolled ones exert greater conflict-force onto the group.

The division of conflict-force into low conflict-weight and high conflict-weight types reveals the unevenness of the theoretical abstract shape of the group. This difference in conflict-weight of the various diagnostic role types may be observed in several experimental studies designed to measure emotion and personality.

THE ACCESSIBLE VERSUS THE IMPEDANCE STATES

The division of low conflict-weight diagnostic types versus their opposite high conflict-weight types was originally observed in a study reported by Kellerman (1965) and Kellerman and Plutchik (1968) which describes the development of a personality test designed to measure the relative activation of each of the eight emotion categories. The test, the Emotions Profile Index (Plutchik and Kellerman, 1974), described in earlier chapters, was administered to three groups of female subjects who varied along a maladjustment continuum. The first group consisted of normal subjects with an absence of psychiatric symptoms. The maladjusted groups consisted of hospitalized patients divided on the basis of moderate or severe psychiatric disturbance.

In this study, a series of personality terms were paired and subjects chose one personality term out of a pair to reflect a best self-description. All personality terms were correlated to their constituent underlying emotions. The average emotions profile of each group was plotted with respect to the eight basic emotion categories. These data generally indicated that the gregarious, timid, trusting, and controlled categories tended to be highly activated in the normal group, while the depressed, aggressive, distrustful, and dyscontrolled categories were hardly activated at all in the normal group. As maladjustment increased the emotions profile changed significantly. Illustrative case examples of individual emotion profiles are offered in Kellerman (1965), Kellerman and Plutchik (1968), and Plutchik and Kellerman (1974).

Figure 7-1 demonstrates a hypothetical "normal" accessible profile and its mirror opposite "disturbed" impedance profile. The terms accessible and impedance are used here as a way of signifying the difference in conflict-weight of each type. Since normal and maladjusted subjects differ in a systematic way with regard to emotion-personality patterns, the pattern exhibited by a normal group may be considered one that reflects its accessibility, while the pattern emerging for disturbed subjects may reflect their overall impeded condition.

An examination of Figure 7-1 shows that the conflict-weight implied by a normal profile cannot be the same as the conflict-weight of its mirror-image disturbed profile. The accessible personality types contain and express emotions that are more frequently seen in normal and otherwise undisturbed populations. The controlled, gregarious, timid, and trusting types express emotions that are typically social and may reflect behavior that is more interpersonal. The dyscontrolled, depressed, aggressive, and distrusting types express emotions characteristic of antisocial, impetuous, and even morbid behavior. Therefore, persons who express the roles defined in chapter 3 of puritan, intellectualizer, romantic, and innocent express less conflict-weight in the group. These roles correspond to the accessible personality dimensions. Persons who occupy the roles of reintegrator, child, scrutinizer, and scape-

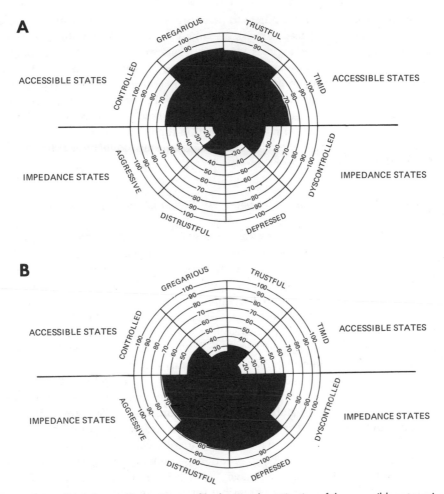

Figure 7-1.   (A) A "normal" emotions profile showing the activation of the accessible categories. (B) A mirror-image "disturbed" emotions profile showing the activation of the impedance categories. The midpoint of the circle represents 0 percent. The outer rim of the circle represents 100 percent.

goater express more conflict-weight in the group. These latter roles correspond to impedance personality dimensions. The findings by Kellerman and Plutchik and others (Tomkins, 1964) that apply to polar personality dimensions also have relevance to the polar role types of the group. The results by Kellerman and Plutchik indicated that "groups varied significantly in the frequency of choices of high and low conflict traits according to theory. Each group had a distinctive emotion profile."

This finding suggests that perhaps the overall basic emotional composition of any system, individual or group, contains elements that are unequally weighted. It is more "normal" for certain emotional patterns to become persistently expressed than it is for others to be expressed. It is more normal and less disturbed to experience and express a preponderance of accessible emotions that it is to experience and express a preponderance of the impeded emotions.

Hence, all the basic emotions in the group as they become expressed through role types produce an imbalance in the conflict nature of the group. The impedance states are more conflictual than are their respective opposite accessible counterparts. They are more severe. It is for this reason that the inequality in role type either must be shown in the manifest group structure or expressed as an abstract or implied shape of the group. Polarity is thus considered to reflect an inequality of opposites in the group structure.

The Accessible versus the Impedance States: Experimental Studies

The Emotions Profile Index has been utilized in many different kinds of studies that by interpolation show the accessible-impedance separation. The test has been used to compare the relative degree of personality differences of psychiatric populations (Sheppard, Fiorentino, Collins, and Merlis, 1969). It has been applied in the study of diagnostic syndromes (Platman, Plutchik, Fieve, and Lawlor, 1969; Fiorentino, Sheppard, and Merlis, 1970). It has been adapted for use with dolphins (Kellerman, 1966), baboons (Buirski et al., 1973; Kellerman, Buirski, and Plutchik, 1974), and chimpanzees (Buirski, Plutchik, and Kellerman, 1978). Finally, it has also been used to diagnose groups (Kellerman and Maliver, 1977; Kellerman and Plutchik, 1978). In all the studies of humans, animals, and groups, the division of the accessible states and the impedance states seems to be a uniformly consistent division.

The application of the Emotions Profile Index categories to groups seemed especially useful because the eight ideal basic role types are conceptualized to contain the eight basic emotion-personality categories. Since the role types of this ideal group composition are divided into accessible versus impedance types, then the mathematical formulation that may be applied to Emotions Profile Index polar categories may also be applied to the division of accessible versus impedance roles of the group; that is, measures of conflict that could be imposed on Emotions Profile Index patterns have relevance to role-conflict measures of the group. This application is also relevant to the problem of plotting the transformational group shape, The new shape may be determined by the actual difference in conflict-weight or conflict-magnitude of the accessible versus the impedance role states.

SUMMARY

The transformational imperatives inherent in the group structure include magnitude differences in role-conflict structure. It is the uneven distribution of group conflict that is reflected in the overall group role composition. This uneven spread of conflict reveals the possibility that the circular group shape only relfects what Chomsky would consider a transformational condition; that is, that the circle is a shorthand method—a condensation as it were—of a more complex shape. First, the circle may be an averaging representation that reflects a balance and smoothing out of the imbalance in conflict-weight differences of the accessible versus the impedance categories. Second, the circular shape of the group is one that may only reflect the regularity in the rise and fall of tension level irrespective of whether this rise and fall was caused by high or low conflict-weighted role types. In the following chapter an attempt will be made to describe how these imperatives are used to transform the apparent circular shape of the group to its theoretical implied one.

The Transformational Shape of the Group: The New Shape

In this chapter, the difference between accessible and impedance polar role types will be formalized by a mathematical relationship. This relationship is a comparison of conflict-magnitude between each of the polar accessible and impedance role types. The derived equation will permit the group's transformational shape to be plotted and viewed graphically and the new shape will be analyzed with reference to its implications for the group structure. This new structure then will be compared to similar models used in other scientific and artistic disciplines. In the final part of the chapter the relation of this new shape to spatial models will be proposed, and prognostic implications of role types will be drawn from these analyses.

CONFLICT-WEIGHT MEASURES OF ACCESSIBLE AND IMPEDANCE STATES

The mathematical relationship of polar role conflict also corresponds to a clinical sense of conflict between accessible and impedance states. This accessible-impedance difference may be understood by creating a set of hypotheses with respect to emotion activation levels on the Emotions Profile Index. These hypothetical activation levels are based upon Emotion Profile Index percent activation levels rather than on percentile ranks. For example, a person whose emotions profile percent "trustful" score is highly activated and whose "distrustful" score hardly activated at all could be perceived to experience a low degree of conflict; that is, if the trustful score were to be completely activated in Figure 7-1 of chapter 7 and the distrustful score entirely unactivated, conflict would be at a minimum. If, on the other hand, the trustful score were not at all activated, but the distrustful score fully activated, conflict would be at its maximum. If both trustful and distrustful were equally activated to the 100 percent point, conflict would not equal 50 percent. Rather, because of the weightedness or impedance quality to the distrustful dimension, its measure of conflict is influenced to a greater extent by its impedance nature as compared to an equal activation of the trustful dimension. This produces a tilt of conflict-balance so that conflict is higher than 50 percent. It is this sort of tilt in the conflict-balance of the group with respect to each of the eight role types that implies its transformational shape.

Table 8-1 is based upon a conventional mathematical procedure of establishing limits in the derivation of an equation. Such an equation is designed to establish a relationship between forces whether physical or psychological. A percent rank order description of polar conflict is presented in this table. This ranking establishes a basis for understanding the nature of conflict between the accessible versus the impedance states so that the "weightedness" differences between these accessible and impedance states may be better understood.

It may be seen in Table 8-1 that conflict scores rise in direct relation to the rise of impedance category scores and indirectly in relation to accessible category scores. This difference presumably reflects the difference in adaptation or coping potential between accessible and impedance states; that is, a rise in conflict scores will tend to correlate positively with a rise in maladjustment and maladaptiveness. The impedance states reflect this impairment in adaptation and coping potential more directly.

Figure 8-1 illustrates the correlations between the high conflict inherent in maladaptive impedance states, and the relatively lower conflict inherent in

Table 8-1. The mathematical limits of the difference in polar conflict-weight for accessible versus impedance states:* A rank ordering of conflict-range from 0 to 100 percent.

RANK ORDER DESCRIPTION OF CONFLICT	ACCESSIBLE DIMENSION† (percent)	IMPEDANCE DIMENSION** (percent)	CONFLICT SCORE (percent)
Minimum conflict	100	0	0
Low conflict	0	0	25
Medium conflict	50	50	50
High conflict	100	100	75
Maximum conflict	0	100	100

*These scores correspond to clinical judgments of the difference in degree of maladjustment between polar accessible and impedance states.

†Accessible dimensions include: trustful, timid, controlled, and gregarious.

**Impedance dimensions include: distrustful, aggressive, dyscontrolled, and depressed.

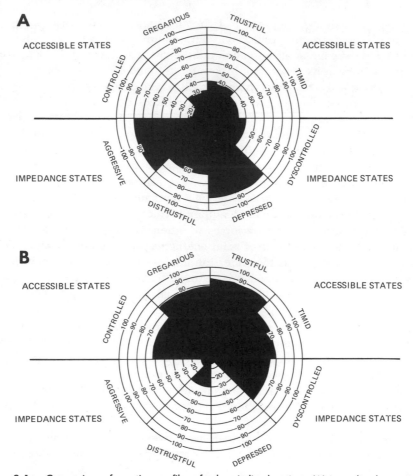

Figure 8-1.   Comparison of emotion profiles of a hospitalized patient: (A) immediately preceding a suicidal attempt; (B) immediately following a suicidal attempt. The activation of impedance categories correlates to the presuicidal period. The activation of accessible categories corresponds to the postsuicidal period. The midpoint of the circle represents 0 percent. The outer rim of the circle represents 100 percent. (Reprinted with permission from the *Journal of Psychiatric Research* 8:127–137, Platman, Plutchik, and Weinstein, Psychiatric, Physiological, Behavioral, and Self-Report Measures in Relation to a Suicide Attempt, copyright 1971, Pergamon Press, Ltd.

the accessible coping states. These profiles reflect a pre- and postsuicidal emotion sketch of a 49-year-old female hospitalized patient (Platman, Plutchik, and Weinstein, 1971). They show a glaring correspondence between the high activation of the impedance states and absence of significant activation in the accessible dimensions, immediately preceding a suicidal attempt. Following the suicidal attempt, with the sudden extirpation of conflict, the profile shows a highly activated accessible pattern with hardly any activation of the impedance dimensions whatsoever. The presuicidal state was reflected in high impedance or maladaptive potential. The postsuidical state was reflected by an absence of great conflict.

This illustration is offered to demonstrate the clinical implications of psychological and emotional conflict as it becomes reflected in the "weightedness" or magnitude of one element of a polar pair against the other. These elements are the weightedness of the accessible emotions versus the impedance emotions.

The Stress and Strain of Conflict

In order to understand and derive all remaining quantitative permutations between polar types the concept of conflict may be divided into two distinct elements. The element of "weight" or magnitude relates to the idea of conflict stress. Magnitude of the conflict refers to the absolute severity or absolute activation of one dimension against the other.

In examining Figure 8-1 it may be seen that each element in a polar pair may have an absolute weight. For example, the trustful accessible dimension may be activated to the 75 percent level. The distrustful impedance dimension also may be activated to 75 percent, but its absolute weight would be more than 75. The activation of impedance states weigh more or are more severe than equal amounts of activation of accessible states, and this is reflected in the stress element of conflict. A person who experiences low trust and high distrust is far more conflicted than one who experiences high trust and low distrust.

Figure 8-1 also shows not only that there are absolute magnitude differences between polar dimensions, but also that the relative activation of polar pairs includes an implicit distance feature. The distance feature contains the idea of conflict-strain and is the second element of conflict. Distance between opposites refers to the net potential momentum one force would have pushing or stretching against the other. It influences the conflict measure in the way that distance influences physical force fields (Caianiello, 1966). For example, each ring on the circle in Figure 8-1 represents 10 percent activation. The center of the circle is equal to zero activation while the outer ring of the circle is equal to 100 percent activation. If the trustful and distrustful dimensions were each activated to 75 percent they would not be 7.5 units each distant from the center zero point. This imbalance is based upon the finding that the impedance part of the circle containing impeded diagnostic states represents an area of the circle that is different than the arc of the circle containing accessible categories. The impedance part of the circle constitutes a condensed area and therefore the stretch of distance from the center point of the circle to an equal point on the circle of either an accessible or impedance state cannot be the same. Just as a given magnitude of any impedance state is greater than the magnitude of its opposite accessible state, so too does a given distance of the impedance state reflect a longer stretch of distance from the center zero point as compared to the same apparent distance for its opposite accessible state. Therefore, 7.5 units from zero on the impedance side of the circle may reflect a truer distance of perhaps twice that of the accessible side. The impedance side may then be 15 units distant from the zero point while its accessible opposite is only 7.5 units distant from the zero point. This distance difference is expressed as the strain element of conflict and may be compared to the distance covered by the stretching of a spring. The important point to remember is that the circle really may be a shorthand group shape. The difference in degree of conflict inherent in accessible versus impedance states reveals that both magnitude and distance differences are not accounted for by the circular form. Impedance states contain both more stress and more strain potential than their equally activated polar accessible counterparts.

The Conflict Equation: K

The derivation of the conflict equation was approached in two ways. First, the terms of the equation were based upon the elements of stress and strain inherent in any polar conflict; that is, the terms were based upon the difference in conflict between an accessible state and its opposite impedance state. Second, clinical estimates of conflict based upon the relative activation of any polar pair correlated highly to quantitative results derived from the conflict score of that polar pair as measured by the Emotions Profile Index. A group of clinicians were able to estimate accurately the amount of conflict that would be expected in a person who for example experienced high trust and low distrust, or low trust and high distrust, or equal amounts of trust and distrust, and these relative comparisons were consistent with actual Emotion Profile scores. Derivation of the equation was guided by the limits set forth in Table 8-1.

The Emotions Profile Index may be used to display any emotional configuration, and particular patterns may be measured in terms of their polar conflict. In terms of group functioning, a similar method may be used. This sort of close correspondence between group functioning and personality has been proposed by Cattell (1956). Cattell coined the term "syntality" to indicate that group structure is analogous to individual personality, and in part the use of the term syntality assumes the concept of group personality. The emotion profiles derived for a therapy group (Kellerman and Maliver, 1977) showed that absolute polar conflict of accessible versus impedance categories can generate a profile implying such a group personality.

In the equation for polar conflict, the *Kellerman Score* represented by the letter K is the designated symbol for conflict. The equation is represented as:

$$K = \frac{\dfrac{I^2 + 20\,I + 1000 - A^2}{10}}{40}\ 10; \text{ or more simply as: } K = I^2 + .5I + 25 - A^2,$$

where K equals conflict, I equals Impedance state and A equals Accessible state. The remaining terms of the equation are designed to convert raw score range in Emotions Profile Index scoring to an absolute percent range of zero to 100.

Table 8-2 presents the K values for a comparison matrix of accessible versus impedance categories in terms of 10 percent differences. Any polarity conflict score may be seen from this table. Scores of the accessible categories of trustful, gregarious, timid, and controlled are located in rows, and scores of impedance categories of distrustful, depressed, aggressive, and dyscontrolled are located in columns. An accessible trustful percent score of 20 as it compares to an impedance percent score of 20 generates a *Kellerman Conflict Score* of 35. An accessible score of 80 as compared to an impedance distrustful score of 20 yields a *Kellerman Conflict Score* of 20, while the opposite configuration, that is, an impedance distrustful score of 80 as compared to an accessible trustful score of 20 yields a *Kellerman Conflict Score* of 80. Such comparisons may be made by referring to Table 8-2.

In the study by Kellerman (1965) and Kellerman and Plutchik (1968), Emotion Profile Index scores were computed for subjects who were divided in terms of their relative degree of maladjustment. This study established the nature of a normal profile in which the accessible dimensions are highly activated and the impedance dimensions only mildly activated. The categories of incorporation, reproduction, protection, and exploration represent these accessible prototype dimensions. They are translated into the personality dimensions of trustful, gregarious, timid, and controlled respectively.

Table 8-2.   *Kellerman scores for each pair of opposite categories.*

		ACCESSIBLE STATES (PERCENT SCORE)*									
		100	90	80	70	60	50	40	30	20	10	0
IMPEDANCE STATES (PERCENT SCORE)†	0	0.0	4.8	9.0	12.8	16.0	18.8	21.0	22.8	24.0	24.8	25.0
	10	5.3	10.0	14.3	18.0	21.3	24.0	26.3	28.0	29.3	30.0	30.3
	20	11.0	15.7	20.0	23.8	27.0	29.8	32.0	33.8	35.0	35.8	36.0
	30	17.3	22.0	26.3	30.0	33.3	36.0	38.3	40.0	41.3	42.0	42.3
	40	24.0	28.7	33.0	37.8	40.0	42.8	45.0	46.8	48.0	48.8	49.0
	50	31.3	36.0	40.3	44.0	47.3	50.0	52.3	54.0	55.3	56.0	56.3
	60	39.0	43.7	48.0	51.8	55.0	57.8	60.0	61.8	63.0	63.8	64.0
	70	47.3	52.0	56.3	60.0	63.3	66.0	68.3	70.0	71.3	72.0	72.3
	80	56.0	60.7	65.0	68.8	72.0	74.8	77.0	78.8	80.0	83.3	81.0
	90	65.3	70.0	74.3	78.0	81.3	84.0	86.3	88.0	89.1	90.0	90.3
	100	75.0	79.8	84.0	87.8	91.0	93.8	96.0	97.8	99.0	99.8	10U.0

*Accessible states include: trustful, timid, controlled, and gregarious.

†Impedance states include: distrustful, aggressive, dyscontrolled, and depressed.

A normal profile is one in which trustful is activated to 80 percent of maximum, gregarious to 80 percent, timid to 70 percent, and controlled to 65 percent. The categories of rejection, deprivation, destruction, and orientation are equivalent to the personality dimensions of distrustful, depressed, aggressive, and dyscontrolled respectively. They represent the impedance dimensions. A normal profile is one in which the dimension of distrustful is activated to 30 percent, the depressed dimension to 25 percent, the aggressive dimension to 15 percent and the dyscontrolled dimension to 40 percent.

Figure 7-1 shows a relatively normal emotions profile and its maladaptive opposite image. The conflict scores based upon the activation levels of the normal profile and its maladaptive mirror-image profile are presented in Table 8-3. This table shows the distinct variation of conflict between the normal profile and its maladaptive mirror-image profile with respect to the conflict differences of accessible and impedance categories.

Figure 7-1 and Table 8-3 vividly portray the profound difference between high accessible and high impedance profiles. The normal profile shows an activation of pleasure and sociability features, reflected in the gregarious and trustful scores, as well as a reasonable activation of caution as reflected in the timid and controlled scores. The limited activation of all impedance categories essentially determines the overall low average conflict of the normal profile as referred to in Table 8-3. The maladaptive mirror-image profile to the normal one displayed in Figure 7-1 shows high activation of depression, suspicion, impulsivity and aggression, and a limited activation of pleasure and caution. Thus it is not surprising that the average overall conflict of the maladaptive profile is high.

The study by Kellerman (1965) and Kellerman and Plutchik (1968) yielded the data from which normative levels of accessible and impedance states in both normal and maladaptive subjects is now established. These normative levels have been supported by data from studies cited earlier. These data have suggested a modification of Plutchik's (1962) original order-

Table 8-3.   A normal emotions profile and its mirror-image maladaptive profile: a comparison of *Kellerman conflict scores* based upon the relation of accessible and impedance states.

	TRUST−DISTRUST (percent)	GREGARIOUS−DEPRESSED (percent)	TIMID−AGGRESSIVE (percent)	CONTROLLED−DYSCONTROLLED (percent)
Normal	80−30	80−25	70−15	65−40
Maladaptive	30−80	25−80	15−70	40−65
Normal*	K = 26	K = 23	K = 20	K = 38
Maladaptive†	K = 78	K = 79	K = 76	K = 64

*The average *Kellerman conflict score* for the normal profile = 27 percent.
†The average *Kellerman conflict score* for the maladaptive profile = 74 percent.

ing of primary emotions. The positions of anger and expectation should be transposed and the positions of fear and surprise should be transposed. All of the figures that are presented here reflect this new approximation.

The Transforming Group Shape

Establishing quantitative normative levels for each personality disposition of a polar pair is important because it suggests that the polar role types of the group also may be understood in the same manner. It then becomes possible to actually plot each role type of the group with reference to a hypothetical tripartate axis, so that the group may be seen in a three-dimensional space. These are the accessible, the impedance, and the conflict axes. The two-dimensional circle of the group may then be seen as a reflection of a deeper structure. This new form reflects conflict-magnitude differences that are exerted onto the group by the presence of accessible and impedance types.

This transpositional method unites basic personality types with those of group role types described in chapter 3. In the accessible category, the trait of trust corresponds to the role type of romantic; the gregarious trait corresponds to the puritan role; the timid trait is equivalent to the role of innocent; and the trait of controlled is the equivalent of the intellectualizer role. In the impedance category, the distrustful trait corresponds to the scrutinizer role; the depressed trait corresponds to the role of reintegrator; the trait of aggressive correlates to the role of scapegoater; and the dyscontrolled trait corresponds to the role of child.

The transformed group shape derives its configuration in three-dimensional space based upon the location of polar types in terms of the respective conflict-force each exerts onto the group surface. The accessible role types are plotted with reference to the normal profile accessible scores seen in Table 8-3, and the impedance role types are plotted with reference to the maladaptive impedance profile scores also seen in Table 8-3.

Emotion-Conflict (K) is a Hyperbolic Paraboloid

The transformational shape of the group is also a representational shape of the Kellerman equation. In physical terms, the equation for K represents the shape of a hyperbolic paraboloid. This shape suggests that polar conflict, whether expressed as polar personality conflict or polar group role-type conflict may also be physically expressed as a hyperbolic paraboloidal form. The group's interactional nature may be viewed with respect to its boundary conditions within this new implied physical shape.

In order to support this formulation it may be useful to ask whether the hyperbolic paraboloidal shape is used in any other scientific discipline as a boundary condition for facilitating the study of interactional effects of any kind. In physics research, for example, the hyperbolic paraboloidal model has been used in the study of the interaction of particles. Walls and Dunn (1974) report a study in which an ion trap was constructed in the form of a hyperbolic paraboloid. Figure 8-2A shows a rendering of this ion trap. The model was able to store ions for long periods of time. The hyperbolic paraboloidal trap was suitable in this experiment because it created a boundary condition in which interactional phenomena could be studied without additional energy entering the field and obscuring effects.

The therapy group boundary condition may be similarly designed to permit a maximal interactional effect among group members. The observation that the group's underlying transformational shape is hyperbolic and parabolic suggests that this particular shape may be compatible with the group's boundary function.

In architectural and in engineering applications, the hyperbolic paraboloidal shape is sometimes used for its elegance and for its capacity to support and distribute great weight. In the therapy group the underlying transformational group shape is one that reveals the difference in magnitude or "weightedness" of role types. As a boundary condition it also may facilitate the dynamic interplay of forces characteristic of an interactional environment.

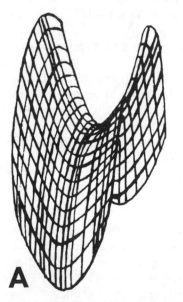

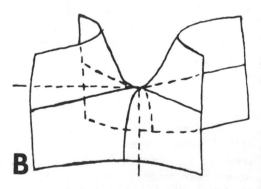

Figure 8-2.   Hyperbolic paraboloidal shape: (A) A common hyperbolic-paraboloidal ion trap (Walls and Dunn, 1974). Ions become trapped and oscillate in the parabolic well. The ion trap becomes an interactional environment for ions and electrons. (B) A simple pattern for constructing a hyperbolic paraboloid (Bers, 1969).

The *Kellerman score* is one that reflects both stress and strain elements of conflict. This score is expressed in the hyperbolic paraboloidal form. Such a form obviously cannot be a circle. It must be assymmetrical representing elements of "weight" and "distance," the stress and strain of conflict respectively. *It is proposed that the hyperbolic paraboloidal form is revealed to be the group boundary form within which the operation of forces inherent in polar personality types become expressed.* The interaction of forces existing in the group's roles is thus enhanced within the hyperbolic paraboloidal implied boundary condition of the group. Figure 8-2A and *B* show two sample hyperbolic paraboloidal shapes.

The two-dimensional apparent circular shape of the group is based upon an ego-defense level of functioning. It locates group members in a circular way and at equidistant points. The implied transformational group shape seen in three-dimensional space is the decondensed or diluted circle—an expression of the implied hyperbolic paraboloid—viewed, as it were, as an uninterrupted surface line. It is not a circular and equidistant positioned shape. Rather it demonstrates an elongation in shape and may be twisting, elliptical, and helicoidal. The new shape is one in which no single area reflects any extra weightedness or conflict-magnitude. This is what is meant by a decondensed circle. It is reconstituted. Before actually plotting this transformational shape in a three-dimensional space the value of spatial models will be considered.

SPATIAL MODELS

The Work of Bales

Several authors have suggested that it is necessary to begin to visualize three-dimensional space in the study of interpersonal behavior (Borgatta, Cattrell, and Mann, 1958; Borgatta and Crowther, 1966; Carter, 1953; and Schutz, 1958). The work of Osgood, Suci, and Tannenbaum (1957) on the semantic differential is perhaps the best known of the research proposing the use of three-dimensional models of personality factors. This sort of model was used to analyze clinical case material.

The most ambitious exploration of interpersonal behavior as understood from a three-dimensional space has been attempted by Bales (1970). Bales has been especially interested in exploring the deepest layers of group structure as seen through a spatial model. To visualize three-dimensional space in the study of interpersonal behavior, appearing and unfolding as it does through the group structure, becomes a scientific imperative for Bales. He states, "In order to understand how personality and group role types relate to each other, we must be able to visualize more than one or two dimensions within which they may differ from each other." There actually has been a plethora of factor analytic studies showing that more than two factors emerge in the study of personality and group behavior (Warren, 1963).

The work by Bales was based upon dual factor analyses of a domain of personality tests and implied traits. Sixty subjects were studied by many different methods. These subjects met in twelve groups of five subjects. They held a series of five two-hour meetings. Each group met with a somewhat different task. There were two interviewing and inference tasks, one somewhat formalized self-analytic task, and two value-dilemma tasks based on clinical cases. Data for all five meetings were pooled for each individual. Individual subjects were plotted on a three-dimensional space according to several personality factors.

One important finding suggested that certain areas of the spatial plot correlated with status position and, by implication, with personality traits and types. Bales found that subjects will generally strive to change their position; they strive to move upward in the space. The location of subjects in the space yielded 26 personality types, and in certain respects this work generated results that paralleled the findings of Strodtbeck and Mann (1956). The 26 types imply spatial areas and are listed in Table 8-4. They are based upon values, attitudes, and motivational style.

A content analysis of these 26 types demonstrates that most contain one or two elements of the eight basic dispositional types. For example, the trustful propensity may be seen to exist in type 3, toward social solidarity and progress; type 4, toward group loyalty and cooperation; type 9, toward emotional supportiveness and warmth; type 11, toward altruistic love; type 17, toward permissive liberalism; type 18, toward trust in the goodness of others; and

Table 8-4. Bales' 26 personality types.

TOWARD:

1.	Material success and power	14.	Individualistic isolationism
2.	Social success	15.	Rejection of social conformity
3.	Social solidarity and progress	16.	Rejection of conservative group belief
4.	Group loyalty and cooperation	17.	Permissive liberalism
5.	Autocratic authority	18.	Trust in the goodness of others
6.	Tough-minded assertiveness	19.	Salvation through love
7.	Rugged individualism and gratification	20.	Self-knowledge and subjectivity
8.	Value relativism and expression	21.	Self-sacrifice for values
9.	Emotional supportiveness and warmth	22.	Rejection of social success
10.	Equalitarianism	23.	Failure and withdrawal
11.	Altruistic love	24.	Withholding of cooperation
12.	Conservative group beliefs	25.	Identification with the underprivileged
13.	Value-determined restraint	26.	Devaluation of the self

Personality trait descriptions are based upon subject's prevailing attitudes and motivations.

type 19, toward salvation through love. Similarly, the distrustful propensity may be seen to exist in type 5, twoard autocratic authority; type 23, toward failure and withdrawal; and type 24, toward withholding of cooperation. One or more of the basic emotion categories are contained within any of the 26 types. Since the 26 types are dispositional types they may be conceived as groupings of traits. The function of the basic emotions in the formation of traits has been elaborated by Reich (1949), and the connection of emotions and traits has been discussed in earlier chapters.

Personality traits contain underlying basic emotions that comprise the nature of the trait itself. Each of the 26 types posited by Bales may be shown to contain basic emotional properties. They may be located in any three-dimensional space in a manner that corresponds to the locations of each of the eight basic emotions or roles. It is proposed that this location system will be consistent, especially since trait behavior is consistent in the personality and persists over time. A three-dimensional space will reflect this consistency whether in the location of traits, roles, or emotions. Furthermore, subjects who are part of any group system may similarly be located in a three-dimensional space in a way that reflects the expression of their basic diagnostic inclinations and attitudes.

The three-dimensional space may increase the power to make relational conclusions of interpersonal behavior and may be especially suited to visualizing the compositional structure of groups with regard to a whole range of variables. The Bales work, reflecting the dimensions of status and power, likeability and task commitment, demonstrated the group's compositional structure with reference to the striving and mobility of members. Members of the group apparently strive to change their positions, and this striving may be traced as location changes in the three-dimensional space.

The tracing of each member's striving direction produced a clear physical upward trend in the space. In addition, this movement revealed several other interesting findings.

> Members are not typically distributed at random or equally throughout the space; more are found on the positive side of the space than on the negative side, and the tendency to be on the positive side is very marked for women as compared to men. More members are found in the forward part of the space than in the backward, and this tendency is more marked for men. On the average, women are further downward, considerably more positive, and slightly backward from the men. Men are about equally distributed between the upward and downward parts of the space, with a few more in the downward part, but women are definitely found more frequently in the lower part of the space. The differences between the positions of men and women are about what might be expected from the cultural stereotypes of the male and female adult sex roles.

Bales' discovery that on the basis of sex stereotypes, women occupy lower positions of status in the space also perhaps implies that even in the role transformations of the therapy work, the resistance to change and working-through is more difficult for women than it is for men. This may be true because of stereotypical rigidities about women inherent in the social system at large regardless of role type.

Bales indicates that the structure of self-analytic groups, "is more like a spiral . . . an irregular web of interconnected group positions." The form or shape of the group structure as a spiral is a tacit recognition that the apparent group structural circular shape may indeed be quite different from its more complex underlying abstract shape. It has prompted Bales to regard the spatial model of group structure as one with power to construct a "higher synthesis" in order to generate new knowledge about important aspects of this structure. "The spatial model, standing for the mathematical model, is the logical structure that gives one a boost in his power to make inferences about relationships." This higher order synthesis becomes more possible when considering the composition of the group in a three-dimensional space.

Group Shape and Process: The Relation of Space and Time

The discovery of fundamental laws of group structure can be advanced by the use of scientific analogies in the formulation of group structure principles. The group may be seen as a microcosm of the environment at large, an issue discussed in earlier chapters. However, the question to be asked now is whether the group may be viewed macrocosmically as well. An analogy to general physical field theory may be useful. One of Einstein's great contributions was his work on the nature of space. Einstein posited an alternate view to the Newtonian idea of an absolute space that cannot be affected by that which it contains. Rather, Einstein posited the notion that the field must be affected by the matter in it; that is, the presence of matter influences the curvature of space (Rindler, 1960). This idea may be used to help develop analogies about the group shape. The shape of the group is not an absolute circle immune to its inner forces. Rather it is a shape that is determined by variation in its diagnostic composition. This is one way in which the group structure is understood as a dynamic model and not a static one.

The model of group structure presented here utilizes the idea of objects becoming portions of space. Caianiello (1966) describes this formulation as one introduced in Descarte's analytical geometry. In relativity theory, a field is characterized by assigning quantities to each part of the space. Within this context, group theory determines all the possible forms of relations of forces in the field. These forms are called field equations. They are partial differential equations and have relevance to the hyperbolic paraboloidal shape of the group. These equations of mathematical physics are called the hyperbolic partial differential equation, the parabolic partial differential equation, and the elliptic partial differential equation. There are also general relativity field theorists who propose curvature to space with hyperbolic and parabolic function—an hypthetical shape (Robertson and Noonan, 1968).

The analogy of group process as a microcosmic reflection of the environment is taken for granted among group therapists. The issue raised here suggests a similar analogy for macrocosmic comparisons; that is, that small group structural properties may reflect macrocosmic structure. The proposition that the hyperbolic paraboloid may exist as the true structural shape of the microcosm called therapy group, may perhaps also be relevant to a proposed shape of the overall physical macrocosmic universe.

General relativity theory also conceives of a macrocosmic four-dimensional space-time continuum. Within this conception, the universe may be seen either as a closed system or as an open one. If a structural form is in the shape of a hyperbolic paraboloid, then an open system is implied in which energy enters and escapes. This conception is expressed in physics: "As the universe expands matter is lost but compensated by creation of new matter" (Bondi, 1961).

The universe of the therapy group as seen in its structural form of the hyperbolic-paraboloid may also be conceived as an open system. However, as described in chapter 4 the system is open only insofar as membership change takes place; that is, older members leave and newer members enter. In this generational movement, elapsed time emerges as the historical continuity element of the group structure. Time becomes a space intersect; that is, time reflects the continuous nature of the group. It is part of the group's infrastructure within the context of the hyperbolic paraboloidal boundary condition. The force exerted by group members who are interacting with dispositionally varied conflict-magnitudes determine this implied shape or boundary condition of the group. In addition, the element of time needs to be symbolized by the presence in the group of a specific infrastructural object. If the aim of the group is to "stay alive," then as a structural factor, time becomes a major variable of the group culture and is a critical factor in the expansion of group life. Time function, therefore, as suggested in chapter 4 exists in the form of the therapist.

The analogies to physical theory drawn here are heuristic devices designed to help penetrate the deepest layers of group structure as they become revealed in the transformational group shape. In the approach developed here the group structure is expressed in a three-dimensional shape. The group process introduces the dimension of time into the group structure. As the group evolves, its shape begins to metamorphose. This metamorphosis is determined, in part, by the ever changing symmetries of the eight basic role types. These role types are interacting, becoming modified, and becoming transformed. They become obliquely arranged and rearranged as a function of the group process. An interesting and compelling similarity of interactional forces in particle theory of physics is called "the eightfold way." It is a theory about the symmetries of elementary particles (Gell-mann and Néeman, 1971). These microcosmic and macrocosmic analogies to the group structure suggest that the formulation of a measurable unity between human and physical phenomena is probably not far fetched.

Zonal Implications of the Space

Interactional effects of group role-types on one another may be traced by their movement from one zonal location to another in the three-dimensional space. Figure 8-3 represents a three-dimensional space showing 26 distinct locations plus the center position, or 27 total locations. The Bales research showed that a three-dimensional space may be represented by a division of zones. A similar idea was shown on a two-dimensional circumplex organization of diagnostic terms (Kellerman and Plutchik, 1978). These terms were correlated to the location of subjects in a therapy group, who were also located on the circumplex. Certain zones reflected accessible diagnostic areas as well as areas of locations of the accessible types. Other zones reflected impedance diagnostic areas as well as areas of locations of the impedance types.

It may be that the location of subjects based upon their diagnostic variation would also show a distinct zonal difference between accessible and impedance role types in the three-dimensional space. This sort of difference suggests certain hypotheses about the adaptational power of any group based upon its compositional texture. For example, the life-span of the group may be considerably shortened if conflict were to increase without regulation. This would imply that more members become located in impedance zones and increase the group's termination potential.

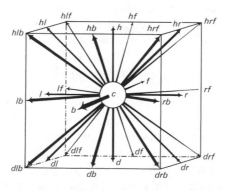

Figure 8-3.   A three-dimensional effort-shape space orientation around the body showing 27 distinct locations. Personality types also may be plotted in the space in order to reveal the location arrangement of polar forces h = high, d = deep, l = left, r = right, b = backward, f = forward, c = centre, hr = high right, db = deep backward, lf = left forward, dr = deep right, hb = high backward, rf = right forward, dl = deep left, hf = high forward, rb = right backward, hl = high left, df = deep forward, lb = left backward, hrf = high right forward, dlb = deep left backward, hlf = high left forward, drb = deep right backward, hlb = high left backward, drf = deep right forward, hrb = high right backward, dlf = deep left forward. (From Laban, 1963. Reprinted by permission of Macdonald & Evans (Publications) Ltd.)

PSYCHOLOGICAL SPACE

Usandivaras (1976) indirectly refers to this life-span implication of group process by proposing that "the mental space of the group is similar to its group space and so the structural aspect of the member's thinking will be an expression of the type of group space." He develops the notion of psychological space which corresponds to the sense of three-dimensional physical space. A system of coordinates, vertical and horizontal lines at right angles, permit the precise placing of objects in the space. This establishes relations of distance, placement, and proportion among them. Of course, "objects" could also refer to members of a therapy group or interrelations of a set of concepts, forces, or personality traits.

Usandivaras considers group space to be representational space which can be experienced as projective space. Projective space may be characterized by properties of perspective and may possess a higher degree of development at the representational level. It is an idea that obliquely reveals another powerful aspect of the group process: that a person occupying any role type may contemplate the eventual recombination of one role into another. This possibility characterizes the group as a meaningful change environment and suggests that group life is profoundly adaptive, and therefore highly selective in evolution. A focus on projective representational space also implies differences in conflict-force of accessible and impedance types as they are expressed in their respective zonal locations. Both Bales and Usandivaras have begun to explore a deeper level of group structure; one in which the internal process of the group is considered to reflect a complex outer shape.

The Icosahedron

The research by Bales ushered in an era of group dynamics and social-psychological research on group process and group structure with respect to a three-dimensional space. The implications of three-dimensional space research have generated a higher conceptual synthesis in other fields. This is seen in the studies of theoretical mathematics, in architectural and engineering applications, in physical and neural models of behavior, as well as in aspects of group theory set forth above.

The three-dimensional space illustrated in Figure 8-3 is used in modern educational dance theory to locate themes concerned with space orientation (Laban, 1963). The design and location points of this space are also ideally suited as reference locations for any group structure. It permits all of Bales' 26 types to be accurately located. It also permits the location of all group dispositional types especially with respect to polarities. The space accounts for 26 locations specifically designated within a three-dimensional space around a center point. An indefinite number of locations may be found within the space.

In this space, Laban located eight basic effort-actions that are part of the effort-shape conceptualization of movement and dance. These eight basic effort-actions become subconscious motifs. They are contrasts of mood that are felt in the effort elements. They are movements of punching, pressing, slashing, wringing, dabbing, gliding, flicking, and floating. They are compounded of motion factors of weight, space, and time, concepts not unlike those used to understand boundary conditions of the group structure described earlier. Thus, Labanotation, the system of dance notation, has incorporated the use of three dimensional space in the understanding and expression of dance structure to the extent of relating emotional dispositions to movement in space (Laban, 1966; North, 1972).

The space of Figure 8-3 represents movement around the body. It combines space for both peripheral and central movements, and divides the space into three planes (Dell, 1977). Figure 8-4 shows these planes: "the vertical or door plane including the dimensions up-down and side-side divides the space in front of the body from the space in back. . . . The horizontal or table plane including the dimensions side-side and forward-backward divides the space of the upper body from that of the lower. . . . The sagittal or wheel plane including the dimensions forward-backward and up-down divides the space on the right side of the body from that on the left" (Dell, 1977).

Figure 8-4 shows the basic division of all three planes. The shape resembles that of a hyperbolic paraboloid presented in Figure 8-2; that is, the hyperbolic-paraboloid contains in its shape the expression of conflicting elements. These elements may be contrasts of emotions, personality traits, members of a therapy group, or a distribution of movement planes as seen in Figure 8-4.

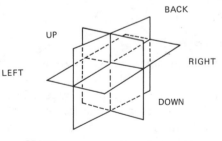

Figure 8-4.   An ichosachedronal construction. (Reprinted from Dell C. *Space Harmony*, by arrangement with the Dance Notation Bureau.) The space around the body may be divided into three planes. The planes form a symmetrical hyperbolic paraboloid with the parabolic well. The vertical or door plane divides the space into front and back. The horizontal or table plane divides the space into upper and lower. The sagittal or wheel plane divides the space into right and left. When the corners of the planes are connected, they form the ischosahedron. The basic diagnostic polarities of the group composition may be represented in various locations of the ichosahedron.

Each of the three planes contains mood or personality trait correlations. For example, application of effort-shape theory to accessible and impedance diagnostic types can imply that the vertical front plane, the horizontal upper plane, and the sagittal right plane are locations in which the accessible traits of trustful, timid, gregarious, and controlled are generally expressed. The vertical back plane, the horizontal lower plane, and the sagittal left plane are locations in which the impedance traits of distrustful, aggressive, depressed, and dyscontrolled are generally expressed. The vertical front plane may reflect an ego-strength plane; that is, persons who demonstrate activity in this plane are generally assertive, proud, and perhaps even strident. The horizontal upper plane may correlate to traits of sociability, empathy, and generally well developed social-interaction skills. Persons who demonstrate activity in this plane generally may have well developed relationships. The sagittal right plane can be one in which activity itself becomes the main ingredient. Doing, as an end in itself becomes rewarding. Persons of this type may be deferential and obedient, and yet need to work to feel worthy. In some ways, the division of the planes and their personality correlates resemble the organization of intrapsychic forces. This proposed relation of the planes to ego-id-superego forces also suggests that characteristic of each plane are locations reflecting these intrapsychic forces.

Dell (1977) states, "When the corners of the three planes are connected, they form an ichosahedron, a geometric model from which various spatial scales and forms can be explored." The ichosahedron is the interconnected space of all personality expression. In it, all primary as well as complex moods may be located in terms of the planes of the divided space. The ichosahedron can be unfolded into an "uninterrupted surface line spread into a plane" (Laban, 1966)—a reconstituted shape.

The location of Bales' 26 types may also be plotted in terms of the three planes. Similarly, the location of each of the eight basic dispositional types containing differing conflict weights may be seen to correspond to specific locations in the various planes of the space.

In transforming the apparent group shape to its hypothetical underlying one, the three-dimensional space into which this transformation takes place may be understood from several points of view. First, it is a space that may be viewed with reference to diagnostic projective zones. Second, it contains planes of the ichosahedron that may have location implications of an intrapsychic and personality trait nature. Third, it enables the hyperbolic-paraboloidal group shape to be graphically seen as an uninterrupted surface line. This line shows the reconstituted shape as a function of conflict (K). This is illustrated in Figures 8-5 and 6. The shape hints at either an elliptical or helicoidal model as a function of the true difference in weightedness and distance between the accessible and impedance basic diagnostic states.

THE TRANSFORMATIONAL SHAPE OF THE GROUP

Figures 8-5 and 6 represent a first approximation to the transformation of the apparent group circular shape to its implied abstract one. This new abstract shape is neither circular nor flat. It seems rather elongated, twisting, and somewhat elliptical.

An examination of this shape demonstrates that the impedance states of dyscontrol, depressed, aggressive, and distrustful cluster in one or two specific zones. The accessible states of controlled, gregarious, timid, and trustful also cluster together in one or two specific zones. The plots of Figures 8-5 and 6 were made by using the normative data of accessible and impedance states given in Table 8-3. The tripartite axes consisted of the accessible, the impedance and the *Kellerman conflict score* for each element of a polar pair. The plot for any state was made by referring to its assigned percent score provided in this table. The same was done for its opposite state percent score. Polar conflict scores then constituted the third axis. A location was established at the intersect point of all three axes for any state.

One new implication of this transformational shape as seen in Figure 8-6B is that the concept of polarity assumes a more complex meaning when viewed in three dimensions. Apparently, polarity reflects the location of forces

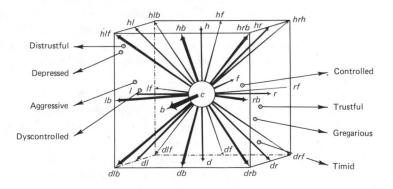

Figure 8-5.   The transformational group shape in a three-dimensional space. The accessible states are all located essentially to the front and to the right of the space. The impedance states are all located to the back and to the upper left of the space. The plots were made on the basis of the data provided in Table 8-3. Line *dlf* to *drf* represents the accessible state axis percent activation with *dlf* representing the zero point. Line *dlf* to *hlf* represents the K value axis with *dlf* as the zero point. Line *dlf* to *dlb* represents the impedance state axis percent activation with *dlf* as the zero point. Locations of personality dispositions follow. Trustful: front to right front. Gregarious: front to right and down. Timid: front to down front deep. Controlled: center, right, and forward. Distrustful: high, left, and back. Depressed: high, left, and back. Aggressive: left, back, and toward center. Dyscontrolled: left, center, and back. (See legend for Figure 8-3 for key to abbreviations.) (Based upon Laban, 1963.)

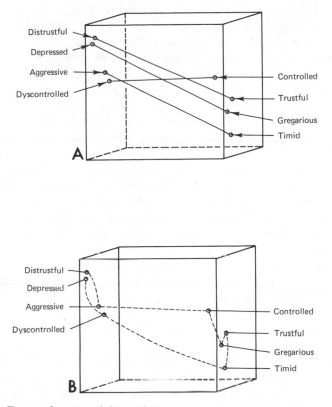

Figure 8-6.   The transformational shape of the group in a three-dimensional space. (A) Location relationship of polar states, indicated by solid lines. (B) An approximation of the new shape. Dotted line reflects an ordering sequence of states. Starting at Gregarious, the dotted line continues to Trustful, Timid, Dyscontrolled, Depressed, Distrustful, Aggressive, Controlled, and finally back to Gregarious.

in a new similarity structure. For example, the gregarious type is located in a zone characterized by relatedness, interactional activity, and sensitivity to others, while its opposite, the depressed type, is located in a zone characterized by withdrawal and instability. The distance between them suggests that in an abstract sense, group members expressing the impedance diagnoses sit, as it were, close to the ceiling and on the far side of the room. Group members reflecting the accessible categories sit, as it were, in their normal group positions. This metaphor of seating is one that may reflect the true alienation of some group members who are of the impedance type. It suggests that the therapeutic help they seek needs to be powerful enough, so to speak, to pull them down from the ceiling and "into the circle."

Another implication of this new group structure arises out of the sense that accessible and impedance diagnostic types existing in the group as polar pairs create a force field that may be defined by the nature of the conflict between all polar pairs. If Bales is correct, it may be expected that persons of the impedance type will want to change their position in the psychological space in the group. This is an interesting hypothesis because it raises the issue of the possibility of changing hierarchical patterns, and in this instance, of modifying an existing force field.

Various researchers of ethological studies have shown that hierarchical patterns are resistant to change (Delgado, 1969; Lorenz, 1966). Furthermore, a common observation of group behavior suggests that the more stable members of the group show unconscious resistance to the forward movement of the more unstable group members despite stated wishes and encouraging statements to the contrary. Spotnitz (1976) refers to this resistance phenomenon and indicates several ways of resolving it. He suggests that the resistance be pointed out, emotional defensiveness challenged, and historical material be brought to bear on the current repetition behavior. However, the key point is that hierarchical and ritualistic order becomes difficult to change. In addition to the traditional therapeutic content intervention, there exists an underlying group structure that reveals a deeper meaning to resistance elements. This structure needs to be addressed in the therapy process if resistance to change is to be overcome.

If this state of hierarchical resistance does indeed exist, how may the force field represented by the distance between accessible and impedance types seen in Figures 8-5 and 6 be sufficiently relaxed so that hierarchical patterns and resistance rituals may be modified? The answer to this question lies in the very nature of the difference between accessible and impedance types.

The first question to be considered refers to the weightedness of the impedance types. What is the quality constituting the essence of this magnitude in the impedance type, and how may this quality be modified? The answer to this question shall be explored and defined in the following chapters. It is an important question to answer, because most practitioners of group therapy are eager to compose groups on the basis of diagnostic heterogeneity in order to ensure the presence of psychological and emotional tension in the group climate. However, the difference in conflict force exerted onto the group by this heterogeneous composition produces the very resistance to change with which therapists and patients struggle. The therapist, therefore, creates a paradox in composing the group. In part, the therapy itself then becomes the creation of a dialectic designed to resolve the paradox.

Diagnostic and Prognostic Implications of Spatial Plots

Figures 8-5 and 6 show the location of polar types in terms of their planes and zones. In addition to distance features, there are also other interesting location differences between polar types. The timid type is located in a deep forward (df) to deep right forward (drf) position. It is opposite the aggressive type who is located in a high left (hl) and backward position. These positions are neither conspicuous nor vulnerable. They reflect a kind of accessibility. Although the aggressive person is an impedance type, the energized quality and volatility expressed by this type prevents such as person from being located in any more obscure area of the space. Timid types, although not terribly vocal, are also located in a positive and visible forward zone.

The controlled type is located in a right central and forward (rcf) area reflecting only a partially inhibitory component. It is opposite the dyscontrolled person, who although an impedance type, is found in a medium left backward (lb) position. This position reflects the "outgoingness" quality expressed through impulsivity.

Implications of these location plots suggest that at least these two impedance types, the dyscontrolled and the aggressive, are more reachable than otherwise might be expected.

Those categories reflecting greatest distance in the field are the trustful versus distrustful and gregarious versus depressed types respectively. In both cases the accessible types, trustful and gregarious, are found at down forward (df) to down right forward (drf) positions reflecting the most positive and interactive part of the entire space. In contrast, the impedance types of distrustful and depressed are found in the high left (hl) to high left back (hlb) positions reflecting the most underdeveloped interactive part of the entire space.

As far as implications for prognosis are concerned, these data suggest that only two of the impedance types, distrustful and depressed, may be quite difficult to reach in the therapeutic endeavor. The other six types, including the two impedance types of dyscontrolled and aggressive, may have better prognoses, a result that is quite contradictory to traditionally held therapy attitudes concerning the poor prognosis of dyscontrolled and aggressive types.

The discussions in this chapter and in chapter 7 have attempted to demonstrate that there may be clinical advantages to viewing the group structure in transformational terms. The intuitive conception of the group as a circular form, then, seems to reflect an ideal more than a reality and seems to raise some important points. First, these discussions suggest that concepts of conflict and tension in the group are not synonymous and perhaps need to be reassessed in the light of the formulations offered here. Second, the relative prognoses of the group's diagnostic composition may also need to be reassessed. These implications, in certain respects, offer new clinical insights and may generate further suggestions for research as well as group composition and therapeutic regulation. These formulations may reveal the value of conceptualizing clinical problems in a new spatial three-dimensional framework.

Implications for the Model of Personality Structure

The elliptical, elongated, and somewhat twisting nature of the transformational group shape suggests that a model of personality may be portrayed in a similar manner. In previous chapters this syntality revealed a series of interconnected relationships between emotions, personality traits, ego-defense mechanisms, basic diagnostic states, and psychosexual stages of development. To this may be added that the system of intrapsychic forces can also be shown to relate to these interconnected personality elements. These intrapsychic forces constitute the essence of the difference in conflict-magnitude of accessible versus impedance states.

In the following chapters, the intrapsychic connection to this system of personality shall be outlined. This analysis will represent a conceptual synthesis, in part derived from an exploration of basic group dispositional types as seen in the three-dimensional space. A basic question is asked by this formulation. If the essence of the extra magnitude of impedance types is known, can this information be therapeutically addressed so that all the impedance types may be subject to essential therapeutic change? It may be that the transformational implied shape of the group represents a truly pretherapeutic condition. The apparent group circular shape may be an expression of eventual therapeutic working-through, a wish as it were, of a time when each basic type is weighted equally. The group starts off in a circle. It really exists, however, as a helicoidal twisting shape reflecting the hyperbolic paraboloidal K differences of basic types. A successful therapy group may therefore be one in which the aim has been to transform the actual group shape, an hyperbolic paraboloid expressed as an elongated, and twisting form, to an "actual" circular one.

9

The Intrapsychic Group: Intrapsychic Conceptions of Group Structure

In the previous chapter it was proposed that the group exists in a state of conflict imbalance. The particular configuration of conflict was related to the role composition of the group. Certain roles were considered to be of low conflict weight, while others were considered to generate a great amount of conflict. The low conflict weighted roles were called accessible types, while the high conflict roles were called impedance types. A fundamental issue was raised regarding the difference between accessible and impeded role types: it was suggested that there is a basic difference between the intrinsic nature of accessible and impedance roles which needs to be identified.

Each role type of the group reflects a corresponding basic emotion, ego-defense mechanism, and diagnostic disposition that is germane to its nature. The intrinsic difference between the accessible type and the impeded type exists on all levels of personality including the levels of emotion, defense, and diagnostic disposition. Differences in conflict magnitude between the accessible and the impeded types imply that certain emotions, defenses, and diagnostic dispositions are of low intrinsic conflict weight, while other emotions, defenses, and diagnostic dispositions are of high intrinsic conflict weight. The imbalance in the role-conflict composition of the group, therefore, may reflect a similar imbalance at all levels of personality structure, including the levels of emotion, ego-defense, and diagnostic type.

It is the purpose of this chapter and the next to show that this conflict imbalance of personality structure and of group structure is based upon the intrapsychic property contained within each emotion, ego-defense, and diagnostic dispositional state and that such a personality program is expressed in basic roles of the group. More specifically, it will be proposed that there are particular emotions, ego-defenses, and diagnostic dispositions which, as part of their development, have emerged with an intrapsychic nature. For example, some emotions may be id emotions while others are superego emotions. This formulation applies to defense mechanisms, roles, and diagnostic dispositions as well.

The difference between the accessible and impedance role types correspondingly will reveal the basic organization of the intrapsychic structure of the group. The first task, in this chapter, however, is to present the varieties of conceptions used to apply intrapsychic formulations to group forces, group function, and group role theory. These ego-id-superego analogues will be explored as a prelude to the exposition and analysis of the relation between accessible versus impedance roles to be presented in the next chapter. It is an analysis of the inherent intrapsychic nature of these roles.

CONCEPTIONS OF THE INTRAPSYCHIC GROUP

Many conceptions have been proposed to show that intrapsychic forces operate in the group setting. Some of these treat the group as a whole organism, as it were, and assign to each intrapsychic element a function in the transference nature of the group; that is, the transference to the group as-a-whole may be to mother-ego, the relation to the therapist may represent a transference to the father-superego, and any individual member of the group may represent some portion of id force (Schindler, 1973). Other conceptions attribute differences in group phase to intrapsychic shifts (Spotnitz, 1976). A third conception relates intrapsychic states to the role composition of the group (Redl, 1942). Apparently there is no uniform conception of the intrapsychic group among researchers. This lack both of a uniform theory and of a consensus of the place of group composition in the formulations of the intrapsychic group will be examined in the following sections. In addition, in the following sections an attempt will be made to trace the influence of intrapsychic forces in the group on the appearance of group role behavior. This will be done by proposing that during group formative periods certain phenomena emerge that help relax rigid group ego forces so that role development is possible.

The development of group process in which the group function affects its formative periods leads to the appearance of roles. Several intervening steps need to be outlined to show this sequence. First, intrapsychic analogues to elements of group structure will be presented. Second, the way in which these ego-id-superego forces are related to group function will be proposed. Third, an attempt will be made to show the causal connection between group function and the vicissitudes of group formative periods, and fourth, the appearance of group role behavior as an expression of group formative periods will be explored. An attempt will then be made to show that the appearance of group roles can reveal the group's underlying intrapsychic and emotional composition.

Ego-Id-Superego Analogues to Elements of Group Structure

First and foremost, most psychodynamically oriented writers basically agree with the proposition that the "psychological organization of groups is fundamentally similar to that of individuals" (Peck, 1963). Freud (1921) originally proposed this issue by positing that groups contain the precise characteristics of control that the ego provides for the individual. Freud's position was that as the group develops, its structure evolves as an ego structure. This group ego structure substitutes for the function of the ego that was yielded by each of its members. The process of identification and yielding of the individual ego to the group ego is also suggested by Bach (1954), and Wolf (1950). Ammon (1977) states this proposition most directly: "the group becomes a real and symbolic embodiment of the ego of its members."

Some authors further develop the idea that group equals ego force. Slavson (1957) emphasizes that "Although the term group ego is usually employed euphemistically, actually there is a group ego which is represented by the leader through the investment in him by the members of the group." Slavson amplifies his idea of investment in the leader by indicating: "The condition of belonging to a group is partial deegotizing of the individual so that a portion of his ego is given up to the group, and especially to the leader as representative. . . . It is out of these discorded portions of the individuals' egos that a group ego emerges. . . . All group action, whether deliberative or uncontrolled is a result of a group's ego."

The group action as it is a function of the group's ego also implies that superego as well as id forces shift and rebalance accordingly. Freud (1914a) described the group's ability to allow individual superegos to be held in abeyance, and Slavson further indicates that, "Superego judgements are weakened in each member by the group's primary code, its sanctions and approval. The libido thus freed is invested in the leader who becomes the representative of the group superego." The implication for therapy in Slavson's formulation relates fundamentally to the idea that as ego accumulates in the group, individual members may express feelings in a more spontaneous manner because they, as part of this large cumulative ego, need not be inhibited by the superego-leader. Wolf (1950) also implies this point: "The total ego of the group appears to permit the ego of each member of the group to experience a greater expression of aggression than in ordinary circumstances." Perhaps the ego of the group helps it to be viable and strong enough so that the expression of id and superego conflict does not threaten to destroy it.

The ego force existing in the cumulative membership is an essential ingredient of the group's viability and survival potential. This ego force is the pulsating system of the group, allowing it to expand and contract, in part also as an expression of id and superego forces that continuously register their impact on the group surface. It is an oscillating condition similar to the boundary condition described by Dunphy (1974) and is a feature of the group's tension regulation function described in chapters 5 and 6. A more resilient ego force enables group functions to emerge.

Superego force resides both in the position of leader (Foulkes, 1964) and in the group-as-a-whole (Durkin, 1964). The part fusion of ego and superego elements in the group-as-a-whole is provided with a rationale by Freud (1921). In considering the group to be an accumulation of individuals who have consensually attributed the same objective in the place of their ego-ideal, Freud ascribes this substitution of individual ego-ideals to a supraobject. This substitution creates the possibility for each group member to be identified with one another in their respective ego. A similar formulation is presented by Grinberg, Gear, and Liendo (1976). The resulting balance of ego and superego allows the group to express negative attitudes (Bach, 1954), or as Wolf (1950) indicates, the group may express aggression. These negative attitudes and aggressive feelings are derived from id sources and their display reminds group members that the spontaneous expression of feelings is permissible. Freedom of emotional expression increases the likelihood for group cohesion to develop and a cohesive group facilitates the unfolding process to the phases of group life. The group's intrapsychic nature may then be considered entrenched. This permits the group to function well. This correlation of group intrapsychic forces to group function will ultimately have an effect on role phenomena generated by group formative periods. It should be noted from this discussion that most authors are vitally interested in locating the ego representations of the group.

Intrapsychic Forces and Group Function

The achievement of group function is equivalent to creating cohesion at various stages of group process. A cohesive group is a well defined intrapsychic group, and this cohesion is expressed in the group's personality. Schindler (1952) discusses group personality in terms of such intrapsychic processes. He proposes that during the phases of group process, the group ego regulates the interaction between the group id and the group superego. The group id is represented by the common needs all group members express, such as needs for security and pleasure. The group superego is generated by the common perception of the leader as father and the group-as-a-whole as mother. Schindler thus implies that the group-as-a-whole may contain ego as well as id and superego elements. This conception is more complex than simply designating separate intrapsychic elements to discrete aspects of group structure.

The cumulative fantasies of group members toward the group-as-a-whole is considered by Bion (1959b) to reflect a perception of the mother figure. Bion's conception is concerned with the shared myths and fantasies of group members as they affect the group process. As Jaques (1955) suggests, the group-as-a-whole is a blank screen onto which members project infantile wishes. Jaques considers the sharing of unconscious fantasy indispensable to the group process. The relation between intrapsychic forces and group function, therefore, is determined in large part by the unconscious joining of the fantasies of group members. This sharing of fantasy suggested by Bion and Jaques has also been considered by Bach (1954) as an issue of id gratification and fusion with the group, by Dunphy (1974) as the common group fantasy, by Kaplan (1967) in the form of "the collective wishes" of the group , later (1966) as an issue of individuation versus fusion, and by Spotnitz (1976) as the common group resistance. Thus, group function and group cohesion are inextricably bound and become crystallized when the intrapsychic forces begin to operate.

Phenomena of Group Formative Periods

Existing group cohesion as expressed by the unconscious joining of fantasies of group members also emerges as the expression of group emotions. Many authors hypothesize that the appearance of group emotions as well as shared fantasies exists and is generated from conflict-free areas of the ego (Scheidlinger, 1964). Kaplan (1967) similarly indicates that the dynamic forces which generate group emotions at certain stages "appear to arise primarily from adaptive processes within the ego rather than as direct derivatives of instinctual conflicts." In many formulations of group phases, the ego function of the group, including the regressive phenomena that exist in the service of the ego, is considered to be the primary force that sets into motion the activity of the group, including the expression and regulation of group emotions. Although there are regressive phenomena occurring during group formative periods in which individual members may perceive the group as the preoedipal mother or father (Durkin, 1964; Kaplan, 1967), Scheidlinger (1964) nevertheless asserts that the group emotions reflect ego adaptations derived from conflict-free areas of the ego. This is an important point, because regressive aspects to group formation reflect a tendency for id forces to fragment the unfolding group process. Again, the group ego formation is essential to group function and to the unfolding of the group's formative stages.

Freud (1921) first indicated that regression constituted the essential character of group formation. This means that ego and superego structures are vulnerable in the group to instinctual forces and by direct implication, to the process of regression. Scheidlinger (1968) agrees with the Freudian position, also indicating that suggestibility and emotional contagion play a part in the regressive probability. Dunphy (1974) amplifies this position and indicates that in the immediate formative group stage interpersonal closeness is resisted by group members, emotional attachment is avoided, and because of the omnipresence of superego, the ego boundaries of the group "are maintained with increasing rigidity." Kaplan (1967) also states, "One of the effects of group formative process upon the ego is the blurring of individual distinctiveness and a tendency for the individual to regress to an immature level of emotional and intellectual functioning." There is therefore considerable feeling that id forces, by implication, permeate the group during formative periods generating strong superego counterforce and a somewhat rigid group ego. Authors such as Kubie (1958) also argue that because free association in the classic sense is absent in the group, the group cannot deal with problems of intrapsychic conflict such as the working-through of authority problems. This position similarly reveals a conception of the group ego as rigid.

Even though regressive phenomena are observable during group formative periods, nevertheless, if the group is diagnostically well composed, a correct intrapsychic balance will emerge and will help facilitate the group process. For example, Hartman and Gibbard (1974b) unequivocally state that "The group composed of normal individuals begins with a far wider range of adaptive capacities than does the infant." It is this oblique reference to the inherently resilient quality of a good group composition that counteracts any deleterious regressive effects to the group formation. The fact that the group begins with adaptive capacities allows the group process to become expressed as a force toward cohesion.

The early group phase is in fact characterized by ego functions. Abrahams (1950) considers this early group phase to reflect relationships to past figures; Bach (1954) sees the early phase as a sensing of behavior problems; Cholden (1953) views it as an attempt to try to understand limits; Dreikurs (1951) perceives it as a time of establishing relationships; Stoute (1950) defines it as a time when resistance appears; and Taylor (1961) sees it as a time of self-revelation. In all of these positions, delay of gratification, scanning behavior, abiding by regulations, and the adjustment of interpersonal relationships are all properties of ego function. It seems that the group-as-a-whole contains a profound measure of ego representation at its very beginnings. This ego phenomenon of the group allows it to accomplish its tasks and sets the stage for the unfolding of role behavior.

Interpersonal Role Behavior and the Intrapsychic Group

Most theories of the group's phases consider the initial group ego function to be one that is rigid and protected. As the group evolves, this rigid ego is transformed into one that is flexible and more viable. The transformation is accomplished through the gradual expression of role interactions and the development of a group culture, a group history, and a continuing interplay of id and superego elements of the group. Rey (1975) addresses this issue and suggests that the understanding of group dynamics can only depend on understanding the intrapsychic shift as the group proceeds. It is possible to monitor this sort of shift only through the exploration and analysis of interpersonal behavior. These intrapsychic shifts affecting individual members are not always easy to trace in the group. Wolberg (1968) indicates that patients absorb new ways of behaving quite automatically. Sometimes patients use the group to gain gratifications, but do not function in an assertive way outside the group. At other times, interpersonal shifts may produce improvement in behavior outside the group while no apparent change is evident within the group. Occasionally, improvement is neither registered within the group nor out of it. Some patients will have to leave the group in order for the changes in intrapsychic balance to be revealed in behavioral effects. This is sometimes true of the paranoid type who may not show any improvement in or out of the group. Nevertheless, the group process itself may create a new reality for such patients quite automatically. It may do this by altering the balance of intrapsychic forces and by altering identifications formed through role shifts. Much of this change will be felt in time even without the patient knowing it.

The focus on the interpersonal as a way of understanding intrapsychic balance is also addressed by Durkin (1964) who states that the result of intragroup transferences tells the therapist "the way in which each member's intrapsychic conflicts were translated into his interpersonal behavior." Knobloch (1968) states this same proposition quite cogently: "Intrapsychic processes are interpersonal processes in a group schema"

The vast literature on interpersonal behavior in the group context is essentially the study of role behavior and role interaction. Group roles, however, need to be understood in terms of their basic intrapsychic nature. In the spirit of Durkin and Knobloch, Ezriel (1952) indicates that the intrapersonal gets expressed in the interpersonal. The differentiation of group roles is generated by the intrapsychic process of introjection and projection. This notion was also proposed by Hartman and Gibbard (1974b). Generating and stereotyping roles through intrapsychic introjection as well as through projection was implied by Wolf et al. (1970) who indicate that the presence of other group members provides the opportunity for each to act as an auxilliary ego for the other. Foulkes (1964) also indicates that group members may play part of ego, id, or superego for each other. One's role is thereby etched in the psyche of the group, in part, by the introjections and projections of group members. These introjections and projections may become especially powerful provided they correspond to particular fantasy roles of group members. Grinberg et al. (1976) call this process of role definition projective identification and projective counteridentification. The group permits an induction of roles through these identification processes.

Zimmer and Shapiro (1972) also recognize the connection between the interpersonal and the intrapsychic. They propose that introjective identification—assuming another's qualities as one's own—and projective identification—attributing one's qualities to another—are the processes that help differentiate roles in the group. The theme of central persons or central roles proposed by Redl (1942) is an example of a role system of group composition that utilizes the concepts of introjection and projection, projective identification and projective counteridentification. These processes, as they help generate the central roles, also contain intrapsychic correlates. Each central role renders service to the ego, the id, or the superego. The central figure is thus a focus of the collective need of the group and constitutes a group valency. For example, the hero as a central figure is one who initiates acts. This sort of initiatory behavior permits other group members to discard their anxieties. The hero thereby renders a service to the ego of group members.

A major theoretical contribution of Redl's work on central figures is his proposition that different roles may reflect either ego, id, or superego dispositions. This implies that any basic role theory of group composition should also reveal the basic underlying intrapsychic organization of the group; and a theory of group roles should consider the effect of group resistance on role development. Some of these effects shall be reviewed in the following section.

Group Resistance and Its Effect on Role Development

Bion (1959a) and Slater (1966) consider the central struggle of the group to be one of individuation versus fusion. As the group evolves, it becomes possible for members to yield to the group ego and yet maintain their own role assignment. As roles become defined they may also be exchanged. This is what Levinson (1959) considers to be an example of ego achievement in the group: the stability of role assignments and innovation in role assignments. In terms of the group resistance, then, role function becomes a compromise between adaptation to existing conditions and the creation of new ones. It is a compromise between the resistance and the working-through process. As Hartman and Gibbard (1974b) indicate, the intrapsychic process of introjection and projection on a group-wide basis will generate psychic boundaries including differentiated roles. The working-through process alters psychic boundaries and creates the possibility for roles eventually to be exchanged. Dunphy (1974) considers such role shifts to be reflected in the modification of intrapsychic structures. Resistance is partially overcome by relaxation of rigid group ego boundaries, by the development of an idealized group image, and by role exchange. Cohesion and group solidarity are then possible.

Spotnitz (1976) observes that the group develops a common neurosis and a common resistance. This veiw is quite correct, although it might be suggested that the group begins with a common neurosis or a common resistance that is determined by its intrapsychic complexion and that is based upon its compositional role structure. Spotnitz further indicates that the instinctual energy of the group is held in check by the neurosis and that this conflict fortifies the resistance. To this may be added that the instinctual energy of the group is held in check by defenses that manage the inordinate superego demands that are also inherent in the group compositional role structure. Again Spotnitz observes that the resistance exposes the patient's psychic history. It also may be added that the specific defenses a group member uses correlate to specific emotions and diagnostic dispositions, and these structures contain corresponding intrapsychic designations. An individual's psychic history, then, may be indirectly traced from any number of interpersonal samples of behavior.

Spotnitz lists five kinds of group resistances: a group ego resistance, a group id resistance, a group superego resistance, a group secondary gain resistance, and a group transference resistance. All of these resistances may be analyzed with reference to the difference in conflict weightedness between accessible and impedance roles. It is proposed that the group's entire intrapsychic resistance, including the five listed by Spotnitz, may only be resolved by a shift in the role assignments of the impedance types, especially with regard to the severe impact of superego strain expressed by scrutinizer-paranoid types and by the reintegrator-depressed types that were discussed in chapter 8. Spotnitz suggests that it may be possible to develop an immunization against toxic group responses or resistances. The immunization may be the giving up of typical defenses used to release emotion in order to manage superego demands and those defenses used to block emotion in order to control id urges. These releasing and blocking functions of defenses shall be examined in the following chapter. The giving up of typical defenses may be the only way of instituting a working-through group therapy condition in which the group ego may fully develop.

From the foregoing it may be seen that the literature on the relation of intrapsychic elements to group role structure and group process is in a state of becoming. For some the group is solely ego. For others the group contains elements of superego as well as id. For some, transference to the group is to a preoedipal parent and for others the transference to the preoedipal parent relates only to the leader, and then only indirectly to the group-as-a-whole. To Schutz (1961b) the leader is ego. To Bion (1961) only the work group is equivalent to ego. To Slavson (1953) the group may be ego as well as collective superego, and to Wolf and Schwartz (1962), the group is ego while the therapist is either superego or id dominated.

In terms of any uniform intrapsychic formulation, two main themes emerge from a review of the group literature. First, it may be assumed that all three intrapsychic influences exist at all points and in some form throughout the group structure and during all phases of the group process even though ego formation is the major intrapsychic focus of most authors. Any unifying theory of the group intrapsychic infrastructure should acknowledge that the group-as-a-whole contains ego as well as id and superego influences; that the leader of the group is endowed with superego transference elements but must also function as part of the group structure, and is therefore also infused with ego

and id qualities; that, similarly, group members constitute individual id re-
sponders, yet identify with superego forces projected onto the therapist, as
well as comprising an individual part of the group-as-a-whole ego structure.
Second, the review of the group process literature suggests that a sequence of
development occurs in the group process that shows the causal connection
between group function, group formative periods, and the appearance of
group roles.

The formation of roles in the group is influenced by each person's developmental history; that is, intrapsychic structures of the personality begin to
appear out of the relative success each person achieves in mastering developmental tasks. Any person's diagnostic pattern, and hence, implied group role,
has its expressive roots in that person's psychosexual developmental history.
The appearance of group roles is therefore intricately tied to the entire personality program of the emotion system. This is a sociobiological as well as a
psychoanalytic conception and is, in part, set forth in the following section.

A Sociobiological View of Intrapsychic Development

In traditional psychoanalytic thought both the ego and superego are later
developments in the process of psychosexuality; that is, the oedipal resolution
is generally seen as determining the final shape of the superego. The position
set forth in this book holds that the basic emotions exist at birth as predispositions, and inherent in their nature are diagnostic, defense, and intrapsychic
elements. This position implies that the main influence at work in the ultimate
connection between emotions and intrapsychic forces exists in shared genetic
codings. There is a second influence between emotion and intrapsychic forces
that becomes apparent as a function of development. These are adaptational
considerations that are part of the developmental process. In certain respects
the predispositional personality structure becomes salient during suitable developmental periods. This means that aspects of the personality structure,
such as intrapsychic forces and emotion, become reinforced and more highly
differentiated during periods of development that require such elements of
personality to become fully expressed. For example, although features of control in the personality such as those expressed in obsessional defenses are provided in the epigenetic program, it may be that these control features are
called forth during the anal psychosexual period of development where controls and the response to demands are prominent. Kaywin (1960) states that
"every developmental stage with its individual functional patterns will become associated with positive and negative tonal (affective) representations.
Thus representations of the various so-called 'psychosexual' zones (oral, anal,
genital) will be laid down." It is these positive and negative "tonal" representations that may also be derived from the emotion-personality structure existing
at birth and which become more salient during specific developmental
periods.

Kaywin ties together in a general way psychosexual development and emotion patterns. What may be emerging is the sense that the differentiation process occurs through psychosexual development but that the intrapsychic apparatus, at least the id and superego, are engraved in the substrate of emotion structure. Stolorow and Lachman (1978) suggest that in terms of defenses, there may be lines of development for each defensive process. The authors state that defense mechanisms are the "end point of a series of developmental achievements." They consider the entire issue of differentiation of the structural apparatus and perceive it to be, in the traditional sense, a function of psychosexual development. It might be added that these lines of development have a starting point that may also be located in the substrate of emotion along with intrapsychic inclinations.

Traditional psychoanalytic understanding and object relations theory consider identification to be an ongoing unfolding process based upon the conflict emerging during each psychosexual period. As the work with conflict confrontation produces character trait formations, superego and ego effects become increasingly visible in the personality. In the formulation proposed here, it is assumed that the entire program in a predispositional sense exists at birth. Therefore, psychosexual conflict can also be inherent in each bipolar pair of emotions. Psychosexual conflict can be more or less intense on the basis of whether the intrapsychic aim of each emotion is achieved; that is, whether the aims of id emotions and superego emotions are achieved. It is proposed here that the extent to which these intrapsychic aims are frustrated in part determines the intensity of psychosexual conflict that emerges during developmental stages. This means that psychosexual conflict is both epigenetically and developmentally determined. In the following chapter the aim of each intrapsychic force will be hypothesized in terms of its effect on the development of psychosexual conflict.

In the foregoing, an attempt was made to understand the intrapsychic designations of various elements of the group structure and to trace a sequence of developmental group processes that presumably lead to the appearance of roles. At this point, the main issue to be explored in group role theory as it relates to intrapsychic structure is the determination of the specific intrapsychic ingredients of each role. Are any roles specifically ego or id or superego ones?

THE INTRAPSYCHIC RELATION BETWEEN BASIC EMOTIONS AND BASIC GROUP ROLES

It was proposed in earlier chapters that when groups fail to achieve an ideal role composition they try to organize themselves so that through a system of role assumptions an ideal role composition may be approximated. The ability of group members to assume roles is made possible by mechanisms of projective identification, projective counteridentification, and introjective identification cited by Grinberg et al. (1976) and Zimmer and Shapiro (1972). In the group an ideal role composition is stimulated by the wishes and by the conscious or unconscious instructions of the therapist. The therapist and the group members may intuitively understand that the group needs to function within a boundary condition consisting of polar forces. These are the polar forces described in earlier chapters consisting of pushes and pulls and of active and passive attitudes. They are expressed as properties of the basic emotion structure of the group and become revealed through the interplay of the eight basic roles of the group. Therefore, in order to understand the specific intra-psychic influence of the basic group roles, the specific intrapsychic force contained in each of the eight basic emotions must first be determined and identified. Since each emotion is part of an entire personality system, then the intrapsychic element inherent in each emotion will also be reflected on each level of this system including the levels of ego-defense and basic roles.

It becomes possible to begin to understand the connection between intrapsychic forces and emotions when the basic emotions are examined as they are revealed in their pure form. They may be seen in their purest states at their highest intensity levels. This formulation was proposed by Plutchik (1962) and is illustrated in a structural form in Figure 2-10. At their highest respective intensity levels, joy and sorrow become ecstasy and grief. Acceptance and disgust become voraciousness and revulsion. Fear and anger become terror and rage, and expectation and surprise become vigilance and amazement.

These high intensity basic emotions become consistently expressed both during wakeful hours and during sleep. However, when the basic emotions are expressed at their highest intensity levels during any dreaming period, the dreamer will awaken from the dream with what is commonly called a nightmare. It is only when the dream's defensive operations are working that the high intensity emotions are controlled. When the dreamer's defenses cannot cope with the dream's stimuli the dreamer will experience a nightmare in which one of the eight basic emotions emerges in its pure form.

It is proposed here that the intrapsychic element of each basic emotion is revealed and may be understood through the analysis of the organization of dreams and nightmares. In the following chapter a theory of nightmares will be presented that attempts to show the intrinsic intrapsychic element of each basic emotion, diagnostic state, and group role.

10

The Intrapsychic Group: A Theory of Nightmares—Intrapsychic Meanings of Diagnostic Types

Freud (1900) first proposed that the dream is the guardian of sleep. Presumably, the dream is designed to organize the amorphous bombardment of stimuli during sleep in a way that renders such stimuli relatively harmless and not unduly disturbing. Since Freud believed that these stimuli reflected neurotic and even psychotic raw material, he hypothesized that the dreamer utilized a system of coping mechanisms called the dream work in order to disguise disturbing primary process material by transforming this material into some benign and relatively innocuous secondary state. This transformation distinguishes the manifest dream from the latent dream. The dream work and its coping mechanisms of displacement, condensation, secondary elaboration, and symbolism theoretically are expressed by all people in all cultures. When these coping mechanisms do not sufficiently disguise the dreamer's primary dream material, sleep will not be successfully guarded, the dream material breaks into consciousness, and the dreamer will awaken with a nightmare.

It is proposed here that the kind of nightmare that awakens the dreamer is not determined solely by a breakdown of the dream work. The kind of nightmare any individual experiences is a function of that person's basic diagnostic disposition. The nightmare is characterized by the basic emotion implied by any diagnostic disposition. The incapacity of the specific ego-defense that manages this basic emotion is the only way in which the nightmare may occur. It is proposed, then, that the nightmare can only crystallize if the specific ego-defense representing that person's diagnosis is impaired while dream work mechanisms are similarly impaired. It is also possible for the dream work to become impaired but for ego-defenses to remain intact in their function as specific emotion coping devices. Under such conditions, the dreamer will experience what is commonly called an anxiety dream, or a disturbed dream, yet one in which the dreamer remains sleeping. In the definition of a nightmare, therefore, it is the emotion and content of the dream that awakens the dreamer. This proposition considerably broadens the notion that nightmares are only dreams of terror. Experience can demonstrate that individuals awaken because of a wide array of dream contents, not all of which are dreams of terror, panic, or fear. In this chapter it will be proposed that the system of nightmares reveals the intrapsychic designation of each emotion, diagnostic state, and group role, and further, shows the intrapsychic function of each basic corresponding defense mechanism.

A PARSIMONIOUS THEORY OF NIGHTMARES

There may be an infinite number of nightmares that are possible for people to dream, yet it is proposed here that this multitude of nightmares may be analyzed essentially with reference to the eight basic personality categories. In the final analysis, there are only eight basic nightmares that it is possible for people to dream. Furthermore, these eight basic nightmares emerge as four polar pairs and reflect, in a consistent fashion, the nature of opposites of the basic system. They will be revealed with their elemental intrapsychic nature. The system of nightmares and its correlation with the levels of emotion, defense, and diagnostic disposition of personality structure suggest a series of postulates.

Postulate 1:   *There are eight basic nightmare themes that correspond to the eight basic categories of the entire emotion-personality system.*

Postulate 2:   *Any basic nightmare is a reflection of the dreamer's current diagnostic state.*

Postulate 3:   *Any of the basic nightmare themes may be experienced.* For example, a passive person may experience nightmares of grief that are characteristic of persons feeling depressed. This is possible because the passive person's feelings at the time of the dream must include depressive elements.

Postulate 4:   *Each nightmare theme reveals the basic intrapsychic nature of each diagnostic state.*

Postulate 5:   *Although there are an infinite number of dream contents, when they become nightmares they reveal only eight basic emotion themes.*

In the following section the system of nightmares will be described and sample nightmares will be presented to illustrate each of the eight typical nightmare categories. These typical nightmares reflect the basic diagnostic states.

The Eight Basic Nightmares

THE MANIC DISPOSITION

The emotion of joy or feelings of pleasure constitute the underlying state of the manic disposition. Reaction-formation is the specific ego-defense designed to manage the pleasure urge. In any dreamer, especially in one with manic feelings, when the bombardment of erotic or pleasurable dream stimuli is too strong, and the defensive reaction-formation not sufficiently applied to manage the stimuli, the dreamer will produce a highly sexualized ecstatic dream content in which all prohibition dissipates. It is likely that a loss of control will result and an orgastic or wet dream will awaken the dreamer. The nightmare is a result of the heightened sexuality that ordinarily would have been managed by some reasonable measure of reaction-formation.

A young man of 22 who was in the process of analyzing various oedipal features of his personality described a sexual obsession he had about a woman five years his senior whom he had known since adolescence. He had always felt extremely attracted to her but believed she would never contemplate any sort of relationship with him other than a casual one. This man was an active, productive, and exuberant person. After some time in therapy, he began to feel more mature and less inadequate. His reaction-formation defense became less severe and he had the following dream after coincidentally meeting this woman at a party.

> I was standing in a room near a couch. There were lots of people around. Denise walked by. She was wearing a tight black woolen sweater and she was big. I felt sexual towards her. The people were milling around but they gradually disappeared and we seemed to be alone. I had my hands out—like they were held out in front of me in a cupped fashion, palms away from me—like you'd help someone on with a coat. We seemed to be sitting on the couch now. She slowly turned towards me, and as she did, I didn't move my hands so that they were slightly cupped and her breasts sort of fit—like a perfect fit. It reminds me of the docking maneuver of one space vehicle with another—a locking together—but it was gentle. I was feeling very excited, extremely excited. I instantly felt that she was firm, and as I got the feeling that she was firm, I had an orgasm and I ejaculated in my sleep. The orgasm woke me up.

This dream-nightmare is one example of many possible eroticized dream contents, all of which will end in an erotic awakening dream-nightmare when the defense of reaction-formation is impaired.

The nightmare itself of each of these contents may be understood as de-rived from a single structural element of personality that involves a specific diagnostic disposition, emotion category, and ego-defense mechanism.

THE DEPRESSED DISPOSITION

The emotion of sorrow or feelings of loss or inferiority constitute the under-lying state of the depressed disposition. Compensation is the specific ego-de-fense designed to manage the feelings of loss, sorrow, or inadequacy. When the bombardment of loss stimuli in any dreamer overpowers the compensatory defense, the dreamer will experience a dream in which grief reflects the dream content. In such dreams, the nightmare occurs with the dreamer awakening while crying or sobbing as a direct result of the dream content. If sobbing or cyring does not result from the nightmare, the loss experience will be reflected in a profound yearning or grieving. In the absence of compensatory mechanisms, nothing is left for the dreamer but weeping or responding to incapacity.

A 30-year-old man who was working-through separation fears and who would consistently defend against any expression of depressive feelings finally admitted to feelings of incapacity. He was afraid to live alone and he usually managed to divert his attention from his fears by engaging in compensatory behavior. Nevertheless, he was somewhat shy and relied heavily on his par-ents for emotional support. The day after he rented his own apartment he had the following dream.

> I can't quite remember all the events. I know my father died. He was dead. It was too much for me to take. I loved him so much and now I would never see him again. I was crying. It seemed that grief was pouring all out of me. I felt miserable. I never experienced such misery. I woke up sobbing with tears streaming down my face. I forgot how I found it out but someone told me he was dead. When I woke up and realized I had a nightmare I was relieved but still sobbing. It was the worst dream I have ever had.

Of the thousands of potential dream contents that are possible in this category, they all may be understood as derived from a specific sequence of events in the personality structure involving emotion, defense, and disposi-tional tendency. In this case all such dreams end in some form of grieving nightmare when the compensation defense is impaired.

In terms of this theory of dreams and nightmares, sexual orgastic or "wet" dreams are the opposite of crying, weeping, or sobbing dreams.

THE PASSIVE DISPOSITION

The emotion of fear constitutes the underlying state of the passive dispo-sition. Repression is the specific ego-defense designed to manage the fear and the passivity. When repression is overcome by excessively threatening stimuli in the dream, the dreamer will experience a nightmare in which terror characterizes the dream content.

A 42-year-old man who lived alone, who never married, and who never really developed enduring relationships, finally met someone who especially appealed to him. He saw this woman for more than two years. In therapy sessions he noticed it was his longest relationship, that friends were asking when they were getting married, and that his "fiance" friend had also mentioned that they would probably marry. At this point he had the following dream.

> I was sleeping in my bedroom and I heard someone break in the front door. I was terrified. I started saying "who is it" but the terror was too much. I felt myself getting out of bed to run somewhere and I woke up mumbling to myself "who is it" which in the dream was said very clearly, but when I heard myself as I woke up, it was just a mumble. I woke up half sitting in the bed.

The relationship this man developed was pushing back the barriers of repression. His terror reflected a deeply felt axiety about allowing someone "in."

Of the multitude of dream contents that may contain themes of threat, the specific nightmare itself, because of the impairment of the repressive defense, will always be characterized by the emotion of terror.

THE AGGRESSIVE DISPOSITION

The emotion of anger constitutes the underlying state of the aggressive disposition. Displacement is the specific ego-defense designed to manage the angry and aggressive feelings. In the absence of any displacement defenses, the dreamer will produce a highly aggressive confrontational or directly rageful dream in which the dreamer is the assertive figure. Of the many dreams in which the dreamer experiences rage directly, the nightmare is always a result of the acting-out or direct expression of the rage.

The same 42-year-old man who awakened with a terror nightmare was expressing the opposite dispositional tendency one year later. He was not yet married but was continuously talking about it in sessions. One month after reporting the following nightmare he was married.

> I was sleeping in my bedroom and again I heard someone break into my house. I immediately remembered that I had dreamt this exact dream before and in a way I then knew it was a dream, but I still couldn't ignore what was happening. I was surprised. I was almost terrified again but I felt something get angry inside of me. The anger became high and strong and I felt my fear dip into the background. I never felt that before in my life. I felt strong and brave and even tough. I dreamed that I got out of bed and said "who is it, come on in I'm ready for you." I dreamed I was standing there with my fists closed as though I was ready to fight. I woke up stirred up but I felt good.

This man was no longer repressing as much as he did and was becoming more assertive. Even though his assertiveness was becoming expressed through anger, nevertheless, the displacement defense of his personality was more restricted and this enabled him to become heroic in the dream. In the absence of the displacement defense all such dream contents will develop into nightmares in which aggression prevails.

Thus, nightmares of terror in which one is threatened are the opposite of nightmares of confrontation or rage in which one is threatening.

THE HYSTERIC DISPOSITION

The emotion of acceptance constitutes the underlying state of the hysteric disposition. Denial is the specific ego-defense designed to manage the high suggestibility inherent in the need to accept and incorporate. It is frequently seen, in a clinical sense, that when denial mechanisms fail to function, the dreamer will reveal tension in a hysterical fashion, and the awakening moment occurs in conjunction with laughing behavior typical of hysterical laughter. The laughter usually reflects an acknowledgement of criticism towards others. Because of the defense of denial such criticism could not be expressed. In the absence of denial, criticism emerges in the form of sarcasm as in the telling of a humorous anecdote.

A 35-year-old man diagnosed as hysteric personality always experienced problems in his relationships with women. He was consistently unable to notice any negative qualities in women. He felt comfortable with men, yet depended on the women in his life for support, for evidence of self-importance, and for self-esteem. He was a happy-go-lucky type with a good sense of humor even though he also was socially immature. He was un-employed for a while and would not acknowledge the seriousness of his situation. After a therapy session in which he "celebrated" his one year unemployment anniversary he reported the following dream.

> I told someone a joke in the dream. I don't know who it was, but the punch line was so funny that I broke up with laughter. It really was hysterically funny. It woke me up laughing. I can't remember what the joke was but it had to do with poking fun at someone.

The nightmare of the hysteric, therefore, is one in which laughing or amusement causes the dreamer to awaken because in the absence of denial the laughter reflects implicit criticism toward another person.

THE PARANOID DISPOSITION

The emotion of disgust constitutes the underlying state of the paranoid disposition. It is a rejection response. Projection is the specific ego-defense designed to manage feelings of self-contempt. When the projection defense becomes impaired, the dreamer will experience feelings of revulsion. The nightmare may be characterized by themes of fragmented body parts—an expression of self-contempt—that the dreamer finds unable to tolerate.

A 38-year-old man who constantly complained of somatic ailments, reported the following dream.

> I was walking along the street and a truck was backing into a driveway. I stopped and waited for the truck to clear the path along the sidewalk so that I could keep on walking. Suddenly I looked down and I noticed some of my clothes were gone. I don't know what happened but I saw my arm fall off. It was split down the middle. There was no blood. Then I looked down and my penis was lying on a table next to me on the sidewalk. It was detached from my body and it also seemed to be split down the middle. I could see the cross section of tissue. I became horrified. I got nauseous and woke up scared.

When the projective defense does not fully operate, feelings of great incapacity and self-contempt emerge in the form of body fragmentation. The sense of incapacity is so great that without the use of the projective device, there is nothing to experience except one's total lack of solidity.

Nightmares of laughter or even detached amusement are the opposite of nightmares of self-contempt reflected in dreams of body fragmentation.

THE OBSESSIVE DISPOSITION

The emotion of expectation constitutes the underlying state of the obsessive disposition. Intellectualization is the ego-defense representing the obsessive defensive syndrome that manages the control feature inherent in the expectancy feeling. When the intellectualized control defenses become impaired, dreams of loss of control characterize the nature of the nightmare.

A 36-year-old woman who was especially controlled and obsessional had the following dream.

> I was high up on a cliff and I was dangerously close to the edge. Without realizing, I lost my footing, and I went over—falling, falling. I woke up.

This same woman reported that when she was a child she would frequently have a dream in which she was in the bathroom about to urinate. She would urinate, only to awaken and realize that she had wet her bed. She was a bedwetter throughout her childhood and each bedwetting incident always would be preceded by the rationale offered by the dream, thereby allowing her to urinate in bed.

Dreams that contain themes of falling or urinating may be referred to as loss of control dreams. They occur because the control defense of intellectualization is impaired.

THE PSYCHOPATHIC DISPOSITION

The emotion of surprise constitutes the underlying state of the psychopathic disposition. Regression is the ego-defense that manages the need to remain impulsive and dyscontrolled. When the regression defense becomes impaired, a nightmare will occur in which the dreamer is unable to move in the dream, is trapped, buried alive, drowning, or paralyzed.

A 25-year-old woman was referred to treatment because of a severe acting-out problem. She was frequently in trouble with her family and friends, and she relied heavily on drugs. She was always on the move and could never fully concentrate. She frequently would complain that things were boring. She did not particularly like the idea that a therapy session was a standard specified period of time. At the second session, she reported the following dream.

> I was in a grave, and I was being buried alive. I couldn't move. I was paralyzed. I tried to scream and woke up.

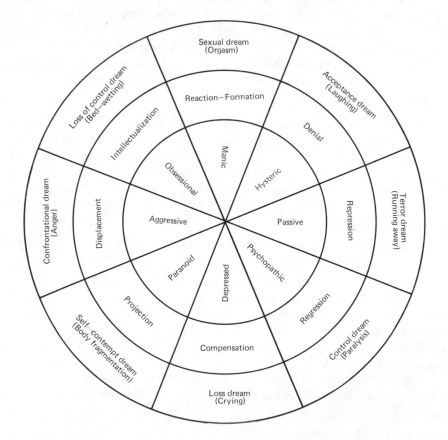

Figure 10-1.   A similarity structure of diagnostic dispositions and dream-nightmare themes. Intervening ego-defenses are indicated.

In another dream, she reported essentially the same nightmare theme except that the dream was one in which she was drowning and was unable to breathe. She again tried to scream and awakened.

In the absence of the regression defense which ensures an impulsive condition the nightmare for this dispositional type consists of themes in which the dreamer is overcontrolled.

Nightmares of loss of control of the obsessional type are thus opposite to nightmares of over control of the psychopathic type.

Figure 10-1 shows the basic polarities of nightmares and reveals that dream structure exists as a similarity structure; that is, those categories of nightmare closer to one another on the circle are more similar, and those categories of nightmare further apart on the circle reflect increasing differences from each other. Opposite categories show the greatest difference of nightmares. In the following section a discussion of how these nightmares reveal intrapsychic designations for each diagnostic type will be proposed.

Intrapsychic Designations for Basic Nightmare Categories

A content analysis of the basic nightmare categories will, quite easily, reveal their elemental intrapsychic nature.

NIGHTMARES OF SEXUALITY REFLECTING ID FORCE

The sexual dream reflecting a great pleasure urge in the absence of the reaction-formation defense reveals the basic id nature of the manic dispositional type. The emotion of joy contained within the manic disposition may therefore be essentially an id emotion. In this sort of dream, sexuality or pleasure is experienced in its fullest id expression. This manic type contains an inherent id nature that is managed by the *impulse blocking defense* of reaction-formation. In the absence of this blocking defense, impulse is released.

NIGHTMARES OF GRIEF OR CRYING REFLECTING SUPEREGO FORCE

This kind of nightmare expresses the opposite of gratification of needs and reveals the depressed type to be a superego one. The emotion of grief in the dream and its corresponding superego sense suggests to the dreamer that a "last chance" has been lost. In the absence of the compensation defense, loss seems irrevocable. The superego force inherent in this type generates feelings of inadequacy. The compensation defense is designed to release impulse in order to increase self-esteem. The grief nightmare, therefore, reveals the superego nature of the depressed type. In this type inherent superego force is managed by the *impulse releasing defense* of compensation. The emotion of sorrow, therefore, may be considered to be a superego emotion.

NIGHTMARES OF LAUGHING REFLECTING ID FORCE

The laughter dream of the hysteric type is a yielding-to-impulse dream. The hysteric type is one who denies any critical feelings toward objects external to self. When the defense of denial is not properly functioning, impulse in the form of criticism toward the environment will be released. Thus, denial is considered to be an impulse blocking device preventing this hysteric type from seeing and expressing any negative feelings to external figures. In the absence of denial a release of impulse toward the environment reveals the id nature of the hysteric. Nightmares include sarcasm or critical wit towards others and it is the experience of surprise in the dream that awakens the dreamer. Such types are surprised to experience any critical feelings at all. The laughter in the dream reflects this surprise as in reactions to the surprise ending to a joke. The awakening moment therefore also reveals the ego-alien nature to the nightmare and suggests that all nightmares represent ego-alien expressions in the personality. In the hysteric type, inherent id force is managed by the *impulse blocking defense* of denial. The emotion of acceptance, therefore, which is the underlying basic emotion of the hysteric, may be considered to be an id emotion.

NIGHTMARES OF FRAGMENTATION REFLECTING SUPEREGO FORCE

The paranoid personality type produces nightmares in which body fragmentation occurs. The fragmentation nightmare is one in which the dreamer experiences body parts either falling off or disintegrating. This sort of nightmare is based upon self-punitive feelings characteristic of the paranoid type. These nightmares occur whenever the projective defense is not functioning properly so that such persons are no longer able to release impulse and criticize the external world. This means that in the absence of the projective defense paranoid types are confronted with a profound sense of inferiority and strong self-critical feelings. These feelings suggest a superego formation inherent in the basic nature of the paranoid type. The dreamer awakens quite disturbed and frightened, and even experiences feelings of revulsion. It is proposed that the paranoid personality containing the central emotion of disgust or rejection and managed by the defense of projection produces a nightmare of fragmentation and is revealed to be a superego dispositional type; that is, a diagnostic type whose inherent superego nature is managed by the *impulse releasing defense* of projection.

NIGHTMARES OF TERROR REFLECTING SUPEREGO FORCE

The threatening terror dream of the passive dispositional type is quite inhibiting and punitive and reflects the superego nature of the emotion of fear. This sort of nightmare occurs when the repression defense is inadequate so that the basic impulse of escape from threatening stimuli fails. Examples of such threatening situations include running in terror from an attacker but being unable to escape quickly enough and dreams of being physically harmed. These are nightmares in which punishment and the feeling of dread prevails. They are superego dreams in which a sense exists that the dreamer is "bad" or will be punished. Repression generally regulates such superego impulses. The sense of dread and terror may be a result of superego pressure in which the dreamer is found in the role of the bad object—an implicit rationale for punishment themes to exist. The emotion of fear is therefore presumed to contain superego elements. It is proposed that the passive personality type in which fear is managed by the defense of repression generates terror nightmares and is revealed to be a superego dispositional type; that is, a diagnostic type whose inherent superego nature is managed by the *impulse releasing defense* of repression.

NIGHTMARES OF RAGE REFLECTING ID FORCE

Nightmares of rage characteristic of the aggressive dispositional type include dreams in which the dreamer is the attacker. These dream contents include violence toward others and overall yielding-to-rage impulses. These are nightmares in which anger, execution of punishment, and a general feeling or inclination to assault exists and they reveal the id nature of the aggressive dispositional type. In the absence of the defense of displacement, anger is expressed in its fullest manner. Instead of expecting punishment in the superego sense, as in the case of the nightmare of the passive type, this aggressive type becomes the attacker, is free of superego prohibitions and because of the absence of displacement is able to express the fullest and most intense form of anger in a direct manner. It is proposed that the aggressive personality whose basic emotion of anger is managed by the defense of displacement produces a nightmare of rage or attack and is revealed to be an id dispositional type; that is, a diagnostic type whose inherent id nature is managed by the *impulse blocking defense* of displacement.

NIGHTMARES OF LOSS OF CONTROL REFLECTING ID FORCE

The loss of control dreams of the obsessional type in which falling or bed wetting are thematic examples, shows that the defense of intellectualization is designed to exert control over what appears to be emotion with an id nature. The obsessive defenses are designed to control impulses and to guard against loss of control. These are blocking defenses. The nightmare of loss of control in which the dreamer awakens suggests that inherent in the basic nature of the obsessive type is an id force. In the absence of controlling defenses underlying id impulses become fully expressed. It may even be suggested that because id impulses inherent in the obsessive type are so intense several symptoms become characteristic of this dispositional tendency. These include rituals, obsessions, compulsions, and ruminations. The control defenses of intellectualization, rationalization, undoing, and sublimation are used to manage any potential breakthrough of such impulse. It is proposed, therefore, that the obsessive personality expressing the central emotion of expectation and managed by the defense of intellectualization produces a loss of control dream and is thereby revealed to be an id dispositional type; that is, to be a diagnostic type whose inherent id nature is managed by the *impulse blocking defense* of intellectualization.

NIGHTMARES OF PARALYSIS OR OVER-CONTROL REFLECTING SUPEREGO FORCE

The psychopathic dyscontrolled type expresses nightmares of over-control. This sort of nightmare includes contents of being unable to move. The nightmare occurs when the regression defense becomes incapacitated. Instead of impulses being released, which is generally the case when regression is effectively working, they become blocked when regression is impaired. The dreamer is awakened by the dream content of paralysis. The dreamer, experiencing a sense that dire consequences exist, feels vulnerable. Instead of freedom of movement which is usually necessary in persons of this type, in the absence of the regression defense, a deadened and dreaded immobility is experienced. It must be remembered that the psychopathic type tries to create external stimulation in order to counteract a "deadened" internalized sense and such attempts are generally made possible by the utilization of the regression defense. The "stopped" condition generates a sense of vulnerability to the full punitive measure of the superego. Parenthetically, it might be suggested that hyperkinetic children whose behavior, insofar as its energized quality is

Table 10-1.   The intrapsychic nature of diagnostic states: the relation of defense to nightmares.

DIAGNOSTIC DISPOSITION	DEFENSE	PURPOSE OF DEFENSE	NIGHTMARE THEME BASED UPON IMPAIRED DEFENSE	INTRAPSYCHIC FORCE REVEALED BY NIGHTMARE
Manic	Reaction-formation	To block impulse	Sexual-orgastic pleasure	Id
Depressed	Compensation	To release impulse	Grief—sobbing	Superego
Obsessive	Intellectualization	To block impulse	Loss of control, falling—bedwetting	Id
Psychopathic	Regression	To release impulse	Paralysis, drowning, being buried alive	Superego
Aggressive	Displacement	To block impulse	Attack—stabbing, hitting	Id
Passive	Repression	To release impulse	Terror—running, escaping	Superego
Hysteric	Denial	To block impulse	Laughing—sarcastic wit	Id
Paranoid	Projection	To release impulse	Fragmentation—body parts falling off	Superego

concerned, resembles the behavior of dyscontrolled types, surprisingly respond to mood energizing medication. Psychodynamically, these mood energizers could be addressing the underlying problem; that is, hyperkinetic activity may be the result of a powerful unconscious motivation to keep moving for fear of being completely paralyzed or "stopped." The mood energizer may thus be addressing the basic underlying fear of the hyperkinetic child of becoming immobilized. It is proposed that the psychopathic dyscontrolled personality containing the central emotion of surprise and managed by the regression defense produces a nightmare of panic-paralysis and is revealed to be a superego dispositional type; that is, a diagnostic type whose inherent superego nature is managed by the *impulse releasing defense* of regression.

Table 10-1 shows the intrapsychic nature of diagnostic states and indicates the blocking or releasing purpose of each defense mechanism. An examination of Table 10-1 will show how defense mechanisms regulate the intrapsychic force of each diagnostic disposition. In Figure 10-2, the intrapsychic elements as they correspond to each of the eight basic dispositional

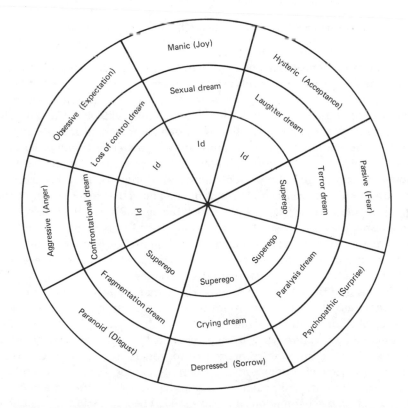

Figure 10-2. The intrapsychic structure of each of the eight basic emotion-dispositional categories. Typical nightmare themes are indicated.

types are shown. Again, the theoretical structure shows the opposition of id
and superego forces for each of the four polar pairs. This is meant to imply that
the basic personality system is consistently paralleled by the id-superego opposition at all levels. For example, it may now be suggested that joy, acceptance, anger, and expectation are id emotions based upon their most intense
expression in the absence of typical defenses. Similarly, sorrow, disgust, fear,
and surprise may be superego emotions, since, in the absence of defense their
intense expression in nightmares reveals superego meaning. It may also be
suggested on the same basis that manic, hysteric, aggressive, and obsessive
diagnoses reflect id states while depressed, paranoid, passive, and
psychopathic diagnoses reflect superego ones. The question now raised by the
analysis of defenses in relation to emotions and diagnostic states is whether
defense mechanisms may be considered, in the traditional psychoanalytic
sense, to be ego-defense mechanisms, or, whether as proposed here, basically
id or superego ones. In the following section the issue of whether defenses are
strictly speaking ego mechanisms shall be further explored.

DEFENSE MECHANISMS AND THE EGO: SOCIOBIOLOGICAL IMPLICATIONS

Although defenses have been referred to throughout this book as ego-defenses, the nightmare system has revealed their functions to reflect either id or
superego aims. In traditional psychoanalytic theory defense mechanisms represent ego operations (A. Freud, 1937; Hartmann, 1959; and Vaillant, 1976).
In the theoretical model presented here, defense mechanisms are regulating
features inherent in emotion and contained within an epigenetic program. It is
proposed that these defenses or defensive inclinations exist before the development of the ego. The present theory also proposes that only the ego in
the intrapsychic apparatus is absent at birth. The ego is, in a manner of speaking, the acculturation of intrapsychic sociobiological forces. The basic defense
mechanisms may be those structures epigenetically given and rooted in the
basic emotion system. The ego forms as a function of development, and defenses simply may become more effective regulators of id and superego emotions as a result of this developmental experience.

Defenses of the ego per se may be those that are utilized in the personality to maintain character formations and trait structure. These are the ego-
defenses of identification, introjection, internalization, and perhaps splitting
and isolation. In Figure 10-2 it may be seen that the personality structure
becomes an infraformation composed of id versus superego. In this respect,
defenses are viewed fundamentally as corresponding to emotions and not to
ego. Even in infants and primates, in the absence of significant ego development, a wide range of emotions are expressed. The expression of emotion does

not require the presence of ego. The ego, in this present model, emerges out of the cumulative conflict generated by the id-superego polarity inherent in the four bipolar pairs of emotion-diagnostic dimensions in each person. *The ego, therefore, is equivalent to conflict, or it is the product of intrinsic conflict between the four bipolar pairs of emotion.* Novey (1959) implies a similar idea by stating that "it is reasonable to postulate that anxiety and other emotions do not come into being in the adult only as full-blown ego operations, but must also exist as transitional states from the drives." The present theory would hold that the entire personality system exists in the substrate of emotion and that the expression of this system is tied to object relations formation and to the vicissitudes of psychosexual development. The defense structure may become salient during suitable developmental periods and these periods may also correspond to ego development. The differentiation process in the personality occurs through the resolution of conflict during these developing psychosexual stages. This differentiation process refers essentially to ego development. However, id and superego predispositional forces are encoded within emotion structure.

Psychosexual conflict becomes resolved on the basis of the extent to which the intrapsychic aims of each emotion is achieved; that is, whether the aims of id emotions and superego emotions are achieved. The ego emerges as one formed by the accumulation of both achieved and frustrated id-superego aims. This ego formation provides the bridge to the appearance of the identification mechanisms used in the development of personality trait structure. These mechanisms include identification and introjection and were cited earlier.

The issue of differentiation of ego formation as a function of developmental considerations is an evolutionary adaptational concept. The issue of an existing id-superego structure rooted in biology is an epigenetic one. Both phenomena as they appear in group life reflect the sociobiological interaction with psychoanalytic principles. Freud obliquely referred to the interaction of epigenetic and evolutionary phenomena by proposing that the content of the unconscious is phylogenetically determined. In this same light the present theory proposes that emotions contain a deep structure that includes regulatory defense features. These are regulators of id and of superego aims. The structure of personality presented here therefore is understood to be encoded at birth and in certain respects awaits its full developmental salience. It is both epigenetic and evolutionary. Thus defense mechanisms are referred to throughout this book as ego-defenses only because of conventional psychoanalytic usage. They perhaps should more accurately be referred to as emotion-defenses.

In the following section, the relationship of intrapsychic forces to psychosexual stages shall be proposed. Specifically, the question of intrapsychic aims during each psychosexual stage shall be hypothesized.

Intrapsychic Aims of Psychosexual Stages

Conventional psychoanalytic thinking regards development of ego, id, and superego to be based upon object relations management within the confines of specific psychosexual stages. The theoretical construction proposed in this chapter suggests that object relations development within the context of psychosexual stages produces refinement of intrapsychic force but does not create intrapsychic force. Intrapsychic force in the form of id and superego formations is presumed to be present at birth. However, they become exercised and expressed, as it were, as a function of the working-through of object relations problems during salient psychosexual stages. This is what is meant by the refinement of intrapsychic forces as a function of development. Development of intrapsychic force as a function of the effects of psychosexual stage conflicts and as a expression of diagnostic dispositional states is proposed in the following formulations.

THE ORAL BIPOLAR DIAGNOSES: MANIC VERSUS DEPRESSED

Karl Abraham (1927) was among the early psychoanalytic pioneers to point out the relationship between the oral psychosexual stage and the manic-depressive diagnoses. The proposed intrapsychic aim of the manic type is to express id impulses inherent in underlying pleasure needs. The extent to which this aim becomes frustrated may determine how much superego becomes generated in the form of depressive, sorrowful feelings. The id aim, to express the basic nature of the manic type or to seek full gratification, cannot ever be fully met. Socialization demands make this id aim impossible to completely fulfill. The frustration of full gratification may create a condition in which some loss is perceived. This perceived loss contains depressive features in which superego elements emerge. Thus, the oral period may generate elements of id and superego based upon socializing demands. The relation of id and superego to diagnostic states was discussed in the earlier section on the intrapsychic analysis of nightmares.

THE ANAL BIPOLAR DIAGNOSES: OBSESSIVE VERSUS PSYCHOPATHIC

It is proposed here that the intrapsychic aim of the obsessive dispositional type is to express underlying id impulse. The extent to which this aim becomes frustrated may determine how much superego emerges in the form of impulses that are withheld. When the control features of the obsessional type frustrate underlying urges for impulses to be expressed, then what remains are "stopping" experiences or superego feelings of "paralysis" previously discussed in the section on the intrapsychic nature of the nightmares of the psychopathic type. In a sense, the particular intrapsychic frustrations of the anal period generate obsessive-psychopathic conflict in the form of an id-superego compromise formation. These quantities of expression of id and superego are also based upon socializing demands.

THE PHALLIC BIPOLAR DIAGNOSES: PASSIVE VERSUS AGGRESSIVE

The aim of the aggressive dispositional type is to express id impulse and release anger directly. This aim cannot be fulfilled because of socialization demands and, in psychoanalytic terms, because of castration fears. When id aims are frustrated during this phallic psychosexual period, it is proposed that superego force in the form of passive, fearful feelings will emerge. The relation of superego force to the passive diagnosis was discussed previously in the section on the intrapsychic analysis of nightmares.

THE OEDIPAL BIPOLAR DIAGNOSES: HYSTERIC VERSUS PARANOID

The aim of the hysteric type is to express id impulses. Incorporation needs may even include the taking in of noxious stimuli. The extent to which such needs are blocked determines how much superego force inherent in opposite and rejecting paranoid features will substitute. This seems to indicate that if acceptance or incorporation fails to occur fully, what is left is superego force in the form of rejection inherent in the paranoid disposition.

Table 10-2 shows the relation between psychosexual conflict stages, diagnoses, and intrapsychic forces. In this table it may be seen that each diagnostic type of any polar pair corresponds to a single psychosexual stage but contains a separate id or superego force.

In summary, it may be proposed that personality trait structure and the refinement of ego/id and superego structure are based upon biological as well as developmental factors. Vicissitudes of psychosexual developmental experiences become superimposed on existing basic personality structure, in part, lending meaning to the psychosexual developmental experience. For example,

Table 10-2.   Relation between psychosexual stages, diagnostic state, and intrapsychic force.

PSYCHOSEXUAL STAGE	DIAGNOSIS	INTRAPSYCHIC FORCE
Oral	Manic	Id
	Depressed	Superego
Anal	Obsessive	Id
	Psychopathic	Superego
Phallic	Aggressive	Id
	Passive	Superego
Oedipal	Hysteric	Id
	Paranoid	Superego

it may be expected that id or superego emotions help make logical those events which evoke them during salient developmental periods. This process further contributes to the refinement of id and superego intrapsychic formation. In a sense, early and ongoing parental identifications and introjections, the basic nature of object relations, generate more differentiated elements of an existing program. Novey (1961) understands this formulation and states the implication incisively: "Although we have every reason to believe that the infant experiences emotion our structural theory has left little room for this belief." However, the present way of viewing the intrapsychic apparatus does allow for the belief that infants may experience the full basic emotion system even with only minimal ego development, and, in addition, may express a refinement of this system as a function of ego development.

The finding that no single basic dispositional type is an ego one, implies an important intersecting point between the intrapsychic underpinnings of individual members of the group with the intrapsychic nature of the group-as-a-whole. This issue will be explored in the following section. It will be proposed that individual members of the group as they constitute an ideal group composition create in the unfolding of their interpersonal role behavior an intrapsychic struggle between opposite role types that reflects a basic struggle between id and superego. The nature of this id-superego struggle, its balancing and rebalancing, and its therapeutic effects apparently help to fuel the group process. *Group interaction becomes the conflict between id and superego. The group structure that develops out of this conflict is the resulting ego. It is an ego in abstraction but exists insofar as the group composition comprises an id-superego conflict arena. The group becomes a new intrapsychic form illustrating how the intrapersonal becomes expressed in the interpersonal. It is an example of the intersecting structures of group psychotherapy and personality.* In the follo· /ing section intrapsychic role designations shall be described in terms of group role composition.

THE INTRAPSYCHIC GROUP ROLE COMPOSITION

Table 10-3 shows each of the basic eight categories with respect to corresponding aspects of personality structure. The relation between group roles, defenses, and the intrapsychic group structure shows how a rich and complex set of phenomena can be simply seen.

The role of puritan is one that utilizes reaction-formation defenses and is basically trying to manage the id nature of the puritan's manic disposition. In contrast the role of reintegrator is one that utilizes compensatory mechanisms to manage the superego nature of this basically depressed reintegrator type. The role of romantic is one in which denial mechanisms are utilized to manage its basic hysteric id nature. In contrast, the role of scrutinizer is one that

Table 10-3. The relation of intrapsychic forces to personality structure.

DISPOSITIONAL TYPE	DEFENSE	EMOTION	NIGHTMARE	INTRAPSYCHIC FORCE	GROUP ROLE
Manic	Reaction formation	Joy	Sexual dream	Id	Puritan
Depressed	Compensation	Sorrow	Crying	Superego	Reintegrator
Hysterical	Denial	Acceptance	Laughter	Id	Romantic
Paranoid	Projection	Disgust	Fragmentation	Superego	Scrutinizer
Aggressive	Displacement	Anger	Attacking	Id	Scapegoater
Passive	Repression	Fear	Fleeing	Superego	Innocent
Obsessive	Intellectualization	Expectancy	Bed-wetting	Id	Intellectualizer
Psychopathic	Regression	Surprise	Paralysis	Superego	Child

203

utilizes projective mechanisms to manage its basic paranoid superego nature. The role of innocent is one that utilizes repression as a defense to manage its basic passive superego nature, while the role of scapegoater is one that utilizes displacement as a defense to manage its basic aggressive id nature. The role of intellectualizer is one which uses control defenses to manage its basic obsessional id nature while the role of the child is one that uses regressive defenses to manage its basic psychopathic superego nature.

The inextricable connection between emotion, defense, and intrapsychic organization allows for a further exploration into the defense infrastructure as it is designed to manage emotion and as it addresses the intrapsychic demand inherent in each basic dispositional role type. Figure 10-3 shows the emergence of the ego in the group as a function of role and id-superego conflict. One implication drawn from this analysis is that the shape of the ego of the group-as-a-whole is determined by the nature of polar role conflict. The ego is the dialectic; it is conflict.

The underlying intrapsychic nature of each role is displayed in a structural form in Figure 10-3. If defenses managing the roles of scapegoater, intellectualizer, puritan, and romantic become impaired, then their respective under-

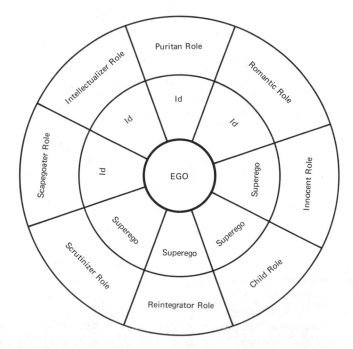

Figure 10-3.   The intrapsychic conflict inherent in the role composition of the group determines the nature of the group's ego. The ego of the group-as-a-whole is therefore a function of all group polar conflict, and is represented in the center space.

lying intrapsychic nature will emerge in the form of corresponding basic emotions of anger, loss of control, sexuality, and self-indulgance respectively—all reflecting derivative id aims. If defenses managing the roles of innocent, child, reintegrator, and scrutinizer become impaired, their respective underlying nature also will emerge in the form of corresponding basic emotions of fear or withdrawal, some form of phobic or paralytic-like behavior, depression, and profound feelings of incapacity—all examples reflecting superego effects.

The difference between id and superego role categories also, for the most part, correspond to the differences between the accessible and impedance dimensions that were discussed in the context of diagnosis and conflict. Before proceeding with an analysis of the intrapsychic nature of the group the intrapsychic function of defenses will be briefly reviewed. The intrapsychic regulatory function of defenses were outlined earlier.

Intrapsychic Function of Ego-Defenses

For the most part, defenses of the accessible categories act to block emotion as a way of controlling id urges. Reaction-formation acts to block responses to pleasure. Denial acts to block responses of a critical nature to external figures. Intellectualization acts to block loss of control. Defenses of the imedance categories, for the most part, act to release emotion as way of controlling superego urges. Compensation is designed to release emotion in order to regain a loss and to overcome inferiority feelings. Projection is designed to release criticism toward others as a way of avoiding painful self-evaluation. Regression is designed to release impulse in order to avoid responding to the controlling requirements of superego demands. These defense mechanisms were discussed in relation to group roles in chapters 5 and 6, and an analysis of blocking and releasing functions of defenses was discussed earlier in the present chapter. There is one exception to the polar conflict system of accessible and impedance states presented here as they correlate either to id or superego aims.

THE EXCEPTIONAL CASE

The one exception in the personality system that attributes id aims to accessible categories and superego aims to impedance categories is in the passive and the aggressive dispositional types. Figure 10-2 shows that not all accessible categories are constituted with an id nature. The passive accessible type is one with a superego nature. The same phenomenon is seen in the impedance categories. Not all impedance states are constituted with a superego nature. The aggressive type has a basic id nature. Thus, in the final analysis, it may be assumed that only *most* of the accessible categories contain basic defenses designed to block emotion in order to manage inherent id intrapsychic force. Similarly, it may be assumed that only *most* impedance categories contain basic defenses designed to release emotion in order to manage underlying superego intrapsychic force. The superego nature of the passive-accessible type creates a positional inconsistency in the personality system. Like other accessible types, an inherent id force would be expected to characterize its nature. It is inconsistent also for the agressive-impedance type to display an id nature. Like other imedpance types, an inherent superego force would be expected to characterize its nature. It is difficult at this point to explain the inelegance of this finding. It may be that when the personality structure is seen in three dimensions as a twisting elliptical shape, each succeeding personality level may be located in this spiralling space at slightly different locations. In three dimensions the structural model may reveal catgegory overlapping. Furthermore, this inconsistency in the intrapsychic character of passive and aggressive types may contribute to the unfolding of a dynamic process in the group.

In previous chapters on the transformational shape of the group it was suggested that a dialectic exists in the group based upon the conflict difference in the weightedness between accessible and impedance types. The question asked was whether conflict could ever be resolved if all the accessible types exerted minimal conflict force onto the group while all the impedance types exerted maximum conflict force onto the group. The proposition that accessible types are really all id types and that impedance types are really all superego types constituted the strength of this dialectic dilemma. However, the dilemma begins to yield when it is suggested that one of the accessible types is actually a superego one while one of the impedance types is really an id type. Instead of four accessible-id types that are structurally locked into position with four corresponding impedance superego types, it may be that the group's compositional structure generates a good deal of polar conflict while simulataneously containing a lever for change in its basic infrastructure.

The placement of passive and agressive types around the circle only becomes inconsistent on the intrapsychic level of personality. However, this inconsistency may reveal a key factor in the group structure permitting it to become responsive to a whole host of therapeutic influences; that is, because of the passive-active ingredients as well as the intrapsychic forces inherent in the passive and aggressive types, a more complex intermingling of accessible and impedance role types becomes possible. The therapeutic lever for change in the group may be defined, in part, as this mutation-like inconsistency. It may be an example of the system of personality structure intersecting group process in a facilitative way. This inconsistent element of the personality system should be further studied.

THE INTRAPSYCHIC NATURE OF THE GROUP

Spotnitz' (1976) focus on the need to work-through deep group resistance elements implies the inordinate impact of superego forces on the group's surface. The variation in conflict force determines the dilemma of working-through inherent in the therapist's creation of a diagnostically hetereogeneous group. The significant superego stress on the group in the form of the superego weightedness of impedance role types, added to the cumulative superego transference toward the therapist, generates a group ego structure highly influenced by superego force. This group ego structure utilizes defenses acting to block emotion and to release emotion in order to maintain a balance of intrapsychic demands that become expressed through interpersonal interaction.

The group as the expression of ego is therefore occupied with the management of urges to release and to block emotion. Because of the inordinate superego pressure in the group reflected in the weightedness of impedance roles, the interaction of blocking and releasing mechanisms are given most attention in the continuing group process. This inordinate superego pressure emanates from the group role composition and from the transferential relationship of the group to the therapist. In previous chapters on the transformational shape of the group it was shown that the impeded role types that generate the greatest superego conflict weight are the scrutinizer-paranoid type and the reintegrator-depressed type. The inordinate amount of superego conflict discharged onto the group emanates from these two sources. The main difficulty presented by superego demands in the group may be defined as one in which inadequacy feelings and potential feelings of loss characterizing reintegrator-depressed types, along with severe feelings of vulnerability and self-contempt characterizing scrutinizer-paranoid types, constitute a main preoccupation of the working-through energies of the group. It is perhaps this condition that characterizes the group's resistance at its deepest levels. To maintain this resistance to working-through, defenses of compensation and projection are utilized to release emotion so that superego urges representing basic depressed and paranoid character structure remain powerful influences in the group.

Durkin (1964) indicates that the defense system is a basic character structure reflecting the balance of id, ego, and superego of each member. To this may be added that the intrapersonal is more easily expressed in interpersonal interaction when, in the group, the presence of an impedance role type is balanced at least by the presence of one opposite accessible type. Such balance implies that the group will not become an intractable superego environment or an especially acting-out environment based upon inordinate id urges. The goal for any member of the therapy group is to reevaluate typical defense postures. In doing this, those members who express roles characterized as superego ones may be able to experience a significant change in their basic character structure. Those who express roles characterized as id roles may also experience change. Therapists who encourage each group member to interact with every other group member are thus asking members to work with projected intrapersonal aspects of their personalities in an interpersonal way. In this way, the status rituals described in earlier chapters can change and hierarchical patterns of relating may become altered.

The working-through of defenses represents a profound change experience and suggests that environmental and developmental influences may indeed be strong enough to modify predispositional id-superego qualities etched in the substrate of emotion. The working-through process therefore reflects a confluence of sociobiological and psychoanalytic phenomena. A final issue to be discussed with respect to the intrapsychic group concerns the relationship of the intrapsychic balance to psychosexual stages of the group process.

PSYCHOSEXUAL GROUP PHASE IN RELATION TO INTRAPSYCHIC BALANCE

In chapter 4 on a genealogical view of group psychotherapy, the first generation of group life was considered to reflect an oedipal stage and as such was related in a dispositional way to paranoid and hysteric themes. Hartman and Gibbard (1974b) also indicate that there is "a paranoid cast in the formation of small groups," and Durkin (1964) also sees the formative group as one that is highly suggestible. Even though Durkin attributes this suggestibility to submissive behavior in response to the fearful perception of the group as a preoedipal mother, high suggestibility also implies that some hysteric quality exists, and this indicates an oedipal cast to the group. Furthermore, it may be that the perception of the group involves not the fear of the preoedipal mother but competition for the oedipal mother. Bion (1959a) also indicates that the group is idealized in the initial phase, and such idealization only can occur if strong hysteric denial ingredients exist in the group's experience. On the basis of the present personality system it is possible to attach intrapsychic significance to the various group generations. Since dispositional types have been intrapsychically designated, and since these same diagnostic dispositions have been related to psychosexual development, it is possible to understand the nature of the intrapsychic balance inherent in the psychosexual stage of each succeeding group generation.

Table 10-4 shows the relation between group generation, psychosexual stage, diagnostic disposition, intrapsychic force, basic emotion, and basic defense. This table shows that each period of psychosexual development is characterized by an intrapsychic conflict between id and superego forces. Apparently the intrapsychic struggle may exist throughout psychosexual development. It supports in part the Kleinian view that the entire intrapsychic apparatus exists at birth.

During the first group generation the diagnostic cast of the group implies paranoid and hysteric themes. The id-superego balance revolves around oedipal issues of competition and loyalty. During the second group generation the diagnostic cast of the group implies passive and aggressive themes. The id-superego balance during this generation concerns phallic themes of assertiveness and envy. The third generation of the group contains a diagnostic organi-

Table 10-4.   The Relationship between group generation and the structure of personality.

GROUP GENERATION	PSYCHOSEXUAL STAGE	DIAGNOSTIC DISPOSITION	INTRAPSYCHIC FORCE	BASIC EMOTION	EGO-DEFENSE
1	Oedipal	Hysteric	Id	Acceptance	Denial
		Paranoid	Superego	Disgust	Projection
2	Phallic	Aggressive	Id	Anger	Displacement
		Passive	Superego	Fear	Repression
3	Anal	Obsessive	Id	Expectancy	Intellectualization
		Psychopathic	Superego	Surprise	Regression
4	Oral	Manic	Id	Joy	Reaction-formation
		Depressive	Superego	Sorrow	Compensation

zation involving obsessive and psychopathic elements. The id-superego balance during this generation of the group involves issues of control, acting-out, and reaction to demands. During the fourth generation of the group the diagnostic organization includes manic and depressive dispositions. The id-superego balance during this group generation revolves around derivative possessing-sexual and deprivation themes.

The Nature of the Ego in Each Group Generation

The "shape" of the group ego is determined differently as a function of the group age; that is, the group ego as it is formed out of id-superego struggles inherent in each psychosexual stage is not a consistent ego. As the group ages, a psychosexual regression occurs and the group, as ego, is affected by this regression.

During the first group generation the ego is one that emerges in the work on loyalty and disloyalty. This struggle reflects the oedipal nature of the intrapsychic balance during this first group generation instigated by hysteric and paranoid themes. Hysteric and paranoid themes generate opposing intrapsychic aims. The proposed intrapsychic hysteric-id aim is to express impulses and begin to generate a critical and evaluative sense of the world. Incorporation aims are pursued even with the intention of absorbing noxious stimuli, and this aim will be generally frustrated because of reality and socialization demands. The extent to which it becomes blocked determines how much superego force inherent in its opposite paranoid-superego disposition will substitute for it. Thus during the oedipal group phase it is likely that the group ego will be determined by the particular nature of incorporation and rejection urges. During the second group generation the ego of the group emerges as one that is concerned with phallic assertion themes. This generation of the group is influenced mainly by aggressive-id and passive-superego aims. When the id aims inherent in aggressive themes are frustrated, it is proposed that superego forces in the form of passive-fearful feelings will emerge. During this phallic phase of the group then, the group ego will be determined by the particular nature of passive-active urges. During the third generation the group ego emerges as one that is expressed in themes of control and in reaction to demands. This anal phase is also defined by issues of acting-out. This generation of the group is influenced mainly by obsessional control themes reflecting underlying id force and by psychopathic dyscontrol themes reflecting underlying superego force. When id aims are frustrated, then superego in the form of impulses that are withheld or inhibited emerge and may cause the group to become inert. In this group generation then, the ego will be determined by the particular nature of controlled and dyscontrolled urges. During the fourth group generation the ego is an oral one and is expressed through themes of "neediness." In this generation of the group, major intrapsychic themes revolve around manic-id aims of attaining pleasure. The extent to which this aim is blocked may determine how much superego becomes generated in the form of depressive-superego force. The id aim, to seek full gratification, cannot ever be fully met. Socialization demands make such id achievement impossible to attain. Thus the group ego will be one in which, to a certain extent, loss is perceived. Depressive superego elements may be experienced by group members during this group generation and the group ego will be determined by the difference members experience between a need to be loved and a corresponding feeling of a lack of fulfillment.

The ego of the group emerges and may be monitored whenever these basic themes are worked on in the group. Although all themes become expressed in each generation of the group, each generation of the group is also characterized by a major theme. Whenever the group is a working group, it may be said to be characterized as an ego group. The work group will be defined as one in which psychosexual themes are crystallized and defensive operations yielded. Whenever the group bypasses appropriate psychosexual themes, defensive operations will obtain and the group may express a high level of resistance. Bion (1959a,b; 1961) essentially postulates a similar model. His work group is an ego group and his assumption groups are id-superego ones.

This chapter has described a theory of intrapsychic forces that are revealed through a theory of nightmares, in which id-superego predispositions exist in an epigenetic structure. It was proposed that this structure is related to emotion, defense, and diagnostic dispositional states and that the entire system may influence the group in profound ways. A main point that has emerged in this discussion concerns the ability of the group's interactional capacity to alter these powerful elements of personality that are contained within the roles of the group. It was suggested that the yielding of defensive operations enables such alterations to take place. The work on defenses is essentially defined as the evaluation of the regulatory blocking and releasing defense functions.

Group Communication: An Introduction

The manner in which the group yields defensive operations so that assumption-like groups become work-like groups may be traced in the communicational structure of the group and in the overall psychosomatic symptom structure of the group; that is, in its interpersonal interactions, members of the group reveal group anxieties and group symptoms that are congruent in many respects to individual psychosomatic symptoms. The group's psychosomatic symptoms are inextricably bound to individual defensive operations and to the geometry of communication in the group. The implication here is that there is a systematic nature to the interpersonal communication of the group, and that this organization of communication also reveals whether the anxiety of the group is being acted-out or is being managed therapeutically.

The group's communicational system shall be reviewed in the following chapters and a system of communicational structures will be proposed. This system will imply that the significant moments of therapy process can be detected even in terms of psychosomatic signals of the group. How the group communicates these signals also reveals that the intrapsychic group is a communicating one.

11

Communicational Structure of Groups: Research Traditions and Focal Conflict Themes

---

The overt or manifest content of a group somehow has never satisfactorily informed therapists of the actual meaning of any interaction. The feeling among therapists and authors persists: what is specifically said in the group is not the only thing going on; that there exists underlying or latent meaning to verbal interaction; and that nonverbal ritualistic communication is also part of the overall group interaction. Authors have attempted to decipher the true meaning of group interaction by examining group transcript data and by applying a whole range of methodological techniques in the analysis of these data. Researchers consistently want to develop new ways to understand the laws and meaning of the communicational structure of the group.

The search for a scientific underpinning to group communication is well expressed by Newcomb (1963): "It is a safe prediction that individuals who are initially strangers to one another will, under conditions assuming that they will become well acquainted, experience many changes in the degree of their attraction toward one another. Such changes, like any others that scientists investigate, presumably occur in orderly ways, and the principles governing both change and nonchange correspond to constancies."

This statement by Newcomb suggests that there are specific rules that may govern the communicational structure in the life of the group. Watzlawick, Beavin, and Jackson (1967) indicate that the group communication should be understood as a transactional event and not simply a reaction to a stimulus, and, Kadis et al. (1968) consider such transactional events to mean that the group communicates on several different levels simultaneously. One level is the literal one or manifest one. The second is interpersonal and includes references to status and role. The third level contains the unconscious meaning to the manifest first level including symbolic transference implications toward other members. Understanding the communication in a group implies access to each of these levels.

This chapter will provide a review of various methods employed to study the several levels and complex structure to group communication. Some of the features that comprise the total contextual fabric of the group's communicational structure include the appearance of focal conflict themes, the expression of anxiety in the group, the appearance of psychosomatic symptomatology and its relation to emotion, the expression of role behavior and dreams, interaction as it relates to the leader-therapist, and the system of communication as it constitutes a communicational group geometry. The overall communicational structure of the group is composed of these features of group life and will also be explored in the following chapters.

ATTEMPTS TO UNDERSTAND GROUP COMMUNICATION: A SURVEY

Translating the manifest communication into its more cogent latent meaning constitutes a Chomskian inverse matrix in which the surface structure of the group communication may be considered analogous to the deeper structure of language (Chomsky, 1972). So far, the only technique not employed in the study of group communication is that of code theory in which deciphering techniques are used to uncover true messages hidden within the manifest content but not beneath it. In this kind of research, the deeper levels of group communication are discovered strictly through the analysis of verbatim transcript data of the manifest content. It is the sort of methodology that Hall (1953) employed in the study of dreams.

Methods of Studying Verbal Interaction

Scores of techniques have been used to study verbal communication and overall interaction in groups. These may be divided into methods of group research from three distinct traditions. The first is that of group process research. This type of research attempts to understand group communication by utilizing experimental approaches with short-term task groups and classroom groups. The second research tradition from which the study of group communication arises is that of family interaction. Patterns of communication are derived that essentially diagnose pathological circuits of family life. Results of such studies are generally used to develop techniques in the treatment of families. The third tradition in group communicational theory is that of research into the psychotherapy group process. Group psychotherapy research in turn is divided into two methods of understanding the communication of the group-as-a-whole. The first approach investigates focal conflict themes of group interaction. The second is that of the psychoanalytic tradition which employs transference interpretations to make sense out of the mainifest group content. All of these traditions derive principles of group communication that have many elements in common.

GROUP PROCESS RESEARCH

There has appeared in the group process literature a plethora of studies that reflect this particular research approach. Bales (1950) used an extensive coding system to understand the true communication in groups and his work tended to influence an entire generation of group process researchers. Leary (1957) attempted to code verbal interaction using categories of analysis of dominance-submission and love and hate. Schutz (1958) used observer ratings and observational systems to code such interaction on the basis of needs for inclusion, control, and affection. Thelen (1954) used a scoring system for group interaction which was based upon Bion's theory of basic-assumption group activity. Dunphy (1966) utilized postmeeting evaluations in studying group communication, and in classroom groups, Mills (1964) used a sign process system, while Mann (1966; Mann, et al. 1967, and 1970) used a member-leader and a member-member scoring system to measure the feelings of subjects.

In a separate series of studies designed to understand member-therapist or member-leader interaction, hypotheses were generated to imply that all communication in the group always has some reference to the leader (Gibbard and Hartman, 1973a, 1973b, 1973c; Mann et al., 1970). This hypothesis also has been independently proposed by Wolf and Schwartz (1962). An example of research designed to evaluate this hypothesis is given by Mann (1966). In his study, all statements that might really be disguised references to the leader were divided into four kinds of statements and into four thematic categories. The analysis demonstrated the complexity of any manifest verbal interaction in the group. The four types of statements were further divided in several ways: four kinds of hostility, including moving against, disagreeing, withdrawing, and guilt-inducing; four kinds of affection, including moving toward, identifying, agreeing, and reparation; three kinds of power relations, including submissive, equality, and dominance; and four ego states, including expressing and denying anxiety, depression, and guilt. Results of the study suggested that group transcript data can indeed be analyzed with respect to assumed leader references. These group process studies sharpened the conviction among researchers that group communicational meaning could only minimally be understood from overt manifest verbal statements, and that the larger syntactical life of the group existed beneath the surface as a deeper layer to the group interaction.

FAMILY COMMUNICATIONAL STUDIES

The second major tradition of group process communication analysis is divided into two parts. First, research into family process interaction was generated by the Palo Alto group. This research consisted of the study of family patterns (Riskin, 1963), the formulation of the double bind theory presented by Bateson, Jackson, Haley, and Weakland (1956, 1963), and, in a new model system of communication, the schizophrenic family (Haley, 1968). Bateson and Jackson (1964) also investigated the implied role behavior of groups. Such studies demonstrated that a series of complementary patterns of interaction or roles exist in groups. The work by Bateson and Jackson suggested that the action of one member of a group has special value in the responsive potential of another member, a comparison similar to the resonance value or role salience proposed by Foulkes (1977). This idea of role complementarity and role resonance has also been reviewed by Kellerman (1977) in a theoretical study of the structure of Shostrom's (1972) mate selection model. In general, in identifying pathogenic family patterns, the research of the Palo Alto group revealed a new way to understand group communication.

The field of family therapy provided the second theoretical arena of group process research into latent communicational patterns. Utilizing psychodynamic and group process formulations, studies were designed to probe the deeper meanings of family communication. Theoretical studies by Ackerman (1958), Bott (1957), and Bowen (1960) provided an impetus for a new generation of work in family therapy. Satir (1965) and Howells (1975) analyzed the family as a treatment unit. Zuk (1971) proposed a theory of a triadic communicational framework in the family, and Ravich (1974) analyzed the issue of complementarity in families as a special communicational phenomenon. A small number of family interactional patterns was proposed by Ehrenwald (1974), and Minuchin et al. (1978) developed a systems family approach for the treatment of anorexia nervosa. Results of these approaches have implications for therapy group process. They have revealed communicational links that include sharing patterns, contagion patterns in which a sharing of pathologies occurs, complementary patterns with implications for role theory, and patterns of resistance against contagion patterns. The structure of Ehrenwald's and Minuchin's conceptions of family communicational patterns also has relevance to therapy group communication in terms of the defense structure that prevents group members from understanding the deeper levels of communicational meaning.

Both the group process and family therapy literature generated principles of underlying themes of group function and pointed the way to the understanding of communicational change as a function of such process.

GROUP THERAPY RESEARCH

The third tradition in group communication research was developed by psychoanalytic group therapists as well as by so-called Tavistockian therapists interested in underyling thematic focal conflicts expressed by the group-as-a-whole. Both psychoanalytic and Tavistockian researchers proposed thematic underlying meanings to group communication about which all manifest material related. In addition, some authors related these thematic focal conflicts to various stages of group development.

Levels of Communication

Bach (1954) enumerates seven specific categories of group communication and assigns a hierarchical meaning to each level. A puritanical first level consists of rational problem solving. The second level includes a direct approach to communication among members in which considerations of etiquette become worked-through. The third level, an indulgence level, permits group members catharsis through laughing and playing and even through the expression of irrational emotions. This third level is an acting-out libidinized one. A fourth level is termed the testing of interpersonal effects. It is a diagnostic preoccupation level where members convey their impressions to one another. This level of communication indicates that a self-perceptive orientation exists as part of the group culture. Level four seems also to be one in which typical defenses become partially worked-through. The fifth level is called the level of contextual associations. Here the group engages in free associations and dreams. The sixth level consists of nonrepressed communicational reactions among members and the seventh involves new problem solving.

Bach attempts to formulate categories of communicational analysis in which deeper layers refer to emotional communication. In such an analysis, the more surface, manifest level of group communication is likely to reveal typical defense patterns. Understanding the deeper levels of this communication can uncover messages of an emotional nature which the surface communication, as a defense communication, is designed to obscure. A partial theoretical validation of this hypothesis is offered by Bach in the proposal that as the group matures, it works toward greater emotional reciprocity and is less concerned with defensive communication. Festinger (1968), in a study of informal communication, also distinguished between two levels of communication. One is emotional and the other nonemotional. According to Festinger, in emotional communication, desire decreases as a result of catharsis. In nonemotional communication desire may not decrease. This conception resembles Bionian ideas of the difference between communication in the work group and the communication that characterizes the basic assumption groups.

Yalom (1970) surveys a system of stages of the group also presented by Parker (1958) and by Tuckman (1965). This system implies that communicational themes may represent each group stage. The first orientation stage, in which the members of the group are concerned with acceptance and approval, seems to contain elements of oral and oedipal features where "oughts" and "shoulds" prevail, but where members depend on the leader for guidance. The second stage is one of group conflict. Here members are concerned with dominance and power. This stage resembles the phallic and anal stages of psychosexual development in which pecking orders seem to develop as a reflection of dominance or assertion themes. The third and fourth stages of harmony and cohesiveness, respectively, again seem to contain oral and oedipal elements in which loyalty issues and issues of obedience prevail. Apparently, the ongoing group contains both progressive and regressive psychosexual elements.

Finally, Ezriel (1973) proposes that all communication in the group may be understood in terms of the required and avoided relationships that each member of the group carries as a reflection of that member's historical character problems. Essentially, Ezriel is positing a communicational paradigm in which knowledge of any member's defensive posture will reveal information about underlying emotions.

The issue of how members of the group communicate emotionally has interested group therapy authors as well as researchers of group process. Writers of both traditions have proposed categories of communicational analyses involving basic focal conflicts of the group. The kinds of responses to these conflict themes that are produced by individual members of the group may also be understood to be a function of role types of the group.

Thematic Categories of Group Communication: The Issue of Focal Conflicts

The salience of focal conflict is cogently described by Foulkes and Anthony (1965): "the group tends to speak and react to a communication as if it were a living entity. . . . All contributions are variations on this single theme, even though the group is not consciously aware of that theme and do not know what they are really talking about." The issue of focal conflict theme is a concept that joins the analysis of individual communication with the communicational analysis of the group-as-a-whole. Stock and Lieberman (1962) indicate that the group focal conflict refers to the "shared, preconsciously maintained fantasies in the group." These themes relate to Bion's (1952) basic assumption groups, and Ezriel's (1950) underlying common group tension. Stock and Lieberman indicate further that, "A group therapy session can be understood in terms of a slowly emerging, shared pre-conscious conflict together with varying attempts to find an adequate solution to the conflict." The surface level of the group's moment to moment communicational interaction is actually considered to contain disguised elements of the deeper focal conflicts: "the focal group conflict is never expressed in direct, explicit, or succinct terms. The manifest content is a vehicle offering masked hints of underlying issues." This difference between manifest and latent communication is related to the difference between the psychology of the group-as-a-whole and that of individual members. "Because the focal conflict characterizes the group rather than any single patient, individual expressions often bear only a tangential or partial relationship to the underlying conflict."

The operation of focal conflict themes assumes at least three phenomena of group life (Stock and Lieberman, 1962). The first phenomenon assumes that free association occurs in the group. The second assumes that the manifest content refers to the here and now, and that the underlying meaning refers to a group wish or focal conflict—a position first asserted by Whitman, Lieberman, and Stock (1960). The third assumption accepts that all elements of the interaction are relevant to the shared, preconscious group focal conflict.

These assumptions make possible the conclusion that, "The group situation consists of a conversation; one comment followed by another and another in which a number of individuals participate. There is usually a surface coherence to these successive comments; that is, the patients can be described as having a conversation about some topic. However the series of comments also can be understood as a sequence of associations which involve a subsurface implication with a coherence of its own . . . all material of the session is relevant to the group focal conflict . . . any comment has both a specific, personal meaning for the individual as well as some implication for the total group . . . when three or four patients react to a topic or a story introduced by one individual, it is relatively easy to make . . . the judgement that the group-as-a-whole is the level on which the communication is relevant." Finally, it is asserted that "there may be a limited number of 'families' of focal conflict." Freudians would propose basic psychosexual themes that reflect these limited number of "families" while Bionians would propose themes reflected in the basic assumption groups. Ezriel would propose an underlying common group tension theme about which members begin to form a common or shared group fantasy. The fantasy would be connected to the emergent required and avoided relationship inherent in the role-conflict composition of the group. Finally, Foulkes and Anthony (1965) propose a group matrix in which the group responds as a whole to the communication of an individual and an individual's communication comes "from the group through the mouthpiece of the speaker."

SOME FOCAL CONFLICT THEMES

Two examples of the appearance and operation of focal conflicts are offered by Stock (1962), Stock and Lieberman (1963), and by Whitman and Stock (1958). The first is a focal conflict that appears as angry feelings toward the therapist along with fear of abandonment and in addition anger on the part of the therapist should the defiance of group members become expressed. The solution is for the group members to join forces and comply in a manner that expresses the anger obliquely, for example, in a passive-aggressive manner. In this way, the focal conflict and its solution replicate exactly the formation and development of character traits in an individual. This paradigm demonstrates theoretically that groups may develop traits reflecting partial resolutions or compromises of its focal conflicts. The paradigm also suggests that groups may develop personality; that is, typical ways of behaving based upon the relationship of the membership to the therapist, and based upon the management by the group of focal conflict tension. This idea also has been proposed by Kellerman and Plutchik (1977) in a theoretical paper outlining a basic system of emotion, defense, and diagnostic dispositional tendencies of therapy group membership. The notion of group personality has also been referred to by Kellerman and Plutchik (1978) in a diagnostic similarity structure analysis of therapy group membership, and by Kellerman and Maliver (1977) who identified and measured the personality profile of the therapy group.

A second example of a focal conflict theme emerging in the group occurs when sexual competitiveness exists in association with the guilt evoked by such needs. The solution is for the group to express the competitiveness in a displaced way, for example, to argue about who in the group is the sickest member.

Kadis et al. (1968) suggest that focal conflicts may emerge in groups during peak moments. The moments of focal conflict pressure are defined by the authors as "G" responses or group phenomenon responses. They include responses to the appearance of a new member, someone attacking the therapist, an attempt to annihilate a group member, fractionation of the group, a change in the status of a member, and subgrouping. It is suggested that moments of focal conflict pressure may also emerge during caroming events in which the group assumes a bandwagon stance, during times of acting-out, and during moments of reactive associations by members. Such focal conflict pressure may also occur in reaction to the appearance and disappearance of defense behavior in terms of multiple transferences, with regard to the homeostasis of the group, and to the feeling of having reached a plateau. Thus, Kadis et al. propose that focal conflict themes may emerge in response to structural as well as group process elements.

The relation of focal conflicts to communicational meaning is, according to most authors, a translation of how emotionality is managed in the group. For example, Durkin (1964) indicates that when the group is formed, the underlying hostility existing in a cross-section of the membership is really a defense against fear of narcissistic injury. This implies that most communication during formative group periods perhaps will exist as focal conflict with regard to the defense of hostility versus the expression of it.

Understanding the focal conflict theme facilitates a deeper understanding of any ongoing communication. The main point, however, is that focal conflict themes consist of historical-emotional material on the latent level that is managed by defense on the surface level. Each interaction can be a communicational sample that reflects the social organization of the group. This social organization is bound by the character defenses of individuals of the group.

Scheflen (1967) indicates that "The social organization for an interaction is not a simple alternation of speaker and listener, but involves kinship and other affiliational systems, dominance hierarchies, territorial arrangements, and other abstractable dimensions." These other abstractable dimensions may actually refer to the role relations of the group, and consequently, inevitably imply emotion-defense relations.

ROLES AND COMMUNICATION

One always may be trying to justify and reinforce a particular role in the group through the expression of typical defensive behavior. Therefore, any member's specific communication in the group will contain deep structure information about the nature of defense and underlying emotion. Communication in the group is related to one's defense regarding underlying transference feelings, or, as Ezriel suggests, regarding the avoided relationship. The extent to which any member of the group is able to blend defenses with group focal conflict depends to a large degree on that member's particular dispositional role quality. According to Foulkes (1977), "The individual resonates in the key to which he is attuned, in which his specific personality structure is set." Resonance is a reflection of diagnostic disposition and role type. It may take place "without any particular message being sent or received, being in fact purely instinctive. . . . It is as if all the events were specifically interrelated with each other in their vital meaning, and showed this interrelationship by resonating."

Bach (1954) also claims that the group's role repertoire is a necessary compositional feature to group structure insofar as it enables the group to maintain its communicational network. He enumerates universal themes in the communicational structure of the group which may correspond to focal themes. These are ambivalent feelings about loving women, hostility, distrust and fear of people, feelings of inferiority and a desire to be average, and blaming others versus accepting responsibility. In addition, Hobbs (1951) suggests that for each theme of the group process there exists both a major participant and some minor participant. It is not clear whether these participants are complementary types or whether they are basically similar types, although Foulkes and Anthony (1965) suggest that resonating in the group is usually associated with complementary relationship between members. For example, any focal conflict power theme will generally resonate with a dominant member as its major pariticipant and a submissive one as its minor participant. Any focal conflict theme involving needs for love and attention may resonate with an elated group member as a major participant and a depressed group member as a minor one. Variations of dominance themes seem to be quite prominant in the focal conflict nature of the group.

Dominance: Role Implications

Schachter (1968) implies that communication to dominant or submissive group members may follow specific patterns. This observation is further developed by Hurwitz, Zander, and Hymovitch (1968), who studied the effects of power on the relations among group members. These authors found that low dominance types: tend to be defensive against high dominance types; experience constraints in their permission or sense of permission to communicate; are expected to participate less, so that when they do it appears more conspicuous—a reference to their actual participation time versus their apparent participation time; and have fewer communications directed toward them. Other studies on the effects of differential positions in power hierarchies upon behavior essentially yield similar data (Kelley, 1951; Lippitt, Polansky, Redl, and Rosen, 1952). In addition, these studies also show that other members lower in the dominance hierarchy are influenced by the more dominant members; that lower dominant members attempt to influence the higher dominant ones but only in an indirect fashion; that the high dominant types will confront other members directly; and, of course, that low dominant types are generally deferential. Similar results have also been derived in ethological studies on the relations between emotions and dominance in baboon and chimpanzee groups (Buirski et al., 1973; Buirski, Plutchik, and Kellerman, 1978), and in the study of a comparison between animal and human group process (Kellerman, Buirski, and Plutchik, 1974).

In terms of the role behavior of high dominant types, Watson (1971) discovered that they send more messages than members who are less dominant. This finding supports the notion that a differential gradient of participation time exists in the group, and may be related to the particular role composition of the group. The issue of the distribution of participation time in the group has also been addressed by Smith (1972) who discovered that feedback is more effective in altering participation rate when given to individuals, but that greater change in perception of other group members resulted from feedback to the group. The study by Smith indicates that communicational structure of the group produces and is subject to individual effects as well as group effects.

Group Resonance and Role Behavior

Many authors have noticed that one member of the group may have an instant affinity for another member, or that one member may share a common pool of experience with another. In the role structure of the group, this sharing of experience may become expressed when certain members assume liaison positions in the group (Ross and Harary, 1955). Such roles also have been cited by Powdermaker and Frank (1953) who describe the "protege patient," that is, one who follows the lead of another or resonates with another. Roles in the group, however, are not immutable, and as group members work-through their particular conflicts a shift in the overall role structure of the group occurs. As the group evolves, these sorts of shifts reflect the resonating role composition of the group. Where two or more members felt a certain affinity for each other in the past, the working-through of conflict produces new sets of alliances, dislocations, and overall role transpositions. The group process is, as Durkin (1957) points out, a changing of communication among members. The changing communication also reflects the ongoing change in role assignment. This point is especially important in view of the ultimate work each member of the group must accomplish. The work in the group must address neurotic transference experiences of each member. Durkin (1964) points out that each member has a childhood which can be shown to influence and affect their communication in the group. As neurotic transference material becomes worked-through, roles shift and communication changes. This entire process reflects the profound nature of the therapeutic experience. One's history becomes reexamined and better understood on the basis of this working-through process. The group, therefore, as a communicational network and as a role network is essentially a transference matrix. Resonance occurs within the transferential mode in the infrastructure of the group and reflects its underlying emotional life. For the most part, resonance is obscured simply because most communication must be exchanged and expressed in secondary process terms, or, as Durkin (1964) points out, "on the level of the member's defense."

The group-as-a-whole will experience its resonating vibration at a deep level only "if the therapist regards the intercommunications as free associations and searches out their latent intent." In such instances the therapist "will have no difficulty in identifying transferences in the group." Even though the transferences may be disguised or appear rational, the therapist will be able to see them (Durkin, 1964). Durkin indicates that the therapist notices these neurotic transferences on the basis of their inappropriate emotional qualities. To this may be added that when the therapist understands the group role composition and its attendant defense structure, then the uncovering and working-through process of neurotic transference is clearer.

In order to understand any communication, the structure of defense syndromes needs to be known. This suggests the proposition that *all communication in the group may be about sources of emotion*. These sources of emotion are located both in individual members and in the group-as-a-whole.

GROUP-AS-A-WHOLE EMOTIONALITY AND RESONANCE

Bion (1961) expressed the relation of focal conflict theme to emotion by stating that each group has its own emotional tension. Each group means each basic assumption group. For example, Bion states that "when a group is pervaded by the emotions of the dependent group the emotional states of the fight-flight group and pairing group are held in abeyance." Bion's conception of basic assumption groups constitutes the major theoretic statement of implied group-as-a-whole focal conflict themes. When the basic assumption pairing group prevails, all communication is assumed to refer to the underlying emotions of hope and sexuality. When the basic assumption fight-flight group prevails, all communication is assumed to refer to emotions of hate and anger. When the basic assumption group of dependency prevails, all communication is assumed to refer to the emotions of guilt and depression. Bion's conception of underlying emotion inherent in the group focal conflict theme also suggests that the group is never really in conflict as to its basic needs. The group is either wholly hateful and angry, or guilty and depressed, or hopeful and sexual. It can never really be hateful and hopeful simultaneously, or sexual and depressed simultaneously. This sort of structural law to group life defines the group as a so-called single-minded body. Once the group is motivated by these infrastructural elements it may assume what appears to be an independent life.

The group, therefore, informs itself in at least three ways, First, it has an interpersonal level in which member to member interaction represents a defensive manifest communication level. Here role behavior as a structural component of group life is most evident. Second, the group has an intrapsychic level in which each member must work-through transference material and rebalance pervasive id-superego conflict. Third, there is also a group level where individual members resonate with underlying focal conflict themes in the Bionian sense. On the group level, Bion's valency is equivalent to Foulkes' resonance. As Stock and Thelen (1958) indicate, Bion's valency on the group level reveals that group members have instant shared experience with other members within one of the three basic-assumption cultures. These levels to group life have also been reviewed by Rose (1963) and related to Horneyian psychodynamic formulations.

The Group Personality: Implications for a Psychosomatic Aspect to Communication

Group therapists have become polarized over the formulation of these so-called distinct levels to group communication. In general, the idea that the group may have a life or a level that as an essential configuration comprises more than just the sum of its parts is the philosophical dividing line between psychoanalytic group psychotherapists and group-as-a-whole psychotherapists.

The argument is made by Wolf and Schwartz (1962) that a fallacy exists in the analogy of the group-as-a-whole to the individual member of the group: "You cannot call individual respiration group respiration, or individual perspiration, group perspiration. Is there a group skin? a group liver? or a group mind? Can there be a group mind without a group nervous system?" One answer to the position enunicated by Wolf and Schwartz is provided by Foulkes and Anthony (1965): "any event in a group must be looked at as something which potentially involves the whole group although it may be expressed in endlessly varying configurations. Symptoms which are located physically in a single individual, so-called 'conversions,' correspondingly appear in the group only negatively as areas of 'no response' so long as their meaning cannot be expressed in words."

It is certainly difficult to propose that the group contains an organ system like a skin. However, von Bertalanffy (1968) and Miller (1969) develop the concept of group boundaries, and in chapter 4, on the genealogical feature of group life, a group membrane or boundary was postulated which tended to be either firm or fragile depending on the extent to which the rules and regulations of the group were respected. In a sense, when an individual expresses dyscontrolled behavior by acting-out, the issue of boundary violation is created. The skin or dermatological system of any single individual or of the group is a boundary between inner and outer environments. In an individual, acting-out of urges and general impulsive behavior correlates with all sorts of dermatological eruptions. For example, Klander (1935) drew a correlation between the character trait of impatience and the appearance of persistent itching. Weiss and English (1957) have reported a similar finding. Their results show that both dyscontrolled aggression and overall intensely felt aggressive impulses correlate with a whole array of dermatological conditions.

The question then becomes: if group members tend to act-out, become generally dyscontrolled, and disrupt the group boundary, does the group also develop so-called psychosomatic boundary symptoms? It may be seen, for example, that groups occassionally show prolonged irritability and acting-out. If the acting-out is allowed to continue there develops a feeling in the group of the need to persevere in the acting-out, to continue, so to speak, to scratch it. The main point here is not to demonstrate that the group has a skin, but that the group contains structure and function, part of which may be affected by phenomena of group life. As the group is affected, symptoms may appear from which a group skin or boundary function may be inferred.

In the foregoing discussion, a review and integration of methods for studying group communication as well as the emergence of group focal conflict themes was outlined. Conceptions were presented that viewed the group as a fully crystallized communicational system expressing its emotion and role program abstractly through its membership and one that shows an organization of symptoms from which analogies to psychophysiological organ systems may perhaps be inferred. The issue of how to understand any hypothetical psychophysiological system has implications for the communicational structure of the group and will be explored in the following chapter.

12

Communicational Structure of Groups: The Psychosomatic System

It has been proposed that the communicational structure of the group reflects its role composition; that the deepest level to group communication comprises the organization of emotions underlying role composition; and that these emotions are managed by defense behavior expressed in manifest communicational content. To this is now added the proposition by Alexander (1950) that "Every emotional state has its own physiological syndrome." Alexander further suggests that certain personality types are predisposed to certain diseases and that "physiological responses to emotional stimuli . . . vary according to the nature of the precipitating emotional state." This is a theory of psychosomatic disorders proposing that specific disorders relate to specific emotions. It is a proposition of the specificity of the psychosomatic process also considered by Kubie (1953).

In this chapter, a system of psychosomatic structure will be proposed. This system, as it functions in individual personality, will be related to the overall structure of emotion, ego-defense, and diagnostic disposition described in previous chapters. The question of how this psychosomatic system is expressed in the therapy group context will then be investigated in a later chapter on the relation of symptoms to group dream analysis.

THE RELATION OF EMOTION, GROUP ROLE TYPE, AND PSYCHOSOMATIC SYMPTOMATOLOGY

An examination of the major texts on psychosomatic organ systems indicates that most authors agree on about eight such systems (Alexander, 1950; Gruenberg et al., 1968; Weiss and English, 1957. These are the respiratory, reproductive, sensory, digestive, skeletomuscular, dermatological, nervous, and cardiovascular systems. Some authors include the hemic, lymphatic, and endocrine, systems, but these correlate to emotionality in only a general way. It is proposed here that a correlation can be determined connecting each of the eight organ systems with one of the eight basic emotions, roles, and defense mechanisms, to reveal an underlying psychosomatic system inherent also in group composition. The organization of this system and of its regulating mechanisms exists as a part of the communicational structure of the group.

Psychosomatic Disorders: Fact and Fiction

All people in all cultures probably experience psychosomatic or psychophysiological symptoms. This proposition is implied in the position of Holt and Winick (1961), who state, "The somatic problem is a defense mechanism of the individual developed as one means of coping with antici-pated overwhelming anxiety." From an empirical point of view, most clinicians would probably agree that in any serious and enduring therapeutic contact such symptoms always appear. Nevertheless, many therapists disregard such evidence and continue to accept the prevailing notion that individuals with psychosomatic symptoms are somehow different from other persons. Bach (1954), for example, distinguishes psychosomatic sufferers from others; Ruesch and Bateson (1951) indicate that "The immature person is the princi-pal bearer of psychosomatic manifestations"; Kadis et al. (1968) even indicate that the presence of more than one person with psychosomatic problems in a therapy group may cause subgrouping among these persons;" and Yalom (1970), with a measure of finality, states that persons with psychosomatic con-ditions are not suitable for group therapy.

This attitude gains its plausibility from a somewhat arbitrary determina-tion that some persons with obvious psychosomatic conditions are substan-tially sicker than others. It would be impossible, however, for any group therapist to screen out patients on the basis of whether or not they display psychosomatic conditions. What sorts of psychosomatic conditions would pa-tients have to show in the first place to exclude them from participating in a group? Would asthma, severe acne, lower back pain, high blood pressure, nervous tics, spastic colitis, migraine, or impotency symptoms eliminate them from group therapy treatment? The answer is that all persons express some psychosomatic symptoms and all patients in therapy groups are included in this category. The important variable in therapy group composition is a rela-tively equal measure of ego-strength among members.

Therapists are impressed by the more obvious psychosomatic expression of symptoms. It is an accepted psychological principle that the appearance of symptoms is the result of anxiety that has been converted and expressed in body language. Blum (1972) points out that these psychosomatic symptoms express symbolic messages. Since the experience of anxiety is so important to therapeutic function, then hypothetically it becomes more difficult for so-called psychosomatic types to work in therapy; presumably they do not experience anxiety. Ammon (1975) describes this age-old bias by stating, "Psychosomatic disturbance is a structural damage of the ego in the sense of a narcissistic deficit, acquired in earliest childhood which is compensated and defended by means of the symptom in a more or less self-destructive manner." Another way of stating this proposition is to say simply that when individuals are anxious, but also unable either to examine or manage their tension, then it may be likely for such persons to experience physical symptoms that in some way are tension equivalents. Spotnitz (1973) says that psychosomatic symptoms may be understood to be acting-out equivalents; that is, whenever basic anxieities cannot be managed they may tend to become expressed in action rather than for tension to continue. Anxiety then may become expressed as a rudimentary or prepsychosomatic condition.

In contrast with the views segregating psychosomatic from other patients, it is proposed here that the appearance of a particular symptom condition will be determined by a person's basic dispositional style. This proposition may apply to all people. All members of therapy groups, including therapists, experience and express psychosomatic reactions. Thus, the assumptions made, to cite differences between sufferers of psychosomatic disorders and others, need to be restated. It is far more reasonable and clinically valid to assume that work in therapy groups allows patients to resolve defensive behavior so that awareness and consciousness prevails over tendencies to repress and to develop psychosomatic symptoms. When one is conscious of intrapsychic conflict, acting-out probability decreases and the appearance of psychosomatic symptomatology also subsides. Hence, work in therapy groups helps patients to lower their overall psychosomatic symptomatology index (PSI). Each group member's PSI will become significantly lower as a function of working-through.

As group generations evolve, the group's PSI also decreases. The Group's PSI is obliquely referred to by Loeser (1957): "The reverberative circuit represents a circular, around the group reaction of high intensity. It may manifest itself . . . by collective anger, by laughter, by silence. The presence of a highly contagious form of emotion is then manifest. It represents the group reaction or group mentality . . . (It) gives way again to normal function as the group seeks its equilibrium, like a homeostatic psychosomatic reaction."

The group's PSI may be conceived as the cumulative psychosomatic reactions of any group session. Coughing, laughing, leaving the room, drowsiness, swiveling in one's chair, etc. may be formed into a frequency hierarchy of psychosomatic symptoms that yields the group's PSI. Two implications become apparent from this conception. First, the nature of the hierarchy can reveal the entire personality pattern of the group because the system of psychosomatic symptoms is correlated to the basic personality system. Second, once a PSI is obtained, it may be used as a master template to view the latent group communication.

Keeping in mind the proposition that all persons may express tension through psychosomatic symptoms, the following section will outline a theory of the structure of psychosomatic symptomatology and its relation to the basic emotion, ego-defense, and diagnostic structure presented in earlier chapters.

Personality Types and Corresponding Psychosomatic Organ Systems

It is proposed that there exist eight basic psychosomatic types to which all psychosomatic symptomatology relates. Some systematic relationships between diagnostic type and psychosomatic symptomatology are offered by Alexander (1950), Gruenberg et al. (1968), and Weiss and English (1957), among many other sources. The entire literature on psychosomatics is highly theoretical. Generally, it lacks a systematic formulation based upon some unifying underlying structural organization. One possible unifying system will be offered in the following section. It should be noted that many of the symptoms listed in the following section and attributed to psychosomatic origins may also develop from physical causes.

In the description of eight basic psychosomatic types presented here, each will be related to emotion, defense, diagnostic disposition, and psychosexual level of development. Based upon the discussion of intrapsychic representation in the previous chapter, each psychosomatic type will also be intrapsychically designated in terms of its basic nature. Futhermore, it is proposed that each role type of the group reflects a particular psychosomatic organ system propensity that may become activated as a response to crisis.

GREGARIOUS VERSUS DEPRESSED

Gregarious: The Respiratory System

The gregarious dispositional type expresses high energy in all social behavior. The group role expressing this type is that of the puritan, the hard worker. Joy and pleasure represent the emotion of this category. Defensively, reaction-formation governs the basic sexual orientation of this type. On a clinical level, the manic disposition expresses the diagnosis of the gregarious type. On an empirical level, clinicians working with tubercular patients and patients with other respiratory problems frequently notice that manic or highly energized paranoid types are unduly represented in this symptom category. The point is that high energy types seem to develop all kinds of respiratory disorders. Weiss and English (1957) also report the appearance of pulmonary tuberculosis in high energy types. They as well as Wittkower (1949) indicate that such patients are fatigued and undernourished. Other respiratory disorders associated with high energy personalities include hyperventilation, colds, allergy, sinusitis, vasomotor rhinitis, asthma, sighing, coughing, and throat clearing. These correlations have been reported as early as 1937 (Halliday, 1937). The high energy or manic quality associated with respiratory disorders has also been related to aggression, ambition, argumentativeness, hysteria, repressed sexual tension, and underachievement.

It is proposed that the gregarious-manic type is dispositionally predisposed toward expressing psychosomatic symptomatology through respiratory disorders.

Depressed: The Reproductive System

The depressed dispositional type shows withdrawal and loss of interest in social behavior. The group role expressing this disposition is that of reintegrator, a person trying to manage experiences of loss and inferiority. Sorrow or grief represent basic emotions of this category. Defensively, compensatory mechanisms govern the basic depressive and loss experiences of this type. Clinicians who work with depressed patients frequently find that impotency, frigidity, menstrual problems, functional infertility, and premature ejaculation are the initial physical complaints offered by such patients. These are also reported by Alexander (1950), Gruenberg et al. (1968), and Weiss and English (1957). Causes of the depressive quality are offered as repressed hostility, fear, shame, hate and disgust.

It is proposed here that the depressive dispositional type may show psychosomatic symptomatology through the organ system that is variably called genitourinary, sexual, or reproductive.

Thus, the opposition of the clinical categories manic and depressed reveal that the respiratory and reproductive systems may correspondingly constitute opposite psychosomatic symptom structures. Their special relation to one another has also been reported by Weiss and English to reveal some similarity in the symbolic meaning of their respective symptoms. Not only are respiratory infections related to intense needs for attention and affection, but so too are depressions correlated to common colds. "It was felt that the emotional stimuli might be the same for both a nasopharyngeal catarrhal secretion and a vaginal catarrhal secretion." There is a similarity of the "living mucosa and the presence of erectile tissue in both the genital and nasal regions." This simultaneous activation of organ systems is also proposed by authors who view the respiratory asthma attack of the manic-energized typed to be the suppressed cry of the depressive type.

Finally, a possible relationship between psychosomatic organ system expression and psychosexual development is offered by Saul (1939): "The dermal and respiratory mechanisms, trends, and relations to the mother are analogous to the oral ones. They are fundamental to an understanding of psychological functioning . . . observations strongly suggest that they play a role in the skin and respiratory allergies similar to that of the oral ones in the gastrointestinal disorders."

It is proposed here that the gregarious-manic and deprived-depressive dispositions express their respective opposite psychosomatic conditions of respiratory and reproductive disorders, and that these psychosomatic conditions perhaps may be better understood as those reflecting psychosexual problems of an oral nature. Problems of depression are also understood by psychoanalysts to reflect derivative oral problems.

CONTROLLED VERSUS DYSCONTROLLED

Controlled: The Skeletomuscular System

The controlled dispositional type expresses feelings of expectation and anticipation as basic emotions. The role expressing this disposition in the group is that of intellectualizer. Defensively, intellectualization and other obsessional mechanisms operate to meet one's needs for control. On a clinical diagnostic level, obsessive highly controlled types seem to develop skeletomuscular disorders. Disorders of arthritis, rheumatism, aches in muscles and joints, lower back pain, muscle cramps, and generalized tension headaches are some examples. The prevailing psychodynamic interpretation of such psychosomatic expressions revolves around needs for control. For example, persons who develop these disorders are considered to be demanding and exacting. They experience great hostility and strong needs to manipulate and sometimes develop compelling feelings to serve others or to act deferentially. Such behavior reflects an attempt to keep hostility repressed. Weiss and English indicate that such persons "relieve the restrictive influence of conscience by serving others." Male patients show "a chronic state of inhibited rebellious hostility. This seems to be a reaction against unconscious dependent feminine trends for which they overcompensate with aggressiveness." There is some evidence that such types are accident prone and behave in ways designed to relieve guilt. The authors further attribute the appearance of skeletomuscular disorders to persons who are uncommunicative. They are unable to fight directly. Therefore they must control their environment completely or "seethe or boil within."

Dyscontrolled: The Dermatological System

Weiss and English also propose that opposite to the controlled type is an impulsive one who tends to act-out conflicts. The dyscontrolled dispositional type is an impulsive type. The role reflecting this type in the group is that of child. The emotion of surprise, defined as a behavioral disorientation, is the basic emotion of this category. The defense of regression permits the dyscontrolled type to persistently express impulse. On a clinical level a psychopathic disposition expresses the diagnosis of the dyscontrolled type. The impulsivity and acting-out characteristic of this type reflects an eruption of sorts through boundaries. Boundary violations are expressed physically in disorders of the skin. Dermatological conditions such as psoriasis are conditions that acting-out patients report. Conditions such as blushing, itching, edema, dermatitis, pruritus, alopecia areata (loss of hair), eczema, excessive sweating of hands and feet, acne, urticaria, nail biting, and eczema of ear, scalp, and nape of neck are some examples of dermatological disorders in acting-out personalities.

Psychodynamically, itching and scratching may be understood to be a symbol sequence of impatience and impulsivity. In an early study, Klander (1935) indicates that masochistic tendencies have a close affinity to the skin in the sensation of pain. Scratching constitutes an expression of the hostile impulse. In pruritus ani and vulvae, itching may reflect an inhibited sexual excitement. Scratching then becomes a source of conscious erotic pleasure and a masturbatory equivalent. It also has been correlated to regression (Gillespie, 1938; Stokes, 1932). In some respects impulsive types are also exhibitionistic. English and Weiss observe that the skin is the border between the inner and outer life and that scratching is related to aggression. Its effect is to "eliminate something unpleasant whether real, fantasied, or figurative."

It is proposed here that the controlled-obsessional type and the opposite dyscontrolled-psychopathic type express their respective psychosomatic disorders through the skeletomuscular and dermatological systems. In a structural sense, then, the skeletomuscular system is opposite to the dermatological system. Furthermore, the basic control and dyscontrol properties of these respective types may be regarded in psychosexual terms as anal derivative elements. Macalpine (1953) and Weiss and English refer to anal derivative dynamics for dermatological conditions. Macalpine states that the "origin can be traced to a reactivation in adult life of infantile fantasies about procreation centering around the anal function which preceeded genital interest and the knowledge of sex." In addition, most clinicians generally understand the issue of obsessional-control and psychopathic-dyscontrol to be one that reflects anal derivative problems.

TIMID VERSUS AGGRESSIVE

Timid: The Nervous System

The timid dispositional type expresses apprehension and fear as basic emotions. The role representing this type in the group is that of the innocent. Defensively, a general repression mechanism enables a person of this type to inhibit both feeling and action. On a clinical level, a passive disposition reflects the diagnosis of the timid type. The defense of repression is utilized to maintain this timid style. A wide variety of nervous system disorders are associated with this type. These include insomnia, fainting, weakness, vertigo, numbness, tingling of extremeties, ringing in ears, ocular and visual phenomena, epilepsy syndrome, and migraines. Correlated trait behavior can include trepidation and lethargy. The level of introspection in such a person is exceedingly low and interpersonal confrontations are scrupulously avoided.

It is proposed that the timid-passive type may show psychosomatic symptomatology through the organ system referred to as the nervous system.

Aggressive: The Cardiovascular System

The aggressive dispositional type expresses or experiences anger and rage as basic emotions. The role representing this type in the group is that of scapegoater. Defensively, displacement mechanisms are designed to manage anger. On a clinical level, this disposition is expressed through direct aggressive behavior or through displaced aggression. Clinicians probably would agree that the aggressive type, whether outwardly angry or inwardly smouldering, is prone to cardiovascular disorders.

The essential psychodynamic of the correlation between the aggressive type and the appearance of cardiovascular problems is proposed by Alexander (1950):

> The individual who has become excessively inhibited under the influence of his early experiences will find it much more difficult to handle his aggressive impulses efficiently in adult life. He will tend to repress all his self-assertive tendencies and be unable to find some legitimate outlet for the expression of these tendencies. The damming up of his hostile impulses will continue and will consequently increase in intensity. This will induce the development of stronger defensive measures in order to keep the pent up aggressions in check. The over-compliant, over-polite, submissive attitudes found in patients with hypertension are precisely such defenses, but they do not prevent the accumulation of tension. Consequently, feelings of inferiority develop which, in turn, stimulate aggressive impulses; and the vicious circle is perpetuated. Because of the marked degree of their inhibitions, these patients are less effective in their occupational activities and for that reason tend to fail in competition with others, so that envy is stimulated and their hostile feelings toward more successful, less inhibited competitors is further intensified.

Saul (1939) proposes the same aggression-cardiovascular correlation offering a similar illustrative case.

Other psychosomatic symptoms of the cardiovascular system may include fainting, palpitation, grinding of teeth, arrhythmia, migraine, high blood pressure, dizziness, and insomnia. Again, Weiss and English attribute these symptoms to an inability to express aggression directly, but within the context of an underlying consistent feeling of resentment and anger. Hamilton (1955) also states that tensions will become expressed through the circulatory system because of chronically displaced rage. This aggressive type has been reported to be overly concerned with social status, prestige and material success (Dunbar, 1943).

It is proposed that the timid-passive type and the opposite aggressive type express their respective psychosomatic disorders through the nervous and cardiovascular systems. Furthermore, it seems evident, as Alexander (1950) points out, that focal themes of the passive and aggressive types relate to issues of assertiveness. In psychosexual terms, this constitutes a phallic level derivative theme.

TRUSTFUL VERSUS DISTRUSTFUL

Trustful: The Sensory System

The trustful dispositional type expresses agreeableness and positive attitudes. The role representing this type in the group is that of romantic. There is a distinct absence of criticality in a person with this diagnosis. Acceptance is the basic emotion of this category. Defensively, denial mechanisms govern the basic suggestibility of this type. On a clinical level, an hysterical disposition expresses the diagnosis of the trustful type. Clinicians working with hysterical patients frequently find that these patients are sensory types and that they actually report many unusual sensory experiences. Some sensory symptoms include vertigo, dizziness, ringing in ears, taste distortion, hysterical deafness, hearing and visual problems including hallucinatory experiences, tunnel vision, blurriness, auras, and hysterical blindness

The sensory system, it is proposed, seems to reflect hysterical diagnostic dynamics.

Distrustful: The Digestive System

The distrustful type expresses suspicion and criticality. The role representing this type in the group is that of the scrutinizer. Disgust and rejection constitute the basic emotions of this category. Defensively, the projection mechanism is designed to keep the external world imperfect so that a personal sense of imperfection remains out of awareness. On a clinical level, the distrust is reflected as a paranoid dispositional style.

There has been much controversy in the literature regarding the basic psychodynamics of paranoid character and associated psychosomatic symptomatology. The paranoid as a projector and as one who expresses disgust as a basic emotion is presumably also making some digestive or gastrointestinal statement. This connection is also made by Alexander and Menninger (1936) in a paper relating persecutory delusions to the digestive system. Persecutory delusions and melancholia were observed in constipated patients who were typically expressing distrust and rejection. The implicit self-instruction the paranoid type expresses is "I must hold on to what I have." Another self-instruction indicates that this person must not take in any foreign substance. Paranoid distrustful types also show a whole set of swallowing problems.

Symptoms of digestive disorders include chronic diarrhea, constipation, spastic colitis, ulcerative colitis, irritable colon, indigestion, peptic ulcers, belching, vomiting, biliary tract problems, and a wide variety of intake swallowing problems starting with exaggerated appetite and progressing to vomiting, nervous vomiting, esophageal neurosis or choking on food, cardiospasm, reporting metalic tastes, and anorexia nervosa. The proposed psychodynamics of digestive tract disturbances have ranged from definitions of dependency reactions to underachievement, frustration, depression, anxiety, the appearance of "feminine" traits in males, and finally reactions of disgust generated by separation problems. Other emotions cited by Alexander relating to gastrointestinal disorders and constituting a paranoid emotion cluster include intense rage, greed, jealousy, and envy. Still other paranoid-obsessive features to this psychosomatic system can include stubbornness, over-ambitiousness, and over-conscientiousness. When the paranoid type becomes exceedingly critical, then, according to Weiss (1944), this individual will behave as though existing conditions cannot be swallowed or tolerated. Some paranoid psychosomatic symptoms, such as swallowing problems, at times also appear to be hysteric.

It is proposed here that the trustful-hysterical type and the opposite distrustful-paranoid type express their respective psychosomatic disorders through the sensory and digestive systems. Furthermore, as a connection to psychosexual level of development, the hysterical-sensory and paranoid-digestive types seem to express oedipal conflict; that is, the hysteric-sensory type is forever loyal and this loyalty is supported in its motive by the high suggestibility and posture of total acceptance of the hysteric. The paranoid-digestive type is loyal to no one, and this lack of loyalty is supported in its motive by the need to criticize. It is this loyalty-disloyalty issue that theoretically ties the hysteric and paranoid types on the psychosexual level. The clear opposition of suggestibility and criticality also shows the polar connection between these types in terms of their respective underlying personality inclinations.

The relationship of psychosomatic organ systems to basic diagnostic types is displayed graphically in Figure 12-1 and the entire system of psychosomatic

Figure 12-1.   The relationship of psychosomatic organ systems to basic diagnostic types.

Table 12-1. The personality system.

PROTOTYPE PATTERN	INCOR-PORATION	REJECTION	DESTRUCTION	PROTECTION	EXPLORATION	ORIENTATION	REPRODUCTION	REINTEGRATION
GROUP ROLE	Romantic	Scrutinizer	Scapegoater	Innocent	Intellectualizer	Child	Puritan	Reintegrator
TRAIT	Trustful	Distrustful	Aggressive	Timid	Controlled	Dyscontrolled	Gregarious	Depressed
DIAGNOSTIC DISPOSITION	Hysteric	Paranoid	Aggressive	Passive	Obsessive	Psychopathic	Manic	Depressed
EMOTION	Acceptance	Disgust	Anger	Fear	Expectation	Surprise	Joy	Sorrow
DEFENSE	Denial	Projection	Displacement	Repression	Intellectualization	Regression	Reaction-formation	Compensation
DREAM—NIGHTMARE	Laughter	Fragmentation	Rageful act	Terror—escape	Release—bed-wetting, falling	Paralysis	Orgasm—sexual dreams	Crying, sobbing
INTRAPSYCHIC STATE	Id	Superego	Id	Superego	Id	Superego	Id	Superego
PSYCHOSEXUAL STAGE	Oedipal	Oedipal	Phallic	Phallic	Anal	Anal	Oral	Oral
PSYCHOSOMATIC SYSTEM	Sensory	Digestive	Cardiovascular	Nervous	Skelto-muscular	Dermatological	Respiratory	Reproductive

235

and personality types including that of group role types is offered in Table 12-1

Schwartz and Wolf (1960) who ask—is there a group liver, group skin, or group mind?—may now be provided with an additional partial answer. Based upon the role composition of the group, a psychosomatic profile for any group may be derived, and this profile will reflect the diagnostic structure of the group. Whether or not group members, or even the therapist for that matter, can perceive the expression of these disorders depends on the extent to which symbolic communication may be understood.

PSYCHOSOMATIC SYMPTOMATOLOGY AND DREAMS: AN INTRODUCTION

Foulkes and Anthony (1965) indicate that the understanding of symptoms and the repressed unconscious is akin to the deciphering of a code. Kanzer (1959) also indicates that the basic symbolic communications of the group are those of somatic conditions and dreams. To this, Greenleaf (1973) adds that dreams have the same structure as symptoms: "they hide and reveal elements of meaning at the same time and employ similar 'condensing and obscuring devices'." This connection was emphasized by Alexander and Wilson (1935) who related dream material to psychosomatic symptoms. Ammon (1977) implies this relationship by stating that "Every dream which is used in the group is . . . an interpretation of the unconscious dynamics of the group event: It expresses both the individual and interpersonal dynamics of the dreamer and of the group-as-a-whole." To understand further the appearance and meaning of somatic conditions in the group, the introduction and utilization of dreams in the group also need to be reviewed. Dreams reveal the connection, in part, to the group's psychosomatic profile and offer one way to understand the meaning of symptoms.

In earlier chapters, the personality system was analyzed in terms of its similarity structure. In this chapter, it was proposed that the psychosomatic component in the personality system is also part of this similarity structure. In this connection, Bion (1961) points out that physical diseases display a similarity or a link that corresponds to the similarity structure of the basic assumption groups. This means that the group's underlying emotion structure is inextricably tied to the system of physical symptomatology—a reference to the connections between the individual personality system, the psychosomatic system and the personality system of the group.

The expression of symptoms in the group, however, may not be easily revealed. Yet, the group-as-a-whole may generate mechanisms—such as the appearance of dreams—that permit its overall PSI to be more readily visible. Bion (1961) states, "The group in the sense of a collection of people in a room, adds nothing to the individual or the aggregate of individuals—it merely reveals something that is not otherwise visible."

In the following chapter an attempt will be made to further understand the presence of psychosomatic symptomatology in the group as it is revealed through work with dreams.

13

Communicational Structure of Groups: The Psychosomatic System and the Special Problem of Dreams

---

The appearance and use of dreams in therapy groups is far from being well understood. Even though most group therapists make use of the dream, there is a basic contradiction between such use in the group and the way in which psychoanalysts work with dreams in individual treatment. Some group therapists use the dream as a way of analyzing patient's conflicts and transferences by involving other group members in the overall associative process (Wolf, 1949, 1950). In fact, Wolf contends that relationships in the group may be cemented through the work with dreams. Other group therapists utilize the manifest content of the dream to understand its basic communication. Both methods raise a fundamental theoretical dilemma.

In this classic statement on the interpretation of dreams, Freud (1900) developed the idea that the manifest content of the dream never reveals its deeper layers. In fact, the manifest content is designed to conceal the deeper meaning of the dream, a position that has often been restated (Altman, 1969; Nagera, 1969). In psychoanalytic terms, asking all group members to associate to a single member's dream implies that the entire group participates in this concealment. Becoming informed exclusively by the manifest content of the dream maintains a fundamentally defensive condition.

The dreamer is the only person who can truly unravel the manifest dream. Altman (1969) indicates that the manifest dream, the dream from above, will produce associations to current experiences, fantasies, and hopes. The dream from below, the latent dream, which is composed of instinctual wishes, inhibitions, and prohibitions can only be reached through the dreamer's associations. This is what is meant by someone having exclusive access to their own dream.

The dream contains the particular id-superego configuration inherent in the dreamer's personality and only the dreamer can uncover deeper self-dream structure. Thus for the group to "take" the dream implies that work on the dream will be composed of material in the dream from above.

It seems clear that the dream is a special kind of material, different from any other group content. Group members generally recognize this difference and there is an idiosyncratic interactional feeling to the group whenever a dream is reported and worked on. It is proposed that the work on dreams tends to interfere with the natural flow of group interaction, and in terms of communicational structure seems to serve the interactional as well as the intrapersonal resistance. The work on dreams in the group, therefore, although viewed by most therapists as useful, must also be viewed as a complicating element of the group process.

DREAMS AND COMMUNICATION IN THE GROUP

Two methods have been proposed to reconcile the work on dreams in the group to the psychoanalytic position with regard to individual dream interpretation. The first is offered by Wolf and Schwartz (1962), who simply advocate doing dream analysis in the group in the same way that it is done in individual treatment; that is, by gathering material mostly from the dreamer. The second is to posit a group dream. That is, to assume that any dream introduced is, in some way, an abstraction of the entire group process. This position considers each person's dream to be a collective group dream. The efficacy of such a theoretical leap certainly is not supported by any great body of data. However, group therapists are, in fact, confronted with the dilemma of the appearance of dream material and the decision about what to do with it. The inclination to consider any person's dream as a true group dream and to rely on its manifest content for meaning is thus quite strong, and provides an explanation for the attempts that have been made to justify such a dream use method.

The Theory of the Group Dream

The most inventive theoretical attempt to reconcile dream use in the group with psychoanalytic precepts of dream interpretation is offered by Klein-Lipshutz (1953) who proposes that dreams of group members resemble dreams of young children in which the manifest and latent contents presumably are identical. The dream is "a vehicle . . . of communication rather than an end in itself." The claim of congruence between manifest and latent content would probably not meet any standard experimental criteria and would probably not be supported by most therapists. However, the Klein-Lipshutz position suggests that the dream need not interrupt the communicational flow of the group because it is only a vehicle of communication. Its ultimate meaning or meanings become less important than its potential galvanizing use. The dream, therefore, is only seen as a group dream: "The dream of one member becomes the property of the group; it is everyone's dream."

This position is echoed by Chalfen (1964) who adds that the therapist never offers any interpretation to the dream but only registers feelings about it. All other patients are helped to become involved in the associative process. Chalfen further states that in the group situation the dream itself emerges from the ongoing interactive process of the group. Zimmerman (1967) develops the concept of the group dream by proposing that any dream introduced by a group member expresses the affect of the entire group. Since all members are identified in their egos, then any dream may reflect the interactions of the entire group. Thus, Zimmerman states: "The dream describes the emotional state of the whole group."

The individual dream that becomes transformed into a group-shared dream has its historical roots in the work of Stekel (1943) and later in the work of Gutheil (1951). Locke (1957) describes this history and indicates that the dream in the group is an abstract statement. "The dream of one is shared by all. . . . Every group member is provided an opportunity to see himself in the group, at work, at home, in the present, in the past, all in the dream of another group member."

Battegay (1977) indicates that "The group dreams show in a concentrated manner the deeper conflicts coming up in a social frame which are linked to early experiences in the primary group of childhood, mostly the family." Finally, Grotjahn (1973) also states that the dream of one member becomes the dream of all members and offers a clinical illustration to demonstrate the validity of this proposition.

A woman of 35 who was pregnant for the first time reported the following dream fragment: "I was giving a big party. Someone made snide remarks and I threw a number of women out."

Grotjahn indicates that the meaning of this dream fragment is quite obvious. In keeping with the position that the dream of one becomes the dream of all, Grotjahn's key transposition is the substitution of 'group' for party, that is, the big party presumably refers to the therapy group. Grotjahn's equation, however, may only be one of several equally relevant interpretations. For example, since Grotjahn indicates that the woman was pregnant for the first time, it seems likely that the seminal latent meaning to "big party" is really "big stomach." Interpreting "big party" as a reference to the group-as-a-whole, then, may reflect only one of several possible interpretations. Another obvious manifest interpretation refers to throwing all the women out of the group perhaps so that she can have the men to herself and ultimately the therapist to herself. This sort of wish can be attributed to a Bionian pairing impulse especially since this woman was pregnant. The point is that the potential intrapersonal meaning to an individual member's dream may become diluted if the dream is immediately usurped by the group-as-a-whole. It is the patient's personal associations alone that offer the most reliable uncovering of the latent meaning.

Therapists who generally understand the dream as reflecting unconscious group themes also perceive work with dreams as producing more frank, open, relevant, and meaningful therapy (Klein-Lipshutz, 1953). Of course, since the underpinning to the manifest dream assumes a latent meaning, then can any dream ever be irrelevant or not meaningful?

The major issue here is that therapists are searching for a way to use dreams in the group. Once the premise is accepted that so-called group dreams are a tangible part of the therapy work, then the link of individual personality to the group system also reinforces therapeutic intervention based upon group focal conflicts; that is, interpretations of the group focal conflict theme has relevance to any member's personal conflicts. Yet most therapists are also aware that when dreams are introduced they tend to generate a more intellectualized ambiance in the group, thereby shifting the work from member-member interaction to an inclination to be deferential to the expert-therapist—a process that slows the group.

The Problem of Dream Use in Therapy Groups

The issue of working with dreams in the group has been considered by many authors who, along with Wolf and Schwartz (1962), recognize the special problem this work creates. Foulkes (1964) acknowledges the paradox of interpreting manifest content in the group as though it had true latent meaning. However, he too feels that the analyst cannot reject the dream no matter what difficulties it presents. If the material is introduced, it must be dealt with by the group. Johnson (1963), however, feels that dreams, free association, and historical information may or may not be employed, depending on the particular group therapy model used. The issue of whether or not to use such material relates to how any particular therapist views the increased resistance in the group whenever dreams are introduced. Klein-Lipshutz (1953) offers one way to undercut this increased resistance. The author suggests that generally dreamers become less defensive if associations to the dream are offered by other members first. This method is of course quite anathema to any analyst who considers a dreamer's personal associations to manifest elements as the only imperative to the unravelling process.

Kadis et al. (1968) also recognize that the reporting of a dream produces greater resistance and defense both in the dreamer and in the other group members, although again, together with Archibald (1954) and Fielding (1967) they insist on accepting any and all material introduced into the group—a compelling point, indeed.

Wolf and Schwartz (1971) also indicate that the object of working with dreams in the group is to "encourage multilateral group analysis." This is accomplished by first having the dreamer associate to manifest elements and then inviting the participation of the other members of the group. Wolf and Schwartz (1970) further point out the difference between a focus on manifest content versus one on latent content: "The greater the exploration of the manifest, the greater the likelihood of emphasizing similarities, homogeneity. The greater the exploration of the latent content, the past, history, psychic determinants, the greater the likelihood of emphasizing individual differences, hetereogeneity, diversity."

Yet, to develop work on latent themes requires time, and as Becker (1964) indicates, the use of dreams in the group and the focus on associations by the dreamer and by all other members raises the question of just how much of the group time may be devoted to any dream. Experienced groups will tend to deal with dreams more efficiently, but Yalom (1970) continues to ask whether dream work can play any useful role in the group. Finally, Mullen (1956) draws a sharp contrast between those who focus on the manifest content with the dream's significance given a group-shared meaning, and the psychoanalytic position that demands a commitment to the unfolding process in order to get at the latent communication. Mullen indicates that a search for meaning of the dream by the group interferes with the group experience. The presentation of the dream and its interpretation have a tendency to produce feelings of alienation in the group. Mullen suggests that keeping to the non-teleological is most important; that is, that a focus on the latent content should constitute the work; associations offered by other group members destroy the latent or true dream. This is a key point because if valid, it assumes that group work on any dream, insofar as that dream is translated and transformed into a group dream, may in fact, obscure the communicational process of the group, and worse, may obliterate it entirely.

Mullan further indicates that in order for the dream to be focused toward its latent content, the therapist must go against the group tendency. This reference to leadership raises the question of how therapists adjust factors such as time spent on a dream, who associates first, nature of interpretations, and overall pacing of a session in which a dream is presented. The therapist can always sense resistance and communicational interference when a dream is introduced, and thus the therapist's virtuosity is invoked whenever a dream is presented. How the therapist manages the group during such interpretive and associative sessions determines the extent to which group communicational flow is permitted to develop naturally.

Dream Use and Group Leadership

A major conceptual contribution to group communicational theory was suggested by Wolf and Schwartz (1962) who proposed that virtually every dream in the group may be a tacit communication to the therapist. This proposition generated the notion of a group to therapist communicational synapse. Thus, any communication in the group, whether between two or more members, may also be a communication to the therapist. Ezriel (1973) amplifies this synaptic principle by suggesting that the therapist must be aware of covert transference manifestations relating directly to the leader but "being diluted by references away from him." According to Ezriel, in every session a need for a required relationship with the therapist emerges. The salient point to this proposition, perceived both by Wolf and Schwartz and by Ezriel, is that the special role of the therapist as it is juxtaposed with the needs of group members becomes the "source of all the patient says and does during that session" (Ezriel, 1973).

Foulkes (1964) also addresses this point. He argues that there are two distinct levels to group communication. The manifest level contains member to member communication or a sort of interaction that may be defined as role to role. Its underlying latent level is a role to leader communication, or a communicational pattern based upon an authority structure. The underlying communication is a metacommunication. The basic transference on this level is that of child to parent. The leader is the catalyst, the interpreter, and the one to activate the analytic and integrative processes of the group. According to Foulkes, the basic synaptic member to therapist communicational structure of the entire group process derives its motive force from the group's magical expectation that the leader will provide all help whenever necessary. Durkin and Glatzer (1973) refine this synaptic proposition by declaring that other authors also consider all transference phenomena to constitute displaced communication to the therapist.

The extent to which this principle of communication operates in the group infrastructure is important because it has direct significance to the art of therapist intervention. It implies, for example, that each therapist intervention may be heard by group members as a reply to some other oblique member to therapist communication. The therapist intervention, therefore, may be understood by group members to contain an identical underlying structure as that of member to member communication.

THE THERAPIST'S INTERVENTION

Durkin (1957) asserts an important group principle when she says, "Since the group processes are natural ones, they will function regardless of whether or not the therapist is aware of them." The question of therapist intervention then becomes an extremely important issue. When the therapist responds in the group, how do the members hear it? Do they integrate the therapist's remarks on a manifest level or do they understand it as a latent communication? The following clinical vignette illustrates this sort of communicational problem:

Marvin, a 37-year-old man, was involved in a heated discussion with Arlene, age 28. After a while, the therapist intervened and asked the group how they felt about whatever Arlene was saying. Suddenly, in the midst of this therapist-sponsored pause, Tom, age 33, opportunistically commented about his own recent social conquests. Tom's comment seemed to relate to the essence of Marvin and Arlene's interaction. Another member then responded to Tom by acknowledging Tom's "harem."

How is this group moment to be understood? The therapist, who was a man, interrupted Marvin and Arlene originally to ask the group a question. When he did that, suddenly something unexpectedly occurred and his question seems to have been ignored. Why did the therapist intervene in the interaction between Marvin and Arlene in the first place? It may be assumed that he wanted to facilitate the group communication by intervening. However, a deeper analysis of this clinical example can show that the therapist separated Marvin and Arlene as a couple in order to focus on Arlene. Tom and others then correctly expressed an unconscious pattern of the group by referring to the therapist's motive or countertransference. This particular unconscious motive of the therapist may have been to keep coupled with each group member and to keep all other potential couples separated. Thus, one member of the group quite correctly referred to the therapist's latent motive by displacing it onto Tom; that Tom had quite a harem, an oblique reference to the therapist's "harem" in the group. Tom represents an object replacement for the therapist simply because it was he who expressed the therapist's covert need, albeit with a seemingly disconnected response. This example also shows that the communicational group structure is multilevelled, and any manifest, disconnected association will contain an understandable latent meaning. Durkin (1957) quite correctly states that "the leader-therapist . . . must guide the whole system of communication" of the group, and this important role implies the need for the therapist to be aware of countertransference problems in order to better understand latent communicational continuity.

This analysis reveals several qualities of the group's communicational structure. First, it distinguishes between the group's manifest and latent communicational levels. Second, it suggests that any seemingly inappropriate remark in the group may have its latent logical link. Third, it reveals that the members of the group may be constantly in touch with both communicational levels at all times. Fourth, it implies that a therapist's intervention may always interfere with the communicational group flow—its natural process. Fifth, it illustrates the therapist's personal psychodynamics, which in the above example, was composed of oedipal competitive elements as well as oral dependent features. The important group dynamic principle, however, suggests that any therapist's interference in the group process will contain some resistance features to overall group communication even if the intervention is well designed, well aimed, and free from countertransference. The therapist, therefore, must always weigh interventions with care. This means that the therapist's role of maintaining suitable conditions for facilitative group communication may not only depend, as Durkin (1964) reports, on the ability to make correct interpretations or to render solutions to focal conflicts, but instead may even depend more on how many of these are made. This point is also noted by Burton (1975), who states that that "therapy is best which interferes the least."

Another major implication of the nature of group communication based upon the psychology of therapist to member intervention relates to the assumption that the therapeutic aim of the group is to help members resolve their conflicts. Yet, as was illustrated above, the therapist, in an attempt to help a group member improve a communication, became an agent of the resistance. The underlying latent message was for group members not to interfere with the therapist's needs and, in fact, not to change. This phenomenon of the group's needing to maintain its resistance—in this case, its inclination to retain all ongoing role functions—has also been pointed out by Yalom (1970). He describes a patient who "had actively worked on the problems of other members for months but steadfastly . . . declined to disclose herself. Finally in one meeting she began to discuss her problems and confessed that one year previously she had been an inmate of a state psychiatric hospital. The therapist responded reflexly, 'Why haven't you told us this before?' This comment, perceived as a punitive one by the patient, served only to reinforce her fear and distrust of others." The question becomes, what might the therapist have done at this point in the patients' group work? Yalom suggests that the therapist "might have commented upon the fact that she now seemed to trust the group sufficiently to talk about herself or might have commented about how difficult it must have been for her previously in the group wanting and yet being afraid to share this disclosure." These remarks are perfectly satisfactory and yet another suggestion might be for the therapist to say nothing. The patient herself has said whatever was the important revelation—she has already done it, as it were, so why say something after the fact?

The decision not to intervene also implies another corollary communicational proposition of the group process; that even helpful comments may carry a covert message including the instruction "not to change." Bion (1961) implies the proposition that all communication contains a "don't-get-well" message. He indicates that the group "hates" to learn through experience. There are also empirical samples of group behavior to suggest that the group indeed needs to maintain its equilibrium and not to change. Some group members use the personal pronoun "we" in suggesting that the cumulative group membership has a unanimously different view of an issue than some single member. The "we" response has been observed by Bach (1954). It usually carries a condescending message so that while the communicational content is "to change," the inflected message is "not to change." Furthermore, whenever a member does begin to show change in behavior, other group members begin to "offer advice": again, as a way of serving the group role resistance. Whenever a silent member finally manages to verbalize something spontaneously, it frequently occurs that the therapist or other group members offer some supportive comment that calls attention to the difference in this member's communicational stance. What such alleged supportive comments tend to do, however, is to convey the covert message, "don't talk!" The therapist especially need not call attention to role changes as they begin to occur.

CONDUCTING THE DREAM

The implication that therapist intervention potentially interferes with the natural group processes makes the problem of conducting the dream in the group particularly difficult. An additional complicating factor of this problem is the position taken by many authors that therapy groups need to be therapist centered. It is the therapist who steers the therapy (Wolf and Schwartz, 1962). Although inviting the entire group to participate in the work done on any one dream the authors nevertheless see the therapist as conducting the dream analysis in an individual psychoanalytic mode. The dreamer gets to associate first. Wolf and Schwartz indicate that the dreamer is encouraged to associate to a dream, and these "associations take precedence over all others and at this point the analyst may have to inhibit the instantaneous reactions of other members."

Bach (1954) is suspicious of the leader-oriented nature of the group. He states that "Unconsciously the group culture is limited and restricted to a leader-follower relationship in which the leader constantly demonstrates his leadership by some sort of superiority in knowing the unconscious." Bach, like Gutheil (1951) and Hobbs (1951), would like the therapist to assume a naive position. "In group practice it is necessary to modify the Freudian dream interpretation technique. . . . Emphasis on a technically complete and 'correct' understanding of dreams fosters a strong dependency on the group therapist which results in undesirable regression." These authors feel that expert interpretations weaken group centeredness and strengthen leader centeredness.

This contrast in opinion as to whether dream use interferes with the group process is further amplified by Bieber (1957), who indicates that work on dreams dilutes the leadership quality from the therapist's position. Kadis et al. (1968) also indicate that the therapist may either work with the dream or avoid it by asking the patient to associate to or to guess what particular significance there is to the dream. The authors feel, in either case, that the therapist's role as interpreter diminishes as the group develops the ability to introspect. Kadis et al. consider a good working group to be one that can overcome practically any obstacles—a compelling position of faith in view of group dynamic and psychoanalytic resistance issues. Bach (1954) agrees fully with this position: "cohesive groups are quite capable of extracting much meaning from dreams. . . . Because every member's associations are naive, neither trained nor intellectual, they are similar to interpretations given under hypnosis."

Thus, use of the dream in group psychotherapy creates theoretical dissension. To ask the dreamer for associations and for the therapist to guide the session accordingly can interfere with the natural communicational flow of the group. For the therapist to assume a naive position and for the group to handle the dream, invariably will support the dream's manifest level which in turn will obscure underlying meaning, despite Bach's position of the intrinsic power of the group. Nevertheless, conducting the dream must be based upon an interaction of individual and group considerations.

THE GROUP DREAM — RESOLUTION TO A DILEMMA

Foulkes and Anthony (1965) recognize that work with dreams in the group creates a contrapuntal force to the overall group process. They indicate that "the leader must address the group process, individual functioning, and the dream at the same time." Mullan (1956) suggests that in order to keep the dream in tune with latent material the group therapist must go against the group's tendency. As group members offer their interpretation to various aspects of the dream, filling out "the therapist's interpretive design," as it were, the basic significance of the dream becomes questionable. Mullan further indicates that the very search for meaning to the dream by the group interferes with the essence of the group experience for each member. The presentation and interpretation of the dream tends to generate an alienation in the group; members focus on thematic material and on intellectual connections and lose sight of each other.

Mullan suggests that keeping to the nonteleological or to the latent affect may be a key to unlocking this dilemma of dream use in the group. The problem is that no technique has yet been developed to do this effectively; that is, in order for latent material to surface in a way that facilitates group process, defenses need to be more easily regulated. To this, Edwards (1977) states that "a technique for focusing on group processes and dreams which includes an understanding of recent ego-psychological theory has not been described." Furthermore, it is proposed here that a fundamental question regarding the meaning of dream use in the group session has not yet even been asked. This question refers to the issue of whether an individual's dream can generate an equivalent dream response from the group-as-a-whole. Such a group-as-a-whole dream response can have special significance to the group process, especially with respect to the problem of conducting dreams. This constitutes an area of group function that has not yet been explored but will be considered presently.

The Individual's Dream Versus the Group's Response

The group's communicational structure is a transformational one. The entire group transcript of a session can be understood as a Chomskian deep structure. Much of it can be reducible to only a few underlying focal themes. The therapist's role is to facilitate this transformation. In orchestrating the session, the therapist's skill lies in keeping time with the meter of the group's reverberating rhythm. This function consists of helping the group, through transformational means, to create fewer surface structure themes from repetitive group interaction. Simultaneously, the therapist also needs to uncover the more cogent person to person interaction so that the chains of analyses or underlying themes may be seen as congruent with group focal conflict themes. In this sense, the group environment is a contrapuntal one composed of parallel lines of development; that is, the few themes of the group are identified by

the transformational work done by the therapist via transference interpretations, deletions, and group-as-a-whole interpretations occurring from deep to
surface and from surface to deep levels of the group communication.

Working on the dream in therapy is a problem that underscores the transformational nature of the group communication. Work on dreams creates a
dilemma only if the group's natural process is stopped. The dream may be
worked on and the ostensible dilemma resolved if certain conditions of the
group process are followed. These conditions will be examined.

When the group's natural communicational processes are activated, an
interactional flow occurs that is experienced by each member as a personal
absorption in the process. During such times, most therapist interventions are
superfluous and frequently serve the group resistance. The natural interactional flow of the group is, in an analogous way, equivalent to individual free-
association in which there exists only limited external interference and
maximum personal absorption. Individuals may be absorbed by good theater
or by interesting literature. During sleep, dreams will absorb the dreamer's
energy and this constitutes a similar sort of in-depth experience in the absence
of self-consciousness. It is the waning of self-consciousness and the deepening
absorption of one's interest that usually determines whether one was at all involved in such a "natural process." During such times, it is the nonteleological
level of communication that becomes more familiar. When one resonates with
the latent communication, then one may be said to be absorbed. It is a time of
noninterference. It is a time in which the unconscious is also more accessible.

In the group, members strive to achieve such absorption experiences.
They most likely will be felt at times when the membership is participating in
an overall thematic way, when the therapist is verbally inactive, when defensive aims of members are not inordinately urgent, and when no single group
member introduces material requiring special attention such as dreams.
Dreams interfere with the natural group processes for all these reasons. Any
person's dream usually omits most of the group membership. Work on group
themes becomes rather forced during such times and the therapist is likely to
be active and supervisory. Intellectualized manifest motifs are then likely to
comprise group-as-a-whole focal themes.

Thus, it must be seen that the introduction of dreams in the group can
generate powerful resistance elements. Whenever a group member introduces
a dream, other group members become immediately defensive. They all may
turn to the therapist. Sometimes they feel as though the therapist should
make an interpretation and, so to speak, "get it over with." Generally, however, the member introducing the dream is immediately elevated in the dominance hierarchy of a group. Except for announcing a pregnancy, there is
probably nothing that can temporarily elevate one's dominance in a group
faster than introducing a dream. A dislocation of the group process occurs and
members perceive the dreamer to be special. It may be that anyone, other
than the therapist, who interferes with the group's natural processes will be
seen as awesome or demanding, or prominent in some other way. Further-

more, the member who introduces the dream has already decided to remain outside the group's inner process. Each member intuitively may realize that to introduce a dream into a session means to stand alone and even perhaps to protest. The essential question, then, is to protest what?

It is proposed here that when individual members introduce dreams they are communicating to the group some termination message. The message might be that they require more personal work, in which case they may be telling the therapist to help them in their transition from one conflict phase to another. Or, they may be indicating some wish to leave the group. In any event, the general message is one that says "I am no longer in the interactional flow of the group." or "I am no longer unself-conscious." Insofar as participation in the interactional flow of the group assumes a lessening of acute self-consciousness and an absorption resembling states of sleep or transcendence, the member who introduces a dream indicates difficulty in participating in this thematic communal enterprise. The message offered may be for the group to shift its focal themes so that the member whose dream it is again may be involved in the uninterrupted group flow.

Working on the dream may indeed inform the dreamer that the group does, in fact, recognize this member's need for additional work. The problem, however, is how to integrate the dream and how to conduct the session so that the resistance dilemma is resolved. Too many interventions and too many dreams will produce a group that is never unself-conscious and such a group cannot survive. Interventions always interrupt and awaken the group from its state of absorption into one of acute self-consciousness. Yet the group member who introduces a dream is already awakened or separate from the overall potential absorption process of the group. In an analogous sense it is as though a person were awakened from a dream because the dream material transformed the dream into a nightmare; that is, the dreamer's defensive structure was not sufficient to keep the dreamer asleep. The dreamer's participation in the group is of a different nature than usual, just as a nightmare is of a different nature than usual night dreams.

In order to understand how a dream might advantageously be treated in a group, the difference between the usual interactional flow of the group and its interruption by the introduction of a dream needs to be further explored. One way to understand this difference is to examine the analogy between the normal interactional group flow as it is analogous to normal night dreams and the introduction of a dream in the group as it is analogous to the appearance of a nightmare. In this way, the meaning of nightmares also may be brought to bear on the group process. The nightmare is different from normal dreaming and reflects characterological changes in the dreamer that are not reflected by normal, undisturbed night dreams. So too does the introduction of a dream change the group's natural interactional process. To study the nightmare as it interferes with the process of natural sleep and dreams may shed some new light on the effect the work of the dream in the group has on the group's natural processes.

CHARACTER STRUCTURE AND DREAMS

It is proposed here that the appearance of a nightmare in an individual signals the modification or transformation of some psychosomatic physical symptom. The nature of the physical symptom is determined by the set of existing defenses and the basic dispositional tendency of the dreamer. These psychosomatic symptoms and the relation of nightmares to dispositional types were explored in the previous chapter and in the chapter on the intrapsychic group. Now it is possible to relate dispositional types, defenses, nightmares, and psychosomatic symptoms.

Impairment of manic and depressed defenses will produce nightmares reflecting modification in respiratory and reproductive symptoms respectively. Impairment of obsessional and psychopathic defenses will produce nightmares reflecting changes in skeletomuscular and dermatological symptoms respectively. Impairment of passive and aggressive defenses will produce nightmares reflecting changes in nervous and circulatory or cardiovascular symptoms respectively. Impairment in hysteric and paranoid defenses will produce nightmares that reflect modifications in sensory and digestive symptoms respectively.

In this sense, a nightmare signals the dissolution of a fixed character formation. This position is consistent with that expressed by Jones (1931) and Mack (1970). Because ones defenses are no longer serving to reinforce a particular character pattern, the appearance of a nightmare means that something has become ego-alien (Altman, 1969). The likelihood is that the ego-alien element is reflected by the dissolution of a physical symptom and the freeing of anxiety. This means that the nightmare signals a change in, or the extinction of, some psychosomatic symptom. Tension has become physically unbound, It may not remain unbound, but could develop into another symptom reflecting a tension rebinding. The occurrence of a nightmare, therefore, will reflect a dissolution of a psychosomatic symptom, the beginning phase of a new one, or both. The following example illustrates this connection.

A 26-year-old female patient reported several nightmares that reflected a breaking through of manic energy. She was an asthmatic who also suffered with bronchitis and other upper respiratory tract disorders. In the nightmares, the manic quality appeared in the form of sexuality and screaming. After reporting the nightmares she was asked whether there was a difference in her respiratory conditions. Surprised by the question, she said that both the nightmares and the total disappearance of all of her symptoms occurred simultaneously two weeks before. The nightmares were generated by some events in her life having direct bearing on her marriage.

Kadis et al. (1968) also indicate that the dream will reveal information on diagnosis and defenses, and Foulkes and Anthony (1965) indicate that symptoms need to be defined by the therapist so that patients can see both sides to the conflict—the need to hide something, a character formation, and the need to have something understood, a potential character reformation. The nightmare signals a moment of character reformation.

Since the introduction of a dream in the group may be understood as an aberration of the group's interactional flow—just as the nightmare is the dream's aberration—then the dream in the group may reflect the fact that some defensive function of the group structure is modified. For example, a preceding group session may have constituted the pivotal event for this change or eruption. The therapist and the group members should expect a change in the psychosomatic profile of the group; that is, when a dream is introduced, it reflects a disturbance—an awakening moment in the group life—and the therapist and the group members should be alert to any spontaneous physical changes in the group. This is similar to the event of a nightmare—an awakening—that signals a change in a psychosomatic condition. It suggests that a decision of noninterference needs to be employed by the therapist in managing the dream at its point of introduction. It does not mean that the therapist is allowing group members to conduct the dream. To wait and to trace the group's activity immediately after the introduction of a dream may reveal the latent communication of the group. The physical expressions of the membership may reflect the group's idiosyncratic way of imposing its own natural process onto the dreamer and the dream and of reabsorbing the dreamer into the group process.

OPERANT RESPONSES TO DREAM MATERIAL: DISPOSITIONAL TYPE, SYMPTOMS AND NIGHTMARES

When a dream is presented in the group, the kinds of unsolicited responses that emerge from group members may depend upon the particular generational phase of the group; that is, the responses may in part depend on the underlying focal conflict of the group. Such themes are generally related to derivative psychosexual material. Second, group members will respond in terms of particular role dispositional qualities that imply specific psychosomatic potentialities. Therefore, whenever a dream is presented, the therapist can listen for samples representing somatic responses. Laughing and fragmentation can reflect oedipal hysteric-sensory and paranoid-digestive responses respectively. Trembling or expressions of feeling cold and intense vocalizing or expressions of dominance can reflect phallic passive-nervous and aggressive-circulatory responses respectively. Silence or inactivity and changing of seats can reflect anal obsessive-skeletomuscular and psychopathic-dermatological responses respectively. Rapid-fire associations and crying can reflect oral manic-respiratory and depressed-reproductive responses respectively.

These comparisons between psychosomatic systems and derived behavior are only first approximations. They are given here to illustrate that group members may respond with a whole array of possible behaviors to the introduction of a dream. Laughter is a sample of hysteric-romantic role behavior. Fragmentation is correlated with paranoid-scrutinizer role behavior. Trembling is an example of passive-innocent role behavior. Shouting or pressured responses reflect aggressive-scapegoater role behavior. Silence is a derived controlled behavior associated with the obsessive-intellectualizer role. Changing of seats constitutes impulsive behavior associated with the acting-out seen in persons with psychopathic-child role behaviors. Intense and energized activity represents manic-puritan role behavior and crying reflects behavior associated with the depressed-reintegrator role. These are the kinds of contents associated with nightmares that correspond to specific dispositional types. They can now also be associated with somatic syndromes.

When the dream is introduced in the group then, members may respond with behaviors that will reflect the psychosomatic profile of the group. Such moments also create opportunities to work-through defensive behavior. Therefore the dream in the group can be viewed as equivalent to a nightmare and this implies that the soil of the group at the point of response to the dream represents a fresh new canvass on which to form new character patterns. Since the tension of the group will be directed toward the dreamer, then the interaction of the group at the point of working on the dream can reflect the therapeutic capacities of the group.

A group with too much levity means that denial mechanisms are keeping the group from seeing something. Responses of dislocation and fragmentation mean that projection mechanisms are maintaining the group as a critical punitive agency. An overabundance of timidity, trembling and passivity in the group implies strong repression while intense gesticulating and shouting may imply the operation of displacement. Silence and excessive therapist participation implies intellectualized control, and acting-out implies regression. Energized activity and pairing attempts imply the operation of reaction-formation while crying or excessive bravado can reflect some problem in the use of compensation. This analysis relates defense to corresponding somatic syndromes.

Kadis et al. (1968) indicate that therapists, regardless of their orientation, will have to respond in some way to the intimate message that dreams convey. However, the therapist's job is extremely demanding when one considers the profound disruptive role dreams can play in the overall communicational structure of the group. The therapist needs to manage the dream in a manner that recognizes its relation to group elements as well as in its importance to the dreamer per se. Wolf and Schwartz (1962) seem to recognize this issue. They engage in dream analysis of the individual in the group and see the dream also as a group dream with various group members in it. They also understand the psychodynamics of the group dream as one in which the entire group membership shares the same unconscious perception.

Treating a dream in the group, therefore, is not simply a matter of deciding whether to invite associations from the dreamer first or from other members first. The central issue of dream interpretation and dream use in the group relates to the interaction of individual personality elements and group elements. Whatever interpretative or associative work that is done on dreams in the group will be enhanced by an understanding of these issues. Working on dreams in the group, therefore, always involves some trade off with regard to the continuity of the group's natural process. In order to minimize the interference of this process, the therapist and group members should focus on group dispositional effects as well as on the dream itself. Just because a dream is introduced does not automatically mean that the therapist should "work on it" as an urgent demand. The therapist should see what the group's response is first.

Stekel (1943) stated, "In the dream we re-experience the past, forget the present and foretell the future." In the group, the reexperience of the past exists in the role traits expressed by any member. Any group member's current state in the group—the existential present state—is always, in part, in the process of becoming. The present is therefore unformed and unhistorical. The aim and direction to the working-through process enables a foretelling of the future, a projected time of new character patterns, a glimpse of which may be gotten in the work on dreams. A much more detailed technique needs to be developed in order to nurture the interaction between individual and group elements demanded by the work with dreams.

In the foregoing, an attempt was made to outline some basis for understanding the appearance of psychosomatic symptomatology in the group. To do this, it was necessary to discuss the special problem of dreams. In the following chapter, member to member communicational patterns will be discussed as they relate to language and emotion, and as they reveal further access to latent content.

14

Communicational Structure of
Groups: Communicational
Patterns—A Group Geometry

Preceding chapters have explored aspects of group communication, focal underlying conflicts, the group's proposed physical or psychosomatic communicational structure, and the special problem of dream use. To these elements must now be added that there may be a geometry to group communication and that an examination of the particular shapes of member to member communication can generate greater access to the latent content of group functioning.

THE SHAPE OF GROUP COMMUNICATION

The observation that a geometry to group communication exists has been indirectly considered with regard to the seating locations of members of the group (Buirski, 1975; Winick and Holt, 1961), and in terms of a variety of mathematical methods that, in a more direct fashion, are used to understand group communication through specific patterns of analysis (Bavelas, 1966; and Cherry, 1961). Buirski suggests that the group's dominance rank will be reflected in the seating arrangement and in the ritualistic patterns to the seating arrangements. Kadis et al. (1968) discuss the geometry of group nonverbal communication. They indicate that various seating positions are inherently meaningful. For example, a member who sits near the door may be conveying feelings about leaving the group; sitting on a couch may indicate a need to feel the presence of other members. Kellerman, Buirski, and Plutchik (1974) also note that members who sit adjacent to the leader may be dependent and passive, while those who sit across from the leader may be oppositional. Steinzer

(1950), in an attempt to examine the space dimension of group communication, found that persons sitting opposite each other have the greatest stimulus value for each other. This idea of interpreting the manner in which group members locate themselves has also produced social-psychological research largely concerned with status and power issues.

The Issue of Dominance: Status and Power

The problem of power relations in the group has been examined in the social-psychological literature with reference to social pressures brought to bear on individual group members (Festinger, Schachter, and Back, 1950), and in terms of theories of social power. In an interesting theoretical exposition, French (1956) and French and Raven (1968) present a theory of social power related to groups generally that may be especially relevant to the communicational rules governing therapy groups. The authors propose the simple axiom that the basis of interpersonal power is in the nature of enduring relationship between person A and person B. Power levers are hypothesized that constitute the bases of any power relationship, and five such power levers are presented. First, a traction power is proposed that simply indicates B's liking for A. Second, expert power is proposed indicating that B thinks A has more knowledge. Third, a reward power is presented that suggests A mediates rewards for B. Fourth, a coercive power suggests that A has the power to mediate punishments for B, and that B accedes to this assumption; and fifth, a legitimate power is proposed in which B believes that A has the right to prescribe B's behavior or opinion.

French and Raven suggest that all communication may be understood with reference to these few assumptive rules. In addition to a set of rules governing member to member interaction, the authors may also have formulated a set of useful laws that determines the behavior of each member to the group therapist. Traction, expert, reward, coercive, and legitimate powers are precisely those that each group member accepts upon entering the group in relation to the therapist. What French and Raven have done, therefore, is to propose a set of axioms that are implicitly accepted by the entire group and that constitute a seminal definition of the communicational underpinning of member-therapist relations. When Wolf and Schwartz and Durkin and Glatzer suggest that all communcation in the group always contains a message to the therapist, the message may be decoded as it were, in terms of the power-relation levers proposed by French and Raven.

One of the implicit interpretations of the power rules developed by French and Raven assumes that all relationships contain some dependency element, and that the disparity in dependency between relating members constitutes the strongest ingredient of the relationship. This issue of disparity is universally seen by authors with reference to a wide variety of group therapy elements. Some of these elements include position of roles, seating locations, and personality tendencies, and these seem to play an important part in the group infrastructure.

The polarity of personality dispositions as they relate to the communicational structure of the group has also been discussed by Bateson (1958). He posits one general communicational principle to indicate that all communicational interchanges are either symmetrical or complementary. A complementary communication involves a relationship in which an assertive member keeps getting more assertive as a submissive one keeps getting more submissive and is called a complementary schismogenesis. Such role reinforcement only occurs when both members relate to each other, hence it is a complementary schismogenesis. A symmetrical schismogenesis, on the other hand, involves a relationship in which both members keep getting more assertive. It is competitive and is defined as an escalation. In therapy groups, the level of group resistance supports complementary type schismogeneses in which role stereotypes are reinforced. This is the "don't-change" message. In contrast, the working-through process retards the development of complementary schismogenesis while confronting the processes involved in any symmetrical or escalating role reinforcement. Within this framework, the communicational analysis of any group session takes into account the power relations between members in terms of their polar role conflicts, and between member and therapist in terms of the stream of underlying messages that are steadily heading toward the therapist from each of the patients. Researchers of group communication have been frequently concerned with the measurement of such communicational patterns.

Measuring Communication

Many ingenious methods have been devised for measuring and understanding the interaction of groups. For example, Cartwright and Zander (1968) suggest that the use of graph theory may permit the deepest structure of the group to be analyzed. They suggest the possibility of preparing a set of concepts for describing the entire group structure. "One can speak with exact meaning about the diameter of a group, the number of levels it has, its degree of connectedness, its vulnerability to splitting and its degree of balance." The use of this sort of group theory has not been applied extensively with therapy groups, but researchers have been interested in citing its relevance to measurement in all social sciences (Harary and Norman, 1953; Harary, Norman, and Cartwright, 1965). Other techniques—unusual in so far as concerns their applicability to group therapy measurement—are included in studies of mathematical representations of group structure (Glanzer and Glaser, 1959), in the use of matrix algebra as a sociometric barometer of group theory (Forsyth and Katz, 1946), and in the use of matrix mathematics to detect cliques within the group (Harary and Ross, 1957). An interactional sociogram technique called the Interaction Chronogram has been developed by Chapple

(1949) and Cox (1973) and is described by Reder (1978). It is a device used to moniter the process of the session with regard to content, affect, and interaction.

According to Bionian group-as-a-whole theorists, the existence of a few underlying focal conflicts in the group implies that the latent level of the group's transcript could be analyzed in a reasonably reliable manner with a variety of analytic techniques. These can include graph theory, matrix algebra, cryptographic theory, binary coding theory, as well as the analysis of psychosexual content within transferential material. There is such a wide consensus among authors regarding the existence of only a few underlying focal themes that a high concurrent validity might be expected from all such analyses.

The state of the art can be estimated by the work of Watzlawick, Beavin, and Jackson (1967). They theorize that groups contain a calculus of communication which is defined by the general laws of communication. "The existence of such a calculus can, in the present state of our knowledge, be compared to that of a star whose existence and position are postulated by theoretical astronomy but has not yet been discovered by the observations." The authors attempt to formalize the communicational rules to group interaction both with regard to general laws governing the group-as-a-whole and in terms of member to member interactions. For example, in terms of role assignments, the authors would propose that every communication has a content as well as a relational aspect to it. There is a manifest and a latent content, and the meta-communicational level of the group carries information about role to role messages and about emotion. An axiom of the calculus therefore is that one cannot not communicate. The idea of an interactional contextual component to emotional communication has also been proposed by DeRivera (1977). The structure of the emotional communication of language may therefore be analyzed in the person to person communication of the group.

Emotion and the Structure of Language

In the structure of language, Lacan (1968) and others propose that phonemes, the smallest distinguishable unit of sounds, are the elementary particles of language. However, it is here proposed that only sounds with valency constitute basic particles or fundamental ingredients of language. In linguistic structure, valency is equivalent to inflection or intonation. Phonemes are therefore not just random sounds but, with intonation, reflect some meaning. Intonation of sound as the basic phoneme or unit of language is the first sign that the human being is a verbally communicating organism and comes equipped with an epigenetic language program just waiting for its developmental salience. Infant babbling always contains intonational nuances. This relation of inflection to sound has also been noticed by social psychologists and by ethologists. Intonation is the emotion of the sound and it is the emotion, not the content, that delivers the greatest portion of the message of the spoken word (Kellerman, 1977c). This is the relational aspect inherent in the communicational system implied by Watzlawick, Beavin, and Jackson (1967).

Lacan indicates that the moment in which desire becomes human is also the moment in which the child is born into language. It might be more useful to postulate that the moment in which emotion takes an object is really the moment in which the child is born into language. It seems clear that emotions become associated with objects during preoedipal intonational periods and it therefore seems that language becomes inextricably tied to the structure of emotion. Since people are born with the capacity for a full complement of emotions, the capacity for language also exists at birth.

All emotion is connected to objects. Because of this connection the structure of emotion contains an interpersonal expressive program. This emotion-object connection suggests that the infant too is born with an interpersonal program. The emotion-object relationship may be a bridge to cognition; that is, knowing is inherent in feeling. It is the connection between the interpersonal and intrapsychic. The operation of emotion in developing or accumulating its repertoire of objects roughly parallels what Lacan calls the developmental movement of "other" to "I." This developmental movement reflects the emergence of ego.

Lacan indicates that the mapping of human relationships determines the laws that regulate the unconscious activities of the mind. The relational meaning to this hypothesis, however, suggest that inborn patterns, abstracted through language and reflecting emotion, are truly what regulates the unconscious activities of the mind. The power of the spoken word, then, as it affects one's daily life is based upon the attachment of emotion to objects and the prying loose of emotions from objects.

The relation of language and emotion thus constitutes an evolutionary advance: to use language—the abstraction of underlying systems—to change those systems. It is evident the basic structure of language needs to be studied in terms of the basic structure of emotions. Some implications of this formulation can be drawn. First, perhaps the distinction between affect and thinking disorders is quite arbitrary, and all disturbance reflected in diagnostic dispositional terms contains underlying emotional conflict. Second, the Lacanian position of language as a symbolic order existing even before the birth of the individual may reflect an inherent sociobiological genetic program. This implies that neuroses and neurotic patterns cannot easily be changed. The difficulty lies in changing a genetic program that is fully expressed in a bizarre talking circuit that was determined by the principles of early object relations in which all emotion was attached to objects. The problem is a thorny one. It is a problem of changing the ritualistic locking in of emotion through language.

In psychoanalytic terms, these changes may occur only when the object and the emotion can be separated. Thus, it becomes important to understand the basic emotion structure of language exising in its historical and rudimentary form on the level of inflected phonemes that are frequently observed in infants; that is, infants who babble express emotion through the intonation of the babbling. This raises the question of the range of these intonations. How many intonational or inflected sounds are there? Does the range of such intonational babbling reflect a specific emotion range and perhaps even an emotion language? It might be proposed that the basic intonational range reflects the basic emotion spectrum. Consequently, there may only be eight basic inflected phonemes that in combination may generate any amount of inflections at all. These may connect to the eight basic bipolar emotions. The system, then, may be related on all levels of personality including the levels of traits, defense, language, and dreams.

This structure may be expressed as a biogenetic program. It is hypothesized here that this basic structure of eight lines of development, in contrast to the Lacanian "mapping" position, determines the laws of the unconscious and may be first observed during intonational babbling. In a metacommunicational sense, the emotion structure underlies the basic personality system and may provide additional understanding of the relational and role communicational structure of the group; that is, communication in the group frequently concerns role to role messages about emotion. Group communication therefore is perhaps more fundamentally an intonational metacommunication.

Communication of the Group-As-A-Whole

Foulkes and Anthony (1965) also suggest that the group process is metacommunicational, and that the meaning to interaction may be understood on the manifest level only by interpreting the group's defensive structure. This structure contains underlying intonational mood as well as thematic content themes. For example, if the group ignores something or denies any critical attitudes in member to member interactions, it may be developing hysteric-like tendencies in order to avoid confronting oedipal loyalty-disloyalty issues. If, on the other hand, the group maintains a rigid critical stance and consistently projects anxiety, its paranoid cast acts, again, to avoid oedipal issues especially with reference to the therapist. If the group experiences discontinuity in that themes get lost from session to session, the group may then be described as a highly repressed one, probably very passive, and in a full fledged phallic resistance. Such a group is inhibiting power themes. Communication in this sort of group may be understood in terms of phallic defensive functioning. If the group displaces aggression onto one or more designated members, the defensive displacement is designed to deflect the group's focus from the therapist—again an example of avoidance of phallic assertion and defiance themes in the transference to the therapist. If the group consistently intellectualizes in order to control emotion the resistance is a derived anal one and all communication may be understood with respect to issues of "not-giving." The therapist again is the object of the transference resistance. If the group acts childish, silly, or even delinquent it again serves the resistance by "not-giving" and all communication may be understood as the avoidance at all cost of any serious confrontation with the therapist.

Even if the group acts as a Bionian work group with a full energy commitment it may be operating with some reaction-formation. Its resistance motive in this case is to avoid any sexual reference to the therapist and to maintain a spirit of work-rewarded dependency. Similarly, if the group operates with strong compensatory mechanisms, it is presumably resisting the experience of loss and also maintaining a dependency condition—a reflection of oral derivative behavior.

To these possible infrastructural communicational rules, Foulkes and Anthony (1965) add that the group may operate on the level of symbolization in which various patients assume intrapsychic roles. Some take the role of superego while others assume the roles of ego and id. The particular correlation of intrapsychic forces to roles of the group has been more fully elaborated in chapter 10 on the intrapsychic nature of the group.

The above defensive group postures refer to the nonteleological or metacommunicational level of the group-as-a-whole. Understanding the group's defensive posture will reveal the emotional message underlying its manifest content. As Back (1961) suggests, the communication is only a repetition of a few main points that occur over and over again by different means. It is suggested here that these few main points reflect the four psychosexual stages that produce four essential focal themes. The four focal themes are further expressed in four polar role types and defended by four polar defensive syndromes. It is proposed that the infrastructural group-as-a-whole communicational system consists of these few patterns and is controlled by these few defensive operations. This suggests that there may only be a limited number of patterns of communication in the group. Authors of group therapy have been interested in determining these patterns.

Member-to-Member Communicational Patterns

The geometry of member-to-member communication has been approached in a variety of ways. Rosenbaum and Berger (1963) report studies in which researchers are interested in determining the actual number of interactional bonds in a group if each member interacts with every other member. This is essentially research into the relationship of group size to group process and represents the point of view that the dyad is the major communicational pattern of the group. The issue of studying dyads or triads in the group has also been discussed by Turquet (1974). Rosenbaum (1974) indicates that the emotional relationships of families may be understood as a "network of interlocking triangles." This particular geometry constitutes a balance phenomenon. As the central triangle changes, so do all other group triangles.

Slavson (1957) considers the geometry of member-to-member communication by positing three essential patterns. One is bilateral in which there exists a reciprocal bilateral interaction. A second is unilateral in which two members are involved in an interaction only by virtue of one contacting the other. A third is called a peripheral contact in which one member obliquely communicates with another. Such a relationship may be said to be obtuse.

DYADS, TRIADS, AND QUADRADS

Kadis et al. (1968) describe four kinds of communication that can be conceived of in geometric terms. The first, a vertical communication, is a bilateral therapist to patient interaction. The second is a horizontal communication in which the therapist uses personal examples and the working-through of personal conflicts as a means of stimulating the group. The third, a triangular communication, is one in which the therapist becomes the apex of any member to member interaction so that the therapist controls all interaction. The fourth, a circular communication, is a more natural and unencumbered interactional process. This model of communication is basically an authority model of group function. Both the vertical and triangular patterns are therapist centered while the horizontal one ignores authority relations but is controlled by the therapist. The circular pattern claims a democracy of group interaction but still allows for therapist regulation.

The question of the number of members that may be involved in any communicational interaction is addressed by Wolf and Schwartz (1971) who postulate three basic geometric patterns to communication: bilateral, where two members are involved in a reciprocal interaction; trilateral, where three members may be reciprocally interacting; and quadrilateral, where four members share an interaction. In a study on interpersonal analysis in groups, Geller (1963) postulates three vectors of communication. These are content vectors, defined by what is said, process vectors, defined by how it is said, and relationship vectors, defined by to whom it is said. Such vectors may also be analyzed with reference to dyadic, triadic, and quadradic communicational patterns.

COMMUNICATIONAL LINK PATTERNS

Foulkes (1964) has proposed that the group is a network, within which patterns of communication exist that enable patients to work-through conflicts. Networks of interaction have also been proposed in the social-psychological literature in studies of leadership and authority relations. Cherry (1961) formulates two major link patterns that are recognizable in large social groups. These are called skeletal structures of large groups. One is a dictatorship star pattern in which a strong central authority radiates to all of the membership of the group individually. This pattern, and its variations, has been described by Foulkes and Anthony (1965) as one that generates isolation, subgrouping, and monopolism and has been taken by Yalom (1970) to imply group fragmentation. Cherry's second basic large group skeletal structure is that of the commercial ring, a simple chain pattern that implies one set of rules for inside the chain and one set for the outside. Figure 14-1 shows the impaired communicational patterns proposed by Foulkes and Anthony and by Yalom, and the fully accessible pattern also suggested by Yalom in which any geometric communicational link may occur.

Other conceptions of link patterns have been proposed by Bavelas (1951). Communication patterns in groups that were short-term and task oriented were studied. The geometric properties of these communication patterns were analyzed with respect to pentagon chains, simple link chains, and variations of hierarchical links. Bavelas concluded that patterns are determined and may be measured by the distance between members and by the number of communicational links between members. The most interesting finding was that "Lines of communication are found to shorten with the integration of the group

A. Facilitative Pattern

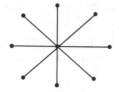

B. Authoritarian Pattern

C. Isolation Pattern   D. Subgrouping Pattern   E. Monopolistic Pattern

Figure 14-1.   Five types of communicational links. A and B are proposed by Yalom (1970), and C, D, and E are proposed by Foulkes and Anthony (1965). Only type A permits all geometric communicational shapes to occur. (From *The Theory and Practice of Group Psychotherapy, 2nd ed.*, by D. Yalom, p. 108, copyright 1975 by Basic Books, Inc., Publishers, New York and *Group Therapy, 2nd ed.*, by S. H. Foulkes and E. J. Anthony, p. 73, copyright 1957, 1965 by S. H. Foulkes and E. J. Anthony.)

as it changes from a mere collection of people, to a leader centered group, and then to a group centered group." Figure 14-2 shows this group process progression as the group becomes more group centered.

According to Bavelas, as the group first convenes, a communicational chain is formed in which the lines of communication may be tabulated in a simple arithmetic manner. Figure 14-2 shows this tabulation. In pattern A, member A to member B is equal to one line, member A to member C is equal to two lines, member A to member D is equal to three lines, and member A to member E is equal to four lines. In the five member group, therefore, any one member needs 10 lines of communication to reach all other members during group formative periods. In pattern B, member A to member B is equal to two lines of communication because the leader occupies the C position. Member A to member C is equal to one line, member A to member D is equal to two lines, and member A to member E also is equal to two lines. In the leader centered group with five members, therefore, any member needs only seven lines of communication to reach all other members. In pattern C, the group centered pattern, any member needs only four lines of communication to reach all other members. Member A to member B is equal to one line, member A to member C is equal to one line, member A to member D is equal to one line, and member A to member E is equal to one line.

How much of this schematic technique of viewing group communication

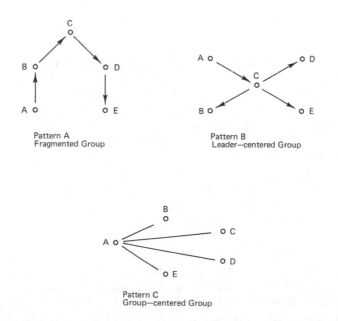

Pattern A
Fragmented Group

Pattern B
Leader—centered Group

Pattern C
Group—centered Group

Figure 14-2.   The group's communicational maturity is reflected in the movement from pattern A to pattern C. Lines of communication shorten as group centeredness develops (from Bavelas, 1951).

may be applied to the communicational structure of therapy groups is not yet clear. However, such studies do suggest that communicational cohesion crystallizes for all members better, and more productively, in group centered groups.

Foulkes and Anthony (1965) state that "as soon as a group is formed, there is an inevitable interaction between members and a need is felt among them to make more and more contact, to establish more and more common ground, to enlarge their understanding of others and to be better understood themselves. These forces all operate toward establishing communication, which in its turn opens up new pathways of contact and new areas of understanding. Communication in a very real sense is this process." In terms of a geometry of group communication then, simple shapes that correspond more to unilateral chain links may not be as relevant to the understanding of the group's communicational structure as are complex shapes that would more closely reflect a group structure of multilateral communication. A bilateral, a triangular, or even a tetradic shape to group communication does not seem to be a sufficient geometry to account for the multiplicity of communicational possibilities in a traditional therapy group of eight members. In the following sections an attempt will be made to develop a rationale for the existence of an ideal communicational geometric shape.

MULTILATERAL GROUP COMMUNICATION

In addition to fantasy material there are essentially two kinds of material that group members can introduce in any group session. First, members may refer to relationships in their lives outside the group which would include current and past experiences with family members, concerns about job, school, etc. The second category of content consists of "inside" references; that is, group members may relate to one another in the "here-and-now" and this can also include references to past group events and even from past group generations. The extreme form of "inside" therapy is practiced by the Tavistock group where treating the group-as-a-whole consists of interpreting group focal themes based upon ongoing group process. The practice of psychoanalysis in groups supported in its pure form by Wolf and Schwartz (1962) and by Durkin and Glatzer (1973) and practiced by most psychodynamically oriented group therapists considers both kinds of group material. Practitioners encourage "inside" interaction more than they encourage members to bring outside material to the group. Resistive groups mostly talk about "outside-things", they are hardly confrontational or interactional or even personal, and they usually dissolve into storytelling. Psychodynamically oriented therapists who practice psychoanalysis in groups will always want to strike a balance between "inside" and "outside" material.

It is proposed here that this particular balance should consist of a focus on the "inside"-group experience for about 65–75 percent of the time and on "outside"-material for about 25–35 percent. This trend toward a three-to-one ratio of "inside" to "outside" material will help create the maximal therapeutic climate for each group member. The desirability for this ratio to occur is based upon the observation that any member's functioning in the group can reflect, to a great extent, that person's behavior outside the group, reflecting that person's character behavior. Encouraging this three-to-one ratio, therefore, permits each member the opportunity to recreate in the group typical patterns of behavior. When this condition is fully realized, the group will then be constituted as a miniuniverse, a microcosm of the "outside" world. This therapeutic condition is the only way in which transference work and therapeutic working-through can take place. The group then becomes a living workshop for each member. It is not exactly equivalent to everyday life, but exists in parallel fashion to everyday life.

Interpretations are frequently made to group members that indicate the transference of intra-group to historical and extra-group relationships. For example, the way in which members react to the group climate is frequently a barometer of the degree to which any member experiences and manages outside relationships. The therapist must be aware in these instances that transference in the group becomes instantly evoked—an illustration of just how strongly parallel lines of development exist between the group climate and one's experience outside the group. Slate (1966) goes so far as to propose that social evolution is entirely recapitulated in the group, and Kadis et al. (1968) even state that patients experience déjà vu in the group because of the parallel between their lives and patterns of behavior in and out of the group. This point has been made by many authors (Johnson, 1963; Weiner, 1974; and Yalom, 1970).

One's degree and kind of involvement in the group directly reflects the nature of that person's closest relationship outside the group. Whenever a group member expresses specific feelings about the group-as-a-whole, the therapist may view such reactions as those containing transferential information. Equally as important is how one conducts personal relations within the group. Role-character behavior will be reflected in the style and emotion of relating, and not only in the specific verbal message. The style of relating or its intonational flavor is the key to the therapy work. It is a true reflection of character behavior and provides the only substantive entree to transference interpretations. For example, a narcissistic and monopolistic person can control an entire group interaction. This person may point toward another group member while talking and looking at still a second group member. Simultaneously, the monopolist may grasp on to the arm of a chair in which a third member is sitting to, so to speak, hold that person still while conducting the defense of a fourth member who may have been unjustly accused by still another fifth member. The remaining two group members may be galvanized in support of the defense of the unjustly accused one. If the therapist points out that this monopolistic person is controlling the entire group and that such behavior also must be occurring outside the group, the interpretation would probably be vehemently denied and defended against. The manifest verbal interaction of the entire group transcript would then be reviewed by the controlling group member and only its content used to logically refute and resist all interpretation. This illustration is designed to indicate that style of behavior relates to underlying emotionality and underlying need systems in a more direct fashion than does overt verbal content interaction. The connection between "inside" and "outside" group work as it may determine an ideal communicational geometry is proposed in the following section.

COMMUNICATIONAL SHAPE AND THE THERAPIST

The important geometric shape to group communication as it relates to transference and to a corresponding working-through of character problems must take into account that the group is a parallel mirror reflection of life, that the shape has relational meaning, and that the therapist must always be part of it.

It is hypothesized here that in one respect the triangular shape is the key shape to group interaction because it permits each communication of the group to be understood as a possible transference communication to the therapist. However the triangular shape only takes into account the "inside" interactional nature of the group. It does not address the notion that all behavior in the group reflects, in a true fashion, one's behavior outside of the group. Thus the triangular shape needs to extend to the "outside." The true geometric shape to the understanding of group communication, then, that takes into account both the ingredient of therapist relevancy to any communication, as well as the ingredient of "inside-outside" equivalence to communication, is a double triangle or a parallelogram. One half of the parallelogram reflects the group interaction while the other half constitutes its reflection in each group member's life and history. The therapist is always part of the triangle in the group and it is accepted that all messages contain hidden transference meaning with regard to the therapist. The parallelogram may be further divided to produce subdivisions that reflect more complex interaction among members. To what extent this geometric conception can generate new understanding of group communicational process ultimately will determine its value as a therapeutic tool.

It should be noted that not everything that transpires in the group contains important messages. Communication and communicational meaning of interaction in the group are always in the process of becoming. What is important is the crystallized moment in which juxtaposition of content and style produce emotion interpreted by the therapist or by other group members to be meaningful. As the group evolves, more and more of its time is valuable to each member. Defense becomes worked-through and crystallized therapeutic exchanges increase in frequency.

The nature of such moments may be analyzed with regard to their geometry in a way that distinguishes between a variety of possible triangles and with regard to the specific meaning to each. It would be interesting to see just what the differences are between these variations of shapes as they relate to role types of the group and especially as they relate to the therapist's position in the shape.

SUMMARY

In the previous four chapters, the communicational structure of the group was explored in terms of its manifest and latent interactional system. An attempt was made to describe this system in terms of phenomena that reveal the group's latent communicational life. Some of these included: the existence of a few group-as-a-whole focal conflict themes, psychosomatic expressions as features of communication in group life, the use of the work on patients' dreams, and the possibility that multilateral interactional patterns constitute an underlying communicational geometry that is welded together by the presence of the therapist.

It is the therapist, that symbol of generational time, of historical access, that presumably provides the therapy group with a tacit reason to exist. The therapist's presence makes the issue of continuity of central importance to each member's working-through process. This continuity, provided in part by the group environment, permits the group member to be part of the therapeutic process. It is the therapist who maintains this environment and it is the therapist who helps create conditions for this environment to become self-perpetuating. Thus the therapy group becomes a powerful cultural environment which, in some respects, eventually absorbs and distributes the authority power of the therapist.

What sort of person is the therapist, whose imputed power has helped create the group process and who also ultimately becomes absorbed by it? The question becomes, who is the therapist?

15

The Group Therapist: Role
Function and
Countertransference

The previous chapters of this book have shown how group life and individual personality systems intersect at many levels of development. The basic structure, role composition, emotions, dispositional types, mechanisms of defense, and intrapsychic nature of these systems have been related to the group's evolutionary process. These systems have been shown to relate also to psychosexual stages of development and to the manifestation of a psychosomatic aspect of group therapy communications.

The group's process is sociobiological. In this view of group therapy life, continuity of group structure and recapitulation of historical elements play the important roles in the consolidation of individual therapy and group process. When the group develops its full structural capacities, it may then constitute a transformational environment. This transcendant or evolutionary sense of the group is reflected in its communicational transformations and by its implied transformational physical shape which is determined by the true variation of the inner forces of the group.

The role of the therapist and its meaning to group life has been cited throughout this book. The therapist as regulator of group tension level, interpreter of transferences and group focal themes, and object of deeply rooted Freudian and even Darwinian identifications, emerges in the group as Redl's chief central figure. Through the therapist, generational experience becomes expressed and the group is assured of its continuity. The therapist as a generational symbol is thus a time equivalent and has access to all the transformations of the group. In an elemental way, the therapist is the group's space intersect;

that is, the therapist as a symbol of time exists within the full experience of all group generations.

In this chapter, the therapist's place in group life will be further explored. The therapist's role will be considered from several perspectives, in terms of the group-process structure in which group effects predominate; the function and power of the leader with regard both to individual and group effects; and the countertransference issues arising out of the therapist's personal unfinished character needs and the strain that the group places on these needs.

GROUP LEADERSHIP AND GROUP STRUCTURE: THE GROUP-AS-A-WHOLE

A geneaological interpretation of group life suggested the hypothesis that the group's aim is to stay alive—to survive. Korten (1962) suggests how this hypothesis incorporates the role of the therapist. He assumes that the group structure generates leadership that is democratic and facilitative when three conditions are met: group goals are of greater importance than individual ones; the overall group need does not place undue stress on the group's goal attainments; and, most importantly, the group's goals do not interfere unduly with the goal of individuals. This position also is proposed by Bales (1950). Usandivaras (1974) further suggests that group solidarity is of overriding importance to the operation of the group process. This element of group structure implies that group members should defer individual aims so that the aims of the group as expressed by the therapist may be accomplished.

Proponents of the view that groups assume an indigenous momentum perceive the therapist to be necessary but not necessarily central in the group's curative process. They stress that given the correct structural elements, the group's natural processes generate a direction which is determined by its survival aim. Gibbard, Hartman, and Mann (1974) state "the therapist must have enough confidence in the evolving work culture of the group, and in the members of the group to endorse one central assumption: if the culture of the group is a generally enabling one, more circumscribed, interpersonal and intrapsychic conflicts will be resolved without the direct, focused attention of the therapist." The authors further state "the therapist's primary responsibility is to the development of a therapeutic group culture."

Parloff (1963) takes exception to such a view. "The group therapist must recognize that although the group's motivational forces and processes provide a potential for change and growth, such changes are not an inevitable, automatic, or inherent condition of groups. Group processes are neither inherently therapeutic nor psychonoxious." Parloff indicates that the group's curative environment is not in any special way generated or endowed by group effects. This theoretical difference expressed by Gibbard, Hartman, and Mann on the one hand, and by Parloff, Wolf, and Schwartz (1962) on the other, contains certain ideological implications. Each side of the dispute may be viewed with regard to particular Skinnerian or Freudian ideologies. The Skinnerian position would emphasize that the group structure is responsible for all attitudes and behavior. Changes in the group structure would inevitably change these attitudes as well as behavior. In this sense the therapist or any other central figure personifies and expresses elements of the group culture and emotion rather than determining them. The Freudian position would stress the shift in intrapsychic balance and the importance of the therapist to the therapeutic transference work. The position taken in this book leaves no doubt that the group structure can be constructed either correctly or incorrectly and the therapy group process will be affected accordingly. It is also certainly clear that the therapist is the chief, central figure around which key transference phenomena revolve. The group therapy process therefore reflects an interpenetration of both Freudian and Skinnerian positions.

Leadership Roles and Group Function

The importance of the leader to group process is further noted by Bennis and Shepard (1974), who indicate that the group may have several leaders during different phases of the process. These catalysts or central persons in leadership roles are capable of approaching the unknowns of new group phases and help the therapist recalibrate the tension level of the group.

According to Bales and Slater (1955), two subleaders emerge in so-called leaderless groups. One presses for task accomplishment and the other addresses the emotional and social needs of members. In the theory of group therapy process presented in this book, it is predominantly the therapist who perceives and addresses the emotional and social needs of the group while the creation of an adequate and natural group infrastructure accounts for the appearance of group phases through which task accomplishment becomes relevant to group process.

The notion of central figures providing leadership roles to satisfy group needs is also seen by Usandivaras (1974), who indicates that the group generally displays a secondary leader; a member who performs the forbidden tasks of the group which are necessary for its survival. For example, the solidarity of the group increases in some way when sexuality is for the most part abolished. This may become partially accomplished with the suppression of competition among men or women. In certain instances and with the support of various central figures, the therapist may assume the sexual role.

In part, Bach (1954) refers to this point in a discussion of flirtation between members. In some respects, flirtation challenges each member to take sides either for or against it; to identify with it or not; to sanction or disapprove of it. Bach suggests that the flirtation tends to create a crisis in the balance of group alliances. In this sense, sexuality can always produce equilibrium problems for the group. Bion would see it as a pairing assumption group within which the therapist as well as the members become subject to the vicissitudes of a focal sexual theme or theme of hope. In contrast, a psychoanalytic explanation would imply that the sexuality of the group need not be either usurped by the therapist or sublimated, and the therapist need not become party to whatever emotions gripped the group at the moment. The therapist's role in a well-constituted group permits unambiguous interpretation. The only task that either the therapist or some other leader/central figure needs to accomplish with respect to sexuality is to prevent acting-out. The management of group tension level during such sexual moments depends entirely on whether the group is galvanized to prevent acting-out.

If the group develops dual central-figure leadership roles, it is the task leader who solves problems and helps to delay gratification. These few functions are frequently expressed by the puritan and intellectualizer role types who work best during Bionian work-group phases. The expressive leader, who may be the therapist or another member such as an accepting romantic type generally seeks agreement and harmony and is eager to eliminate discontent and criticality. According to Bales and Slater (1955), when both central leadership figures are sympathetic with each other, the group will generate a balanced equilibrium in which the status heirarchy within the membership will be stable. The roles of task leader and expressive leader are also occasionally performed by the same person, either the therapist or some other central leadership figure (Borgatta, Couch, and Bales, 1954; Slater, 1955).

It is important to examine the concept of central figures as they constitute role expressions of the group. Redl (1942), in his important paper on this subject, never fully described the relationship among central figures or the correlation between central figures and particular group phases. For example, Bennis and Shepard (1956) point out that "while the potential for certain kinds of leadership is always present, each kind becomes salient only at a certain point in the life of the group." This point is also made by Lieberman, Yalom, and Miles (1973) and by Turquet (1974). Bion (1961) expresses the extreme position by proposing that leaders are only accepted when their attitudes are congruent with the attitudes of the basic assumption group, and not when they lead the group in the sense of goal-oriented work activity. He states that the group is only suggestible to a leader if such leadership "falls within the terms of the active basic assumption. . . . if it does not, the group will ignore it." Bion further indicates that the behavior of members during basic assumption group work is characterized by a loss of individuality and distinctiveness, and this phenomenon applies to the therapist as well. The very serious implication here is that the normal group process contains such strong and overpowering forces that even the therapist is hopelessly governed by them. This view is certainly quite different than that expressed by Parloff (1963), who does not attribute any special significance to forces and potentialities which may be inherent in the so-called natural group process.

Whether or not the group possesses a force of its own, there is no doubt that the therapist is somehow in part, responsible for this force and, according to Bion, even overcome by it. It is frequently expressed in the response of group members to the therapist and is another feature of the overall theory of group structure.

Response to the Therapist

In a basic communicational sense, even Bion's assumption cultures imply a geometric shape to the group's essential transference meaning. The assumption groups of dependency, fight–flight, and pairing indicate that group behavior at any given moment is concerned with one of these emotional problems. It may be more relevant to say that each assumption culture constitutes a message to the therapist. The dependency group needs the leader, the fight–flight group struggles with the leader, and the pairing group in its transferential sense is sexual toward the leader.

These are powerful responses to the role of leader. They are rooted in the group structure in the sense that the leader constitutes a link with history, a generational continuity. Rey (1975) defines this role of the therapist as representing a special inner object of the group, "a meta-system with regard to the system of members." Slavson (1957) addes that, "In a therapy group, the therapist is the recipient of libidinal and other types of transference feelings and is an object of dependency. He is therefore the target of periodic positive, negative and ambivalent feelings." One implication of Slavson's perception of the leader's position is that different types of leaders may permit certain responses to emerge while inhibiting others. Furthermore, patients attribute godlike powers to therapists (Kaplan and Roman, 1963). Hartman and Gibbard (1974b) have indicated that in the Bionian sense, if therapists do not live up to expectations, they become instant objects of hostility. Foulkes and Anthony (1965) add that patients want the therapist to "help them, gratify, advise, inhibit, condemn, mediate, align with them, and to feed them. They want him to be: mindreader, punisher, attacker, sympathetic and inspirer." Underlying these wants and expectations is the unqualified feeling that more than anything else, patients want therapists to play the role of past family members. Patients need the group to be a transference environment and to this end will endow the therapist with parental attributes. According to Yalom (1974), patients also have a desire to possess the therapist solely.

The slightest behavior on the therapist's part may produce group upheavals. Hartman and Gibbard (1974b) suggest that even the leader's silence can generate great anxiety, and Slater (1966) adds that silence can generate feelings of abandonment and consequent intense hostility. As a group effect, hostility toward the leader is apparently one of the main transference ingredients of member response to therapist. This transferential phenomenon is expressed in most communicational triangles and also reflects the patient's transferences outside the group.

RESENTMENT TOWARD THE THERAPIST: EGO-DEFENSE AND RESISTANCE

Freud (1921) proposed that "each member is bound by libidinal ties on the one hand to the leader . . . and on the other hand to the other members of the group." Slavson (1957) amplifies the Freudian thesis by indicating that the leader is equivalent to the group ego and the group ego is an accumulation of portions of each member's ego. One way that the therapist has to diagnose resistance in the group is to estimate whether or to what extent the group ignores and denies the leader in terms of either actual presence or influence (Spotnitz, 1976).

This resistance may be a group response to the therapist. If it contains elements of reaction-formation and compensation, then it is likely to have a dependent cast and the group will be resentful about abandonment anxieties. In this case the resistance is oral and will generate derivative oral group-focal themes. If the resistance contains elements of intellectualization and regression, then it is likely to be expressed through withholding or acting-out behavior. In this case the group will resent the therapist for presumably demanding too much. In such instances the resistance is anal and the focal theme of the group will similarly reflect these derivative anal themes. If the resistance contains elements of repression and displacement, then it is likely to be expressed through passive and aggressive derived phallic themes. If the resistance contains elements of denial and projection, then it is likely to be expressed through group focal themes of competition and loyalty—disloyalty. In this case the resistance is oedipal. This sort of transference matrix reveals derived focal themes of the group's generational development. The first generation oedipal phase is composed of competition and loyalty themes; the second generation phallic period contains passive–aggressive and assertion themes; the third generation reflects anal focal themes of control and acting-out; and the fourth oral generation contains dependency themes. Although each generation is characterized by a major theme, all other psychosexual themes may also be represented. The issue of the psychosexual stages of the group, including the observation that psychosexual conflicts are also expressed in terms of group stages, has been discussed by Applebaum (1963).

In all group resistance, the assumption shared by members is that the therapist harbors covert motives. This allegedly hidden agenda of the therapist (Hinton, 1970; Mann, 1974) permits patients to feel justified in their resentment toward the therapist. In fact, Freud (1921) proposed that the leader ultimately would be attacked. If the leader were not attacked, he then assumed the existence of a therapeutic anomaly. It is Freud's position that in the transferential sense the leader has to disappoint group members and cause them to be angry. To this point, Slater (1966) indicates, in terms of a collective unconscious, that man's social and religious evolution is recapitulated in the small group and therefore the leader tends to be defied and rebelled against. Gibbard, Hartman, and Mann (1974) offer an explanation of this response to the therapist in anal derivative, Freudian psychosexual terms. They indicate that each member's "groupiness" constitutes an ambivalent condition, and "he must fix the blame for his own defenses on something or someone other than the group—on a single member of the group, on the leader." The ambivalence is in the obsessional nature of the transference of member to group and of member to leader, and it reflects an anal derivative symptom of group life; that is, each member's response of resentment toward the therapist accumulates in the group. Even though the therapist may be quite democratic, members enter the group with the feeling that it is fundamentally a psychological and emotional autocracy. According to Lippitt and White (1960), hostility is likely to increase under such predisposing conditions.

It seems clear that each member's relation to the therapist needs to be worked-through. Freud (1921, 1939) and other authors such as Bach (1954), Foulkes (1948), and Gordon (1951) have suggested that ties toward the leader need to be resolved if member-to-member relationships are to develop. These authors focus on the working-through of authority problems as the first step in character restructuring. Bennis and Shepard (1974) also state that "those components of group life having to do with intimacy and interdependence cannot be dealt with until those components having to do with authority and dependence have been resolved." A therapist who intervenes too much prevents member-to-member relationships from developing. A therapist who does allow relationships between members to develop also keeps the group hostility level from escalating inappropriately.

DEVELOPING PEER-ORIENTED RELATIONSHIPS

The therapist recedes more and more into the background as the group works-through its authority conflicts. According to Yalom (1970), this work may be traced in terms of stages of group activity. The first stage is orientation, in which group members depend on the therapist in their overall search for structure. The second stage is conflict, in which dominance themes and the general role organization of the group emerge. The third stage expresses the effects of the working-through of authority conflicts. Here the differences among members are obscured and an inter-member–interpersonal role harmony predominates in the group culture. The final stage is one of high cohesiveness. Slater (1966) suggests that at this point, the group membership has developed its therapeutic work to the extent that identification with the leader as a central figure has been relinquished; and as a result of this work, each group member has established greater individuation. Winnicott (1971) also

indicates that the process of merging and individuation is a natural development among human beings. The idea of the group as a transitional object (Kosseff, 1975) is fully expressed when the group develops group centeredness and
becomes peer dominated.

The group's process of working-through authority problems in order to
become a peer-oriented environment depends largely on the therapist's function in the group. According to Redl (1942), the group's vital processes are
affected by the therapist's functions and the kind of leadership which they
produce. These leadership functions affect the group's formation and maintenance, and even its disruption, depending on how they are carried out. Such
functions, for which the therapist is responsible, presumably operate through
"mechanisms of identification, cathexis, guilt reduction, impulse control and
the incorporation of the superego." Apparently Redl believes that the
working-through of authority problems corresponds to a rebalancing of id–
superego forces in the group so that its ego-strength continues to become more
and more resilient.

THE FUNCTION OF THE THERAPIST

The general thesis presented in this book leads inexorably to the conclusion that the chief role or function of the leader is to guard the evolutionary
process of the group. The leader is responsible for ensuring that the group
structure becomes realized through the group process, and also in part becomes guided by that process. The group may then express its inner nature,
and under such circumstances its infrastructural mechanisms can be fully
utilized.

The therapist must be able to allow the group to proceed from being
leader centered to being group or peer centered. When this goal of therapy is
achieved, entire group sessions may be experienced without any verbal interaction from the therapist. To this point Turquet (1974) suggests that the
leader must create a unique psychosocial position in the group by not becoming either overly involved or detached. The group structure can be so well
arranged that its direction and movement almost dictate to each member the
extent to which any interaction is authentic. The group process can become
self-perpetuating. It presumably may function according to its own best interests and this is an evolutionary and sociobiological implication of the group
process.

This view of the importance of a correct group structure is underlined by
the postulates of Foulkes (1973) and Schutz (1961b), who compare the
therapist's function in the group to aspects of individual mental life. Their
analogy can only be applied if, as Foulkes suggests, the group reflects the
matrix of an individual's mental life. Schutz similarly states that "the leader-

ship functions in the small group are the same as the ego functions within an individual personality." Schutz further outlines the overall role of the therapist by suggesting that it is the therapist who enables the group to fulfill any function that the group is not doing for itself.

The Therapist in the Beginning

Therapy groups as Bach (1954) states, "do not develop a therapeutic work culture without a professional therapist-leader who understands not only the transference process, personality structure and defense mechanisms, but who is also perceptive of group dynamics and interpersonal communication problems." Bach further implies that the search for general principles will better permit the therapist to integrate the process of group life with that of personality structure. To this point, Wolf and Schwartz (1959) add that in psychoanalyic groups, "there is structure, process and content, and . . . each is related to the others." These relationships are more coherently managed when the therapist is able to conceptualize both the process of the group and the structure of individual personality.

To understand and develop deeper conceptualizations about the intersection of group psychotherapy and personality, Bach states, "it is inevitable that we must add a new level of conceptualization without losing the lessons gained from the traditional personality frame of reference." He suggests a series of questions. The first is: "What therapeutic significance to the individual patient does a given process in group dynamics have?" It is partly answered by the previous discussions on how individual functioning is affected by (a) underlying group focal conflicts, (b) psychosexual regression in relation to group generationality, and (c) the working-through of oedipally based authority conflicts during a group's formative periods. Bach's second question refers to the therapist's role in securing the group's natural process. He asks, "What are the practical implications of management of therapy groups from concepts of group life?" A partial answer to this question resides in the discussion of the therapist's role in permitting the group's correct structural underpinning to unfold. This includes an entire range of therapist activities, from the therapist's awareness of the ideal compositional role arrangement of the group to allowing the group to work in the absence of a didactic atmosphere. The third question Bach asks refers to the hypotheses-generating nature of the group process as it sheds new light on individual personality. He asks simply, "What can we learn about personality from group therapy?" A partial answer to this question is also offered in the discussions of how various levels of personality are evoked and displayed in the group.

All the issues raised by Bach's rhetorical queries become instantly relevant at the beginnings of group therapy life. It is true, as Cartwright and Zander (1968) say, that "a group is a collection of individuals who have relations to one another that make them interdependent to some significant degree."

However, this interdependence may be short-lived. The group contains potentially powerful forces that seek consensus, obedience, and an overall orchestration of feelings. The therapist must be aware of such forces and not tacitly support them (Burton, 1975). The therapist needs to be alert to the working-through process even at the formative stage of therapy. Patients do not work-through irrational transferences immediately. However, the only way in which the therapist can maintain a correct therapeutic perspective of the group is to define it as a transference environment rather than simply as a collection of individuals with an interest in one another. The therapist must begin with the idea that the therapeutic task of the group is to rework historical distortion. In addition, the therapist must ensure the group's survival by at least attending to its composition.

Both Freud and Redl, among many others, consider the group to be a congealed environment on the basis of membership agreement about who the leader is. The agreement of the members that the therapist is leader of the group can only be obtained if they also agree that the therapist understands their needs and provides the group with the direction and encouragement which enables them to begin to function. The group membership may then also instantly resonate with the style and presence of the therapist. When the membership decides in a collective unconscious way that the therapist will not or cannot fulfill either individual or group needs, then Bionian phenomena immediately begin to appear. These include defiance, resentment, acting-out, and oppositional behavior among the members. Unfortunately, the abandonment breach that members may perceive in the therapist's relation to them is almost impossible to repair. Abandonment is probably the most powerful generator of group rage. Try as the therapist may, once these Bionian phenomena with respect to abandonment surface, they join the natural transference resistances and at that point the power of the group may be permanently usurped. When the resistance dominates the group in such a form, it will likely prevail. The resistance leader will usually be the most conflicted member and will lead the group to its permanent demise—its termination.

The therapist has to maintain focus on the goal and purpose of both the group and the individual transference work. Only on this basis can the membership agree that the leader of the group is the therapist and not some other designated central resistance-leader figure. Otherwise, as Bion (1955) indicates, the group searches for a leader and there is leadership by default. A variation on this theme of abandonment is also presented by Hartman and • Gibbard (1974a), who indicate that the group may reinforce this sort of abandonment resistance by object-relations splitting in the transference. The group thus perceives itself and the therapist as separate authority objects: the group will be the good object and the therapist will be perceived as the bad object. Bach (1954), who also observes this phenomenon, indicates that therapists cannot lead by default and they must not in turn engage in a "clinical voyeurism"; that is, therapists must not be passive or inert.

If this particular kind of initial resistance occurs, in which the therapist is the bad object, the group's personality becomes salient. The group will appear rigid and resentful and will seem to be behaving with what Freud (1921) referred to as the "group mind."

Kanter (1976) suggests that during formative group phases the therapist needs to meet the object anxieties of each member, develop a therapeutic alliance with each member, and develop group cohesion. The issue of cohesion is obviously of concern to many therapists who wish to avoid the debilitating effects of abandonment anger that the membership may develop. Yalom (1970) indicates that it is the therapist's job "to help the group develop into a cohesive unit with an atmosphere maximally conducive to the operation of . . . curative factors." The curative factors are acceptance, support, hope, universality, altruism, interpersonal feedback, testing, and learning. If the therapist generates movement in the group process, then the group's interactional nature will develop and these curative features will be activated by the members themselves. Thus the therapist fosters cohesion as an abstraction of the process in which the members of the group begin to function with each other in a therapeutic manner.

Wolf and Schwartz (1959) indicate that in a cumulative sense patients are able to resist the therapist's initial countertransference problems. As discussed in earlier chapters, Kosseff (1975) amplifies this proposition by defining the group in object-relations terms as an equivalent transitional object: implied in the group structure is the notion that some degree of separation exists between the cumulative group and the therapist. In this sense, the individual patient does not feel engulfed by the power imputed to the therapist. This proposition is supported by social psychological studies of group dynamics (Bird, 1940; Gouldner, 1950). Cartwright and Zander (1968) also indicate that leadership is determined by the behavior of people who aid in setting, facilitating, and implementing group goals; in improving interaction among members; and in not yielding uncritically to the therapist's authority.

Thus, the therapist in the beginning phase of the group needs to help the members start to interact, set off the group process, and begin to connect individual aims with group goals. This means that the therapist's main role is to regulate group processes as they touch on both the individual members and the group-as-a-whole.

The Therapist as Regulator

There are two major regulatory functions that the therapist performs. The first is a group structure function which is accomplished through the interpretation of defensive behavior occurring throughout the role manifestations of the group. As the therapist intervenes and interprets defensive behavior, the equilibrium of the group is affected. The result of the therapist's behavior is that it introduces a disequilibrium in the group. Astrachan (1970) describes this function and Vassiliou and Vassiliou (1976) call it a catalytic-regulatory function. As defensive behavior becomes expressed and worked-through, tension rises and falls and the group's equilibrium is generally in a state of readjustment. Kanter (1976) also describes this particular function and indicates that the therapist must define roles but refute role stereotypes; that is, a person may express feelings in a spontaneous way but not be allowed to become rigid and stereotyped in a particular role. In this process, the therapist's regulatory job is to point out defensive behavior. According to Kanter, the therapist does this by defining, clarifying, locating, correcting, building, promoting, encouraging, formulating, evoking, specifying, and emphasizing during the interactional process. These are some of the ways that Kanter proposes to deal with "displacement, reaction-formation and denial of affect." They also are some of the ways, it may be added, of dealing with projection, repression, intellectualizaton, regression, and compensation. Durkin (1964) quotes Ezriel as simply stating that the leader defines each role a member takes in order to point to a defense.

The need to regulate the group's equilibrium is dictated by a need to continue to develop homeostatic mechanisms in the group. This issue is discussed in chapters 6 and 7. The therapist discharges this regulatory role by conducting the group with an unambiguous style. The therapist's aim is, as von Bertalanffy (1969) suggests, to control the permeability of the group. The group therefore needs to experience a maximum informational exchange, the main element of which is emotional. In order for maximum emotional information to be exchanged, defense mechanisms need to be worked-through. In Ezriel's terms (1973), this occurs when the required, avoided, and calamitous relationships coalesce into a rational pattern.

Finally, this homeostatic regulatory function becomes a profound therapeutic tool when it is used to undo defenses and to work-through neurotic transference on a deep historical level—the level that combines the "there and then" with the "here and now." These are the so-called genetic explanations, and they are risky because they require more than just a perfunctory comment from the therapist. They require in-depth intervening. They tend to stop the flow of the group as any therapist's intervention will do. Yalom (1970) warns that these historical references are not as profitable as here-and-now interpretations. However, if the therapist is skilled enough to know when and how to make the correct trade-off between stopping the group and rendering a deep genetic interpretation, then the rewards of such attempts far outweigh their hazards. Rey (1975) points out quite correctly that group interpretations tend to structure the group and individual interpretations are only destructive to the individual member's ultra-stable structures. These ultra-stable structures are character formations, traits, and defenses, and they can only be addressed through deep genetic transferential interpretations. These interpretations are interventions that attempt to work-through early object distortions and to rework the distortions of one's history.

The second major regulatory function of the therapist is to adjust specific mechanisms of the group and to try to encourage a shaping of behavior in individuals. Foulkes (1968) amplifies this definition. He says that the therapist's "task is to keep the situation . . . therapeutic, that is to say, to preserve individuals from harm through excessive reactions or incompatible selection, to see that what is learned is made meaningful and can be used constructively." What this means is that the therapist needs to help individuals by softening, excepting, accepting, and even by scolding. These kinds of responses need to be made without manipulation or condescension. It is a point about which Shapiro and Birk (1967) offer a disclaimer. They unequivocally state, "therapy without manipulation is an image which disappears on close scrutiny." Yet one may ask whether behavior which is not spontaneous is necessarily manipulative. It is not necessary for the therapist as regulator to reveal to group members any underlying model of psychological understanding. This, however, does not qualify as manipulation.

SOME REGULATORY FUNCTIONS

Krech and Crutchfield (1948) have listed 14 regulator functions of a leader: executive, planner, policy maker, expert, external group representative, controller of internal relationships, purveyor of rewards and punishments, arbitrator, exemplar, group symbol, surrogate for individual responsibility, ideologist, father figure, or scapegoat. Obviously many more can be listed. Bach (1954) claims that regardless of how many individual leadership functions are enumerated, they can all be analyzed with reference to three general functions: procedural, catalytic, and interpretive. For example, the therapist as guide is either a technical expert or a model-setting participant (Yalom, 1970) and this role is both interpretive and catalytic. Similarly, the leader should be able to help the group deal with interpersonal needs either by instruction or by example (Schutz, 1961b).

Group members gradually learn that the therapist is able to solve problems and to help the group solve them (Applebaum, 1967). One related task is to maintain a blending of diagnostic forces in the group both by selection procedures and occasionally by the leader's assumption of a role that seems to be absent in the group. This function also is procedural and catalytic. Yalom (1970) observes that there are times when a role is not filled and certain leaders will begin unconsciously to fill it themselves. In fact, Yalom indicates that the leader will then behave in a way that corresponds to the particular behavior of the role being assumed. This point is quite interesting since some group therapists report that when they have occasionally changed their usual seat for one located elsewhere in the circle, their rate of verbal interaction drastically increased, only to subside again after some group member pointed out the change. The therapists in these cases began to act like a patient—an indication, perhaps, of underlying yearnings. All in all, the leader's regulatory functions will affect group structure issues or issues of individual transference work.

This role assumption feature of the therapist's function also can contain hidden countertransferential problems. These are conflicts of the therapist that may interfere with the overall therapy group process. Because the group is a transference environment and the therapist is its central figure, and because of Freudian and Bionian phenomena—how the group-as-a-whole responds to the therapist—and the therapist's own incomplete personal development, the potential for countertransference is always dormant and impending. Its basic impulse is frequently in the process of being evoked, in part because the therapist is endowed by the group membership with special powers. In fact, the therapy environment itself may be defined as one in which the group imputes power to the therapist (Whitaker and Lieberman, 1964; Foulkes, 1975). This central role in which power is a core attribute provides the context for an examination of overall countertransference leadership issues.

COUNTERTRANSFERENCE

The need for a therapist to have undergone a psychotherapy experience and to have examined in detail personal problems, character and defensive functioning, and areas of incomplete development was first stressed by Freud (1910, 1912). There are many attempts in the psychological literature to define countertransference and distinguish it from the usual transference definition applied to patients. Some authors do not distinguish countertransference from ordinary transference; they simply consider it the therapist's transference to the patient as expressed in some activity (Schilder, 1930). Schwartz and Wolf (1964) suggest that a therapist's countertransference may occur in order to satisfy the patient's transference needs. On the other hand, a different sort of countertransference may be expressed by the therapist who automatically has to frustrate such needs. Yet Schwartz and Wolf insist on Locke's (1961) bilateral or crosstransference definition. They state that "transference requires by law a complementary response. . . . countertransference is descriptive of behavior induced in the therapist which is responsive to transference and provides the patient transference satisfaction."

Another way to define countertransference is as irrational unconscious responses on the part of the therapist to certain phenomena of the group process. These are unconscious needs and attributes of the therapist (Reich, 1951) which may be illicited in some bilateral manner, or in terms of some response to group focal themes that are not necessarily bilateral. In any case, illusory needs of the analyst which become primary in the group's immediate work are expressed in the countertransference (Schwartz and Wolf, 1964). Wolf and Schwartz (1975a) list some generally common countertransference problems.

1. The therapist may relate to the group as his own family.
2. The therapist may demand activity out of his own depression.

3. The therapist may make the group homogeneous by seeing them as one patient.
4. The therapist may not listen to patients.
5. The therapist may want to be the only child or may treat patients as only children.
6. The therapist may require patients to be shaped in his own image.

Of course such problems focus the group on the therapist's needs.

Countertransference reactions of the therapist produce immediate effects. Group members sense that they are not being understood and that the process of therapy may not be working for any of them. Furthermore, such countertransference may be the only possible way in which the group fails to become a transference environment for each of its members. The countertransference destroys whatever communicational triangles exist because the therapist no longer occupies a special place in all communication. In fact, during countertransferential moments, the therapist undermines the microcosm of the real world that the group represents for each member. Countertransference in its many forms may destroy the communicational parallelogram that is intrinsically characteristic of group structure.

The Psychosexual Component to Countertransference Themes

Slavson (1950), like Wolf and Schwartz (1975a), outlines a few general kinds of countertransference. The first kind is negative and it includes feelings of irritation, anxiety, and disapproval. The therapist conveys a moodiness to the group by expressing such feelings. The second kind is positive: the therapist may favor certain patients and compliment them or otherwise express special preference. The third kind of countertransference concerns the therapist's personal goals for the group. The therapist may set certain aims for the group and then express an inordinate desire to see the group meet such goals.

These three kinds of countertransference as well as others may be analyzed further within the context of derived psychosexual themes. That is, there may be only a few underlying themes to countertransference, and these are the same derivative psychosexual themes that are used to understand all patient communication—the oral, anal, phallic, and oedipal derived themes.

Derivative oral themes of countertransference are reflected when therapists show needs for instant gratification and generally demonstrate problems in delay. Burton (1975) indicates that compulsive acts of introducing innovative techniques may reflect the therapist's need to escape from intimacy. It can be a counterphobic acting-out on the part of the therapist. It also seems to contain a strong oral component, as though magical wishes had overcome the therapist. In part, this phenomenon is reminiscent of Slavson's "aim-attachment"; that is, needing the group to improve as the therapist consistently seeks feedback and confirmation. A variation of this theme has the therapist unconsciously inducing the group to express their appreciation.

The defenses used by the therapist to permit such unconscious motives to exist include reaction-formation and compensation. Reaction-formation keeps aim-attachment needs in a prominent place within the therapist's need system. Under such conditions, the therapist is either overly active in reflecting the puritanical work ethic (as in the manic disposition) or he is keen on obtaining laudatory comments which reflect compensatory strivings indicative of inadequacy or depressive dispositions. The latter sort of need also represents a continual effort at reintegration which tends to obscure the therapist's own fears of abandonment. In nonverbal communication, the therapist may search for approval in the faces of individual group members. In general, the themes of oral countertransference will contain elements of dependency, disappointment, or depression, especially since the therapist is seen by the group members to be a source for solutions. The omnipotent therapist, a variation on this theme, will disappoint the group (Liff, 1975). This countertransference also is seen by Burton (1975).

> Therapists become sensitized to emotional suffering and to problem solving by their own problem family structure in which holistic solutions to childhood problems were never really found. This left them with an unconscious residue, or charge-mission, to solve all persons' family problems.

The strain placed on the therapist who experiences such a countertransference conflict is quite great.

Christ (1975) and Liff (1975) further describe the charismatic leader as someone who embodies these particular countertransference problems. The charismatic leader intervenes too much and promises deliverance. There is "an over-identification with the deprived helpless group members who have to be healed and cured; thus the leader indirectly acts out his own self-restitutional fantasies" (Liff, 1975). In addition, Liff indicates that the therapist sees the group-as-a-whole "as his own idealized parent who will feed back adoring love." This presumably constitutes the maniclike oral derivative countertransference. The antidepressive acting-out seen by Wolf and Schwartz (1975) is also referred to by Liff. Countertransference elements in the charismatic leader's personality thus may be revealed through restitutional or compensatory strivings representing the antidepressive oral derivative behavior to the countertransference.

Derivative anal themes of countertransference are expressed in excessive withholding and controlling behavior. In a variation of this theme, the therapist ignites confrontations so that patients then act out the therapist's wishes. This constitutes the dyscontrol part to the countertransference. Themes of this type frequently reflect the therapist's ambivalence. Because the therapist may need patients' adoration, it will be a struggle also to permit a patient to leave the group. The therapist wants to; yet cannot. This point has been made by Hadden (1953), Kadis et al. (1968), and Wolf and Schwartz

(1959). In another controlling countertransferential behavior, the therapist does not allow any direct expressions of hostility to occur, and may intervene in the group by talking too much in order to deflect angry feelings (Spotnitz, 1976; Yalom, 1970).

The defenses used by the therapist to achieve these specific counter-transference aims include intellectualization and regression. Intellectualization allows the therapist to rationalize, intervene, and compartmentalize all distasteful reactions. It is the major defense of the controlling type of behavior. Regression permits the therapist to express irritability provoke confrontations, and deflect anger.

Derivative phallic themes are expressed mostly in conflict of power. The therapist may become over-impressed with both real or endowed power, or may become fearful of power. Freud (1921) referred to this issue in *Group Psychology and the Analysis of the Ego*. He suggested that the archetypal father prevented his sons from expressing sexual tendencies directly and this led to sexual abstinence and ties among siblings. It was a process resulting in the creation of a substitute individual psychology; and in a sense it constitutes an evolutionary trace to group behavior. The point that phallic and implied castration themes underlie power issues in the therapist's countertransference has been understood by Grotjahn (1950) and Wolf and Schwartz (1962) to express itself as the therapist's over-identification with group members. In this case, the strategem that leadership may become expressed "through the exercise of influence over followers" (Cartwright and Zander, 1968) is taken too seriously by the therapist. The response is to do just that—either to exercise power or become terrified of it. Countertransference responses are expressed by behavior reflecting either position in the extreme. Exercising power over patients reflects the therapist's confusion between aggression and assertion. Withdrawing from patients reflects the therapist's passivity and fear of assuming the parental role. The therapist should be able to appropriately address the cumulative force of the group-as-a-whole. In the absence of aggression and withdrawal, phallic countertransference themes will not crystallize.

The defenses used by therapists to achieve either of these particular phallic countertransference aims include displacement and repression. Displacement permits the therapist to continually express aggression as a way of ventilating neurotic power needs. The therapist actually may become a scape-goater. The defense of repression causes the therapist to relinquish any reasonable authority role. The therapist then becomes ineffective. The use of repression in phallic countertransference behavior is strictly an exercise in therapist passivity, even though some leaders rationalize their passivity by considering patient participation to absolve them from maintaining a posture of noninvolvement (O'Day, 1974).

Derivative oedipal themes are expressed in pairing behavior, in idealization of individual patients or of the group, in the suppression of rivals, and in the derision of members. Burton (1975) states that the therapist "needs to adore someone in a way he doesn't find—and cannot find—at home actually or historically." This need to adore is also an idealization need. It denies reality considerations of relationships. Therapists sometimes express this need by encouraging selected contact with members immediately following the group session. If this contact occurs regularly even for a few minutes, it is surely countertransferential and constitutes a Bionian pairing issue. Another expression of the oedipal countertransference theme is offered by Usandivaras (1974), who indicates that the leader of the group must eliminate any rival; otherwise there is a risk to the leadership position as well as to the group's survival.

When therapists are derisive toward group members, they are involved in desperate countertransference behavior designed to elevate themselves and to deflect experiences and feelings of intimacy. The defenses used by therapists to achieve such oedipal countertransference aims include denial and projection. The use of denial allows the therapist to be a romantic and to seek only pleasant relationships. On the other hand, the use of projection allows the therapist to become a scrutinizer so that no intimacy can develop especially since the experience of intimate feelings can create existential self-doubt. It is this sort of therapist, the one with oedipal countertransference, who seeks to eliminate all rivals.

There may be many other countertransference themes that can be examined, but it is proposed here that they all can be analyzed with reference to only these few psychosexual categories.

Of the many countertransference themes enumerated by Schwartz and Wolf (1964), more than one-third seem to reflect intellectual control needs of the therapist. Another third seems to reflect compensatory needs of the therapist, and the last grouping reflects passive and withdrawal needs. The appearance of these themes may affect the homeostasis of the group. This point bears some resemblance to the findings by Kellerman et al. (1974), that patients in groups seem to create a condition of homeostasis around the traits of caution, agreeableness, and assertion—themes which are also subject to psychosexual analysis.

Generational Considerations

Bennis and Shepard (1956) indicate that each group member expresses characteristic patterns of relating to authority. The first phase of therapy is dominated by members who are submissive and show dependent patterns. These patients need strong leadership and strong rules to satisfy their needs. The second phase of the group is dominated by members who are aggressive and defiant and show counter-dependent patterns. The third phase of the group process is dominated by members who lead the group to compromise and resolution. However, the central latent anxiety of the group during formative periods "concerns feelings toward the leader who is seen as omnipotent." This sense of omnipotence defines all countertransference within the context of a basic power theme. It is a theme that ultimately may become part of the group structure; the leader has both real and imputed powers, and such power in the unfolding of group generations affects the nature of normative psychosexual themes.

The position held by Bennis and Shepard suggests a generational implication of countertransference problems as they are expressed through derivative psychosexual themes. Schwartz and Wolf (1964) provide a method of understanding how these themes are evoked. They consider identification and projection to constitute the primary mechanisms that permit a countertransferential circuit to exist in the group.

Thus, in terms of the retrogressive model of group life presented in chapter 4 of this book, in the first oedipal generation the group will be idealistic and critical. During this time the therapist also expresses oedipal problems through identification and projection. The therapist becomes the romantic who uses denial and idealizes, or the scrutinizer who uses projection and criticizes. During the second phallic generation, the group will be assertive or passive. Through mechanisms of identification and projection, the therapist also may express phallic problems and assume the roles of either the innocent who through repression is withdrawn, naive, and passive; or the scapegoater who through displacement is aggressive, exploitative, and spilling over with power. During the third anal generation the group will be controlled or dyscontrolled. Through the same mechanisms of identification and projection, the therapist may assume a controlling stance and become the intellectualizer, or may create confrontations as a way of maintaining regressive acting-out and become the child. During the oral fourth generation, members seek support and understanding. With the use of reaction-formation, they want to work; or through compensatory mechanisms, they need to avoid a sense of loss or potential abandonment. Using mechanisms of identification and projection, the therapist presents the group with formidable work tasks and becomes the puritan, or continues to seek approval and becomes the reintegrator. In actuality, all psychosexual themes become expressed in all group generations. This suggests that the focal theme of a particular group generation will only tend to call forth its corresponding countertransference response in the therapist over other possible responses. Group generations contain major and minor psychosexual group themes and major and minor countertransferential themes.

The intersection of aspects of the therapist's personality with those of group process raises the final question of who the therapist really is. What sort of personality should the therapist have in order to minimize countertransference problems? Can there be much variation in the personalities of therapists, given the necessary therapeutic functions that must be undertaken if the group is to thrive? Finally, can specific personality features of therapists such as traits, emotions, attitudes, and styles be enumerated? The following chapter will address these questions.

16

The Group Therapist: Personality Style

What sort of person is the therapist? What are the qualities that enable the therapist to facilitate the special process of group life and the therapy that group members undergo in that process? The structure of the group determines to a certain extent how the therapist is seen. Yet there is no doubt that certain therapists resonate with the group most of the time while others do not. Some facilitate the group's natural processes while other therapists tend to interfere with them. In this chapter the differences among group therapists will be described and an attempt will be made to delineate the kind of group therapist whose functioning is germane to the therapy group process, and in part becomes determined by that process.

After the group has developed its cultural attitudes, patients begin to work independently and with only a minimum of therapist activity. This means that the therapist will frequently be a less than active participant. Often the entire group will experience the work in a resonating fashion. During such moments there is authenticity to the effort each group member is making, and a simultaneous loss of self-consciousness which therapists frequently admire (Mann, 1974; Searles, 1965; Winnicott, 1958). The authentic group work is the struggle that emerges for each group member. It has been regarded as compelling by such diverse researchers of the group process as Bales (1970), Bion (1959a), Slater (1966), and Wolf and Schwartz (1962). Mann (1970) describes such moments in terms of work, and states "Work is a precious, if fragile accomplishment." The therapist is usually emotionally moved when observing this struggle, as Searles (1965) indicates, and in turn responds to the work seriously. These are moments of working-out and working-through defenses. During defensive maneuvers, therapists are generally not sympathetic. It is only when feelings are conveyed in the most open, direct, and honest way that therapists become emotionally affected.

THE PERSONALITY AND STYLE OF THE THERAPIST

Wolf and Schwartz (1975b) indicate that the leader's behavior should be governed by simplicity, honesty, and straightforwardness. Fielding (1975) calls it "credibility." This credibility is evoked in the therapist by the patients' struggles. If the group structure is set into motion correctly, then the culture of the group will gradually develop so that this powerful therapeutic climate becomes increasingly a fact of group life. The therapist who attends to the details, moods, and implicit struggles within each session is likely to experience such reflective and moving moments. But the therapist cannot continuously intervene: the therapist must permit the group's process to unfold—to let it happen. Group structure alone cannot produce this state of the group; it is the therapist who nurtures the group, understands it, gives it focus, and encourages its growth. The therapist is responsible for the character flavor of the group's personality.

To experience this compelling congruence with the work of the group, therapists need to identify with the group and to have values that they strive in some way to convey. Wolf and Schwartz (1962) enumerate these values. They indicate that therapists want patients to be introspective and interactive. They also want a democracy to exist within the group structure, and a pluralistic and tolerant attitude to exist among the group members. Finally, therapists want the group to strive for reality and fulfillment. There are certain kinds of therapists who are able to help the group develop these values.

Personality Features

Wolf (1963) indicates that the resonating and facilitating kinds of therapists will be intuitive and empathic; they will not have any pretension or compulsive need to lead; and they will be able to withstand attack and criticism. To this must be added what Wolf and Schwartz imply about therapists' values and the fact that the therapist implicitly must have high hopes for the group. Even the therapist who hopes that the group will do well does not go far enough. The therapist must start with the axiom of hope that as long as the work and structure of the group are well constituted, then the group begins with the assumption of success. Even though Liff (1975) is wary of the charismatic leader, he offers a description of such a personality which may be applied in part to the ideal group therapist. This kind of therapist is unshakable in faith and hope with regard to the profundity of the group's work. Liff states that the charismatic leader "radiates a buoyant and stubborn self-confidence, an unshakable belief in success, an enthusiasm which provokes and evokes enthusiastic responses from the group participants." In this same spirit, Grotjahn (1975) indicates that the therapist looks the group in the eye and fights for its soul.

The therapist must be committed to the idea of diversity (Wolf et al., 1975). The notion of pluralism and diversity also applies to the therapist's ability to withstand both the positive and negative emotional approaches that patients make. It is perfectly desirable for the therapist to be a charismatic type provided that a need for universal acclaim and love is correspondingly unnecessary. Charistmatic types who need such a consensus are intervenors (Bach, 1961; Christ, 1975; Kadis et al., 1968; Liff, 1975; Schwartz, 1965b). They need, as Schwartz (1965b) says, to "inspire followership" and they assume that their goals are everyone's goals.

The therapist must expect to be occasionally disliked. Being disliked is sometimes the only way one can experience any individuality. The therapist's absence of fear and tolerance of the feelings patients harbor are qualities with which patients quickly identify. The identification allows group members to yield defensive behavior quickly. In this regard the therapist needs to be real. The therapist may respond as someone who cannot answer all questions, needs time to pin things down, and reserves the right to be wrong. Patients need to see these qualities. They reflect the therapist's own struggle and work in the group's process.

Here is a sampling of the positive personality attributes of the therapist cited by many authors: the therapist should be a promoter of diversity (Wolf et al., 1975); should be authentic, trusting and trustful, and have accurate empathy (Truax and Mitchell, 1971); should establish warm, accepting, and understanding relationships (Yalom, 1970); should be able to be spontaneous and yet maintain distance (Durkin, 1964); should have the capacity to regulate the group by being an active target, comforter, frustrator, pointer-outer, questioner, interpreter, explainer, teacher, persuader, director, manager, succoring mother, punitive father, and entertainer (Foulkes and Anthony, 1965); and should be a completer. The therapist does or becomes whatever is necessary to facilitate the group's movement: "the general properties of a leader become simply those functions required to maintain a certain kind of equilibrium between outer reality and interpersonal needs and the conflict-free functions of the group" (Schutz, 1961b).

Other references to the therapist's personality are that the therapist needs to have empathy and genuineness, and should prize the patient (Rogers and Wood, 1974). The "therapist is an experiencer —he is a vital, stubborn fighter for life. . . . The therapist is an artist in his science . . . the artistic improvisation and syntheses of the psychotherapist are the same as with any artist." The therapist should be bright and conversant with personal unconscious problems in order to avoid countertransference and "not be afraid of his or patient's demons" (Burton, 1975). The therapist must not be afraid of love and must be intuitive (Usandivaras, 1974). The good therapist can be attentive to group effects as well as to individual psychoanalytic problems, should discriminate action from acting-out, and needs "to consider the history of the group" (Kanter, 1976). The leader needs to be a resource person, clarifier, benevolent authority, stimulator of emotional confrontation, and director of structured experiences; the leader should speak the language of the normative group, empathize, be perceptive, self-aware, warm, eager, and intelligent (Bass, 1960; MacLennan, 1975). Leaders should have empathy, respect, concreteness, genuineness, congruence, trust, warmth, positive regard, immediacy, and the capacity to confront (Truax and Carkhuff, 1967). Yalom and Lieberman's data (1971) from encounter group research reveal that successful leaders are high carers, give good feedback, medium structure, and encourage emotional and aggressive confrontation.

This survey of the literature on qualities of effective therapists may be analyzed in terms of three general categories. First, authors consider the general style of therapists and then enumerate them. Qualities such as intuition, empathy, authenticity, trustfulness, and spontaneity are examples. Second, authors consider the wishes and implementing style of the therapist. Examples of such qualities are that the therapist has high hopes for the group and is proud of it. Examples in terms of style are that the therapist fights for the group, shows a stubborn self-confidence, and regulates the group. Finally, the therapist brings a system of values to the group that includes a belief in the value of diversity, a belief in the value of understanding and working-through unconscious conflicts, an absence of trepidation about being disliked, and a sense of the importance of providing feedback. The mentality, the wishes and style, and the values of the therapist constitute a framework within which the personality of the therapeutic therapist may be understood.

Leadership Variation

In many studies of leadership, authors list contrasting personality and emotional characteristics of leaders that distinguish them from nonleaders (Carter et al., 1950). Bird (1950) lists 79 traits characterizing the behavior of leaders. In an early study of leadership (Stogdill, 1948), leaders were seen to excel nonleaders in intelligence, scholarship, dependability, responsibility, activity and social participation, and socio-economic status. Stogdill's results seem partly based upon the function and role inherent in the leadership position and in the amount of professional training required to assume such positions.

Leadership has been studied extensively in the social-psychological literature in terms of differential effects in the variation of leadership (Kahn and Katz, 1960; Katz and Kahn, 1966; Likert, 1961). A general conclusion drawn from these studies stresses that patients' behavior vary as a function of leadership style and philosophy (White and Lippitt, 1960). In a study on leadership style (Yalom and Miles, 1973), three kinds of leaders were defined: those who energized the group and emphasize stimulation; providers who show interpretative and caring concerns; and social engineers who stress management of the group. It was the providers who produced the greatest change and lowest risk for patients. In another study by White and Lippitt (1962), it was shown that disruptive subgrouping and scapegoating were generated in groups conducted by authoritarian and restrictive leaders. A psychoanalytic analysis of the authoritarian therapist (Wolberg, 1968) also indicated that such leaders demand obedience and tend to discourage growth and self-assertiveness.

Some other potentially deleterious qualities of leadership are suggested by Grotjahn's (1971) rhetorical questions: Is the therapist active or passive? Does the therapist have mood swings? Is the therapist optimistic or pessimistic? Does the therapist have a sense of humor? Is the therapist witty or dull, tolerant or intolerant, puritanical or adventuresome, tender or strict, spontaneous or rigid? Presumably a therapist who is moderately active, without mood swings, optimistic, having a sense of humor, tolerant, trustful, and spontaneous is the better therapist. Therapists who express opposite qualities presumably generate undue pathological conflicts in the group.

SOME NEGATIVE LEADERSHIP FEATURES

Wolf and Schwartz (1962) are concerned about both the overly aggressive and the self-devaluing types of leaders. Christ (1975) and Liff (1975) express concern about the charismatic type of leader who may create a dependent group because of narcissistic, counter-phobic, and antidepressive needs. Burton (1975) adds that depression is the mood state that therapists consistently need to fight. Therapists who always seek to gratify oral needs of patients reveal their own oral problems as well as masochistic problems (Glatzer, 1962). Such therapists are also frequently consensus seeking, disappointing, and vulnerable to attack. Finally, according to Fried (1973), leaders who withdraw into long silences "eventually produce chaotic, psychotic-like behavior." Such leaders will generate abandonment rage in the group which will become expressed as Bionian fight–flight phenomena. The most disruptive kind of therapist for the group process, however, is one who acts-out. Acting-out may be a result of bona fide psychopathic tendencies or it may be a countertransferential and counterphobic response to thematic material of the group process.

Any of these leadership failures cannot produce or provide a guardianship to the history and well being of the group. The needs of such leaders also raise the question of therapist's needs generally. What sorts of life experience motivate therapists to conduct groups, and does the therapist have any special needs which may only be satisfied through such a function and role?

The Therapist's Profile

The issue of the need system and values of the therapist has been reviewed largely from the writings of Wolf and Schwartz (1959, 1962, 1975b; Wolf et al., 1975). Another practical approach to the understanding of the therapist's need profile has been offered by Burton (1975). He describes six variables of satisfaction. The first is defined as an intrapsychic variable. Therapists have access to the subtle balance of forces in their patients and they obtain satisfaction in the knowledge of such profound contact. The second variable is sensual–interpersonal, in which therapists experience a sense of special excitement in the entire therapeutic endeavor with patients. The third variable is called intellectual–rational. Therapists receive satisfaction by the stimulation generated from intellectual discourse and conceptualization. The fourth variable is a research–creative one. Therapists experience joy during moments of insight in their work. The fifth variable is cultist–fraternal: satisfaction is obtained from belonging to the special cult or organization of psychotherapists. The sixth variable is a satisfaction with a comfortable income.

Burton also claims a "metaphysical hunger" as part of the profile of therapists' needs—that is, a comfortableness in hearing confessions, a need for two families, an absence of mental illness in the therapist's personal family, the need to create a pleasant work environment by personally decorating one's office with objects that are loved, cases that are selected carefully, a work week designed to the needs and temperament of the therapist, and other professional activities for diversion and growth.

The therapist should like the work. It should resonate with personal needs, history, and continued personal growth. Wolf et al. (1975) also describe some of the satisfaction issues pointed out by Burton. These authors state that the therapist's attitude toward life is reflected in an identifiable overall style.

The Therapist's Personality Structure

Implications generated from the review of desirable therapist qualities, countertransference issues, and therapist needs suggest that of the eight basic dispositional styles discussed throughout this book, only a blending of some may correctly reflect the personality of the potentially ideal therapist. Of the impeded diagnostic dispositions, the paranoid, aggressive, depressed, and psychopathic ones do not represent personality styles which alone may generate potentially positive therapist qualities. On the contrary, each of these styles reflect critical, angry, sorrowful, and impulsive features of personality. Of the accessible diagnostic types, the passive personality may cause Bionian fight–flight groups insofar as patients will begin to feel abandoned, the therapist's role will be usurped, and overall resistance will undermine the group. The therapist with hysteric personality features demonstrates high suggestibility and will similarly not be able to control the direction of the group. The manic personality type is potentially charismatic with an enormous work objective. This sort of therapist may be able to help accomplish the goals of the group. The obsessive type who expresses control features and a circumspect intellectual view of the group also may be able to help the group accomplish its goals.

A diagnostic construction of the ideal therapist will demonstrate a blending of dispositions. This ideal therapist can be defined as a somewhat deferential, respectful, yet firm and assertive person. Such a person can exercise control and direct the group when necessary, inspire a therapeutic work atmosphere, and, generate a sense of loyalty and pride in the therapeutic work developing out of the group process. This diagnostic blending consists of some hysteric features which are expressed in the sense of loyalty and pride that the therapist shows and in the therapist's quality of deference. It also includes some aggressive and control features expressed in the therapist's ability to be firm and assertive and to control and direct the group when necessary. These propensities are inherent in the aggressive and obsessive personality styles. Finally, the therapist needs to be able to generate motivation, work, and enthusiasm—an ability seen in some energized manic types, and in certain respects symptomatic of manic qualities.

Thus it appears that the successful therapist expresses a mixture of hysteric, aggressive, obsessive, and manic dispositional tendencies and may draw upon the derived behavior of each tendency whenever necessary. This finding correlates with the proposal in chapter 10, on the intrapsychic nature of the group, that most accessible dispositions which are free from underlying superego influence include the hysteric, obsessive, and manic types. In chapter 8 the aggressive disposition, which is impeded was also considered free from superego influence. It was considered to be an exceptional case in the overall network of personality structure. In analyzing the ideal therapist personality structure, this exceptional case appears again. Thus therapist's personality shows basic freedom of expression because of the relative absence of superego pressure. Despite its id complexion on the behavioral and defense levels, the therapist's personality is not anarchistic and chaotic; it is governed by defense mechanisms that correspond to its particular dispositional blend. The ideal therapist responds for the most part with defenses of denial, displacement, intellectualization, and reaction-formation. The therapist's hopes for the group are partly maintained through the use of the denial, as a feature of the hysteric's romantic yearning and sense of loyalty. Displacement permits the therapist to redirect anger and to manage the dominance and power involved in the therapeutic position. Intellectualization aids in the implementation of controls, and reaction-formation converts sexual energy into work energy and aim attachment. Three accessible defenses are designed to moderate impulse and one impedance defense is designed to release impulse.

Although all people express aspects of each basic dispositional type, personality is generally composed of varying proportions of the basic emotions. In terms of the therapist's ideal personality, emotions represented to a greater extent are acceptance, anger, anticipation, and joy. These emotions reflect hysteric, aggressive, obsessive, and manic dispositions respectively. The emotions represented only minimally are disgust, fear, surprise, and sorrow; these reflect the paranoid, passive, psychopathic, and depressed dispositions.

In summary, the therapist needs to respond to a greater extent with hysteric, aggressive, obsessive, and manic tendencies and to a lesser extent with paranoid, passive, psychopathic, and depressed tendencies. On the level of emotion, the therapist responds to a greater extent with acceptance, anger, anticipation, and joy; and to a lesser extent with disgust, fear, surprise, and sorrow. On a defense level the ideal therapist primarily utilizes denial, displacement, intellectualization, and reaction-formation. Projection, repression, regression, and compensation are utilized to a lesser extent. These latter defenses are not active because the diagnoses and corresponding emotions associated with them are not strongly characteristic of such a therapist's personality.

This personality construction also implies that there are psychosexual derivative qualities to the therapist's character style which include oral, anal, phallic, and oedipal features. They are implied by the psychosexual designations of each dispositional quality. The ideal therapist is psychologically, emotionally, and intuitively conversant with all thematic and focal psychosexual themes that emerge throughout any group-life phase.

The therapist also assumes an image in the group and in some respects becomes a mythic figure. The question that remains to be asked refers to the nature of the image that is projected onto the therapist. This question will be addressed in the following section.

Therapeutic Identification with the Leader

A sense that the therapist is a special person emerges when the therapist expresses traits, needs, and general qualities attributed to ideal leaders. While Bion does not share this sense of the leader, Freud underscores it. Bion essentially considers the leader's power to be derived only insofar as the leader and all other members of the group are similarly influenced by the assumption groups and their prevailing emotions. Freud saw the leader as a hypnotist— someone who supersedes any underlying coercive force. Freud viewed the therapist as a resonator who senses the needs and aspirations of each patient. Such a therapist can convey a sense of hope to the group. This therapist expresses all the personality characteristics of ideal leaders reviewed in previous sections. This therapist offers each member of the group a glimpse of some great aspiration which can be attained by work and struggle in the group. Sociohistorical examples of giving aspiration or hope to the world are offered by

Freud, who held out the promise of self-knowledge; by Marx, who offered the promise of social understanding; and by Einstein, who offered the promise of a knowledge of universal cosmic relationships.

When therapists convey aspiration to group members, the entire process of identification with the leader is strengthened. A new reality of possibilities for each patient is created. Patients begin to feel that their relationship to the therapist is important to their improvement (Feifel and Eells, 1963). After some working-through takes place, the quality of optimism and work possibility becomes infused into the fabric of each patient's strivings, and dependence on the therapist for improvement may be reduced. The aspiration-giving therapist is one with a program (Bach, 1954). When a therapist has a program for the group, activity and interaction increase. This sort of therapist may also convey a personal life style which corresponds to the style and program used for the group (Burton, 1975).

Patients perceive the authenticity of the therapist's personality. They begin to admire the therapist's strength of purpose, insight, overall depth, and gentleness. The therapist must be able to think aloud, and to say that the group is a good one. Admitting that not enough is known at certain points so that answers cannot be immediately forthcoming also helps patients realize that the therapy is in the work—that it is the work. The therapist must make a point to modify, change, or refute an interpretation whenever necessary, and to allow patients to witness these modifications. Patients must see the therapist's optimism, love of life, and love of people. The therapist can play and cry, and as Burton (1975) states, must consider life to be a treasure. The therapist needs to respond in the here-and-now as well as to interpret the historical transference. In terms of response style, the therapist needs to be as direct and nondirect as the situation requires. The therapist should love to look at faces.

A strong therapist is not omnipotent. Therapists who seek to obtain omnipotent power produce, as Yalom (1970) suggests, impotent patients. Thus it is exceedingly important for the therapist to accept and acknowledge fallibility and for patients to witness this process. In some respects, the admission of fallibility has more power than the pose of omnipotence. The fallible therapist can also express humor in the group with regard to fallibility. Therapists who are strong and positive in their focus are able to be humorous even and especially at their own expense. They neither tell jokes nor fish for compliments. During times of confusion they may acknowledge a personal lapse in the control of the group. When something was pursued which turned out not to be fruitful, they can readily say so.

The therapist must make sure the group is aware that all knowledge of cause and effect is not known beforehand, and that answers or solutions to problems take time to form. Interpretations and connections made by the therapist reveal themselves in the ongoing process and are in part spontaneously created. The therapist is both an inventor and discoverer. Identification with the leader therefore can be therapeutic.

Some Special Touches

The therapist needs to create a climate where everyone has a chance to express needs. In this respect, the therapeutic therapist is not really one who loves all patients, but one who is allowed to be loved. To permit access—to permit emotional contact—takes great health and self-assurance. It constitutes the essence of therapist self-disclosure without involving the therapist in prosaic confessionals. This quality permits therapists to see patients leave the group gracefully even though their therapy work is incomplete in the objective sense. Some patients may only be able to work to a certain point. They may need time to contemplate and live with the amount of therapy work already accomplished; or because of age, ego-strength level, or the particular blend of conflicts, they may not have the capacity to do any further work at that time. Therapists need to be circumspect and wise enough to view patients on an individual basis.

From this point of view, the therapist needs to be sensitive and fully cognizant of each patient's work and progress, and must be able to help each patient calibrate both the pace and the nature of personal work in the group. Bach (1954) refers to the possibility of coaching patients in this connection. This point is one of the most underinvestigated in the psychoanalytic group therapy literature. Implied in the construction of the ideal therapist's personality and style is the notion that therapists should help each patient to develop techniques of participation and to define personal work. Bach's suggestion of coaching patients may be excellent.

Variations in the training, depth, and intelligence of therapists account for some differences in the success of groups. The more brilliant and perceptive the therapist, the more lucid and visible insights and interpretations become. Yet style is important. As Foulkes and Anthony (1965) suggest, sometimes therapists need to sit on their intelligence and feelings in order to allow patients to arrive at their own conclusions. This also means that at times the therapist has to follow the group (Foulkes, 1975). Frequently the therapist consults patients for certain insights, and encourages the patient to take the lead. The wise therapist knows when and whom to choose for these assignments. Of all therapist qualities other than training and education, wisdom and style are the most important.

The Enigmatic Self-image of the Therapist

Effective group therapists probably have a sense of themselves as being somehow different than the other people in the group. The basic element of this difference lies in the role distinction between therapist and group member. Group members discuss their lives and all their contrasting experiences. The therapist may not participate in the same way. The therapist appears to be professionally sound and steeped in the therapy work. This is the patient's basic image of the therapist. However, the therapist often reveals through style and relatedness something especially different and unusual, and patients then wonder about the therapist's past experiences. This intuition on the part of patients is quite strong.

Most therapists who are defined by all the qualities of the previous discussion generally see themselves as quite enigmatic. These special therapists are a study in contrasts. Generally they have lived and had experiences quite apart and far afield from that of the therapy room. They generally are proficient in other ways and in completely different modalities. The point is that therapists frequently fix upon something in their histories that defines their position and role as being different and somehow contributing to the distillation of this enigmatic quality. Thus the therapist can simultaneously be a dancer and scholar, an accomplished performer of Yiddish poetry and a psychoanalyst, an athlete, a teacher and a group therapist—all in one. So can any patient. However, patients cannot be enigmatic; their aim is to be known. The therapist as a reflective figure partly derives wisdom from the anonymity generated by role specificity and consequently by a self-image characterized here as enigmatic. Therapists who conceive of their persona in this fashion can make a profound therapeutic contribution to the group. This contribution can influence important personality transformations; transformations that emerge out of therapy conditions that are powerful within the group process.

Transition

The therapist is the archeologist and historian of the group's life. This guardianship reflects an involvement in the entire working-through process for individuals and in ensuring the continuity of the group process. The therapist is also a teacher and conductor of the group's work. This role reflects the tasks of locating patients' defenses and orchestrating an ongoing group process. The therapist is at the point of intersect between group psychotherapy process and individual personality structure. Since it was proposed that the function of group life is to ensure the evolutionary path of the family (chapter 6, on the nature of ego defenses), then the core concept of this therapeutic role is continuity. In Freud's *Group Psychology and Analysis of the Ego* (1921), he proposed that the group forms itself through the identification of members with one another based on their emotional ties with the leader. *In Totem and Taboo* (1913), he provided a basis for the appearance of family life in the proposition that a "penitential renunciation of parricide and incest" resulted from an attack on the father-leader followed by remorse. In *The Interpretation of Dreams* (1900), he said, "Behind this childhood of the individual we are promised a picture of phylogenetic childhood—a picture of the development of the human race, of which the individual's development is in fact an abbreviated recapitulation influenced by the chance circumstances of life." Thus, according to Freud, the continuity of history is generational and axiomatic. As suggested in chapter 4 on the genealogical view of group psychotherapy, the therapist has special access to the relativity of this psychological evolution. This access constitutes a context for the therapist's skills and for the expression of wisdom, and it further enables the group to exercise its intelligence. Thus the leader of the group symbolizes the group's historic and even prehistoric continuity, represents the goal of group survival, and is an over-arching symbol of the evolutionary force of time.

This view of the group as a structure designed in evolution to preserve and improve overall family life is relevant to sociobiological theory as advanced by Wilson (1975). The Wilsonian sociobiological view proposes that the group as an institution is designed to preserve and protect its constituent gene pool. The group is loyal only to itself and not to other groups, unless altruism toward other groups contributes to its own survival. The thesis of this book offers an alternate hypothesis, even though the sociobiological formulations made here have proposed that the fundamental elements of personality structure are rooted in biology. It proposes that the personality system is predispositional, exists at birth and is composed at least of emotion, defense, diagnostic inclination, and intrapsychic force. In this regard, the question this book has attempted to answer is whether personality structure rooted in biology can be transformed by cultural forces inherent in the therapy group process. Conventional sociobiological formulations would predict that the group would try to retain this personality structure. Yet, the therapy group as an evolutionary laboratory may be able to resolve this difficult problem and its transformational capacities may imply alternate sociobiological conceptions.

The group seeks to eliminate any significant variation in its constituent role "gene" pool by tending to organize itself as if it were ideally composed and by trying to retain a defensive status-role composition. Yet the group also seems to want to change its role "gene" pool by working-through defenses and by shifting role positions. The group's only aim is to work in order to generate transformations among its members. The interaction of group psychotherapy and personality is the process through which these transformations take place. The main transformational effect becomes visible as a result of the working-through process. Groups begin as aggregates of strangers who are covertly exploitative and competitive with one another and overtly obedient to authority. These groups show status-resistance problems in which some members occupy roles that are valued and coveted while others express roles that are considered inferior and in some ways even reinforced. Gradually and generationally, as the group develops a work ethic, status needs of members dissolve and the authority power of the leader becomes distributed among the members of the group. For the most part, the direction as well as the therapeutic effects of the group at this point are assumed by the membership. The therapist becomes in some respects a titular leader. However the leader is an over-arching symbol and not merely a passive influence on the group. It is the leader who may create deleterious conditions that potentially reinforce defensive functioning so that personality structure, rooted in biology and expressed through group roles, seems immutable. When defensive patterns are reinforced, members retain their role positions, status needs, and exploitative motives. In this sense, more conventional sociobiological predictions will prevail.

However, when the leader helps to reinforce a group culture in which defensive patterns are confronted, then members may relinquish status needs shift their role positions, and experience transformations of personality. Under these change conditions, culture becomes an overpowering force and the inclinations inherent in the biological predispositional personality program of individuals can also be correspondingly transformed. This means that type of leadership is essential. The presence of a laissez faire leader in a group will permit members to function defensively. Under such conditions, a biological rationale that cites scientific evidence to justify an exploitative nature to humankind would seem natural to assume. However, when the leader establishes the necessary therapeutic cultural conditions set forth throughout this book for defense confrontation and resolution to occur, then a therapeutic work ethic will characterize the group life. Under such conditions, powerful personality changes can occur.

This therapeutic change condition is a triumph of culture over biology. Sociobiological principles then, are not only those that would predict immutable biological effects. This finding suggests that the essential study of sociobiology may be the analysis of cultural conditions that can alter biologically determined programs and conditions that can reinforce such programs. It also suggests that the biological predispositional personality program may be an opaque and faintly inked one onto which cultural experiences impress themselves only to then reveal those "impressed" parts of the program. Impressions made upon the biological-genetic program may be transformed by cultural forces, and other impressions than may be made.

The group process of "impression making" is defined as the therapy work. The aim of the group is now also defined as a work aim. Thus the aim of the therapy—of all therapy—is not to eliminate anxiety or to help make people happy. The aim is to help people work and struggle better, to help in the raising of consciousness and consequently to help generate personality transformations. In the group's beginning stage, there is an environment where, in social Darwinian terms, members may feel that only the fittest survive. When defensive, status, and authority problems are resolved, the group becomes an environment—a social structure—in which as Thoreau suggests, it is fitting for all to survive. The therapy group is an evolutionary communal celebration.

REFERENCES

ABRAHAM, K. Psychoanalytical studies on character formation. In *Selected papers on Psychoanalysis*. London: Hogarth Press, 1927.

ABRAHAMS, J. Group psychotherapy: Implications for direction and supervision of mentally ill patients. In Muller, T. (Ed.), *Mental health in Nursing*. Washington: Catholic Univ. Press, 1950.

ABRAHAMS, J., AND VARON, E. *Maternal Dependency and Schizophrenia: Mothers and Daughters in a Therapeutic Group*. New York: International Universities Press, 1953.

ACKERMAN, N. W. *The Psychodynamics of Family Life: Diagnosis and Treatment of Family Relationships*. New York: Basic Books, 1958.

ACKERMAN, N. W. Transference and countertransference. *Psychoanalysis and the Psychoanalytic Review*, 1959, *46* (3): 17–28.

ACKERMAN, N.W. Psychoanalysis and group psychotherapy. In Rosenbaum, M., and Berger, M. (Eds.), *Group Psychotherapy and Group Function*. New York: Basic Books, 1963.

ACKERMAN, N.W. The future of family psychotherapy. In Ackerman, N., and Sherman, S. (Eds.), *Expanding Theory and Practice in Family Therapy*. New York: Family Service Assn. of Amer., 1967.

ALEXANDER, F. *Psychosomatic Medicine*. New York: W. W. Norton and Co., Inc., 1950.

ALEXANDER, F., AND FRENCH, T. *Psychoanalytic therapy: Principles and Applications*. New York: Ronald Press, 1946.

ALEXANDER, F., AND MENNINGER, W. C. Relation of persecutory delusions to the functioning of the gastro-intestinal tract. *Journal of Nervous and Mental Disease*, 1936, *84:* 541.

ALEXANDER, F., AND WILSON, G. W. Quantitative dream studies; a methodological attempt at quantitative evaluation of psychoanalytical material. *Psychoanalytic Quarterly*, 1935, *4:* 371–407.

ALTMAN, L. L. *The Dream in Psychoanalysis.* New York: International Universities Press, Inc., 1969.

AMMON, G. Analytic group psychotherapy as an instrument for the treatment and research of psychosomatic disorders. In Wolberg, L. R., and Aronson, M. L. (Eds.), *Group Therapy 1975—An Overview.* New York: Stratton Intercontinental Medical Book Corp., 1975.

AMMON, G. Ego-psychological and group dynamic aspects of psychoanalytic group psychotherapy. In Wolberg, L. R., Aronson, M. L., and Wolberg, A. R. (Eds.), *Group Therapy 1977—An Overview.* New York: Stratton Intercontinental Medical Book Corp., 1977.

ANTHONY, E. J. Age and syndrome in group psychotherapy. *Journal of the Long Island Consultation Center, 1,* 3: 1960.

APONTE, H. AND HOFFMAN, L. The open door: a structural approach to a family with an anorectic child. *Family Process,* 1973, *12* (3): 1–44.

APPLEBAUM, S. A. The pleasure and reality principles in group process teaching. *British Journal of Medical Psychology,* 1963, *36:* 1–7.

APPLEBAUM, S. A. The world in search of a leader: an application of group psychology to international relations. *British Journal of Medical Psychology.* 1967, *40:* 381–392.

ARCHIBALD, H. C. Therapy groups as dream content. *Group Psychotherapy,* 1954, *7:* 146–147.

ARGYRIS, C. Conditions for competence acquisition and therapy. *Journal of Applied Behavioral Science,* 1968, *4:* 147–179.

ARLOW, J. A. Ego psychology and the study of mythology. *Journal of the American Psychoanalytic Association,* 1961, *9:* 371–393.

ARONSON, M. Resistance in individual and group psychotherapy. *American Journal of Psychotherapy,* 1967, *21:* 86–95.

ARONSON, M. The leader's role in focusing. In Liff, Z. (Ed.), *The Leader in the Group.* New York: Jason Aronson, 1975.

ARONSON, M. L. Acting-out in individual and group psychotherapy. *Journal of the Hillside Hospital,* Jan. 1964, *XIII:* No. 1.

ARONSON, M. L., FURST, H. B., KRASNER, J. D., AND LIFF, Z. A. The impact of the leader on group process. *American Journal of Psychotherapy.* 1962, *16:* 460–468.

ASTIGUETA, F. D. The use of nicknames in delineating character patterns in group psychotherapy. In Wolberg, L. R., Aronson, M. L., and Wolberg, A. R. (Eds.), *Group Therapy 1977—An Overview.* New York: Stratton Intercontinental Medical Book Publishers, 1977.

ASTRACHAN, B. M. Towards a social systems model of therapeutic groups. *Social Psychiatry,* 1970, *5:* 110–119.

BACH, G. R. *Intensive Group Psychotherapy.* New York: Ronald Press Co., 1954.

BACH, G. R. Observations on transference and object relations in the light of group dynamics. *International Journal of Group Psychotherapy,* 1957, *7:* 64–76.

BACK, K. W. Power, influence and pattern of communication. In Petrullo, L., and Bass, B. M. (Eds.), *Leadership and Interpersonal Behavior.* New York: Holt, Rinehart and Winston, 1961.

BALES, R. F. *Interaction process analysis: A Method for the Study of Small Groups.* Reading, Mass.: Addison-Wesley, 1950.

BALES, R. F. Adaptive and integrative changes as sources of strain in social systems. In

Hare, A. P., Borgatta, E. F., and Bales, R. F. (Eds.), *Small Groups*. New York: Knopf, 1955.

BALES, R. F. *:Personality and Interpersonal Behavior*. New York: Holt, Rinehart and Winston, 1970.

BALES, R., AND SLATER, P. Role differentiation in small decision-making groups. In Parsons, T., et al. (Eds.), *Family Socialization and Interaction Process*. Glencoe, Ill.: Free Press, 1955.

BALES, R. F., STRODTBECK, F. L., MILLS, T. M., AND ROSEBOROUGH, M. E. Channels of communication in small groups. *American Sociological Review*, 1951, *16:* 461–468.

BASS, B. M. *Leadership, Psychology and Organizational Behavior*. New York: Harper & Row, 1960.

BATESON, G. *Naven*, 2nd ed. Palo Alto, Calif. Stanford University Press, 1958.

BATESON, G., AND JACKSON, D. D. Some varieties of pathogenic organization. In Jackson, D. D, (Ed.), *Communication, Family and Marriage: Human Communication, Vol. 1*. Palo Alto, Calif.: Science and Behavior Books, Inc., 1968.

BATESON, G., JACKSON, D. D., HALEY, J., AND WEAKLAND, J. H. Toward a theory of schizophrenia. *Behavioral Science*, 1956, *1* (4): 250–264.

BATESON, G., JACKSON, D. D., HALEY, J., AND WEAKLAND, J. H. A note on the double bind. *Family Process*, 1963, *2* (1): 154–161.

BATTEGAY, R. The group dream. In Wolberg, L. R., Aronson, M. L., and Wolberg, A. R. (Eds.), *Group Therapy 1977—An Overview*. New York: Stratton Intercontinental Medical Book Corp., 1977.

BAVELAS, A. Communication patterns in task-oriented groups. In Lerner, D., and Lasswell, H. D. (Eds.), *The Policy Sciences*. Palo Alto, Calif.: Stanford University Press, 1951.

BAVELAS, A. A mathematic model for group structure. In Smith, A. G. (Ed.), *Communication and Culture*. New York: Holt, Rinehart & Winston, 1966.

BECK, A. T., WARD, C. H., MENDELSON, J. E., MACK, J. E., AND ERBAUGH, J. R. Reliability of psychiatric diagnosis: 2. A study of consistency of clinical judgments and ratings. *American Journal of Psychiatry*, 1962, *119:* 351–357.

BECKER, B. J. Dreams in group psychoanalysis. *Psychoanalysis in Groups*. 1964, *1* (2): 22–35.

BECKER, W. C., AND KRUG, R. S. A circumplex model for social behavior in children. *Child Development*, 1964, *35:* 351–396.

BELL, G. B., AND FRENCH, R. C. Consistency of individual leadership position in small groups of varying membership. In Hare, A. P., Borgetta, E. F., and Bales, R. F. (Eds.). *Small Groups*. New York: Knopf, 1955.

BELL, J. E. *Family therapy*. New York: Jason Aronson, 1975.

BENNE, K. D. Comments on training groups. In *Research Reports and Technical Roles*. #21. Boston: Boston University Press, 1958.

BENNIS, W. G., AND SHEPARD, H. A theory of group development. *Human Relations*, 1956, *9:* 415–437.

BENNIS, W. G., AND SHEPARD, H. A theory of group development. In Gibbard, G. S., Hartman, J. J., and Mann, R. D. (Eds.), *Analysis of Groups*. San Francisco: Jossey-Bass, 1974.

BERGER, M., AND ROSENBAUM, M. Notes on help-rejecting complainers. *International Journal of Group Psychotherapy*, 1967, *17:* 357–370.

BERNE, E. *Games People Play*. New York: Grove Press, 1964.

BERS, L. *Calculus.* New York: Holt, Rinehart and Winston, 1969.

BIEBER, T. B. The emphasis on the individual in psychoanalytic group therapy. *International Journal of Social Psychiatry.* 1957, *II* (4): 275–280.

BION, W. Experiences in groups. *Human Relations,* 1948, 1: 314.

BION, W. Experiences in groups. III. *Human Relations,* 1949, *2,* 13–22.

BION, W. R. Group dynamics: a review. *International Journal of Psychoanalysis.* 1952, *33:* 235–247.

BION, W. R. Group dynamics: a review. In Klein, M., et al. (Eds.), *New Directions in Psychoanalysis.* New York: Basic Books, 1955.

BION, W. R. *Experiences in Groups.* New York: Basic Books, London, Tavistock, 1959a.

BION, W. R. *Experiences in Groups and Other Papers.* New York, Basic Books, 1959b.

BION, W. R. *Experiences in Groups.* New York: Basic Books, 1961.

BIRD, C. *Social psychology,* New York: Appleton-Century, 1950.

BISHOP, B. M. Mother-child interaction and the social behavior of children. *Psychological Monographs,* 1951, *65* (11): 1.

BLOCH, D. A. Nathan W. Ackerman: the first family paper. In Wolberg, L. R., and Aronson, M. L. (Eds.), *Group Therapy 1974—An Overview.* New York: Stratton Intercontinental Medical Book Corp., 1974.

BLOCK, J. Studies in the phenomenology of emotions. *Journal of Abnormal and Social Psychology,* 1957, *54:* 358–363.

BLUM, L. H. *Reading Between the Lines: Doctor-Patient Communication.* New York: International Universities Press, Inc., 1972.

BOGDANOFF, M., AND ELBAUM, P. L. Role lock: dealing with monopolizers, mistrusters, isolates, helpful Hannahs, and other assorted characters in group psychotherapy. *International Journal of Group Psychotherapy,* 1978, *28* (2): 247–261.

BONDI, H. *Cosmology.* Second Edition. New York: Cambridge University Press, 1961.

BONNER, H. *Group Dynamics: Principles and Application.* New York: Ronald Press, Inc., 1964.

BORGATTA, E. F., CATTRELL, JR., L. S., AND MANN, J. H. The spectrum of individual interaction characteristics: an interdimensional analysis. *Psychological Reports,* 1958, *4:* 279–319.

BORGATTA, E. F., COUCH, A. S., AND BALES, R. F. Some findings relevant to the great man theory of leadership. *American Sociological Review,* 1954, *19:* 755–759.

BORGATTA, E. F., AND CROWTHER, E. *A Workbook for the Study of Social Interaction Process.* Skokie, Ill.: Rand McNally & Co., 1966.

BORGATTA, E. F., AND ESCLENBACH, A. Factor analysis of Rorschach variable and behavior observation. *Psychological Reports,* 1955, *3:* 129–136.

BOSZORMENYI-NAGY, I. A theory of relationships: experience and transaction. In Boszormenyi-Nagy, I., and Framo, J. (Eds.), *Intensive Family Therapy,* New York. Harper and Row, 1965.

BOTT, E. *Family and Social Network.* London: Tavistock Publications Ltd., 1957.

BOWEN, M. *A Family Concept of Schizophrenia.* New York: Basic Books, 1960.

BOWEN, M. Psychotherapy with schizophrenia in the hospital and in private practice. In Boszormenyi-Nagy, I., and Framo, J. L. (Eds.), *Intensive Family Therapy.* New York: Harper and Row, 1965.

BOWEN, M. Family psychotherapy. In Howells, J. G. (Ed.), *Theory and Practice of Family Psychotherapy.* New York: Brunner/Mazell, 1971.

BRENNER, C. Affects and psychic conflict. *The Psychoanalytic Quarterly,* 1975, *XLIV* (1): 5–28.

BRONOWSKI, J. *Science and Human Values*. New York: Harper and Row, 1965.

BROSS, R. B. Termination of analytically oriented psychotherapy in groups. *International Journal of Group Psychotherapy*, 1959, *3:* 325.

BUIRSKI, P. Some contributions of ethology to group therapy: dominance and hierarchies. *International Journal of Group Psychotherapy*, 1975, *25* (2): 227–235.

BUIRSKI, P., KELLERMAN, H., PLUTCHIK, R., WEININGER, R., AND BUIRSKI, N. A field study of emotions, dominance, and social behavior in a group of baboons (Papio anibus). *Primates*, 1973, *14* (1): 67–78.

BUIRSKI, P., PLUTCHIK, R., AND KELLERMAN, H. Sex differences, dominance and personality in the chimpanzee. *Animal Behavior*, 1978, *26:* 123–129.

BURT, C. The factorial study of emotions. In Reymert, M. L. (Ed.), *Feelings and Emotions*. New York, McGraw-Hill Book Co., 1950.

BURTON, A. *The Patient and the Therapist —New Light on the Psychotherapist*. Sacramento, Calif.: Hamilton Psyche Press, 1975.

BYCHOWSKI, G. *Evil in Man: the Anatomy of Hate and Violence*. New York: Grune and Stratton, 1968.

CAIANIELLO, E. R. Field theory. In Besancon, R. M. (Ed.), *Encyclopedia of physics*. New York: Reinhold Publishing Corp. 1966, 261–264.

CARSON, R. C. *Interaction Concepts of Personality*. Chicago: Aldine, 1969.

CARTER, L. Leadership and small group behavior. In Sherif, M., and Wilson, M. O. (Eds.), *Group Relations at the Crossroads*. New York: Harper and Row, 1953.

CARTER, L. The behavior of leaders and other group members. *Journal of Abnormal and Social Psychology*, 1958, *46:* 256–260.

CARTER, L., HAYTHORN, W., SHRIVER, B., AND LANZETTA, J. The behavior of leaders and other group members. *Journal of Abnormal and Social Psychology*, 1950, *46:* 589–595.

CARTWRIGHT, D., AND ZANDER, A. (Eds.). *Group Dynamics:* Research and Theory. New York: Harper and Row, 1968.

CATTELL, R. B. New concepts of measuring leadership. In Cartwright, D., and Zander, A. (Eds.), *Group Dynamics*. Evanston, Ill.: Row Peterson & Co., 1956.

CHALFEN, L. The use of dreams in psychoanalytic group psychotherapy. *Psychoanalytic Review*, 1964, *51:* 125–132.

CHAPPLE, E. D. The interaction chronogram: its evolution and present application. *Personnel*, 1949, *25:* 295–307.

CHERRY, C. *On Human Communication*. New York: Science Editors Inc., 1961.

CHOLDEN, L. Group therapy with the blind. *Group psychotherapy*, 1953, *6:* 21.

CHOMSKY, N. *Language and Mind*. New York: Harcourt Brace and World, 1972.

CHRIST, J. Contrasting the charismatic and reflective leader. In Liff, Z. (Ed.), *The Leader in the Group*. New York: Jason Aronson, 1975.

COLEMAN, J. C. *Abnormal Psychology and Modern Life*. New York: Scott Foresman and Co., 1956.

COUCH, A. The psychological determinants of interpersonal behavior. In *Proceedings of the XIV International Congress of Applied Psychology*. Copenhagen, August 13–19, 1961.

COX, M. The group therapy interaction chronogram. *British Journal of Social Work*, 1973, *3:* 243–256.

DARWIN, C. *On the Origin of Species*. (Everyman's Library.) London: Dent and Sons, 1956. Originally published 1859.

DELGADO, J. M. R. *Physical Control of the Mind*. New York: Harper and Row, 1969.

DELL, C. *Space Harmony*. New York: Dance Notation Bureau, Inc., 1977.

DERIVERA, J. D. *A Structural Theory of the Emotions*. New York: International Universities Press Inc., 1977.

DIAMOND, S. *Personality and Temperament*. New York: Harper and Row, 1957.

DREIKURS, R. Family group therapy in the Chicago community child guidance centers. *Mental Hygiene*, 1951, *35:* 291.

DREIKURS, R. Group psychotherapy from the point of view of Adlerian psychology. In Rosenbaum, M., and Berger, M. (Eds.), *Group Psychotherapy and Group Function*. New York: Basic Books, Inc., 1963.

DUNBAR, F. *Psychosomatic Diagnosis*. New York: Hoeber, 1943.

DUNPHY, D. C. Social change in self analytic groups. In Stone, P., Dunphy, D. C., Smith, M., and Ogilvie, D. (Eds.), *The General Inquirer: A Computer Approach to Content Analysis*. Cambridge, Mass.: M.I.T. Press, 1966.

DUNPHY, D. C. Phases, roles and myths in self-analytic group. *Journal of Applied Behavioral Sciences*, 1968, *4:* 195–226.

DUNPHY, D. C. Phases, roles, myths in self-analytic groups. In Gibbard, G. S., Hartman, J. J., and Mann, R. D. (Eds.), *Analysis of Groups*. San Francisco: Jossey-Bass, 1974.

DURKHEIM, E. *The Division of Labor*. New York: The Free Press of Glencoe, 1933.

DURKIN, H. E. Towards a common basis for group dynamics: group and therapeutic processes in group psychotherapy. *International Journal of Group Psychotherapy*, 1957, *7:* 115–130.

DURKIN, H. E. *The Group in Depth*. New York: International Universities Press, 1964.

DURKIN, H. E. Current problems of group therapy in historical context. In Wolberg, L. R., and Aronson, M. L. (Eds.), *Group Therapy 1974—An Overview.*. New York: Stratton Intercontinental Medical Book Corp., 1974.

DURKIN, H. E., AND GLATZER, H. T. Transference neurosis in group psychotherapy: the concept and the reality. In Wolberg, L. R., and Schwartz, E. K. *Group Therapy 1973—An Overview*. New York: Intercontinental Medical Book Corp., 1973.

DWORWIN, J. The alternate session in group psychotherapy. *Voices: The Art and Science of Psychotherapy*, 1969, *5:* 105–107.

EDWARDS, N. Dreams, ego psychology and group interaction in analytic group psychotherapy. *Group*, 1977, *1:* 32–47.

EHRENWALD, J. Family dynamics and the transgenerational treatment effect. In Wolberg, L. R., and Aronson, M. L. (Eds.) *Group Therapy 1974—An Overview*. New York: Stratton Intercontinental Medical Book Corp., 1974.

ERIKSON, E. H. *Identity and the Life Cycle*. Psychological Issues, Monograph #1. New York: International Universities Press, 1959.

EZRIEL, H. A psychoanalytic approach to group treatment. *British Journal of Medical Psychology*, 1950, *23:* 50–74.

EZRIEL, H. Notes on psychoanalytic group therapy: interpretation and research. *Psychiatry*, 1952, *15:* 119–126.

EZRIEL, H. Experimentation within the psychoanalytic session. *British Journal of Philosophy and Science*, 1956, *7:* 29–48.

EZRIEL, H. The first session in psychoanalytic group treatment. *Nederlands Tydskrift voor Geneeskunde*, 1957, *111:* 711–716.

EZRIEL, H. Psychoanalytic group therapy. In Wolberg, L. R., and Schwartz, E. K. (Eds.),

Group Therapy 1973—An Overview. New York: Intercontinental Medical Book Corp., 1973.

FEIFEL, H., AND EELLS, J. Patients and therapists assess the same psychotherapy. *Journal of Consulting Psychology,* 1963, *27:* 310–318.

FENICHEL, O. *Problems of Psychoanalytic Technique.* New York: W. W. Norton Co., 1941.

FENICHEL, O. Neurotic acting out. *Psychoanalytic Review,* 1945a, *19:* 197–206.

FENICHEL, O. *The Psychoanalytic Theory of Neurosis.* New York: W. W. Norton Co., 1945b.

FESTINGER, L. Informal social communication. In Cartwright, D., and Zander, A. (Eds.), *Group Dynamics.* New York: Harper and Row, 1968.

FESTINGER, L., SCHACTER, S., AND BACK, K. *Social Pressures in Informal Groups.* New York: Harper and Row, 1950.

FIELDING, B. Dreams in group psychotherapy. *Psychotherapy: Theory, Research and Practice,* 1967, *4:* 74–77.

FIELDING, B. The leader and change. In Liff, Z. (Ed.), *The Leader in the Group.* New York: Jason Aronson, 1975.

FIELDSTEEL, N. D. Family therapy—individual therapy: a false dichotomy. In Wolberg, L. R., and Aronson, M. L. (Eds.), *Group Therapy 1974—An Overview.* New York: Stratton Intercontinental Medical Book Corp., 1974.

FIORENTINO, D., SHEPPARD, C., AND MERLIS, S. Emotion profile index (EPI) pattern for paranoid personality types: cross validation and extension. *Psychological Reports,* 1970, *26:* 303–308.

FORSYTH, E., AND KATZ, L. A matrix approach to the analysis of sociometric data: Preliminary report. *Sociometry,* 1946, *9:* 340–347.

FOULKES, S. H. *Introduction to Group Analytic Psychotherapy.* London: William Heinemann Ltd.; New York: Grune and Stratton, 1948.

FOULKES, S. H. Concerning leadership in group analytic psychotherapy. *International Journal of Group Psychotherapy,* 1951, *1:* 319.

FOULKES, S. H. The application of group concepts to the treatment of the individual in the group. In *Topical Problems of Psychotherapy,* Vol. 2. New York: Basel and Karger, 1960.

FOULKES, S. H. *Therapeutic Group Analysis.* New York: International Universities Press, 1964.

FOULKES, S. H. Psychotherapy and group psychotherapy. In Kadis, A. L., Krasner, J. D., Winick, C., and Foulkes, S. H. *A Practicum of Group Psychotherapy.* New York: Hoeber Medical Division, Harper and Row, 1968.

FOULKES, S. H. The group as matrix of the individual's mental life. In Wolberg, L. R., and Schwartz, E. K. (Eds.), *Group Therapy 1973—An Overview.* New York: Intercontinental Medical Book Corp., 1973.

FOULKES, S. H. The leader in the group. In Liff, Z. (Ed.), *The Leader in the Group.* New York: Jason Aronson, 1975.

FOULKES, S. H. Notes on the concept of resonance. In Wolberg, L. R., Aronson, M. L., and Wolberg, A. R. (Eds.), *Group Therapy 1977—An Overview.* New York: Stratton Intercontinental Medical Book Corp., 1977.

FOULKES, S. H., AND ANTHONY, E. J. *Group Psychotherapy.* London: Penguin, 1957.

FOULKES, S. H., AND ANTHONY, E. J. *Group Psychotherapy: The Psychoanalytic Approach.* Baltimore: Penguin Books, 1965.

FRANK, J. Some values of conflict in therapeutic groups. *Group Psychotherapy*, 1955, *8:* 142–151.

FRANK, J. D. Some determinants, manifestations, and effects of cohesiveness in therapy groups. *International Journal of Group Psychotherapy*, 1957, *7:* 53–63.

FRANK, J., AND ASCHER, E. The corrective emotional experience in group therapy. *American Journal of Psychiatry*, 1951, *108:* 126–131.

FRANK, J. D., et al. Behavioral patterns in early meetings of therapeutic groups. *American Journal of Psychiatry*, 1952, *108:* 771–778.

FRAZIER, S. H. *A Psychiatric Glossary*. Washington, D. C.: American Psychiatric Assoc., 1975.

FREEDMAN, M., LEARY, T., OSSORIO, A., AND COFFEY, H. S. The interpersonal dimension of personality. *Journal of Personality*, 1951, *20:* 143–161.

FRENCH, J. R. P. A formal theory of social power. *Psychological Review*, 1956, *63:* 181–194.

FRENCH, J. R. P., AND RAVEN, B. The bases of social power. In Cartwright, D., and Zander, A. (Eds.), *Group Dynamics*. New York: Harper and Row, 1968.

FREUD, A. *The Ego and the Mechanisms of Defense*. London: Hogarth Press, 1937.

FREUD, S. The interpretation of dreams. In Strachey, J. *The Complete Psychological Works of Sigmund Freud*. Standard Edition, *4, 5,* 1953, London: Hogarth Press, Originally published 1900.

FREUD, S. Three essays on the theory of sexuality: Infantile sexuality. In Strachey, J. (Ed.), *The Complete Psychological Works of Sigmund Freud*. Standard Edition, *19,* 1961, London: Hogarth Press, Originally published 1905.

FREUD, S. Character and anal eroticism. In Strachey, J. (Ed.), *The Complete Psychological Works of Sigmund Freud*. Standard Edition, *9,* 1959, London: Hogarth Press, Originally published 1908.

FREUD, S. The future prospects of psychoanalytic therapy. In Strachey, J. (Ed.), *The Complete Psychological Works of Sigmund Freud*. Standard Edition, *11,* 1957, London: Hogarth Press, Originally published 1910.

FREUD, S. Psychoanalytic notes on an autobiographical account of a case of paranoia. In Strachey, J. (Ed.), *The Complete Psychological Works of Sigmund Freud*. Standard Edition, *12,* 1958, London: Hogarth Press, Originally published 1911.

FREUD, S. Recommendations to physicians practicing psychoanalysis. In Strachey, J. (ED.), *The Complete Psychological Works of Sigmund Freud*. Standard Edition, *12,* 1958, London: Hogarth Press, Originally published 1912.

FREUD, S. Totem and Taboo. In Strachey, J. (Ed.), *The Complete Psychological Works of Sigmund Freud*. Standard Edition, *13,* 1953, London: Hogarth Press, Originally published 1913.

FREUD, S. On the psychopathology of everyday life. In Stachey, J. (Ed.), *The Complete Psychological Works of Sigmund Freud*. Standard Edition, *6,* 1960, London: Hogarth Press, Originally published 1914a.

FREUD, S. Remembering, repeating and working through. In Strachey, J. (Ed.), *The Complete Psychological Works of Sigmund Freud*. Standard Edition, *12,* 1958, London: Hogarth Press, Originally published 1914b.

FREUD, S. Group psychology and the analysis of the ego. In Strachey J. (Ed), *The Complete Psychological Works of Sigmund Freud*. Standard Edition, *18,* 1955, London: Hogarth Press, Originally published 1921.

FREUD, S. Neurotic mechanisms in jealousy, paranoia and homosexuality. In Strachey J. (Ed), *The Complete Psychological Works of Sigmund Freud.* Standard Edition, *18,* 1955, London: Hogarth Press, Originally published 1922.

FREUD, S. Inhibitions, symptoms and anxiety. In Strachey J. (Ed), *The Complete Psychological Works of Sigmund Freud.* Standard Edition, *20,* 1959, London: Hogarth Press, Originally published 1926.

FREUD, S. Libidinal types. In Strachey J. (Ed), *The Complete Psychological Works of Sigmund Freud.* Standard Edition, *21,* 1961, London: Hogarth Press, Originally published 1931.

FREUD, S. Constructions in analysis. In Strachey J. (Ed), *The Complete Psychological Works of Sigmund Freud.* Standard Edition, *23,* 1964, London: Hogarth Press, Originally published 1937.

FREUD, S. Moses and monotheism. In Strachey J. (Ed), *The Complete Psychological Works of Sigmund Freud.* Standard Edition, *23,* 1964, London: Hogarth Press, Originally published 1939.

FRIED, E. Some aspects of group dynamics and the analysis of transference and defenses. *International Journal of Group Psychotherapy,* 1965, *15:* 1.

FRIED, E. Group bonds. In Wolberg, L. R., and Schwartz, E. K. (Eds.), *Group Therapy 1973 —An Overview.* New York: Stratton Intercontinental Medical Book Corp., 1973.

FRIED, E. The narcissistic beginning of the therapy group. In Wolberg, L. R., Aronson, M. L., and Wolberg, A. (Eds.), *Group Therapy 1976 —An Overview.* New York: Stratton Intercontinental Medical Book Corp., 1976.

FROMM, E. *Escape from Freedom.* New York: Farrar and Rinehart, 1941.

FROMM, E. *Man for Himself.* New York: Rinehart, 1947.

GARD, J. G., AND BENDIG, A. W. A factor analytic study of Eysenck's and Schutz's personality dimensions and psychiatric groups. *Journal of Consulting Psychology,* 1964, *28:* 252–258.

GELLER, J. J. Concerning the size of therapy groups. In Rosenbaum, M., and Berger, M. (Eds.), *Group Psychotherapy and Group Function.* New York: Basic Books, Inc., 1963.

GELL-MAN, M., AND NEEMAN, Y. The eightfold way. New York: W. A. Benjamin, 1972.

GERSCOVICH, J. Catalyzation of group process through strategic arrangement of group composition. In Wolberg, L. R., Aronson, M. L., and Wolberg, A. R. (Eds.), *Group Therapy 1976 —An Overview.* New York: Stratton Intercontinental Medical Book Corp., 1976.

GIBBARD, G. S. Individuation, fusion and role specialization. In Gibbard, G. S., Hartman, J. J., and Mann R. D. (Eds.), *Analysis of Groups.* San Francisco: Jossey-Bass, 1974.

GIBBARD, G. S., AND HARTMAN, J. J. Relationship patterns in self-analytic groups. *Behavioral Science,* 1973a, *18:*335–353.

GIBBARD, G. S., AND HARTMAN, J. J. The Oedipal paradigm in group development: a clinical and empirical study. *Small Group Behavior,* 1973b, *23:*305–354.

GIBBARD, G. S., AND HARTMAN, J. J. The significance of utopian fantasies in small groups. *International Journal of Group Psychotherapy,* 1973c, *23:*125–147.

GIBBARD, G. S., HARTMAN, J. J., AND MANN, R. D. *Analysis of Groups.* San Francisco: Jossey-Bass, 1974.

GIBBARD, G. S., HARTMAN, J. J., AND MANN, R. D. The dynamics of leadership. In Gibbard, G.

S., Hartman, J. J., and Mann, R. D. (Eds.), *Analysis of groups*. San Francisco: Jossey-Bass, 1974.

GILLESPIE, R. D. Psychological aspects of skin disease. *British Journal of Dermatology*, 1938 *50*(1):1–16.

GLANZER, M., AND GLASER, R. Techniques for the study of group structure and behavior. I. Analysis of structure. *Psychological Bulletin*, 1959, *56*:317–332.

GLATZER, H. The relative effectiveness of clinically homogeneous and heterogeneous psychotherapy groups. *International Journal of Group Psychotherapy*, 1956, *6*:258–265.

GLATZER, H. Acting-out in group psychotherapy. *American Journal of Psychotherapy*, 1958, *12*:87–105.

GLATZER, H. Handling narcissistic problems in group psychotherapy. *International Journal of Group Psychotherapy*, 1962, *12*:448–455.

GOFFMAN, E. The moral career of the mental patient. *Psychiatry*, 1959, *22*:123–142.

GOLDFARB, W. Principles of group psychotherapy. *American Journal of Psychotherapy*, 1953, *7*:418–432.

GOLDMAN, G. D. Some application of Harry Stack Sullivan's theories to group psychotherapy. In Rosenbaum, J., and Berger, M. (Eds.), *Group Psychotherapy and Group Function*. New York: Basic Books, 1963.

GOLDSTEIN, A., HELLER, K., AND SECHREST, L. *Psychotherapy and the Psychology of Behavior Change*. New York: John Wiley and Sons, 1966.

GORDON, T. Group centered leadership and administration. In Rogers, C. *Client-Centered Therapy*. Boston: Houghton Mifflin Co., 1951.

GOULDNER, A. (Ed.), *Studies in Leadership*. New York: Harper and Row, 1950.

GREENACRE, P. *Emotional Growth*. New York: International Universities Press, 1971.

GREENLEAF, E. 'Senoi' dream groups. *Psychotherapy: Theory Research and practice*, 1973, *10*: No. 3, 218–222.

GRINBERG, L. Projective identification and projective counter-identification in the dynamics of groups. In Wolberg, L. R., and Schwartz, E. K. (Eds.), *Group Therapy 1973 — An Overview*. New York: Stratton Intercontinental Medical Book Corp., 1973.

GRINBERG, L., GEAR, M. C., AND LIENDO, E. C. Group dynamics according to a semiotic model (I.R.M.) based on projective identification and counter-identification. In Wolberg, L. R., Aronson, M. L., and Wolberg, A. R. (Eds.), *Group Therapy 1976 — An Overview*. New York: Stratton Intercontinental Medical Book Corp., 1976.

GROTJAHN, M. The process of maturation in group psychotherapy and in the group therapist. *Psychiatry*, 1950, *13*:62–67.

GROTJAHN, M. *Psychoanalysis and the Family Neurosis*. New York: W. W. Norton & Co., Inc., 1960.

GROTJAHN, M. The qualities of the group therapist. In Kaplan, H. I., and Sadock, B. J. *Comprehensive Group Psychotherapy*. Baltimore: The Williams and Wilkins Co., 1971.

GROTJAHN, M. Selected clinical observations from psychoanalytic group psychotherapy. In Wolberg, L. R., and Schwartz, E. K. (Eds.), *Group Therapy 1973 — An Overview*. New York: Stratton Intercontiental Medical Book Corp., 1973.

GROTJAHN, M. Growth experiences in the leader. In Liff, Z. (Ed.), *The Leader in the Group*. New York: Jason Aronson, 1975.

GRUENBERG, E. M., et al. *Diagnostic and Statistical Manual of Mental Disorders,* 2nd ed. Washington, D.C.: American Psychiatric Association, 1968.

GUILFORD, J. P., AND ZIMMERMAN, W. S. Fourteen dimensions of temperament. *Psychological Monographs,* 1956, *70,* No. 10, Whole No. 417.

GUNTRIP, H. *Schizoid Phenomena, Object Relations and the Self.* New York: International Universities Press, 1969.

GUTHEIL, E. A. *The Handbook of Dream Analysis.* New York: Liveright Publishing Corp., 1951.

GUTTMAN, L. A new approach to factor analysis: the radex. In Lazarsfeld, P. F. (Ed.), *Mathematical Thinking in the Social Sciences.* Glencoe, Ill.: Free Press, 1954.

HADDEN, S. B. Countertransference in the group therapist. *International Journal of Group Psychotherapy,* 1953, *4*:417–423.

HALEY, J. The family of the schizophrenic: a model system. In Jackson D. (Ed.): *Communication, Family and Marriage,* Vol. 1. Palo Alto, Calif.: Science and Behavior Books, 1968.

HALL, C. S. *The Meaning of Dreams.* New York: Harper and Row, 1953.

HALLIDAY, J. L. Approach to asthma. *British Journal of Medical Psychology,* 1937, *17*:1.

HAMILTON, M. *Psychosomatics.* New York: John Wiley & Sons, 1955.

HANDLON, J. H., AND PARLOFF, M. B. The treatment of patient and family as a group: is it group psychotherapy? *International Journal of Group Psychotherapy,* 1962, *12*:132–141.

HARARY, F., AND NORMAN, R. Z. *Graph Theory as a Mathematical Model in Social Science.* Ann Arbor, Mich.: Institute for Social Research, 1953.

HARARY, F., NORMAN, R. Z., AND CARTWRIGHT, D. *Structural Models, and Introduction to the Theory of Directed Graphs.* New York: John Wiley & Sons, 1965.

HARARY, F., AND ROSS, I. C. A procedure for clique-detection using the group matrix. *Sociometry,* 1957, *20*:205–215.

HARE, A. P. A study of interaction and consensus in different sized groups. *American Sociological Review,* 1952, *17*:261–267.

HARE, A. P. *Handbook of Small Group Research.* New York: Free Press of Glencoe, 1962.

HARTLEY, E. L. An exhortation: group process analysis: In Rosenbaum, M., and Berger, M. (Eds.), *Group Psychotherapy and Group Function.* New York: Basic Books, Inc., 1963.

HARTMAN, J. J., AND GIBBARD, G. S. A note on fantasy themes in the evolution of group culture. In Gibbard, G. S., Hartman, J. J., and Mann, R. D. (Eds.), *Analysis of Groups.* San Francisco: Jossey-Bass, 1974a.

HARTMAN, J. J., AND GIBBARD G. S. Anxiety, boundary evolution and social change. In Gibbard, G. S., Hartman, J. J., and Mann, R. D. (Eds.), *Analysis of Groups.* San Francisco: Jossey-Bass, 1974b.

HARTMANN, H. *Ego Psychology and the Problem of Adaptation.* New York: International Universities Press, Inc., 1959.

HEALY, W., BRONNER, A. F., AND BOWERS, A. M. *The Structure and Meaning of Psychoanalysis.* New York: Knopf, 1930.

HEBB, D. O. *A Textbook of Psychology.* Philadelphia: W. B. Saunders Co., 1966.

HERBERT, E. L., AND TRIST, E. L. The institution of an absent leader by a students' discussion group. *Human Relations,* 1953, *6*:215–248.

HINTON, W. *Iron Oxen.* New York: Vintage, 1970.

HOBBS, N. Group-centered psychotherapy. In Rogers, C. *Client-Centered Therapy*. Boston: Houghton Mifflin Co., 1951.

HOLMES, R. The university seminar and the primal horde. *British Journal of Sociology*, 1967, *18*:135–150.

HOLT, H. AND WINICK, C. Group psychotherapy with obese women. *Archives of General Psychiatry*, 1961, *5*:156.

HOMANS, G. C. *The Human Group*. New York: Harcourt, Brace & Co., 1950.

HORNEY, K. *Neurosis and Human Growth*. New York: W. W. Norton & Co., Inc., 1950.

HOWELLS, J. G. *Principles of Family Psychiatry*. New York: Bruner/Mazel, 1975.

HURWITZ, J. I., ZANDER, A. F., AND HYMOVITCH, B. Some effects of power on the relations among group members. In Cartwright, D., and Zander, A. (Eds.), *Group Dynamics*. New York: Harper and Row, 1968.

ILLING, H. A. C. G. Jung on the present trends in group psychotherapy. In Rosenbaum, M., and Berger, M. (Eds.), *Group Psychotherapy and Group Function*. New York: Basic Books, Inc., 1963.

JACKSON, D. The question of family homeostases. *Psychoanalytic Quarterly*, 1957, *90*(Suppl. 31):79–96.

JACKSON, D. Family interaction, family homeostasis and some implications for conjoint family psychotherapy. In Masserman, J. H. (Ed.), *Science and Psychoanalysis*. New York: Grune and Stratton, Inc., 1959.

JACKSON, D., AND WEAKLAND, J. H. Conjoint family therapy; some considerations on theory, technique, and results. *Psychiatry*, 1961, *24*:30–45.

JAQUES, E. Social systems as a defense against persecutory and depressive anxiety. In Klein, M., Heimann, P., and Money-Kyrle, R. E. (Eds.), *New Directions in Psychoanalysis*. New York: Basic Books, Inc., 1955.

JOHNSON, J. A. *Group therapy: A Practical Approach*. New York: McGraw-Hill Book Co, 1963.

JONES, E. *On the Nightmare*. London: Hogarth Press, 1931.

KADIS, A. Reexperiencing the family constellation in group psychotherapy. *American Journal of Individual Psychology*. 1956a, *10*:63–68.

KADIS, A. The alternate meeting in group psychotherapy. *American Journal of Psychotherapy*, 1956b, *10*:275–291.

KADIS, A., KRASNER, J. D., WINICK, C., AND FOULKES, S. H. *A Practicum of Group Psychotherapy*. New York: Hoeber Medical Division, Harper and Row, 1968.

KADIS, A., AND WINICK, C. The role of the deviant in the psychotherapy group. *International Journal of Social Psychiatry*, 1960, *6*:227.

KAHN, R., AND KATZ, D. Leadership practices in relation to productivity and morale. In Cartwright, D., and Zander, A. (Eds.), *Group Dynamics: Research and Theory*. New York: Harper and Row, 1960.

KANTER, S. The therapist's leadership in psychoanalytically oriented group therapy. *International Journal of Group Psychotherapy*, 1976, *26*(2):139–147.

KANZER, M. The recollection of the forgotten dream. *Journal of the Hillside Hospital*, 1959, *8*:74–85.

KAPLAN, S. R. Therapy groups and training groups: similarities and differences. *International Journal of Group Psychotherapy*, 1967, *17*:473–504.

KAPLAN, S. R., AND ROMAN, M. Characteristic responses in adult therapy groups to the introduction of new members: a reflection on group process. *International Journal of Group Psychotherapy*, 1961, *11*:372–381.

KAPLAN, S. R., AND ROMAN, M. Phases of development in an adult therapy group. *International Journal of Group Psychotherapy*, 1963, *13*,:10–26.

KATZ, D., AND KAHN, R. *The Social Psychology of Organizations*. New York: John Wiley & Sons, 1966.

KAUFF, P. The termination process: its relationship to the separation-individuation phase of development. *International Journal of Group Psychotherapy*, 1977, *27*(2):3–18.

KAUFMAN, C. Some ethological studies of social relationships and conflict situations. *Journal of the American Psychoanalytic Association*. 1960, *8*(4):671–685.

KAYWIN, L. An epigenetic approach to the psychoanalytic theory of instincts and affects. *Journal of the American Psychoanalytic Association*, 1960, *8*(4):613–658.

KELLERMAN, H. Relating emotions and traits in the measurement of maladjustment. *Proceedings of the 73rd Annual Convention of the American Psychological Association*. 1965, 229–230.

KELLERMAN, H. The emotional behavior of dolphins, Tursiops truncatus: implications for psychoanalysis. *International Mental Health Research Newsletter*. 1966, *8*(1):1–7.

KELLERMAN, H. Relating suicidal potential to 'flight into health states.' *Transnational Mental Health Research Newsletter*, 1976a, *18*(2):15–16.

KELLERMAN, H. The sociobiology of group psychotherapy and the physics of group boundary structure. Paper delivered at the Association of Science, Psychotherapy and Ethics. New York, November 1976b.

KELLERMAN, H. In Wolman, B. B. (Ed.), *International Encyclopedia of Neurology, Hate and Psychiatry, Psychoanalysis and Psychology*. New York: Von Nostrand Reinhold Co., 1977a.

KELLERMAN, H. Shostrom's mate selection model, the Pair Attraction Inventory, and the Emotions Profile Index. *Journal of Psychology*, 1977b, *95*:37–43.

KELLERMAN, H. Communication and emotion. Paper delivered at the *Postgraduate Center for Mental Health Professional Meeting* on Lacan and Psychoanalysis. New York, 1977c.

KELLERMAN H., BUIRSKI, P., AND PLUTCHIK, R. Group behavior in a baboon troop: implications for human group process. In Wolberg, L. R., and Aronson, M. L. (Eds.), *Group Therapy 1974 —An Overview*. New York: Stratton Intercontinental Medical Book Corp., 1974.

KELLERMAN, H., AND MALIVER, B. L. Measurement of emotion and trait behavior in a therapy group. *Group Process*, 1977, *7*:245–255.

KELLERMAN, H., AND PLUTCHIK, R. Emotion-trait interrelations and the measurement of personality. *Psychological Reports*, 1968, *23*:1107–1114.

KELLERMAN, H., AND PLUTCHIK, R. The meaning of tension in group therapy. In Wolberg, L. R., Aronson, M. L., and Wolberg, A. R. (Eds.), *Group Therapy 1977 —An Overview*. New York: Stratton Intercontinental Medical Book Corp., 1977.

KELLERMAN, H., AND PLUTCHIK, R. Personality patterns of drug addicts in a therapy group: a similarity structure analysis. *Group*, 1978, *2*(1):14–21.

KELLEY, H. H. Communication in experimentally created hierarchies. *Human Relations*, 1951, *4*:39–56.

KERNBERG, O. A psychoanalytic classification of character pathology. *Journal of the American Psychoanalytic Association*, 1970a, *18*:800–822.

KERNBERG, O. Factors in the psychoanalytic treatment of narcissistic personalities. *Journal of American Psychoanalytic Association*, 1970b, *18*:51–85.

KERNBERG, O. F. A systems approach to priority setting of interventions in groups. *International Journal of Group Psychotherapy*, 1975, *25*(3):251–275.

KLANDER, J. V. Psychogenic aspects of diseases of the skin. *Archives of Neurology and Psychiatry*, 1935, *33*:221.

KLEIN, M. Mourning and its relation to manic depressive states. In *Contributions to Psychoanalysis, 1921–1945*. London: Hogarth Press, 1948.

KLEIN-LIPSHUTZ, E. Comparison of dreams in individual and group psychotherapy. *International Journal of Group Psychotherapy*, 1953, *3*:143–149.

KNOBLOCH, F. Toward a conceptional framework of a group centered psychotherapy. In Reiss, B. F. (Ed.), *New Directions in Mental Health*, Vol. 1. New York: Grune and Stratton, Inc., 1968.

KORTEN, D. C. Situational determinants of leadership structure. *Journal of Conflict Resolution*, 1962, *6*:222–235.

KOSSEFF, J. W. The leader using object relations theory. In Liff, Z. (Ed.), *The Leader in the Group*. New York: Jason Aronson, 1975.

KRECH, D., AND CRUTCHFIELD, R. *Theory and Practice of Social Psychology*. New York: McGraw-Hill Book Co., 1948.

KUBIE, L. S. The problem of specificity in the psychosomatic process. In Deutsch, F. (Ed.), *The Psychosomatic Concept in Psychoanalysis*. New York: International Universities Press, 1953.

KUBIE, L. S. Some theoretical concepts underlying the relationships between individual and group psychotherapies. *International Journal of Group Psychotherapy*, 1958, *8*:319.

LABAN, R. *Modern Educational Dance*. London: MacDonald and Evans, Ltd., 1963.

LABAN, R. *The Language of Movement: A guidebook to Chorentics*. Boston: Plays, Inc., 1966.

LACAN, J. *Ecrits*. New York: W. W. Norton & Co., 1968.

LACHMAN, F. M., AND STOLOROW, R. Idealization and grandiosity: developmental considerations and treatment implications. *The Psychoanalytic Quarterly*, 1977, *45*:565–587.

LASSWELL, H. D. The psychology of Hitlerism as a response of the lower middle class to continuing insecurity. In Swanson, G., Newcomb, T. M. and Hartley, E. L. (Eds.), *Readings in Social Psychology*. New York: Holt, 1952.

LEARY, T. *Interpersonal Diagnosis of Personality*. New York: Ronald Press, 1957.

LEARY, T., AND COFFEY, H. S. Interpersonal diagnosis. Some problems of methodology and validation. *Journal of Abnormal and Social Psychology*, 1955, *50*:110–124.

LEDER, R., AND SCHWARTZ, E. K. The developmental stages of a therapy group and their implications for social living. In Riess, B. F. (Ed.), *New Directions in Mental Health*. Vol. 2. New York: Grune and Stratton, Inc., 1969.

LEOPOLD, H. S. Selection of patients for group psychotherapy. *Americal Journal of Psychotherapy*, 1957, *11*:634–637.

LEOPOLD, H. S. The problem of working through in group psychotherapy. *International Journal of Group Psychotherapy*, 1959, *9*:287–292.

LEVINSON, D. J. Role, personality and social structure in the organizational setting. *Journal of Abnormal and Social Psychology*, 1959, *18*:170–180.

LEWIN, K. *A dynamic theory of personality*. New York: McGraw-Hill Book Co., Inc., 1935.

LEWIN, K. *The principles of Topological Psychology.* New York: McGraw-Hill Book Co., Inc., 1936.

LEWIN, K. Constructs in psychology and psychological ecology. *University of Iowa Studies in Child Welfare,* 1944, *20*:3–29.

LEWIN, K. *Field Theory in Social Science.* New York: Harper and Row, 1951.

LIEBERMAN, M. A., YALOM, I. D., AND MILES, M. B. *Encounter Groups: First Facts.* New York: Basic Books, 1973.

LIFF, Z. The charismatic leader. In Liff, Z. (Ed.), *The Leader in the Group.* New York: Jason Aronson, 1975.

LIKERT, R. An emerging theory of organization, leadership and management. In Petrullo, L., and Bass, B. (Eds.), *Leadership and Interpersonal Behavior.* New York: Holt, Rinehart and Winston, 1961.

LINDT, H. The nature of therapeutic interaction of patients in groups. *International Journal of Group Psychotherapy,* 1958, *8*:55–69.

LINDT, H., AND SHERMAN, M. Social incognito in analytically oriented group psychotherapy. *International Journal of Group Psychotherapy,* 1952, *2*:209–220.

LIPPITT, R., POLANSKY, N., REDL, F., AND ROSEN, S. The dynamics of power. *Human Relations,* 1952, *5*:37–64.

LIPPITT, R., AND WHITE, R. *Autocracy and Democracy.* New York: Harper and Row, 1960.

LOCKE, N. The use of dreams in group psychoanalysis. *American Journal of Psychotherapy,* 1957, *11*:98–110.

LOCKE, N. *Group Psychoanalysis.* New York: New York University Press, 1961.

LODGE, G. T. A method for the dynamic representation of personality data. *Journal of Projective Techniques,* 1953, *17*:477–481.

LODGE, G. T., AND GIBSON, R. L. A coaction map of the personalities described by H. Rorschach and S. J. Beck. *Journal of Projective Techniques,* 1953, *17*:482–488.

LOESER, L. H. Some aspects of group dynamics. *International Journal of Group Psychotherapy,* 1957, 7:5–19.

LORENZ, K. *On Agression.* New York: Harcourt Brace, 1966.

LORR, M. Relation of treatment frequency and duration to psychotherapeutic outcome. In Strupp, H., and Luborsky, L. (Eds.), *Conference on Research in Psychotherapy.* Washington, D.C.: American Psychological Association, 1962, 134–141.

LORR, M., AND McNAIR, D. M. An interpersonal behavior circle. *Journal of Abnormal and Social Psychology,* 1963, *67*:68–75.

LUCHINS, A. *Group Therapy: A Guide.* New York: Random House, 1967.

LUNDGREN, D. C. Trainer style and patterns of group development. *Journal of Applied Behavioral Science,* 1971, 7:689–709.

MACALPINE, I. Pruritis Ani: A psychiatric study. *Psychosomatic Medicine,* 1953, *15*:499.

MACK, J. E. *Nightmares and Human Conflict.* Boston: Little, Brown and Co., 1970.

MacLENNAN, B. W. The personalities of group leaders: implications for selection and training. *International Journal of Group Psychotherapy,* 1975, *25*(2):177–183.

MANN, R. D. The development of the member-trainer relationship in self-analytic groups. *Human Relations,* 1966, *19*:85-115.

MANN, R. D. The identity of the group researcher. In Gibbard, G. S., Hartman, J. J., and Mann, R. D. (Eds.), *Analysis of Groups.* San Francisco: Jossey-Bass, 1974.

MANN, R. D., GIBBARD, G. S., AND HARTMANN, J. J. *Interpersonal Styles and Group Development.* New York: John Wiley & Sons, Inc., 1967.

MANN, R. D., et al. *The College Classroom.* New York: John Wiley & Sons, Inc., 1970.

McDOUGALL, W. *The Group Mind.* London: Cambridge University Press, 1921.

MENDELL, D. Family therapy, a synergistic systems approach. In Wolberg, L. R., and Schwartz, E. K. (Eds.), *Group Therapy 1973 — An Overview.* New York: Stratton Intercontinental Medical Book Corp., 1973.

MILLENSON, J. R. *Principles of Behavioral Analysis.* Macmillan, New York: Collier-Macmillan: London, 1967.

MILLER, J. G. Living systems: Basic concepts. In Gray, W., and Rizzo, N. D. (Eds.), *General Systems Theory and Psychiatry.* Boston: Little, Brown and Co., 1969.

MILLS, T. M. *Group Transformation: An Analysis of a Learning Group.* Englewood Cliffs, N.J.: Prentice Hall, 1964.

MILLS, T. M. Observation. In Gibbard, G. S., Hartman, J. J., and Mann, R. D. (Eds.), *Analysis of Groups.* San Francisco: Jossey-Bass, 1974.

MINUCHIN, S., ROSMAN, B. L., AND BAKER, L. *Psychosomatic Families: Anorexia Nervosa in Context.* Cambridge, Mass., Harvard University Press, 1978.

MOOS, R. H., AND CLEMES, S. R. A multivariate study of the patient-therapist system. *Journal of Consulting Psychology,* 1967, *31*:119–130.

MULLAN, H. The nonteleological in dreams in group-psychotherapy. *Journal of the Hillside Hospital,* 1956, *5:*480.

MULLAN, H. Status denial in Group psychoanalysis. In Rosenbaum, M., and Berger, M. *Group Psychotherapy and Group Function.* New York: Basic Books, Inc., 1963.

MULLAN, H. D., AND ROSENBAUM, M. *Group Psychotherapy.* New York: Free Press of Glencoe, 1962.

MURRAY, H. A. Toward a classification of interaction. In Parsons, T. and Shils, E. A. (Eds.), *Toward a General Theory of Action.* Cambridge, Mass.: Harvard University Press, 1954.

NAGERA, H. *Basic Psychoanalytic Concepts on the Theory of Dreams.* New York: Basic Books, 1969.

NEWCOMB, T. M. Stabilities underlying changes in interpersonal attraction. *Journal of Abnormal and Social Psychology,* 1963, *66*:376–386.

NORTH, M. *Personality Assessment through Movement.* London: MacDonald and Evans Ltd., 1972.

NOVEY, S. A clinical view of affect theory in psychoanalysis. *The International Journal of Psychoanalysis,* 1959, *40*:1–11.

NOVEY, S. Further considerations on affect theory in psychoanalysis. *The International Journal of Psychoanalysis,* 1961, *42,* Parts I-II:21–31.

NOWLIS, V. Mood: behavior and experience. In Arnold, M (Ed.), *Feelings and Emotions: The Loyola Symposium.* New York: Academic Press, Inc., 1970.

O'DAY, R. The T-group trainer: A study of conflict in the exercise of authority. In Gibbard, G. S., Hartman, J. J., and Mann, R. D. (Eds.), *Analysis of Groups.* San Francisco: Jossey-Bass, 1974.

OSGOOD, C. E., SUCI, G. J., AND TANNENBAUM, P. H. *The Measurement of Meaning.* Urbana, Ill.: University of Illinois Press, 1957.

OSTOW, M. The structural model: ego, id and superego. *Annals of the New York Academy of Sciences.* 1959, *76*:1098–1134.

PARKER, S. Leadership patterns in a psychiatric ward. *Human Relations,* 1958, *11*:287–301.

PARLOFF, M. B. Group dynamics and group psychotherapy. The state of the union. *International Journal of Group Psychotherapy,* 1963, *13*:393–451.

PARLOFF, M. B. Advances in analytic group therapy. In Marmor, J. (Ed.), *Frontiers of Psychoanalysis*. New York: Basic Books, Inc., 1967.

PECK, H. B.The role of a psychiatric day hospital: a group process approach. *American Journal of Orthopsychiatry*, 1963, *33*:482–493.

PINES, M. Group therapy with difficult patients. In Wolberg, L. R., and Aronson, M. L. (Eds.), *Group Therapy 1974—An Overview*. New York: Stratton Intercontinental Medical Book Corp., 1974.

PLATMAN, S. R., PLUTCHIK, R., FIEVE, R. R., AND LAWLOR, W. Emotion profiles associated with mania and depression *Archives of General Psychiatry*, 1969, *20*:210–214.

PLATMAN, S. R., PLUTCHIK, R., AND WEINSTEIN, B. Psychiatric, physiological, behavioral and self-report measures in relation to a suicide attempt. *Journal of Psychiatric Research*, 1971, *8*:127–137.

PLUTCHIK, R. Some problems for a theory of emotion. *Psychosomatic Medicine*, 1955, *17*:306–310.

PLUTCHIK, R. Outlines of a new theory of emotion. *Transactions of the New York Academy of Science*, 1958, *20*:394–403.

PLUTCHIK, R. The multifactor analytic theory of emotion, *Journal of Psychology*, 1960, *50*:153–171.

PLUTCHIK, R. *The Emotions: Facts, Theories and a New Model*. New York: Random House, 1962.

PLUTCHIK, R. Emotions, evolution and adaptive processes. In Arnold, M. (Ed.), *Feelings and Emotions: The Loyola Symposium*. New York: Academic Press, Inc., 1970.

PLUTCHIK, R. A structural model of emotions and personality. Paper presented at the American Psychological Association meeting, New Orleans, 1974.

PLUTCHIK, R., AND KELLERMAN, H. *The Emotions Profile Index: Test and Manual*. San Francisco: Western Psychological Services, 1974.

PLUTCHIK, R., AND KELLERMAN, H. The nature of tension in small groups. Paper presented at the International Organization for the Reduction of Group Tension Meeting; Eastern Psychological Association Conference, New York, 1976.

PLUTCHIK, R., KELLERMAN, H., AND CONTE, H. A structural theory of ego defenses and emotions. In Izard, C. E. (Ed.), *Emotions and Psychopathology*. New York: Plenum Press, 1979.

PLUTCHIK, R., AND PLATMAN, S. R. Personality connotations of psychiatric diagnoses. *Journal of Nervous and Mental Disease*, 1977, *165*:418–422.

POWDERMAKER, F. B., AND FRANK, J. D. *Group Psychotherapy*. Cambridge, Mass.: Harvard University Press, 1953.

RABKIN, R. *Inner and Outer Space: Introduction to a Theory of Social Psychiatry*. New York: W. W. Norton & Co., Inc., 1970.

RAVICH, R. A. The origins of the concept of complementarity in Nathan Ackerman's family process theory. In Wolberg, L. R., and Aronson, M. L. (Eds.), *Group Therapy 1974—An Overview*. New York: Stratton Intercontinental Medical Book Corp., 1974.

REDER, P. An assessment of the group therapy interaction chronogram. *International Journal of Group Psychotherapy*, 1978, *2*:185–193.

REDL, F. Group emotion and leadership. *Psychiatry*, 1942, *5*:573–596.

REDL, F. Diagnostic group work. *American Journal of Orthopsychiatry*, 1944, *14*:53–67.

REICH, A. On countertransference. *International Journal of Psychoanalysis*, 1951, *32*:25–31.

REICH, W. *Character Analysis*. New York: Farrar, Straus and Giroux, 1949.

REY, J. H. Intrapsychic object relations: the individual and the group. In Wolberg, L. R., and Aronson, M. L. (Eds.), *Group Therapy 1975: An Overview*. New York: Stratton Intercontinental Medical Book Corp., 1975.

RICE, A. K. *The Enterprise and Its Environment*. London: Tavistock Publications, 1963.

RINDLER, W. *Special relativity*. New York: John Wiley and Sons, 1960.

RINGWALD, J. W. An investigation of group reaction to central figures. In Gibbard, G. S., Hartman, J. J., and Mann, R. D. (Eds.), *Analysis of Groups*. San Francisco: Jossey-Bass, 1974.

RISKIN, J. Methodology for studying family interaction. *Archives of General Psychiatry*, 1963, *8*:343–348.

ROBERTSON, H. P., AND NOONAN, T. W. *Relativity and Cosmology*. Philadelphia: Saunders, 1968.

ROGERS, C. R., AND WOOD, J. K. Client-centered theory: Carl R. Rogers. In Burton, A. (Ed.), *Operational Theories of Personality*. New York: Bruner/Mazel, 1974.

ROSE, S. Horney concepts in group psychotherapy. In Rosenbaum, M., and Berger, M. (Eds.), *Group Psychotherapy and Group Function*. New York: Basic Books Inc., 1963.

ROSENBAUM, M. The family under attack in an era of family therapy (or whatever happened to the family?). In Wolberg, L. R., and Aronson, M. L. (Eds.), *Group Therapy 1974—An Overview*. New York: Stratton Intercontinental Medical Book Corp., 1974.

ROSENBAUM, M., AND BERGER, M. *Group Psychotherapy and Group Function*. New York: Basic Books, Inc., 1963.

ROSENTHAL, D., FRANK, J., AND NASH, E. The self-righteous moralist in early meetings of therapy groups. *Psychiatry*, *1954*, *17*:215–233.

ROSOW, H. M., AND KAPLAN, L. P. Integrated individual and group therapy. *International Journal of Group Psychotherapy*, 1954, *4*:381–392.

ROSS, I. C., AND HARARY, F. Identification of the liaison persons of an organization using the structure matrix. *Management Science*, 1955, *1*:251–258.

RUESCH, J., AND BATESON, G. *Communication: The Social Matrix of Psychiatry*. New York: W. W. Norton and Co., Inc., 1951.

RYCROFT, C. *Psychoanalysis Observed*. London: Constable and Co., Ltd., 1966.

SATIR, V. The family as a treatment unit. *Confina Psychiatrica*, 1965, *8*:37–42.

SAUL, L. J. Hostility in cases of essential hypertension. *Pschosomatic Medicine*, 1939, *1*:153.

SCHACHTER, S. Deviation, rejection and communication. In Cartwright, D., and Zander, A. (Eds.), *Group Dynamics*. New York: Harper and Row, 1968.

SCHAEFER, E. S. Organization of maternal behavior and attitudes within a two dimensional space—an application of Guttman's radex theory. *American Psychologist*, 1957, *12*:401.

SCHAEFER, E. S. A circumplex model for personality development. *American Psychologist*, 1958, *13*:327–328.

SCHAEFER, E. S. A circumplex model for maternal behavior, *Journal of Abnormal and Social Psychology*, 1959, *2*:226–235.

SCHAEFER, E. S. Converging conceptual models for maternal behavior and for child behavior. In Glidewell, J. C. (Ed.), *Parental Attitudes and Child Behavior*. Springfield, Ill.: Charles C Thomas, 1961.

SCHAEFER, E. S., AND PLUTCHIK, R. Interrelationships of emotions traits and diagnostic constructs. *Psychological Reports*, 1966, *18*:399–410.

SCHAFFER, J. B. P., AND GALINSKY, M. D. *Models of Group Therapy and Sensitivity*. Englewood Cliffs, N.J.: Prentice Hall, 1974.

SCHEFLEN, A. E. On the structuring of human communication. *American Behavioral Scientist*, 1967, *10*(8):8–12.

SCHEIDLINGER, S. Identification: the sense of belonging and of identity in small groups. *International Journal of Group Psychotherapy*, 1964, *14*:271–306.

SCHEIDLINGER, S. The concept of regression in group therapy. *International Journal of Group Psychotherapy*, 1968, *18*:3–20.

SCHINDLER, W. The "group personality" concept in group psychotherapy. *International Journal of Group Psychotherapy*, 1952, *2*:311–315.

SCHINDLER, W. Socio-biological reflections on group psychotherapy on the family pattern. In Wolberg, L. R., and Schwartz, E. K. (Eds.), *Group Therapy 1973 —An Overview*. New York: Stratton Intercontinental Medical Book Corp., 1973.

SCHLOSBERG, H. The description of facial expressions in terms of two dimension. *Journal of Experimental Psychology*, 1952, *44*:229–237.

SCHLOSBERG, H. Three dimensions of emotion. *Psychological Review*, 1954, *61*:81–88.

SCHMERTZ, J. A. Psychology of the id. *Journal of Clinical Issues in Psychology*, 1976, *7*(2):1–8.

SCHUTZ, W. C. *FIRO: A Three-Dimensional Theory of Interpersonal Behavior*. New York: Holt, Rinehart and Winston, Inc., 1958.

SCHUTZ, W. On group composition. *Journal of Abnormal and Social Psychology*, 1961a, *62*:275–281.

SCHUTZ, W. C. The ego, FIRO theory and the leader as completer. In Petrullo, L., and Bass, B. M. (Eds.), *Leadership Interpersonal Behavior*. New York: Holt, Rinehart and Winston, Inc., 1961b.

SCHWARTZ, E. K. Group psychotherapy: the individual and the group. *Psychotherapy and Psychosomatics*, 1965a, *13*:142–149.

SCHWARTZ, E. K. Leadership and the psychotherapist. *Topical Problems in Psychotherapy*, 1965b, *5*:72–79.

SCHWARTZ, E. K. Group psychotherapy: the individual and the group. In Riess, B. F. (Ed.), *New Directions in Mental Health*, Vol. 2. New York: Grune and Stratton, 1969.

SCHWARTZ, E. K., AND WOLF, A. Psychoanalysis in groups: The mystique of group dynamics. In Stokvis, B. (Ed.), *Topical Problems in Psychotherapy*, Vol. 2. Basel and New York: S. Karger, 1960.

SCHWARTZ, E. K., AND WOLF, A. On countertransference in group psychotherapy. *Journal of Psychology*, 1964, *57*:131–142.

SCHWARTZ, E. K., AND WOLF, A. The interpreter in group therapy: conflict resolution through negotiation. *Archives of General Psychiatry*, 1968, *18*:186–193.

SCOTT, J. P. *Animal Behavior*. Chicago: University of Chicago Press, 1958.

SEARLS, H. F. *Collected Papers on Schizophrenia and Related Subjects*. New York: International Universities Press, 1965.

SELIGMAN, M., AND DESMOND, R. The leaderless group phenomenon: A historical perspective. *International Journal of Group Psychotherapy*, 1975, *3*:277–290.

SHAPIRO, D., AND BIRK, L. Group therapy in experimental perspective. *International Journal of Group Psychotherapy*, 1967, *17*:211–224.

SHEPPARD, C., FIORENTINO, D., COLLINS, L., AND MERLIS, S. Comparison of emotion profiles as defined by two additional MMPI profile types in male narcotic addicts. *Journal of Clinical Psychology*, 1969, *25*:186–188.

SHERWOOD, M. Bion's experience in groups: a critical evaluation. *Human Relations,* 1964, *17*:113–130.

SHOSTROM, E. L. *Pair Attraction Inventory.* San Diego, Calif.: Educational and Industrial Testing Service, 1971.

SHOSTROM, E. L. The measurement of growth in psychotherapy. *Psychotherapy,* 1972, *9*(3):194–198.

SHOSTROM, E. L., AND KAVANAUGH, J. *Between Man and Woman.* Los Angeles: Nash Publishing, 1971.

SLATER, P. E. Role differentiation in small groups. *American Sociological Review,* 1955, *20*:194–211.

SLATER, P. E. *Microcosm: Structural, Psychological and Religious Evolution in Groups.* New York: John Wiley & Sons, 1966.

SLAVSON, S. R. *Analytic Group Psychotherapy.* New York: Columbia University Press, 1950.

SLAVSON, S. R. Common sources of error and confusion in group psychotherapy. *International Journal of Group Psychotherapy,* 1953, *3*:3–28.

SLAVSON, S. R. Criteria for selection and rejection of patients for various types of group psychotherapy. *International Journal of Group Psychotherapy,* 1955, *5*(1):1.

SLAVSON, S. R. Are there 'group dunamics' in therapy groups? *International Journal of Group Psychotherapy,* 1957, *7*:131–154.

SLAVSON, S. R. *A Textbook in Analytic Group Psychotherapy.* New York: International Universities Press, 1964.

SMITH, K. H. Changes in group structure through individual and group feedback. *Journal of Personality and Social Psychology,* 1972, *24*:425–428.

SPARKS, J. Allogrooming in primates: a review. In Morris, D. (Ed.), *Primate Ethology.* New York: Doubleday, Anchor Press, 1969.

SPECK, R. V., AND ATTNEAVE, C. *Family Networks.* New York: Random House, 1973.

SPITZ, H., AND KOPP, S. Multiple psychotherapy. *Psychiatric Quarterly Supplement,* 1957, *31*:295–331.

SPOTNITZ, H. Acting out in group psychotherapy. In Wolberg, L. R. and Schwartz, E. K. (Eds.), *Group Therapy 1973 — An Overview.* New York: Stratton Intercontinental Medical Book Corp., 1973.

SPOTNITZ, H. *Psychotherapy of Pre-Oedipal Conditions.* New York: Jason Aronson, 1976.

STAGNER, R. *Psychology of Personality.* New York: McGraw-Hill Book Co., Inc., 1948.

STEINZOR, B. The spatial factor in face to face discussion groups. *Journal of Abnormal and Social Psychology,* 1950, *45*:552–555.

STEKEL, W. *The Interpretation of Dreams,* Vol. 1. New York: Liveright Publishing Corp., 1943.

STERNBACH, O. The dynamics of psychotherapy in the group. *Journal of Child Psychiatry,* 1947, *1*:91–112.

STOCK, D. Interpersonal concerns during the early sessions of therapy groups. *International Journal of Group Psychotherapy,* 1962. *12*:14–20.

STOCK, D. A survey of research on T-groups. In Bradford, C. P., Gibb, J. R., and Benne, K. D. (Eds.), *T-Group Theory and Laboratory Method: Innovation in Reeducation.* New York: John Wiley & Sons, 1964.

STOCK, D., AND LIEBERMAN, M. A. Methodological issues in the assessment of total-group phenomena in group therapy. *International Journal of Group Psychotherapy,* 1962, *12*:312–325.

STOCK, D., AND THELEN, H. A. *Emotional Dynamics and Group Culture.* New York: New York University Press, 1958.

STOCK, D., WHITMAN, R. M., AND LIEBERMAN, M. A. The deviant member in therapy groups. *Human Relations,* 1958, *11*:341–372.

STOGDILL, R. Personal factors associated with leadership: a survey of the literature. *Journal of Psychology,* 1948, *25*:35–71.

STOKES, J. H. The nervous and mental component in cutaneous disease. *Pennsylvania Medical Journal,* 1932, *35*:229.

STOLOROW, R. D., AND LACHMAN, F. M. The developmental prestages of defenses: diagnostic and therapeutic implications. *Psychoanalytic Quarterly,* 1978, *47*:73–102.

STOUTE, A. Implementation of group interpersonal relationships through psychotherapy. *Journal of Psychology,* 1950, *30*:145.

STRODTBECK, F. L., AND MANN, R. D. Sex role differentiation in jury deliberations. *Sociometry,* 1956, *19*:3–11.

STRUPP, H. H. *Psychotherapists in Action.* New York: Grune and Stratton, 1960.

SUTHERLAND, J. D. Notes on a psychoanalytic group therapy: I. Therapy and training. *Psychiatry,* 1952, *15*:111–117.

TAYLOR, F. K. The therapeutic factors of group analytic treatment. *Journal of Mental Science,* 1951, *96*:976.

TAYLOR, F. K. *The Analysis of Therapeutic Groups.* London: Oxford University Press, 1961.

TEICHER, A. The role of group process in the study of personality development. *Group Process,* 1972, *4*(2):7–18.

THELEN, H., ET AL. *Methods of Studying Group Operation.* Chicago: Human Dynamics Laboratory, 1954.

TOMKINS, S. S. *Polarity Scale.* New York: Springer Publishing Co., 1964.

TRUAX, C. B., AND CARKHUFF, R. R. *Toward Effective Counseling and Psychotherapy: Training and Practice.* Chicago: Aldine, 1967.

TRUAX, C., AND MITCHELL K. Research on certain therapist interpersonal skills in relation to process and outcome. In Bergin, A., and Garfield, S. (Eds.), *Handbook of Psychotherapy and Behavior Change.* New York: John Wiley & Sons, 1971.

TUCKMAN, B. Developmental sequence in small groups. *Psychological Bulletin,* 1965, *63*:384–399.

TURNER, W. J. Some phylogenetic roots of human behavior. *Transactions of the New York Academy of Science,* 1957, *20*:192–198.

TURQUET, P. M. Leadership: the individual and the group. In Gibbard, G. S., Hartman, J. J., and Mann, R. D. (Eds.), *Analysis of Groups.* San Francisco: Jossey-Bass, 1974.

USANDIVARAS, R. J. The argonauts expedition and groups. In Wolberg, L. R., and Aronson, M. L. (Eds.), *Group Therapy 1974—An Overview.* New York: Stratton Intercontinental Medical Book Corp., 1974.

USANDIVARAS, R. J. Group space and the structure of thinking. In Wolberg, L. R., Aronson, M. L., and Wolberg, A. R. (Eds.), *Group Therapy 1976—An Overview.* New York: Stratton Intercontinental Medical Book Corp., 1976.

VAILLANT, G. E. Natural history of male psychological health. V. The relation of ego mechanisms of defense to adult adjustment. *Archives of General Psychiatry,* 1976, *33*:535–545.

VASSILIOU, G., AND VASSILIOU, V. G. Introducing disequilibrium in group therapy. In Wolberg,

L. R., Aronson, M. L., and Wolberg, A. R. (Eds.), *Group Therapy 1976—An Overview*. New York: Stratton Intercontinental Medical Book Corp., 1976.

VON BERTALANAFFY, L. *General Systems Theory*. New York: Braziller, 1968.

VON BERTALANAFFY, L. General Systems theory and psychiatry: an overview. In Gray, W., and Rizzo, N. D. (Eds.), *General Systems Theory and Psychiatry*. Boston: Little Brown, 1969.

WALLS, F. L., AND DUNN, G. H. Storing ions for collision studies. *Physics Today*, August 1974, 30–35.

WARREN, N. Toward an adequate taxonomy of personality attributes: Replicated factor structure in peer nomination personality ratings. *Journal of Abnormal and Social Psychology*, 1963, 66:574–583.

WATSON, D. Reinforcement theory of personality and social system: Dominance and position in a group power structure. *Journal of Personality and Social Psychology*, 1971, 20:180–185.

WATZLAWICK, P., BEAVIN, J. H., AND JACKSON, D. D. *Pragmatics of Human Communication*. New York: W. W. Norton & Co., Inc., 1967.

WEINER, M. F. Genetic versus interpersonal insight. *International Journal of Group Psychotherapy*, 1974, 24(2):230–237.

WEISS, E. Cardiospasm: A psychosomatic disorder. *Psychosomatic Medicine*, 1944, 6:58.

WEISS, E., AND ENGLISH, O. S. *Psychosomatic Medicine*. Philadelphia: W. B. Saunders Co., 1957.

WHITAKER, D. S., AND LIEBERMAN, M. A. *Psychotherapy Through the Group Process*. New York: Atherton Press, 1964.

WHITE, R., AND LIPPITT, R. *Autocracy and Democracy*. New York: Harper and Row, 1960.

WHITE, R., AND LIPPITT, R. Leader behavior and member reaction in three social climates. In Cartwright, D., and Zander, A. (Eds.), *Group Dynamics: Research and Theory*. New York: Row, Peterson, 1962.

WHITMAN, R. M. Psychodynamic principles underlying T-group process. In Bradford, L. P., Gibbs, J. R., and Benne, K. D. (Eds.), *T-Group Theory and Laborabory Method: Innovation in Reeducation*. New York: John Wiley & Sons, 1964.

WHITMAN, R. M., LIEBERMAN, M. A., AND STOCK, D. The relation between individual and group conflict in psychotherapy. *International Journal of Group Psychotherapy*, 1960, 10:259–286.

WHITMAN, R. M., AND STOCK D. The group focal conflict. *Psychiatry*, 1958, 21:269–276.

WILSON, E. O. *Sociobiology: the New Synthesis*. Cambridge, Mass.: Harvard University Press, 1975.

WINICK, C., AND HOLT, H. Seating position as non-verbal communication in group analysis. *Psychiatry*, 1961, 24:171.

WINICK, C., KADIS, A. L., AND KRASNER, J. D. Training and professional practice of American group psychotherapists. *International Journal of Group Psychotherapy*, 1961, 11:419.

WINNICOTT, D. W. Transitional objects and transitional phenomena. *International Journal of Psychoanalysis*, 1953, 34:89–97.

WINNICOTT, D. W. *Collected Papers*. New York: Basic Books, London: Tavistock, 1958.

WINNICOTT, D. W. *Playing and Reality*. New York: Basic Books, 1971.

WITTKOWER, E. *A Psychiatrist Look at Tuberculosis*. London: The National Association for the Prevention of Tuberculosis, 1949.

WOLBERG, L. R. The influence of the therapist's personality on treatment outcome. In Riess, B. F. (Ed.), *New Directions in Mental Health,* Vol. 1. New York: Grune and Stratton, 1968.

WOLBERG, L. R. *The Technique of Psychotherapy,* Third ed. Part 2. New York: Grune and Stratton, 1978.

WOLF, A. The psychoanalysis of groups. *American Journal of Psychotherapy,* 1949, *3*:525–58.

WOLF, A. The psychoanalysis of groups. *American Journal of Psychotherapy,* 1950, *4*:16–50.

WOLF, A. The psychoanalysis of groups. In Rosenbaum, M., and Berger, M. (Eds.), *Group Psychotherapy and Group Function.* New York: Basic Books, 1963.

WOLF A. The role of the leader in the advanced and terminal phases of group psychotherapy. In Liff, Z. (Ed.), *The Leader in the Group.* New York: Jason Aronson, 1975.

WOLF, A. AND SCHWARTZ, E. K. Psychoanalysis in groups: the role of values. *American Journal of Psychoanalysis,* 1959, *19*, 1:38–*51*.

WOLF, A., AND SCHWARTZ, E. K. *Psychoanalysis in Groups.* New York: Grune and Stratton, 1962.

WOLF, A., AND SCHWARTZ, E. K. Psychoanalysis in groups. In Kaplan, H. I., and Sadock, B. J. (Eds.), *Comprehensive Group Psychotherapy.* Baltimore: The Williams and Wilkins Co., 1971.

WOLF, A., AND SCHWARTZ, E. K. The leader and countertransference, In Liff, Z. *The leader in the Group.* New York: Jason Aronson, 1975a.

WOLF, A., AND SCHWARTZ, E. K. The role of the leader as psychoanalyst. In Liff, Z. (Ed.), *The Leader in the Group.* New York: Jason Aronson, 1975b.

WOLF, A., SCHWARTZ, E. K., McCARTY, G. J., AND GOLDBERG, I. A. *Beyond the Couch: Dialogues in Teaching and Learning Psychoanalysis in Groups.* New York: Science House, 1970.

WOLF, A., SCHWARTZ, E. K., McCARTHY, G., AND GOLDBERG, I. The leader as human being. In Liff, Z. (Ed.), *The Leader in the Group.* New York: Jason Aronson, 1975.

WOLMAN, B. B. Group psychotherapy with latent schizophrenics. *International Journal of Group Psychotherapy,* 1960, *10*(3):301.

WOODWORTH, R. S. *Experimental Psychology.* New York: Holt, 1938.

WOODWORTH, R. S., AND SCHLOSBERG, H. *Experimental Psychology.* New York: Holt, 1954.

YALOM, I. D. A study of group therapy drop-outs. *Archives of General Psychiatry,* 1966, *14*:393–414.

YALOM, I. D. *The Theory and Practice of Group Psychotherapy.* New York: Basic Books, 1970.

YALOM, I.D., HOUTS, P. S., ZIMERBERG, S. M., AND RAND, K. H. Prediction of improvement in group therapy: an exploratory study. *Archives of General Psychiatry,* 1967, *17*:159–168.

YALOM, I. D., AND LIEBERMAN, M. A study of encounter group casualties. *Archives of General Psychiatry,* 1971, *25*:16–30.

YALOM, I. D., AND MILES, M. B. *Encounter Groups: First Facts.* New York: Basic Books, 1973.

YALOM, I. D., AND RAND, K. Compatability and cohesiveness in therapy groups. *Archives of General Psychiatry,* 1966, *13*:267–276.

ZIEFERSTEIN, I., AND GROTJAHN, M. Psychoanalysis and group psychotherapy. In Fromm-Reichman, F., and Moreno, J. L. (Eds.), *Progress in Psychotherapy*. New York: Grune and Stratton, Inc., 1956.

ZIMMERMAN, D. Some characteristics of dreams in group analytic psychotherapy. *International Journal of Group Psychotherapy*, 1967, *17*:524–535.

ZIMMER, J., AND SHAPIRO, R. Projective identification as a mode of perception and behavior in families of adolescents. *International Journal of Psychoanalysis*, 1972, *53*:523–530.

ZUK, G. H. *Family Therapy: a Triadic Based Approach*. New York: Behavioral Publications, 1971.

Author Index

325

Subject Index

Page numbers in *italics* refer to figures; page numbers followed by t refer to tables.

a
b
c
d
e
f
9 g
0 h
1 i
8 2 j